16th Linguistic Annotation Workshop (LAW-XVI)

Held at LREC 2022

Marseille, France
24 June 2022

Editors:

Sameer Pradhan
Sandra Kubler

ISBN: 978-1-7138-6125-6

Printed from e-media with permission by:

Curran Associates, Inc.
57 Morehouse Lane
Red Hook, NY 12571

CURRAN ASSOCIATES INC. proceedings .com

Some format issues inherent in the e-media version may also appear in this print version.

Printed with permission by Curran Associates, Inc. (2023)

For permission requests, please contact the Association for Computational Linguistics at the address below.

Association for Computational Linguistics
209 N. Eighth Street
Stroudsburg, Pennsylvania 18360

Phone: 1-570-476-8006
Fax: 1-570-476-0860

acl@aclweb.org

Additional copies of this publication are available from:

Curran Associates, Inc.
57 Morehouse Lane
Red Hook, NY 12571 USA
Phone: 845-758-0400
Fax: 845-758-2633
Email: curran@proceedings.com
Web: www.proceedings.com

LREC 2022 Workshop
Language Resources and Evaluation Conference
20-25 June 2022

The 16th Linguistic Annotation Workshop
24 June 2022
(LAW-XVI)

PROCEEDINGS

Editors:
Sameer Pradhan
Sandra Kübler

Proceedings of the 16th Linguistic Annotation Workshop (LAW-XVI 2022)

Edited by:
Sameer Pradhan and Sandra Kübler

For more information:
European Language Resources Association (ELRA)
9 rue des Cordelières
75013, Paris
France
http://www.elra.info
Email: lrec@elda.org

Message from the Workshop Organizers

The Linguistic Annotation Workshop (LAW) is organized annually by the Association for Computational Linguistics' Special Interest Group for Annotation (ACL SIGANN). It provides a forum to facilitate the exchange and propagation of research results concerned with the annotation, manipulation, and exploitation of corpora; work towards harmonization and interoperability from the perspective of the increasingly large number of tools and frameworks for annotated language resources; and work towards a consensus on all issues crucial to the advancement of the field of corpus annotation. These proceedings include papers that were presented at LAW XVI, held in conjunction with the 13th LREC in Marseille, France, on June 24, 2022.

The series is now in its sixteenth year. The first workshop took place in 2007 at the ACL in Prague. Since then, the LAW has been held every year, consistently drawing substantial participation (both in terms of paper/poster submissions and participation in the actual workshop) providing evidence that the LAW's overall focus continues to be an important area of interest in the field, a substantial part of which relies on supervised learning from gold standard data sets. This year's LAW has received 28 submissions, out of which 20 papers have been accepted to be presented at the workshop.

In addition to oral and poster paper presentations, LAW XVI also features a panel on this year's special theme—*The Impact of Multimodal Language Understanding on Annotation Practices and Representations.* Recent years have seen rapid improvements in performance of machine learning models across multiple modalities of communication such as, text, speech, images, video, gestures, etc. Improvements in unsupervised representation and learning have resulted in state of the art models needing less manually annotated data for training. However, the need for high quality, manual annotations for capturing multiple layers of information surrogates across various signals, including linguistic, is unlikely to go away. On the contrary, annotation practices, guidelines and representations will need to be adapted, extended, to address the challenges brought about by a richer landscape of phenomena. Historically these communities have existed as separate islands, and have crafted solutions that satisfy local research and application needs. The evolution of next generation, situated language understanding systems is likely to create a greater demand on the availability, and ease of use of such multimodal annotations and frameworks.

Our thanks go to SIGANN, our organizing committee, for its continuing organization of the LAW workshops, and to the LREC 2022 workshop chairs for their support. Most of all, we would like to thank all the authors for submitting their papers to the workshop and our program committee members for their dedication and their thoughtful reviews.

— Sandra Kübler and Sameer Pradhan

Organizers

Sameer Pradhan (University of Pennsylvania and `cemantix.org`, USA)
Sandra Kübler (Indiana University, USA)
Ines Rehbein (University of Mannheim, Germany)
Amir Zeldes (Georgetown University, USA)

Program Committee:

Julia Bonn (University of Colorado, Boulder, USA)
Santiago Arróniz (Indiana University, USA)
Emmanuele Chersoni (Hong Kong Polytechnic University)
Jonathan Dunn (University of Canterbury, New Zealand)
Kilian Evang (Heinrich-Heine University Düsseldorf, Germany)
Annemarie Friedrich (Bosch, Germany)
Kim Gerdes (Université Paris-Saclay, France)
Jena D. Hwang (Allen Institute for AI, USA)
Nancy Ide (Vassar College, USA)
Mikel Iruskieta (University of the Basque Country)
John Lee (City University of Hong Kong)
Adam Meyers (New York University, USA)
Jiří Mírovský (Charles University, Czech Republic)
Philippe Muller (Institut de Recherche en Informatique de Toulouse, France)
Skatje Myers (University of Colorado, Boulder, USA)
Kemal Oflazer (Carnegie Mellon University, Qatar)
Maciej Ogrodniczuk (Polish Academy of Sciences, Poland)
Antonio Pareja-Lora (Universidad de Alcalá de Henares, Spain)
Miriam R.L. Petruck (ICSI, USA)
Michael Roth (University of Stuttgart, Germany)
Manfred Stede (University of Potsdam, Germany)
Daniel Swanson (Indiana University, USA)
Bonnie Webber (University of Edinburgh, USA)
Michael Wiegand (Alpen-Adria-Universität Klagenfurt, Austria)
Fei Xia (University of Washington, USA)
Nianwen Xue (Brandeis University, USA)
Deniz Zeyrek (Middle East Technical University, Turkey)
He Zhou (Indiana University, USA)
Heike Zinsmeister (University of Hamburg, Germany)
Yilun Zhu (Georgetown University, USA)

Table of Contents

Workshop Program

Friday, June 24, 2022

8:45–9:00 ***Opening Remarks***

9:00–10:30 ***Session I—Paper Presentations***

9.00–9:15 *Automatic Approach for Building Dataset of Citation Functions for COVID-19 Academic Papers*
Setio Basuki and Masatoshi Tsuchiya

9:15–9:30 *The Development of a Comprehensive Spanish Dictionary for Phonetic and Lexical Tagging in Socio-phonetic Research (ESPADA)*
Simon Gonzalez

9:30–9:50 *Extending the SSJ Universal Dependencies Treebank for Slovenian: Was it Worth it?*
Kaja Dobrovoljc and Nikola Ljubešić

9:50–10:10 *Converting the Sinica Treebank of Mandarin Chinese to Universal Dependencies*
Yu-Ming Hsieh, Yueh-Yin Shih and Wei-Yun Ma

10:10–10:30 *Desiderata for the Annotation of Information Structure in Complex Sentences*
Hannah Booth

10:30–11:00 ***Coffee Break***

11:00–11:40 ***Session II—Paper Presentations***

11:00–11:20 *The Sensitivity of Annotator Bias to Task Definitions in Argument Mining*
Terne Sasha Thorn Jakobsen, Maria Barrett, Anders Søgaard and David Lassen

11:20–11:40 *NLP in Human Rights Research: Extracting Knowledge Graphs About Police and Army Units and Their Commanders*
Daniel Bauer, Tom Longley, Yueen Ma and Tony Wilson

Friday, June 24, 2022 (continued)

11:40–12:40 ***Session III—Posters***

Advantages of a complex multilayer annotation scheme: The case of the Prague Dependency Treebank
Eva Hajicova, Marie Mikulová, Barbora Štěpánková and Jiří Mírovský

Introducing StarDust: A UD-based Dependency Annotation Tool
Arife B. Yenice, Neslihan Cesur, Aslı Kuzgun and Olcay Taner Yıldız

Annotation of Messages from Social Media for Influencer Detection
Kevin Deturck, Damien Nouvel, Namrata Patel and Frédérique Segond

Charon: a FrameNet Annotation Tool for Multimodal Corpora
Frederico Belcavello, Marcelo Viridiano, Ely Matos and Tiago Timponi Torrent

Effect of Source Language on AMR Structure
Shira Wein, Wai Ching Leung, Yifu Mu and Nathan Schneider

12:40–14:00 ***Lunch Break***

14:00–15:00 ***Session IV—Panel on Annotating Multimodality***

15:00–16:00 ***Session V—Paper Presentations (Long; in Person)***

15:00–15:20 *Midas Loop: A Prioritized Human-in-the-Loop Annotation for Large Scale Multilayer Data*
Luke Gessler, Lauren Levine and Amir Zeldes

15:20–15:40 *How "Loco" is the LOCO Corpus?Annotating the Language of Conspiracy Theories*
Ludovic Mompelat, Zuoyu Tian, Amanda Kessler, Matthew Luettgen, Aaryana Rajanala, Sandra Kübler and Michelle Seelig

15:40–16:00 *Putting Context in SNACS: A 5-Way Classification of Adpositional Pragmatic Markers*
Yang Janet Liu, Jena D. Hwang, Nathan Schneider and Vivek Srikumar

16:00–16:30 ***Coffee Break***

Friday, June 24, 2022 (continued)

16:30–18:10 ***Session VI—Paper Presentations (Long; Virtual)***

16:30–16:50 *Building a Biomedical Full-Text Part-of-Speech Corpus Semi-Automatically*
Nicholas Elder, Robert E. Mercer and Sudipta Singha Roy

16:50–17:10 *Human Schema Curation via Causal Association Rule Mining*
Noah Weber, Anton Belyy, Nils Holzenberger, Rachel Rudinger and Benjamin Van Durme

17:10–17:30 *A Cognitive Approach to Annotating Causal Constructions in a Cross-Genre Corpus*
Angela Cao, Gregor Williamson and Jinho D. Choi

17:30–17:50 *Automatic Enrichment of Abstract Meaning Representations*
Yuxin Ji, Gregor Williamson and Jinho D. Choi

17:50–18:10 *GRAIL—Generalized Representation and Aggregation of Information Layers*
Sameer Pradhan and Mark Liberman

Proceedings of the 16th Linguistic Annotation Workshop (LAW-XVI) @LREC 2022, pages 1–7
Marseille, 24 June 2022

Automatic Approach for Building Dataset of Citation Functions for COVID-19 Academic Papers

Setio Basuki, Masatoshi Tsuchiya
Department of Computer Science and Engineering, Toyohashi University of Technology
1–1 Hibarigaoka, Tempaku-cho, Toyohashi 441-8580, Aichi, Japan
{setio,tsuchiya}@is.cs.tut.ac.jp

Abstract

This paper develops a new dataset of citation functions of COVID-19-related academic papers. Because the preparation of new labels of citation functions and building a new dataset requires much human effort and is time-consuming, this paper uses our previous citation functions that were built for the Computer Science (CS) domain, which consists of five coarse-grained labels and 21 fine-grained labels. This paper uses the COVID-19 Open Research Dataset (CORD-19) and extracts 99.6k random citing sentences from 10.1k papers. These citing sentences are categorized using the classification models built from the CS domain. The manually check on 475 random samples resulted accuracies of 76.6% and 70.2% on coarse-grained labels and fine-grained labels, respectively. The evaluation reveals three findings. First, two fine-grained labels experienced meaning shift while retaining the same idea. Second, the COVID-19 domain is dominated by statements highlighting the importance, cruciality, usefulness, benefit, consideration, etc. of certain topics for making sensible argumentation. Third, discussing State of The Arts (SOTA) in terms of their outperforming previous works in the COVID-19 domain is less popular compared to the CS domain. Our results will be used for further dataset development by classifying citing sentences in all papers from CORD-19.

Keywords: citation function, citing sentence, COVID-19, state of the art.

1. Introduction

Citation functions represent the reason why authors of academic papers cite previous works. Valenzuela et al. (2015) stated that the citations should not be treated equally. This is because citations indicate different roles, e.g., introducing the background, comparing and contrasting between studies, using or extending of existing methods, criticizing the previous works, etc. The existence of citations plays an important role in the preparation of a research manuscript since it helps the authors understand the big picture of a topic (Qayyum & Afzal, 2018), position their proposed research in the broad literature (Lin & Sui, 2020), and show their research novelty (Tahamtan & Bornmann, 2019). Moreover, citations can indicate the quality of proposed research (Casey et al., 2019; Raamkumar et al., 2016). Therefore, providing appropriate citations requires serious attention to support research dissemination.

There is a continuous development in designing labels for Rhetorical Structures (RS) and building datasets in the medical domain. Existing works have designed RS and developed the dataset (Alliheedi et al., 2019; Dayrell et al., 2012; Dernoncourt & Lee, 2017; Green, 2015; Jia, 2018; Kim et al., 2011; Liakata, 2010; Shatkay et al., 2008; Wilbur et al., 2006). However, several issues appear in these works. The first issue is that not all these RS were developed based on full text papers; several works built the RS using only papers' abstracts. The second issue is that most of the RS were not specifically designed for *citing sentences* (i.e., sentences which contain citation marks). Since the existing RS covers both *citing sentences* and non-*citing sentences*, the number of labels is considered small, which causes several potential missing *citation functions* being accommodated—the last issue. Moreover, due to the COVID-19 pandemic, the number of published papers covering this topic has significantly increased. Existing RS is not designed specifically for this purpose, and this has become an additional issue. Considering this, we aim to develop a new dataset of *citation functions* that contains more detailed labels, covers full text papers, and is specific for the COVID-19 domain.

Designing new labels of citation functions and building a new dataset is challenging. This is because we need to provide large, labeled training data, which is time-consuming, expensive, and requires much human effort. To obtain the labeled instance with less effort, this paper uses our previous labels of *citation functions* that have been built based on Computer Science (CS) papers. Note that the process to design the labels was accomplished prior to and has not become part of this paper. The developed labels consist of five *coarse-grained* labels and 21 *fine-grained* labels. By using these labels, we obtained classification models with accuracies of 83.6% and 90.1% for *coarse-grained* labels and fine-grained labels, respectively. This paper uses these models to categorize *citing sentences* on COVID-19-related papers obtained from the COVID-19 Open Research Dataset (CORD-19) (Lu Wang et al., 2020).

Through completing this research, we deliver several contributions:

- The automatic classification of *citation functions* on COVID-19 domain achieved accuracies of 76.6% for *coarse-grained* label and 70.2% for *fine-grained* labels.
- The experimental results show that several *fine-grained* labels experienced a meaning shift (the expansion of the labels' definition while remaining in the same idea).
- The COVID-19 domain is dominated by statements highlighting the importance, cruciality,

usefulness, benefit, consideration, etc. of certain topics for making sensible argumentation.

- We noticed that discussing State of The Arts (SOTA) in terms of outperforming previous studies in the COVID-19 domain is less popular compared to the CS domain.
- Lastly, we released a final dataset consisting of 99.6k labeled *citing sentences*[1].

This paper uses two main terms: *citing paper*, which is used to define the paper citing other papers, and *cited paper*, which is used to define the papers cited by the *citing paper*.

2. Dataset Development

This section describes how our proposed dataset of *citation functions* is developed. The dataset consists of several parts, the first of which concerns the obtainment of data sources of COVID-19-related papers. The second part describes the labels of *citation functions*, and the last part builds the dataset of *citation functions* on COVID-19 domains.

2.1 COVID-19-related Papers

This paper uses a collection of papers from the COVID-19 Open Research Dataset (CORD-19) (Lu Wang et al., 2020). Initially, this dataset provided 28k papers. The present number of papers has significantly increased during the continuous development. The CORD-19[2] collected papers from several sources (e.g., PubMed Central (PMC), PubMed, and the World Health Organization's COVID-19 Database). Moreover, it contains a collection from preprint servers such as bioRxiv, medRxiv, and ArXiv. This paper uses the latest version of the dataset **(version: 2021-12-20)** from JSON parsed from the full text of 314,391 (PDF) and 243,652 (PMC) papers. The distribution of CORD-19 is shown in Figure 1.

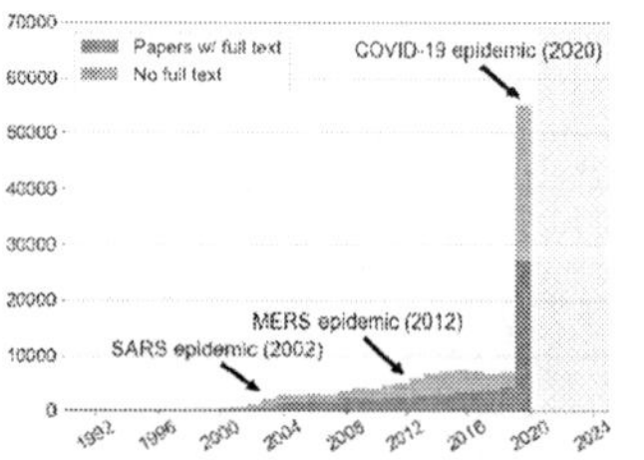

Figure 1: The paper distribution in CORD-19. The x axis depicts year, and the y axis depicts the number of papers. This figure is taken from Lu Wang et al.'s work (2020).

2.2 The Labels of Citation Functions

The labeling scheme of *citation functions* used in this paper is obtained from our previous research. The dataset used to develop the scheme is obtained from Färber et al. (2018), which provided 90,278 papers from ArXiv in the CS domain from January 1993 until December 31, 2017. Since this data source provides all parsed sentences from research papers, we perform *filtering* to separate the *citing sentences* and non-*citing sentences*. The *filtering* is performed using regular expressions based on certain citations tags. In this stage, we obtained around 1.6 million instances of *citing sentences*.

Our proposed labels of *citation functions* are developed through three steps: top-down analysis, bottom-up analysis, and annotation experiment. While the top-down analysis reviews the definitions of the labels from existing works, e.g., *background, usage,* and *comparison,* the bottom-up analysis is performed to identify the *citing sentence* patterns on the dataset. At this point, we obtained an initial dataset consisting of 5,669 samples. Next, we conducted the pre-annotations experiment to develop and finalize both labels of citation guidance and the annotation guidance. The final labels themselves consist of two categories: five *coarse-grained* labels and 21 *fine-grained.* The *coarse-grained* labels represent the generic idea of the *citation functions*, which are divided into *background* for stating certain topics, *citing paper work* for focusing on what is done by author, *cited paper work* to show what has been done by previous works, *compare and contrast* to discuss the similarity between the citing paper and the cited paper, and *other* for all categories that do not match the above criteria. To obtain more specific functions, these *coarse-grained* categories are broken down into *fine-grained* categories.

The annotation step was performed by two annotators who have master's degrees in Computer Science. They were provided with annotation guidance which covers an introduction to the task, labeling examples, and checking mechanism for the annotators' understanding. For the real experiment, the annotators are supplied with an excel spreadsheet that consisted of 421 random *unlabeled citing sentences*. Our experiment shows that the inter-annotator agreement shows 88.59% for *coarse-grained* labels and 72.44% for *fine-grained* labels. Moreover, Cohen's Kappa shows 0.85 for *coarse-grained* labels and 0.71 for fine-grained labels.

Coarse-grained Label: Background
Describes the *citing sentences* referring to the theory, principle, concept, topic, problem, etc. from cited papers.
Fine-grained Label: • **(atr0) definition**: explains the definition of general theory, principle, concept, topic, problem, etc. *example:* Gianna <citation> is a precursor visual environment for modeling CSP. • **(atr1) suggest**: provides the reader with suggestions to refer, see more details, and explore other cited papers. *example:* The interested reader may dig deeper on this subject by referring to <citation>. • **(atr2) judgment**: highlights the positivity/negativity, usefulness/non-usefulness, etc. of concepts, topics, problems, etc. *example:* The n-coalescent has some interesting statistical properties <citation>. • **(atr3) technical**: explains how a theory, principle, concept, topic, problem, etc. is applied. *example:* The WMF model <citation> learns the latent factors by preserving the personalized rankings. • **(atr4) trend**: explains the significance of the research topic, theory, principle, concept, topic, problem, etc. *example:* CNN has been gaining attention and is now used in many text classification tasks <citation>.
Coarse-grained Label: Citing Paper Work
What is proposed by the author?
Fine-grained Label:

[1] https://github.com/tutcsis/COVID-19

[2] https://www.semanticscholar.org/cord19/download

- **(atr5) corroboration**: while proposing a research topic, citing paper cites cited paper. *example:* To do this we build upon the concept of continuous regression <citation>.
- **(atr6) based on**: states that the citing paper follows, considers, is built based on, or is inspired by the cited paper. *example:* Here we follow closely the definition of GPs given by <citation>.
- **(atr7) use**: cites paper use, implements, employs, or adopts the concept, dataset, technique, etc. *example:* The proof systems we use were originally defined in <citation> which is the presentation we follow.
- **(atr8) extend**: the citing paper extends, adapt, improves, adds, or modifies the cited paper's work. *example:* Our proposed method (multiCCA) extends the bilingual embeddings of <citation>.
- **(atr9) dominant**: the citing paper outperforms the cited paper. *example:* Our PredNet model outperforms the model by <citation>.
- **(atr10) future**: mentions the future plan of the citing paper. *example:* In fact, we plan in the future of reproducing all the algorithms in Common2 <citation>, in that spirit.

Coarse-grained Label: Cited Paper Work

What is done by the cited papers?

Fine-grained Label:

- **(atr11) propose**: describes the proposed research by the cited paper. *example:* <citation> used CCA to learn bilingual lexicons from monolingual corpora.
- **(atr12) success**: highlights the success of the cited paper. *example:* <citation> successfully extracts body appearance and topology from synthetic and real input.
- **(atr13) weakness**: highlights the weakness of the cited paper. *example:* The limitation of <citation> is that the traffic is assumed always cross directional.
- **(atr14) result**: describes the result of the cited paper (neutral). *example:* In 1994, Kosaraju <citation> reported another solution to this problem.
- **(atr15) dominant**: states the superiority of the cited paper when compared to the citing paper. *example:* However, <citation> performs better than our method on class accuracy.

Coarse-grained Label: Compare and Contrast

The citing paper and the cited paper are compared and contrasted.

Fine-grained Label:

- **(atr16) compare**: describes the similarity between citing and cited papers. *example:* Recent work by Xia <citation> is independent from, and closely related to, our work.
- **(atr17) contrast:** describes the differences between citing and cited papers. *example:* However, unlike <citation> we did not observe an increased convergence speed.

Coarse-grained Label: Other

This label is prepared for *citing sentences* that do not match all criteria.

Fine-grained Label:

- **(atr18) comparison**: comparison between cited papers (whether similarities or differences between them). *example:* This idea was first proposed by Google <citation> and was then further developed by <citation>.
- **(atr18) multiple_intent**: *citing sentences* have two or more citation marks for different intents. *example:* It is noteworthy that while <citation> fared better than our system with the SemEval data, our system outperformed <citation> on the OEC dataset.
- **(atr18) other**: this label is designed for *citing sentences* that do not meet all of the label categories described above. *example:* The first one is due to Valtr <citation>.

Table 1: The labels of *citation functions* on CS domains.

2.3 Dataset Development in COVID-19 Domains

The proposed dataset of COVID-19 domains is built using an automatic approach by following several steps. **The first step** is preparing the source of the papers. In this step, we do a simple data analysis to gather a deep understanding of the parsed JSON structures of CORD-19. Following this, the analysis is accompanied by *filtering* to select only *citing sentences*. **The second step** is classifying all extracted *citing sentences* using the best models obtained from the dataset of the CS domain. These models were obtained by experimenting with several machine learning (ML) approaches such as Logistic Regression and Deep Learning based on Long Short-Term Memory (LSTM) architecture. Considering the limitations of available instances, we consider using pre-trained word embedding that is both non-contextual, such as Glove (Pennington et al., 2014), word2vec (Mikolov et al., 2013), and fasttext (Bojanowski et al., 2017) and contextual such as the Bidirectional Encoder Representations from Transformers (BERT) (Devlin et al., 2019) and work by Beltagy et al. (2019). **The last step** is verifying the automatically labeled *citing sentences* by performing a random selection of 475 instances and checking the predicted labels manually.

3. Experiment Results

This section explains the results of the automatic classification used to build a dataset of *citation functions* of the COVID-19 domain. The results are divided into several parts: brief information about classification models developed using the CS domain, the automatic classification of *citing sentences* of the COVID-19 domain, and the evaluation of classification through a manual label check. Note that, the classification in the CS domain and the COVID-19 domain is done through two stages, namely the *filtering* stage and the *fine-grained* stage. While the *filtering* stage is used to classify the *citing sentences* into two categories, i.e., *Other (atr18)* and *No-Other (atr0-atr17)*, the *fine-grained* stage is applied to classify the *citing sentences* belonging to *No-Other* class into 18 *fine-grained* classes. Finally, the proportional distribution of labeled instances and a discussion of results are also presented.

3.1 Classification Results for CS Domain

Here, we demonstrate the best results for classifications in the CS domain. In the *filtering* stage, BERT and SciBERT showed identical accuracies of 90.12%, as shown in Table 2. To achieve these accuracies, both methods used different settings as shown in Table 3.

Methods	Accuracy	Macro avg precision	Macro avg recall	Macro avg f1
BERT	90.12	71.58	**85.15**	75.99
SciBERT	**90.12**	**74.53**	82.72	**77.73**

Table 2: The best results on filtering stage.

Techniques	Parameters
BERT	$2e^{-5}$; batch 64; imbalance
SciBERT	$3e^{-5}$; batch 32; balance

Table 3: Best parameters on the filtering stages.

In the *fine-grained* stage, the best result was obtained by using SciBERT by 83.64%, as shown in Table 4 and the hyperparameters is shown in Table 5.

Methods	Accuracy	Macro avg precision	Macro avg recall	Macro avg f1
BERT	80.95	80.98	82.40	81.06
SciBERT	**83.64**	**83.46**	**85.35**	**84.07**

Table 4: The best results on fine-grained classification.

Techniques	Parameters
BERT	$3e^{-5}$; batch 32; imbalance
SciBERT	$3e^{-5}$; batch 32; balance

Table 5: Best parameters on the fine-grained classification.

3.2 Dataset on the COVID-19 Domain

The classification experiment is conducted on 99.6k instances generated from 10.1k parsed paper files (JSON format). The automatic classification begins with the extraction of all the sentences in the JSON files. Next, all extracted sentences are filtered to keep only *citing sentences*. Similar to the dataset on the CS domain, the classification is then applied by following two classification stages, namely the *filtering* stage and the *fine-grained* stage. To measure the accuracy of labeled instances, we perform a manual label check on 25 random samples for each label, for a total of 475 samples (18 fine-grained labels + 1 other label).

After completing the manual label check, we obtained accuracies 76.63% and 70.20% for *coarse-grained* labels and *fine-grained* labels, respectively. The accuracy of *coarse-grained* labels is easily obtained by summing the proportion of correctly and wrongly *fine-grained* labels. Since each label in the *fine-grained* labels has the same number of instances, it is easy to use the confusion matrix to compare each label's accuracy, as shown in Figure 2. The highest number of correctly predicted labels is achieved by the label *technical*, with 24 correct predictions and only a single incorrect prediction. In contrast, the label *cited_paper_dominant* has the lowest number of correctly predicted labels with only nine correct and 16 incorrect predictions.

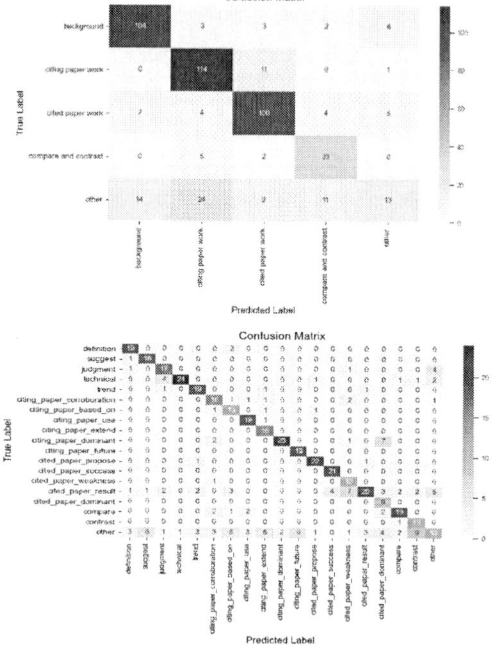

Figure 2: Confusion Matrix of manually label checking for (top) *coarse-grained* labels and (bottom) *fine-grained* labels.

Fine-grained Labels	Number of Instances		Label Proportion	
	CS Domain	COVID-19 Domain	CS Domain	COVID-19 Domain
definition	55,508	3,151	4.18%	3.77%
suggest	51,987	355	3.91%	0.42%
judgment	215,428	**37,885**	16.21%	**45.34%**
technical	85,374	5,557	6.42%	6.65%
trend	66,594	6,579	5.01%	7.87%
citing_paper_corroboration	113,488	2,571	8.54%	3.08%
citing_paper_based_on	55,878	531	4.20%	0.64%
citing_paper_use	115,215	1,114	8.67%	1.33%
citing_paper_extend	28,779	241	2.17%	0.29%
citing_paper_dominant	24,823	294	1.87%	0.35%
citing_paper_future	5,439	424	0.41%	0.51%
cited_paper_propose	**243,031**	5,442	**18.29%**	6.51%
cited_paper_success	34,505	2,128	2.60%	2.55%
cited_paper_weakness	15,054	1,072	1.13%	1.28%
cited_paper_result	154,394	15,063	11.62%	18.03%
cited_paper_dominant	**3,215**	**31**	**0.24%**	**0.04%**
compare	39,364	677	2.96%	0.81%
contrast	20,909	439	1.57%	0.53%
Total	**1,328,985**	**83,554**	**100%**	**100%**

Table 6: The distribution comparison of automatically labeled instances in CS domain and COVID-19 domain. The comparison consists of two parts: (a) the number of instances on each label and (b) the proportion of instance on each label to the total instances in the dataset.

Applying classification models built from CS papers to COVID-19 related papers results in two consequences. The first consequence is that there is a decrease of *fine-grained* label accuracy from 83.64% in CS domain to 70.2% in COVID-19 domain. The second consequence is that two *fine-grained* labels experienced a meaning shift: the label *citing_paper_dominant* and the label *citing_paper_future*. The definition of the label *citing_paper_dominant* changed from expressing the *citing paper's* performance over *cited paper* to discussing the success of *citing paper*, with or without comparison. On the other hand, the definition of the label *citing_paper_future* changed from stating the future plan of the *citing paper* to a general recommendation without specifying whether it is done by *citing paper* or *cited paper*.

3.3 Citation Functions Distribution

To give more analysis on the current COVID-19 dataset, in Table 6 we show a comparison of the distribution datasets in the CS domain and COVID-19 domains. Note that, the distribution in this table represents the number of automatically labeled *citing sentences* in the datasets. The current dataset in this paper consists of 99,691 labeled instances, of which *No-Other* label has 83,554 instances and the *Other* label 16,137 instances. Since the labels of *citation functions* are designed for CS papers, it is worth determining whether the classification models are effective for domains related to COVID-19. Instead of using the number of instances to compare both datasets, this paper uses the proportion of labels as indicators due to the datasets having different sizes.

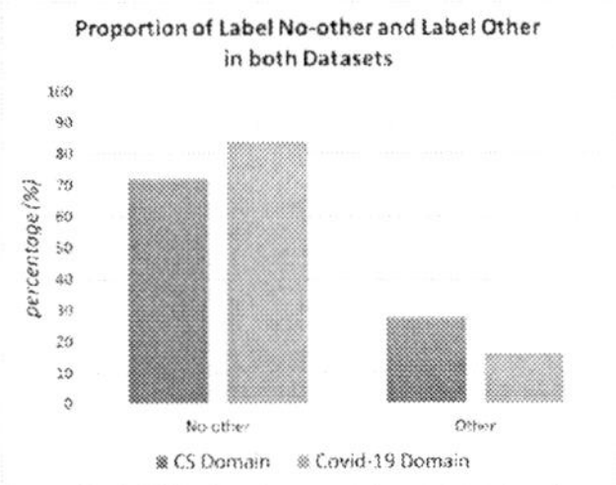

Figure 3: Proportion Comparison between *No-Other* and *Other* labels.

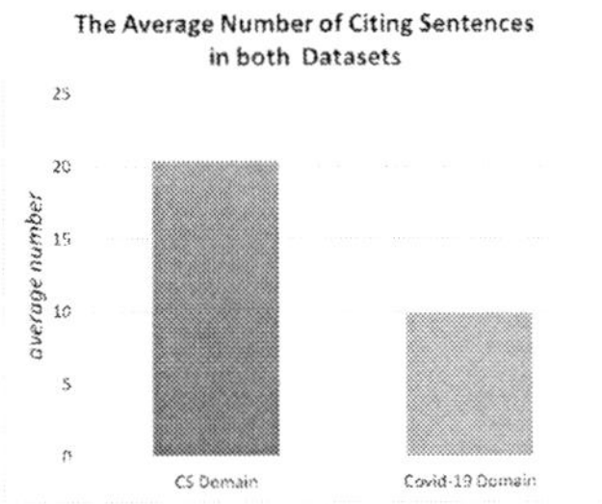

Figure 4: The average number of *citing sentences* in each paper

First, the comparison is done on the *filtering* stage to show the percentage of *No-Other* vs *Other* labels as depicted in Figure 3. In this figure, it is seen that both domains share the same trend in that the proportion of *No-Other* label much higher than *Other* label. Surprisingly, the label *judgment* in the COVID-19 domain has a proportion of almost half at 45.34%. In second place, the label *cited_paper_result* has 18.03% of proportion. The rest of labels constitute less than 10% of the proportion. Furthermore, there are eight labels have only under 1% of the proportion, with the lowest proportion obtained by the label *cited_paper_dominant* with 0.04%, which is equivalent with 31 instances. The CS domain faces a similar situation in that this label has the lowest proportion at 0.24%. However, this proportion is not as severe as in the COVID-19 domain. In the dataset of CS domain, the distribution trend is varied among labels, and no single label exceeds 20% of the proportion.

Another comparative indicator between both domains is the average number of *citing sentences* in each paper. Figure 4 demonstrates that the CS domain has a higher number of citing sentences than the COVID-19 domain. To be more specific, the dataset of CS domain consists of 1,840,815 *citing sentences* extracted from 90,278 papers, while the dataset of COVID-19 domain contains 99,691 *citing sentences* extracted from 10,102 papers.

3.4 Discussion

The experiments conducted in this paper reveal several notable findings. The first finding is a phenomenon of meaning shift in two *fine-grained* labels. This corroborates the assertion that even as this paper achieves acceptable accuracies, there still exists an issue regarding the labels' compatibility between two domains. Next, the large proportion of label *judgment* (constituting almost half of dataset) indicates that *citation functions* in the COVID-19 papers are dominated with statements highlighting the importance, cruciality, usefulness, benefit, consideration, etc. of certain topics for making sensible argumentation. Conversely, the smallest proportion, represented by the label *cited_paper_dominant,* which is followed by several labels with proportions less than 1% (e.g., *compare, citing_paper_extend, contrast, citing_paper_dominant,* and *citing_paper_based_on*) indicates that discussing State of the Arts (SOTA) in the COVID-19 domain is less popular compared to the CS Domain. This trend is supported by the average number of *citing sentences* in the CS domain being higher than in the COVID-19 domain, which emphasizes the fact that discussing the SOTA needs more *citing sentences* and *cited papers*.

4. Conclusion

This paper developed the dataset of *citation functions* using *citing sentences* extracted from COVID-19 related papers. Instead of designing new labels of *citation functions* from scratch and preparing training data, this paper uses our previously developed labels and applied the best ML models that have been built from the CS domain. The experiments show that the application of labels of the CS domain to the COVID-19 domain is promising. Furthermore, the evaluation for obtaining the automatic labeling accuracies uncovers several notable patterns such as label compatibility between two domains, the dominant citation roles on each domain, and the relation between a *citing paper* and the SOTA. For future work, we intend to apply the labels and the models to all papers in the CORD-19 dataset.

5. Acknowledgements

This research is supported by the Toyohashi University of Technology – Japan and Amano Institute of Technology Scholarship.

6. Bibliographical References

Alliheedi, M., Mercer, R. E., & Cohen, R. (2019).

Annotation of Rhetorical Moves in Biochemistry Articles. *Proceedings of the 6th Workshop on Argument Mining*, 113–123. https://doi.org/10.18653/v1/W19-4514

Beltagy, I., Lo, K., & Cohan, A. (2019). Scibert: A pretrained language model for scientific text. *Proceedings of the 2019 Conference on Empirical Methods in Natural Language Processing and the 9th International Joint Conference on Natural Language Processing (EMNLP-IJCNLP)*, 3615–3620. https://doi.org/10.18653/v1/D19-1371

Bojanowski, P., Grave, E., Joulin, A., & Mikolov, T. (2017). Enriching Word Vectors with Subword Information. *Transactions of the Association for Computational Linguistics*, *5*, 135–146. https://doi.org/10.1162/tacl_a_00051

Casey, A., Webber, B., & Glowacka, D. (2019). A Framework for Annotating 'Related Works' to Support Feedback to Novice Writers. *Proceedings of the 13th Linguistic Annotation Workshop*, 90–99. https://doi.org/10.18653/v1/W19-4011

Dayrell, C., Candido, A., Lima, G., MacHado, D., Copestake, A., Feltrim, V. D., Tagnin, S., & Aluisio, S. (2012). Rhetorical move detection in english abstracts: Multi-label sentence classifiers and their annotated corpora. *Proceedings of the 8th International Conference on Language Resources and Evaluation, LREC 2012*, 1604–1609.

Dernoncourt, F., & Lee, J. Y. (2017). *PubMed 200k RCT: a Dataset for Sequential Sentence Classification in Medical Abstracts*. 308–313. http://arxiv.org/abs/1710.06071

Devlin, J., Chang, M. W., Lee, K., & Toutanova, K. (2019). BERT: Pre-training of deep bidirectional transformers for language understanding. *Proceedings of NAACL-HLT 2019*, 4171–4186. https://doi.org/10.18653/v1/N19-1423

Färber, M., Thiemann, A., & Jatowt, A. (2018). A high-quality gold standard for citation-based tasks. *Proceedings of the Eleventh International Conference on Language Resources and Evaluation (LREC 2018)*, 1885–1889. https://www.aclweb.org/anthology/L18-1296

Green, N. (2015). Identifying Argumentation Schemes in Genetics Research Articles. *Proceedings of the 2nd Workshop on Argumentation Mining*, 12–21. https://doi.org/10.3115/v1/w15-0502

Jia, M. (2018). Citation Function and Polarity Classification in Biomedical Papers. *The University of Western Ontario*. https://ir.lib.uwo.ca/etd/5367/

Kim, S. N., Martinez, D., Cavedon, L., & Yencken, L. (2011). Automatic classification of sentences to support Evidence Based Medicine. *BMC Bioinformatics*, *12*(SUPPL. 2). https://doi.org/10.1186/1471-2105-12-S1-S5

Liakata, M. (2010). Zones of conceptualisation in scientific papers: a window to negative and speculative statements. *Proceedings of the Workshop on Negation and Speculation in Natural Language Processing*, 1–4. https://www.aclweb.org/anthology/W10-3101

Lin, K. L., & Sui, S. X. (2020). Citation Functions in the Opening Phase of Research Articles: A Corpus-based Comparative Study. *Corpus-Based Approaches to Grammar, Media and Health Discourses*, 233–250. https://doi.org/https://doi.org/10.1007/978-981-15-4771-3_10

Lu Wang, L., Lo, K., Chandrasekhar, Y., Reas, R., Yang, J., Eide, D., Funk, K., Kinney, R., Liu, Z., Merrill, W., Mooney, P., Murdick, D., Rishi, D., Sheehan, J., Shen, Z., Stilson, B., Wade, A. D., Wang, K., Wilhelm, C., … Kohlmeier, S. (2020). CORD-19: The Covid-19 Open Research Dataset. *Proceedings of the 1st Workshop on NLP for COVID-19 at ACL 2020*.

Mikolov, T., Sutskever, I., Chen, K., Corrado, G., & Dean, J. (2013). Distributed Representations of Words and Phrases and their Compositionality. *Conference on Neural Information Processing Systems*. https://papers.nips.cc/paper/2013/file/9aa42b31882ec039965f3c4923ce901b-Paper.pdf

Pennington, J., Socher, R., & Manning, C. D. (2014). GloVe: Global Vectors for Word Representation. *Proceedings of the 2014 Conference on Empirical Methods in Natural Language Processing (EMNLP)*, 1532–1543. https://doi.org/10.3115/v1/D14-1162

Qayyum, F., & Afzal, M. T. (2018). Identification of important citations by exploiting research articles' metadata and cue-terms from content. *Scientometrics*, *118*, 21–43. https://doi.org/10.1007/s11192-018-2961-x

Raamkumar, A. S., Foo, S., & Pang, N. (2016). Survey on inadequate and omitted citations in manuscripts: A precursory study in identification of tasks for a literature review and manuscript writing assistive system. *Information Research*, *21*(4). http://informationr.net/ir/21-4/paper733.html

Shatkay, H., Pan, F., Rzhetsky, A., & Wilbur, W. J. (2008). Multi-dimensional classification of biomedical text: Toward automated, practical provision of high-utility text to diverse users. *Bioinformatics*, *24*(18), 2086–2093. https://doi.org/10.1093/bioinformatics/btn381

Tahamtan, I., & Bornmann, L. (2019). What do citation counts measure? An updated review of studies on citations in scientific documents published between 2006 and 2018. In *Scientometrics* (Vol. 121). Springer International Publishing. https://doi.org/10.1007/s11192-019-03243-4

Valenzuela, M., Ha, V., & Etzioni, O. (2015). Identifying meaningful citations. *Association for the Advancement of Artificial Intelligence (AAAI)*.

Wilbur, W. J., Rzhetsky, A., & Shatkay, H. (2006). New directions in biomedical text annotation: Definitions, guidelines and corpus construction. *BMC Bioinformatics*, *7*, 1–10. https://doi.org/10.1186/1471-2105-7-356

7. Language Resource Reference

Lu Wang, L., Lo, K., Chandrasekhar, Y., Reas, R., Yang, J., Eide, D., Funk, K., Kinney, R., Liu, Z., Merrill, W., Mooney, P., Murdick, D., Rishi, D., Sheehan, J., Shen, Z., Stilson, B., Wade, A. D., Wang, K., Wilhelm, C., … Kohlmeier, S. (2020). CORD-19: The Covid-19 Open Research Dataset. *Proceedings of the 1st Workshop on NLP for COVID-19 at ACL 2020.*

Proceedings of the 16th Linguistic Annotation Workshop (LAW-XVI) @LREC 2022, pages 8–14
Marseille, 24 June 2022

The Development of a Comprehensive Spanish Dictionary for Phonetic and Lexical Tagging in Socio-phonetic Research (ESPADA)

Simon Gonzalez
The Australian National University
Canberra, Australian Capital Territory, Australia
u1037706@anu.edu.au

Abstract

Pronunciation dictionaries are an important component in the process of speech forced alignment. The accuracy of these dictionaries has a strong effect on the aligned speech data since they help the mapping between orthographic transcriptions and acoustic signals. In this paper, I present the creation of a comprehensive pronunciation dictionary in Spanish (ESPADA) that can be used in most of the dialect variants of Spanish data. Current dictionaries focus on specific regional variants, but with the flexible nature of our tool, it can be readily applied to capture the most common phonetic differences across major dialectal variants. We propose improvements to current pronunciation dictionaries as well as mapping other relevant annotations such as morphological and lexical information. In terms of size, it is currently the most complete dictionary with more than 628,000 entries, representing words from 16 countries. All entries come with their corresponding pronunciations, morphological and lexical tagging, and other relevant information for phonetic analysis: stress patterns, phonotactics, IPA transcriptions, and more. This aims to equip socio-phonetic researchers with a complete open-source tool that enhances dialectal research within socio-phonetic frameworks in the Spanish language.

Keywords: pronunciation dictionary, forced alignment, Spanish dialects, socio-phonetics, annotation tools

1. Introduction

Within current research frameworks in socio-phonetics, workflows are becoming more and more complex due to the amount of data to be processed and the specialisation that the field is experiencing. This has been strongly influenced by the rapid advances in speech processing technologies readily available to be used. One area that has experienced a great level of specialisation is the forced alignment of natural speech data (Bailey 2016; Fruehwald, 2014), which is now widely used in socio-phonetic research (cf. DiCanio et al, 2012; Gonzalez et al, 2018; Strunk et al, 2014). The goal of the forced alignment process is to create time-aligned segmentations at the phonemic level, following acoustic parameter transitions between units, and derived from orthographic transcriptions at the utterance level (Fromont & Hay, 2012; Gonzalez et al., 2018; Kisler et al, 2017; McAuliffe et al., 2017; Reddy & Stanford, 2015). In this sense, the accuracy of the alignment strongly depends on the level of accuracy of the transcription, which works best when it is transcribed annotating the closest to the spoken speech.

An important component of the forced alignment process is the pronunciation dictionary. This stores all the phonemic representation of the segments that will be aligned in the speech data. In the case of English, there are publicly available dictionaries that represent English phonemes in different ways. One well-known available tool in English is the CMU dictionary (CMU, 2016), which uses an encoding from the ARPABET system, representing vowels with two uppercase symbols (e.g. IPA /e/=ARPABET 'EH'[1]) , and consonants with one or two uppercase symbols (e.g. /d/='D'; /h/='HH'). Another one is the Disc option within the CELEX dictionary (Baayen el al., 1995), which uses one letter or number to represent a phoneme (e.g. /eɪ/ = '1'; /tʃ/ = 'J'). After establishing the segments, the next step in the forced alignment process is to annotate all available words in the dictionary, which is also referred to as g2p (grapheme-to-phoneme conversion), and it is the process of converting orthographic text into its corresponding phonological transcription.

1.1 Challenges in Pronunciation Dictionaries

Here we present four of the relevant challenges when deciding how to annotate words. The first challenge is the type of phonemic representation, whether following more orthographic-oriented conventions, as the CMU, or more IPA-oriented conventions. For example, the word "cat" has three phonological segments: starting with a consonant, followed by a vowel, then ending in another consonant. This can be represented using the phonemic representation /kat/, but we can also use 'KAT'. This last use has been preferred because of computational practicalities, due to having simpler encodings than IPA symbols.

The second challenge is the question on what are the phonological elements that we represent in the annotation. One of them is stress marking. In languages where the same vowel can be in stressed and unstressed syllables, as in Russian and Spanish, for example, one question is whether we represent stress in the annotation or not. In a study on Russian (Gnevsheva et al., 2020), it was found that when the annotation reflected the stress differences in words, the accuracy of the forced alignment improved. Results like this are in line with the selection by some forced aligners to use dictionaries that represent stressed and unstressed syllables for their words.

When it comes to annotating socio-phonetic variation, the challenges become more pronounced. This is especially crucial when deciding the type of annotation since inaccuracies, or errors, in the forced alignment output must be traced back to the real cause: either inaccuracies in the forced alignment algorithm, or mismatches between the speech signal and the transcription. For example, if we

[1] Across this paper, IPA transcriptions will follow the conventional // for phonemes and [] for allophonic transcription. Orthographic spellings will be represented with double quotation marks " ", and pronunciation dictionary entries with single quotation marks ' '.

want to annotate the word "car", we can either annotate it to reflect rhotic variants, such as American English, where the annotation would be 'kAr' [kaɹ], or it can be annotated to represent non-rhotic variants, such as Australian English 'kA' [kɐ:]. This has been approached in three different ways. In one approach, researchers used a rhotic model on a non-rhotic accent, and then did the corresponding corrections post hoc after the alignment (MacKenzie & Turton, 2020). In other approaches, the acoustic model of a non-rhotics variant was used for another non-rhotic variant, as in Fromont & Watson (2016), where the model from British English was used to forced align New Zealand English. A final approach is when the acoustic model is trained on the non-rhotic variant itself, as in Gonzalez et al. (2020), where they trained the acoustic model on the same data, then used this model to force align the data in Australian English.

A final challenge is related to the stage following the forced alignment process. The forced-aligned data is a preparation process to then analyse it in the light of socio-phonetic questions, which can be on specific segments (vowels and consonants), but also on higher levels, such as morphology, syntax or suprasegmentals (e.g., prosody). This means that the level of annotation does not stop at the pronunciation dictionary, but also has an impact at the word and syntactical levels. It is common practice to do this work after the alignment by doing a new wrangling of the data, using other resources available that map aligned words with their corresponding lexical information, such as word type and part of speech classification. However, when trying to map outcome data to new sources, and using new tools, results are prompt to have more errors in the final product of the wrangling process.

1.2 Spanish Pronunciation Dictionaries

All these challenges are latent for any language that can be forced aligned, and in this paper, we focus on Spanish and its variants. Here, we assess these factors in relation to Spanish research, and we also look at the current advancements on pronunciation dictionaries. We discuss the areas of improvement and present the results of the development of a resource that aims to contribute to the work on forced alignment (and further) on Spanish socio-phonetic research. The aim is to develop a tool that can be used for two stages: the first one is for the preparation of data for forced alignment, and the second one is for lexical and grammatical tagging (POS) of the forced aligned output. We expect that such a tool can facilitate the transition stage from forced alignment to further analysis without loss of any data and the avoidance of mapping inconsistencies.

2. Related Work

In this socio-phonetic revolution, many technologies and resources have been developed across different languages to achieve great accuracy from annotated dictionaries. A seminal work on this type of annotations has been done for CELEX (Baayen el al., 1995). It contains information on four levels:

- Orthography: shows spelling variations for all corresponding words.
- Phonology: shows corresponding phonological transcriptions, and corresponding variations in pronunciation. It also includes syllable information such as syllable structure and stress types, e.g. primary stress.
- Morphology: shows the derivational and compositional structures for all words, showing their inflectional paradigms.
- Syntax: shows the word class, and all word class-specific subcategorizations, with their corresponding argument structures.

This is an extensive work on linguistic annotation available for English, Dutch, and German. To our knowledge, there is not a version for Spanish available in CELEX.

In terms of pronunciation dictionaries used in forced alignment, there have been great advances in both English and Spanish. For English, state of the art available aligners includes MFA (McAuliffe et al., 2017), MAUS (Kisler et al, 2017), FAVE (Rosenfelder et al., 2014), LaBB-CAT (Fromont & Hay, 2012), and DARLA (Reddy & Stanford, 2015). For Spanish, MFA and faseAlign (Wilbanks, 2021) are two widely used aligners[2]. In this paper, we assess only the phonetic dictionaries available for each of these. We do not evaluate their accuracy[3].

2.1 TalnUPF

MFA has two available dictionaries. The first one is the *TalnUPF Spanish IPA* dictionary, and its annotations use IPA symbols, showing stress information. A sample[4] of the dictionary is shown below.

Word	***Annotated pronunciation***
matamoros	m a t a m ˈo ɾ o s
torreón	t o r e ˈo n
campeche	k a m p ˈe ʧ e
zúñiga	θ ˈu ɲ i ɣ a
guasave	g w a s ˈa β e
allende	a ɟ ˈe n d e

Table 1: Sample pronunciation dictionary from *TalnUPF IPA*

The second dictionary available is the *TalnUPF Spanish gpA* dictionary. Contrary to the previous one, this uses alphabetic letters (similar practice as in the CMU dictionary) and not IPA symbols. An important observation is that there is no stress specification in this dictionary, contrary to the IPA version. In addition, like the IPA version, it makes a distinction between monophthongs and semivowels, as seen in the sample below, where the letter "u" in the word "guasave" is represented with the

[2] Other aligners used for Spanish data include EasyAlign (Goldman, 2011), LaBB-CAT (Fromont & Hay, 2012), and PraatAlign (Lubbers & Torreira, 2016).

[3] Gonzalez, S., Grama, J. and Travis, C.E. (2020). Comparing the performance of forced aligners used in sociophonetic research. *Linguistics Vanguard*, vol. 6, no. 1

[4] These words in the dictionary samples were chosen to be compared to the ones given by Wilbanks (2021) for faseAlign.

semivowel 'w'. This is compared to the vowel /u/, that is represented as 'u' in the word "zúñiga".

Word	*Annotated pronunciation*
matamoros	m a t a m o rf o s
torreón	t o r e o n
campeche	k a m p e tS e
zúñiga	T u n~ i G a
guasave	g w a s a V e
allende	a L e n d e

Table 2: Sample pronunciation dictionary from *TalnUPF gpA*

In terms of individual segments, the letter "ñ" uses two separate symbols: 'n~', which is the palatal nasal /ɲ/. The dictionary also makes the correct distinction between single and complex trills in Spanish: simple (/ɾ/='rf') and complex (/r/='r'). Another distinction is the alveolar /l/ using the lowercase 'l', and the upper case 'L' to represent the palatal lateral /ʎ/ or the palatal fricative /ʝ/, depending on the variant. The third characteristic is that the palato-alveolar affricate /tʃ/ is represented with the two letters 'tS'. Since Spanish voiced stops /b, d, g/ are lenited in intervocalic positions ([β, ð, ɣ], respectively), the dictionary accurately makes the distinction between intervocalic contexts and non-intervocalic, for example, "vaca"='baka', "abeja"='aVexa'. This is the same for the other voiced plosives: 'b' and 'V', 'd' and 'D', and 'g' and 'G'. This distinction is also implemented in the IPA version of the same dictionary. In terms of Spanish variants, since it is based on Castilian Spanish, it represents the labiodental voiceless /θ/='T' and the velar voiceless fricative /x/='x', as in the word "jarrazo"= 'x a r a T o'.

2.2 faseAlign

The dictionary used in faseAlign follows a similar structure to the *TalnUPF Spanish gpA* dictionary. The similarity is that there is no stress specification in the annotation, but it differs from the TalnUPF in that it does not make a distinction between monophthongs and semivowels, as seen in the words "guasave" and "zúñiga", both of which use the same phonemic representation 'u' for "u".

Word	*Annotated pronunciation*
matamoros	m a t a m o r o s
torreón	t o R e o n
campeche	k a m p e CH e
zúñiga	s u NY i g a
guasave	g u a s a b e
allende	a y e n d e

Table 3: Sample pronunciation dictionary from *faseAlign*

Another major difference is that it does not make the intervocalic distinction for voiced stops, this is, it gives the same representation regardless of their phonological context. In this sense, faseAlign gives a more phonemic representation whereas TalnUPD focuses on a more phonetic one. In terms of the other phonemes, it represents complex trills with an upper case 'R' and the single one with the lower case 'r'. The palato-alveolar affricate is 'CH', the palatal nasal 'NY', and palatal lateral 'y'. Finally, in terms of Spanish variants, faseAlign targets Latin-American dialects where there is no /θ/ and /x/. In the case of /θ/, most of the variants realise it the same as /s/ (called *seseo*, where /θ/ and /s/ merge to /s/), and /x/ is realised as /h/.

3. Assessment on Current Tools

When considering that the stage of forced alignment is a transitional stage to prepare the data for phonetic analysis, we assess the available tools in relation to an overall view. It is very important to note that these resources are not necessary lacking for the tasks they carry out, but rather we propose here to improve phonetic annotations that can be easily adapted to most Spanish variants and combine these with other linguistic annotations.

In terms of the lexical and grammatical tagging, CELEX offers great functionality. However, as observed before, it is not available for Spanish. We therefore propose to create an annotated dataset of Spanish words that have the following six features available:

- Orthography: showing spelling variations for all corresponding words based on dialectal differences.
- Phonology: showing corresponding phonological transcriptions, and corresponding variations in pronunciation. The variants can be modified as needed by the users. This flexibility allows us to adapt the dictionary to a virtually infinite number of dialectal phenomena.
- Syllable divisions: showing syllabic information such as syllable structure and stress types.
- Stress: showing the stress pattern of words.
- Morphology: showing the derivational and compositional structures for all words.
- Syntax: showing the word function in the sentence.

The aim of the dictionary is to be both comprehensive and flexible to be used on any documented Spanish variant. In the table below, we show the functions available in the three dictionaries discussed, and the areas where we aim to contribute with this tool.

Tool	*Different Variants*	*Alphabetic annotations*	*Semi-vowels distinction*	*Stress annotations*	*Voiced Stops distinction*
fase Align	Yes	Yes	No	No	No
Taln gpA	No	Yes	Yes	No	Yes
Taln IPA	No	No	Yes	Yes	Yes

Table 4: Feature comparison for the three pronunciation dictionaries for Spanish data.

4. Aims of the Paper

By implementing these improvements in the annotations, our final product includes both phonetic/phonological layers, as well as grammatical/lexical layers, compared to CELEX. We have called it *ESPADA ([E]Spanish*

[A]nnotation [Da]ta). The first advantage is that all these will be available in one resource, which minimises inaccuracies and inconsistencies in data mapping, and offers users the opportunity to change between all available dialectal options without recreating new pronunciation dictionaries.

Based on a preliminary literature review on major dialectal variants, we identified major phonological contexts which capture regional variants, and they are described as follows[5]:

- Stress: choose annotations with or without stress information.
- Voiced Stops Lenition: choose whether Voiced Stops are only represented in their phonological form /b, d, g/ or with their lenited intervocalic counterparts [β, ð, ɣ].
- Semivowels: specify whether semivowels are represented with only their phonological forms /i, u/, or with their phonetic representations [j, w].
- /ʝ/: choose variants where /ʝ/ is realised as /ʎ/.
- /θ/: choose variants where /θ/ and /s/ are distinctive, or where they merge into /s/.
- /x/: choose variants where /x/ is realised as /h/.
- /s/: choose /h/ in contexts where the /s/ is debuccalized (Morris, 2000). In this case, we have chosen the phonological context where this has been most commonly observed: in post-nuclear position, such as "las"=/las/->/[lah], as in Chile and Venezuela.
- /ɾ/: choose to represent /ɾ/ as /l/ in post-nuclear position (also known as lambdacism), which has been observed in some Caribbean dialects (Guitart, 1997), such as in Cuba and Puerto Rico (e.g. "porque"=/poɾke/->[polke]).

5. Methodology

The Spanish lexicon was extracted from two freely available sources. The first one is all the entries from the *Diccionario de la Real Academia de la Lengua Española* (REAL ACADEMIA ESPAÑOLA, 2021), and the text file was compiled by Domínguez (2015). The second database was available from the *LibreOffice* software (Foundation, T. D, 2020). This database contains word entries, ordered in alphabetic order. A great advantage of this resource is that there is a folder for each of the 16 countries available. This can be maximised in our research by selecting to use a pronunciation dictionary customised for a specific Spanish variant, following the dialectal features presented in the previous section. In our approach, we use countries as a proxy for dialectal variants, mainly in terms of orthographic spelling and words used in a specific country. The other way of using this is by merging two or more countries sources to encompass more accurate lexicon. For example, this can be used in the case where there is a study focusing on Caribbean Spanish, which would include Cuba, Colombia, Dominican Republic, Puerto Rico, Panama, and Venezuela (cf. Álvarez et al., 2009; Núñez-Méndez, 2021). In this case, users can choose these countries to create a single pronunciation dictionary.

The data processing was done in RStudio (R Core Team, 2021), by applying a wide range of scripts developed by the main author. The following section describes the segmentation and classification of the data, from words to their corresponding lexical and grammatical tagging.

5.1 Word Level

The phonology of Spanish allows an almost one to one correspondence when assigning individual letters to individual phonemes. This makes the computational process of annotation more reliable and accurate. This also considers the fact that in standard orthography, there are only two diagraphs in Spanish: "ch" (/tʃ/), and "ll" (/ʎ/ or /ʝ/). Another adjustment is the letter "h", which is silent in Spanish. Apart from these exceptions, the other letters can have a one-to-one representation between letters and phonemes. The main motivation for this approach is to allow the expansion of this dictionary and facilitate the automation of adding new entries, in which the algorithm can identify the letters and then create a pronunciation representation from there.

This process has its own challenges. The main one is when we create phonemic representations of borrowed words from another language. For example, the English word "today", following the automatic parsing would be 't o d a j', but this must be corrected to 't u d e j', if the aim is to reflect pronunciations that are closer to source language. In the current version, we have identified these words in a semi-automatic way, but we aim to fully automate this process in future versions. However, due to the open-source nature of the dictionary and its expandability option, this can be done by users as needed.

Another important aspect of standard Spanish orthography is the writing of the acute accent[6] in written words. This was maximised in our computational approach. The rules of orthography help identify where the stress is located within the syllable, which is the main function of the accent in Spanish[7]. However, not all stressed syllables are indicated with an accent. In those cases, these are exceptions when the accent is not written, and the stressed syllable can still be identified following the orthographic rules. This is expanded in Section 5.5.

[5] Here we do not make a clear-cut distinction between European and Latin-American Spanish. The first reason is because there are features that appear in some dialects within Spain that are also found in dialects of Latin-America. Also, Spanish in Latin-America is not homogenous since there are many distinct dialects, and characterising Latin-American Spanish as one single variant is inaccurate. However, with these features we aim to capture major dialectal distinctions, and new distinctions can be added to the dictionary.

[6] In this paper, we will use the word "accent" to refer to the *orthographic* marking in Spanish, and we will use the words "variant" and "dialect" to refer to the *speech-related* differences. We will also use the word "stress" for the *phonetic* emphasis of syllables within words.

[7] This is an important difference between accents in Spanish and other languages such as French. In French, for example, accents are used to indicate the nature of the vowel (open/close), whereas in Spanish is to indicate phonological stress.

Taking into consideration the orthographic rules, we then proceeded with the phonemic mapping. The first step was to break down each word into the individual letters. Each letter then was mapped to a pronunciation counterpart, which represents the phonemes. For this, all "h" letters were excluded since this affects the identification as shown below. For this mapping, we created representations that are one single letter per phoneme, which is similar to the CELEX annotation, with a combination of upper- and lower-case letters. Having one-to-one letter mapping facilitates analysis in further stages, for example, when counting characters, which is effective at dealing with transcriptions with no space between characters. Here, each individual letter would represent a single phoneme, thus the total number of characters would represent the total number of phonemes.

5.2 Vowel Classification

Vowels were classified into two groups: monophthongs or semivowels. If a vowel is not in contact with another vowel, then it was assigned its corresponding value as a monophthong. But if it was in contact with another vowel, it was classified as either a vowel or a semivowel. This depended on the stress pattern represented by the accent. If the vowel being classified did not carry the accent/stress, then it was assigned to the semivowel category. If it carried the accent, then it kept its monophthongal classification.

5.3 Consonant Classification

Our consonant classification process aimed to capture the main phonetic variations presented in Section 4. It does not mean to be exhaustive and further additions can be implemented in future versions of the tool. For the consonants, with only two exceptions, they were assigned their corresponding phonological representation following their orthography, for example, "p"='p', "m"='m'. The first exception was the letter "c". It can represent either a fricative (/s/ or /θ/) or a stop (/k/). If it was before "a, o, u", it was assigned 'k'. In the other cases it was either /s/ or /θ/, depending on the Spanish variant.

The second exception was on the voiced stops /b, d, g/. First, all contexts of "g" before "e, I", (similar to "c"), were assigned to 'h' or 'x' (depending on the variant), which is the case that before these vowel letters it is pronounced /h/ or /x/. Further, if "b, d, g" were between vowels, then they were converted to upper case 'B, D, G', respectively, to represent their intervocalic nature (lenited forms [β, ð, ɣ]).

5.4 Syllable Breakdown

The first step towards syllable breakdown was to identify the vowels in each word and then assign their onsets and codas. For onset and codas, Spanish allows up to two consonants in each cluster (Sheperd, 2003). In terms of the nucleus, at the phonetic level, a semivowel ([j, w]) can be before and after the nucleus, or both in the case of triphthongs. These rules follow the formula below.

$$O_{((C1)\,C2)}\,N_{(S)\,V\,(S)}\,C_{(C1\,(C2))}$$

For example, in the word "transporte", the vowel 'a' can take 'tr' as the onset. For the coda, the maximum it can have is two consonants, if it is the right cluster. In this case, 'ns' is a legal cluster. /p/ therefore starts the following syllable. In this syllable, even when it can take two consonants in the coda position, the cluster 'rt' is not a legal cluster in Spanish. Thus, the second syllable makes its boundary between 'r' and 't', leaving 't' as the onset of the last syllable. The final syllable breakdown is represented below:

trans|por|te
CCVCC|CVC|CV

5.5 Stress Assignment

The next step was to annotate the stressed syllable for each word. As mentioned before, Spanish orthography is an accurate guideline for making syllabic breakdown and stress patterns. The location of a stress is counted in Spanish from right to left, i.e. from the final syllable backwards. There are three positions a stress can take in word stems (Eddington, 2004): last syllable (*aguda*, e.g. "limón"), penultimate syllable (*grave*, e.g. "casa"), and antepenultimate (*esdrújula*, e.g. "búsqueda")[8].

In our process, the first step was to identify the location of an accent in the word. For those words that had the accents, the corresponding syllable was classified as stressed. If there was no accent, then it was identified following the rules of orthography. The first step was to identify whether the word ended in 'n', 's' or vowel. If this was the case, then the stress fell in the penultimate syllable. If the word ended in any other letter, then the stress was assigned to the last syllable.

5.6 Phonotactics and IPA Annotations

For the phonotactic labelling, we converted all vowels to V and all consonants to C. For the IPA notation, we converted each letter to their corresponding IPA representation. This was done with both syllabic divisions and without, and also by adding the order or segments for a more precise annotation. This allows to do searchers like: getting all consonants that appear as the second element of a consonant cluster (C1[C2]V).

5.7 Morphological and Lexical Annotation

This section describes the classification of all words based on their morphological and lexical information. For this, we implemented Natural Language Processing techniques in R through scripts developed by the main author. We used the UDPipe R package (Straka and Straková, 2017), and we used the GSD model for Spanish. This library is widely

[8] There are rules that include a fourth group: *sobre-esdrújulas*, which are argued that have the stress in the fourth or fifth syllable. However, these are generally a stem with suffixes. For example, "ágilmente" has two morphemes: "ágil" + "mente". This has an impact on the pronunciation pattern where the syllable "-men-" can have a secondary stress. Because of this, most of the literature agrees that there are only three places of stress in Spanish. For more on secondary stress see

used for tasks such as tokenization, tagging and lemmatization for many languages. We used this package to label all words in the dictionary. The distributions of the main lexical categories are presented in the figure below with the corresponding final counts across all the dictionary.

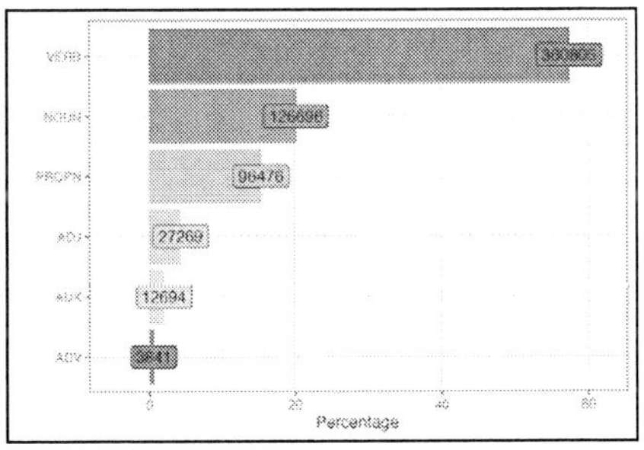

Figure 1: Distribution of Lexical Categories in the final dictionary, with their corresponding counts.

6. Results

All these steps and data processing stages, give a final dictionary with 628,300 entries, fully annotated and readily available for Spanish data research. The dictionary (ESPADA) can be accessed here:

https://github.com/simongonzalez/ESPADA

A sample of the entries and the columns is shown in Table 5 below.

Entry	*POS*	*Base*	*Phonotactics*	*IPA*
aarón	PROPN	a r O n	V CVC	a ron
con	ADP	k O n	CVC	kon
gris	NOUN	g r I s	CCVC	gris
la	DET	l A	CV	la
mesa	NOUN	m E s a	CV CV	me sa

Table 5: Sample Data from the final dictionary file.

The dictionary contains entries for 16 Spanish speaking countries. If only the entries for a given dialect are chosen, there is an average of 58,876 words per country, with varying total numbers, as shown in Figure 2. This gives users the option to select the dialect, or group of dialects, that best apply to the forced alignment process.

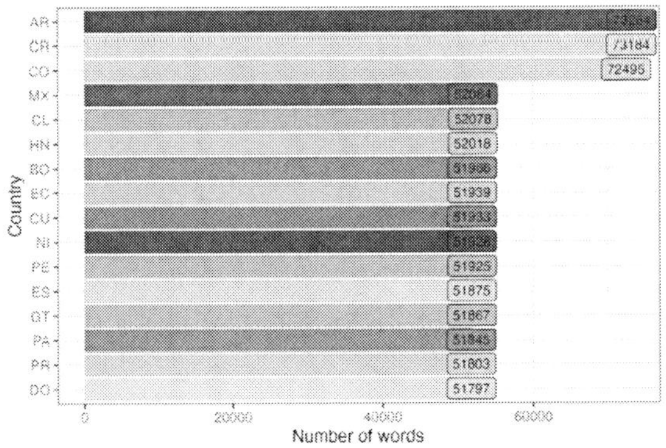

Figure 2: Word Distributions across Countries, with Argentina having the greatest number of entries and Dominican Republic with the least.

7. Conclusions

In this paper, we presented the development of a Spanish dictionary for phonetic and lexical tagging in socio-phonetic research. With this tool, researchers can have the maximum freedom to choose the dictionary that is the most representative of the data to be forced aligned, and then analysed in further stages. It has been our aim to facilitate the process of forced alignment and data wrangling for meaningful and accurate phonetic analysis. The open-source nature of this project also allows users to make the necessary changes to capture the complexity of phonetic variation in Spanish dialects.

8. Future Directions

This paper presents the development of the tool. Future work will aim to evaluate this dictionary with the other dictionaries compared in this paper. This will also include the assessment on the alignment accuracy across different Spanish dialects, especially in socio-phonetic studies.

9. Acknowledgements

We would like to acknowledge *The International Association for Forensic Phonetics and Acoustics (IAFPA)* for funding the main project encompassing this work. We give our thanks for their invaluable support. We also want to thank the two anonymous reviewers for their comments and suggestions. Their contribution has improved this paper in innumerable ways and saved us from many errors. Those that inevitably remain are entirely our own responsibility.

10. Bibliographical References

Aguilar, L. (1999). Hiatus and diphthong: Acoustic cues and speech situation differences. *Speech Communication*. 28. 57-74. 10.1016/S0167-6393(99)00003-5.

Álvarez, A., Obediente, E., and Rojas, N. (2009). Subdialectos del Español Caribeño de Venezuela: Prosodia e identidad regional. *Revista Internacional de Lingüística Iberoamericana* Vol. 7, No. 2 (14)

Baayan, H., Piepenbrock, R. and Gulikers, L. (1995). The CELEX Lexical Database (Release 2, CD-ROM). University of Pennsylvania, Philadelphia: *Linguistic Data Consortium*.

Bailey, G. (2016). Automatic detection of sociolinguistic variation using forced alignment. *University of Pennsylvania Working Papers in Linguistics*, 22 (2). Article 3. Retrieved from https://repository.upenn.edu/pwpl/vol22/iss2/3

DiCanio, C., Nam, H., Whalen, D.H., H. Bunnell, T., Amith, J.D. and Castillo Garcia, R. (2012). Assessing agreement level between forced alignment models with data from endangered language documentation corpora. *INTERSPEECH-2012*, Portland Oregon, 130–133

Domínguez, Giusseppe. (2015). *Diccionario de la RAE en modo texto plano.* https://www.giusseppe.net/blog/archivo/2015/10/29/diccionario-de-la-rae-en-modo-texto-plano/

Eddington, D. (2004). *Spanish Phonology and Morphology: Experimental and Quantitative perspectives*, John Benjamins Publishing Company

Foundation, T. D. (2020). *LibreOffice Writer*. Retrieved from https://www.libreoffice.org/discover/writer/

Fromont, R. and Hay, J. (2012). LaBB-CAT: An annotation store. *Proceedings of the Australasian Language Technology Workshop*, 113–117.

Fromont, R. and Watson, K. (2016). Factors influencing automatic segmental alignment of sociophonetic corpora. *Corpora* 11(3). 401–431.

Fruehwald, J. (2014). Automation and sociophonetics. Talk presented at *Methods in Dialectology XV*. Groningen: University of Groningen. Retrieved from https://jofrhwld.github.io/papers/methods_xv/#

Gnevsheva, K., Gonzalez Ochoa, S. and Fromont, R. (2020). Australian English Bilingual Corpus: Automatic forced-alignment accuracy in Russian and English'. In *Australian Journal of Linguistics*, vol. 40, no. 2, pp. 182-193.

Goldman, J.-Ph. (2011). EasyAlign: an automatic phonetic alignment tool under Praat, *Proceedings of InterSpeech*, September 2011, Firenze, Italy

Gonzalez, S., Travis, C.E., Grama, J., Barth, D. and Ananthanarayan, S. (2018). Recursive forced alignment: A test on a minority language. In Julien Epps, Joe Wolfe, John Smith & Caroline Jones (eds.), *Proceedings of the 17th Australasian International Conference on Speech Science and Technology*, 145–148.

Gonzalez, S., Grama, J. and Travis, C.E. (2020). Comparing the performance of forced aligners used in sociophonetic research. *Linguistics Vanguard*, vol. 6, no. 1, pp. 20190058. https://doi.org/10.1515/lingvan-2019-0058.

Gorman, K., Howell, J. and Wagner, M. (2011). Prosodylab-Aligner: A Tool for Forced Alignment of Laboratory Speech. *Canadian Acoustics*. 39.3. 192–193.

Guitart, J.M. (1994). Las líquidas en el caribe hispánico y la variación como alternancia de códigos. *Boletin del Instituto Caro y Cuervo* 49(2). 229–244.

Kisler, T., Reichel, U.D. and Schiel, F. (2017). Multilingual processing of speech via web services. *Computer Speech & Language* 45. 326–347.

Lubbers, M. and Torreira, F. (2016). *Praatalign: an interactive Praat plug-in for performing phonetic forced alignment*. Retrieved from https://github.com/dopefishh/praatalign

MacKenzie, L. and Turton, D. (2020). Assessing the accuracy of existing forced alignment software on varieties of British English, *Linguistics Vanguard, 6*

McAuliffe, M., Socolof, M., Mihuc, S., Wagner, M. and Sonderegger, M. (2017). Montreal Forced Aligner: Trainable text-speech alignment using Kaldi. *INTERSPEECH-2017*, Stockholm Sweden, 498–502

Morris, R.E. (2000). Constraint Interaction in Spanish /s/-Aspiration: Three Peninsular Varieties. *Hispanic Linguistics at the Turn of the Millennium: Papers from the 3rd Hispanic Linguistics Symposium*, ed. by Héctor Campos, Elena Herburger, Alfonso Morales-Front & Thomas J. Walsh. Somerville, MA: Cascadilla.

Núñez-Méndez E., Koike D.A., and Muñoz-Basols, J. (2021). Sociolinguistic approaches to sibilant variation in Spanish, Routledge

R Core Team (2021). R: A language and environment for statistical computing. *R Foundation for Statistical Computing*, Vienna, Austria. URL https://www.R-project.org/.

REAL ACADEMIA ESPAÑOLA: *Diccionario de la lengua española*, 23.ª ed., [versión 23.5 en línea]. https://dle.rae.es

Reddy, S. and Stanford, J. (2015). Toward completely automated vowel extraction: Introducing DARLA. *Linguistics Vanguard* 1(1). 15–28.

Rosenfelder, I., Fruehwald, L., Evanini, K., Seyfarth, S., Gorman, K., Prichard, H. and Yuan, J. (2014). *FAVE (Forced Alignment and Vowel Extraction) Program Suite* v1.2.2 10.5281/zenodo.22281.

Schiel F. (1999): Automatic Phonetic Transcription of Non-Prompted Speech, *Proc. of the ICPhS 1999*. San Francisco, August 1999. pp. 607-610.

Sheperd, M.A. (2003). *Constraint Interactions in Spanish Phonotactics: An Optimality Theory Analysis of Syllable-Level Phenomena in the Spanish Language*. Retrieved from https://doi.org/doi:10.7282/T3W9585Q

Straka, M. and Straková, J. (2017). Tokenizing, POS Tagging, Lemmatizing and Parsing UD 2.0 with UDPipe. In *Proceedings of the CoNLL 2017 Shared Task: Multilingual Parsing from Raw Text to Universal Dependencies*, Vancouver, Canada, August 2017.

Straka, M., Hajič, J. and Straková, J. (2016). UDPipe: Trainable Pipeline for Processing CoNLL-U Files Performing Tokenization, Morphological Analysis, POS Tagging and Parsing. In *Proceedings of the Tenth International Conference on Language Resources and Evaluation (LREC 2016)*, Portorož, Slovenia, May 2016.

Strunk, J., Schiel, F. and Seifart, F. (2014). Untrained forced alignment of transcriptions and audio for language documentation corpora using WebMAUS. In Nicoletta Calzolari, Khalid Choukri, Thierry Declerck, Hrafn Loftsson, Bente Maegaard, Joseph Mariani, Asuncion Moreno, Jan Odijk & Stelios Piperidis (Eds.), *Proceedings of the Ninth International Conference on Language Resources and Evaluation, LREC'14*, 3940–3947. Reykjavik, Iceland

Wilbanks, E. (2021). *faseAlign* (Version 1.1.11) [Computer software]. Retrieved Apr 17, 2021 from https://github.com/EricWilbanks/faseAlign.

Proceedings of the 16th Linguistic Annotation Workshop (LAW-XVI) @LREC 2022, pages 15–22
Marseille, 24 June 2022

Extending the SSJ Universal Dependencies Treebank for Slovenian: Was it Worth it?

Kaja Dobrovoljc, Nikola Ljubešić
University of Ljubljana
Jozef Stefan Institute
kaja.dobrovoljc@ff.uni-lj.si
nikola.ljubesic@ijs.si

Abstract

This paper presents the creation and the evaluation of a new version of the reference SSJ Universal Dependencies Treebank for Slovenian, which has been substantially improved and extended to almost double the original size. The process was based on the initial revision and documentation of the language-specific UD annotation guidelines for Slovenian and the corresponding modification of the original SSJ annotations, followed by a two-stage annotation campaign, in which two new subsets have been added, the previously unreleased sentences from the ssj500k corpus and the Slovenian subset of the ELEXIS parallel corpus. The annotation campaign resulted in an extended version of the SSJ UD treebank with 5,435 newly added sentences comprising of 126,427 tokens. To evaluate the potential benefits of this data increase for Slovenian dependency parsing, we compared the performance of the classla-stanza dependency parser trained on the old and the new SSJ data when evaluated on the new SSJ test set and its subsets. Our results show an increase of LAS performance in general, especially for previously under-represented syntactic phenomena, such as lists, elliptical constructions and appositions, but also confirm the distinct nature of the two newly added subsets and the diversification of the SSJ treebank as a whole.

Keywords: Slovenian, treebanks, dependency syntax, dependency parsing, Universal Dependencies, annotation guidelines, annotation campaign, data evaluation

1. Introduction

Manually annotated language data are essential to the development and evaluation of natural language processing tools. For syntactic analysis in particular, these mostly involve parsed corpora (treebanks), in which surface word forms bear additional information on their morphological and syntactic characteristics with the structure of a sentence described as a tree-like graph.

To overcome the various drawbacks rising from the multitude and heterogeneity of treebank annotation schemes, especially in the field of multilingual parser development, cross-lingual learning and research on language typology, the Universal Dependencies (UD) initiative (De Marneffe et al., 2021; Nivre et al., 2016) proposed a universal inventory of grammatical categories and guidelines for their application to facilitate consistent annotation of similar constructions across languages.

As of the latest release (Zeman and others, 2022), the UD scheme has been applied to more than 200 treebanks in over 130 languages and has contributed to important scientific advances in natural language processing and linguistics alike. This includes the reference SSJ treebank for written Slovenian (Dobrovoljc et al., 2017), which has been used in modelling several state-of-the-art parsing tools worldwide (Zeman et al., 2018). The treebank, first released in UD v1.2 in 2015, included 8,000 parsed sentences comprising of 140,670 words, placing it in the top third of UD treebanks ranked according to data size.

Within the project Development of Slovene in a Digital Environment (DSDE)[1] aimed at meeting the needs for computational tools and services in the field of language technologies for Slovenian, more than 5,000 new sentences have been added to the SSJ treebank to increase the size of manually annotated training data and thus encourage further advances in the field of Slovenian language technology.

In this paper, we present the results of this latest activity by describing the creation of the new version of the SSJ Universal Dependencies Treebank for Slovenian, which has been substantially improved both in terms of size and the quality of annotations. After a brief presentation of the original version of the treebank in Section 2, we present the extensively documented and slightly revised language-specific UD guidelines for Slovenian in (Section 3) which were implemented to the original treebank (Section 4) and used in the subsequent two-stage annotation campaign described in Section 5. We then evaluate the NLP relevance of the resulting dataset by comparing the performance of a dependency parsing tool trained on both versions of the SSJ treebank in Section 6, and conclude with a short discussion on whether our results justify the labour-intensive data extension typical of treebank annotation in general (Section 7).

2. Original SSJ UD Treebank

The original SSJ UD treebank has been created by a semi-automatic conversion from the reference ssj500k training corpus for Slovenian (Krek et al., 2020b),

[1] `https://slovenscina.eu/en`

a balanced collection of texts sampled from the FidaPLUS corpus (Arhar Holdt, 2007), a predecessor of the 1-billion-word Gigafida reference corpus of contemporary written Slovene (Krek et al., 2020a). The ssj500k corpus includes fiction, non-fiction and periodical texts dating from 1990 to 2000, which have been manually annotated on various levels of linguistic annotation (Krek et al., 2020b), including lemmatization, morphosyntactic tagging and dependency parsing in accordance with the JOS annotation scheme (Erjavec et al., 2010).

The ssj500k conversion from JOS to UD was based on a broad set of mapping rules for all three annotation layers (part-of-speech categories, morphological features and dependency relations),[2] the conversion to UD dependencies required highly fine-grained rules given the several significant distinctions between both annotation schemes (Dobrovoljc et al., 2017), including a much more detailed set of dependency relations in UD (37 labels) in comparison to JOS (10 labels).

As a result, the full ssj500k corpus was automatically converted to UD part-of-speech categories and morphological features with only the instances of the verb *biti* 'be' requiring manual disambiguation (Dobrovoljc et al., 2019) between *AUX* and *VERB* part-of-speech tags. On the other hand, due to the limited coverage of the the mapping rules for syntax, not all JOS-parsed sentences could be converted automatically, especially those exhibiting complex or rare phenomena pertaining to clausal coordination, juxtaposition and predicate ellipsis.

Consequently, only around two thirds of the 13,411 JOS-parsed sentences in ssj500k have been fully converted to UD, which resulted in the original SSJ UD treebank containing 8,000 sentences and 140,670 tokens. Despite the continuous improvements of the SSJ UD annotations since its first release in 2015, the size of the dataset remained unchanged. The 3,411 unreleased partially converted sentences from ssj500k were thus the obvious starting point for the recent extension of the SSJ UD dataset for Slovenian, as described in Section 5.1.

3. Slovenian UD Guidelines Revision and Documentation

With the exception of the online language-specific guidelines for UD morphology annotation published with the initial SSJ release (pertaining to the now obsolete Version 1 of the UD guidelines (Nivre et al., 2016)), the guidelines for Slovenian UD dependency annotation have only been documented implicitly – in the form of the rule-based conversion scripts from JOS to UD annotations (Section 2) and the resulting SSJ dataset. To bridge this gap and provide the necessary documentation in support of both annotation and exploration of Slovenian UD data, the official Slovenian UD guidelines have now been exhaustively documented for all layers of annotation, by describing the general annotation guidelines and its application to specific constructions in Slovenian.

In the process, a few changes to the original UD annotation principles for Slovenian were also introduced to make them better compliant with the universal guidelines and the annotation principles adopted by similar languages, mostly relating to comparative constructions, emphasizing adverbials, sentence-initial discourse phenomena and expletives.

For example, the Slovenian guidelines for the *expl* relation, which was previously used for labelling all instances of the reflexive pronouns *si* and *se* '(to) oneself', have now been improved so as to distinguish between true expletives (e.g. reflexive clitics as part of inherently reflexive verbs or passive constructions) and pronouns occurring as objects (Figure 1).

The official Slovenian UD guidelines are freely available both in Slovenian (as a standalone document)[3] and English (as part of the official UD website).[4] In addition to the category-based description of the universal guidelines and its application to specific examples in Slovenian, the guidelines document also features a construction-based appendix, in which the treatment of specific syntactic phenomena is addressed, including the challenging constructions identified within the annotation campaign described in Section 5.

4. Revision of the SSJ Treebank

In the data preparation stage, the original SSJ treebank annotations were manually improved to implement the newly proposed changes in the annotation guidelines (Section 3) and remove the previously identified annotation mistakes and inconsistencies arising from the original conversion (Section 2). Among others, these included conflicting annotations of paratactical and coordinating clauses, direct and indirect objects, appositional structures, specific multi-word expressions, and a relatively high number of unjustified non-projective relations.

For each of the approximately 30 identified types of issues, various heuristics were used to identify sentences with potentially problematic annotations, which were then manually inspected and corrected in accordance with the guidelines. In the process, 1,670 relations in the original SSJ dataset have been corrected, the distribution of which reflects the structures mentioned above, as two thirds of the corrections pertained to the *advmod*, *nmod*, *obl*, *parataxis*, *appos* and *expl*

[2] The rules and conversion scripts from JOS to UD are available at `https://github.com/clarinsi/jos2ud`.

[3] The document will be published in accordance with the DSDE project timeline as part of the official project website. The preliminary version is available at `http://tiny.cc/ud-sl_guidelines`

[4] `https://universaldependencies.org/`

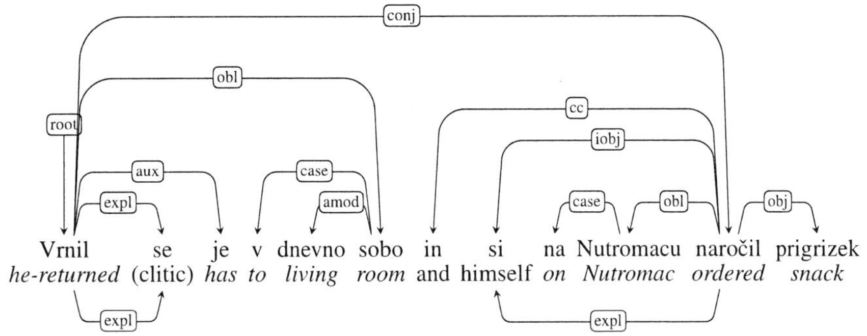

(He returned to the living room and ordered himself a snack from Nutromac.)

Figure 1: Example sentence from SSJ illustrating the change of Slovenian UD guidelines for the expletive *expl* relation from the initial treebank release (below) to UD release v2.10 (above).

relations. This manual work resulted in the slightly revised version of the original SSJ treebank, which was used as the basis for subsequent new data addition described in the sections below.

5. Extension of the SSJ Treebank

The extension of the old SSJ treebank was performed in two subsequent stages, in which new sentences from the ssj500k corpus were added and a new ELEXIS subset was created. In both stages, the data annotation was performed using the ssj500k-compliant Q-CAT corpus annotation tool (Brank, 2022), which was upgraded to also support the CONLL-U format, while the curation stage was performed using the WebAnno (Eckart de Castilho et al., 2016) web-based tool hosted by CLARIN.SI.[5]

5.1. Extension 1: Semi-Converted ssj500k

In the first stage of the project, the 3,411 sentences from the original ssj500k corpus which had not been fully converted from JOS to UD dependency trees at the time of original SSJ compilation (see Section 2) were manually inspected so that the tokens with missing (unconverted) UD dependency annotations were also labeled. Specifically, the semi-converted dataset included 95,194 tokens, out of which 22,377 tokens (23.5%) were initially labeled as *unknown* dependents of the root node (Figure 2). This means that on average 6.6 dependency relations per sentence had to be manually created from scratch, while the existing relations were also checked for the accuracy of conversion.

The process was designed as a multi-annotator annotation campaign, in which each sentence was annotated by two independent annotators (pre-trained linguists) and the final curator in case of disagreements. Although it is difficult to report on the inter-annotator agreement given the specificity of the task (manual corrections of partially converted data), on average, the two annotators agreed on 92.1% annotations (87,675 out of 95,194 tokens). For the *unknown* relations in particular, the absolute agreement was much lower (80.5% or 18,023 out of 22,377 tokens), but it was expected given the complexity of the task (annotation of the most complex syntactic constructions in long sentences).

In total, the activity resulted in 22,377 newly added dependency relations and 4,623 corrected dependency relations in the semi-converted ssj500k subset, amounting to 27,000 (28.4%) tokens with corrected annotations. Almost one half of the previously unlabeled (*unknown*) were punctuation tokens (*punct*), which was expected given the original mapping rules, where punctuation attachment was performed after most other sentence annotations were known. This includes the identification of the sentence *root* element, which is the second most frequent type of unconverted tokens (12%), followed by *parataxis* (9%) and (mostly clausal) coordination (*conj*, 6%), confirming the type of constructions reported to be the most challenging at the time of the original ssj500k conversion to SSJ (Section 2).

On the other hand, most corrections of successfully converted labels pertained to change of head attachment for adverbial modifiers (*advmod*, 20% of all corrections) and punctuation (16%), while most label corrections involved the switch from nominal modifiers (*nmod*) to prepositional adjuncts (*obl*, 4%), with other corrections being more equally distributed across individual relations. This, however, does not necessarily reflect the accuracy of the original rule-based conversion, given the semi-converted sentences do not reflect the final output for the fully converted sentences, as illustrated by the inter-dependent rules for punctuation attachment in the paragraph above.

Given the long learning curve related to this relatively complex annotation task, the speed of the annotators varied from an average of 11 sentences (307 tokens) per hour in the beginning of the first stage to approximately 15 sentences (419 tokens) per hour at its completion.

5.2. Extension 2: ELEXIS

In the second stage of the project, the second new SSJ subset was created based on the ELEXIS-WSD-

[5] https://www.clarin.si/webanno/.

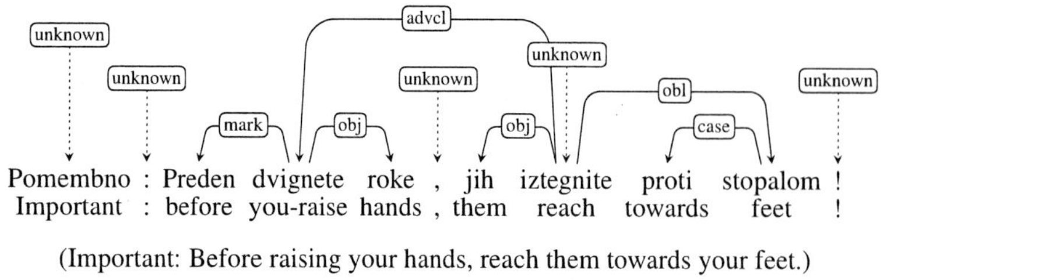

Figure 2: An example of a semi-converted ssj500k sentence with some missing (*unknown*) dependency annotations.

SL corpus, the Slovenian subset of the ELEXIS parallel sense-annotated dataset (Martelli et al., 2021) extracted from WikiMatrix (Schwenk et al., 2021), a large open-access collection of (translated) parallel data derived from Wikipedia. The corpus comprised of 2,024 Slovenian sentences (31,237 tokens) with manual annotations of tokenization, lemmatization and JOS morphosyntactic annotations.

For UD morphology (POS tags, morphological features), the existing mapping scripts (Section 2) were used for conversion from JOS to UD, followed by a manual disambiguation of the AUX and VERB instances of the verb *biti*. Afterward, the dataset was parsed with UD dependency relations using the classla-stanza parsing tool (Ljubešić and Dobrovoljc, 2019) trained on the concatenation of the available data, i.e. the slightly revised original SSJ treebank (Section 4) and the new ssj500k-based extension (Section 5.1).

The automatically parsed ELEXIS dataset was then manually checked by three annotators and the final curator. In the process, 1,534 dependency relations have been manually corrected (854 for wrong head, 252 for wrong relation and 428 for both), mostly pertaining to constructions labeled as *nmod*, *advmod*, *obl*, *conj* and *punct*. The indirectly observed parsing accuracy (95%) was in line with the expected parser performance on standard written texts (see, for example, evaluations reported in Table 3), and was also reflected in the annotation speed (an average of 37.5 sentences per hour) and a relatively high inter-annotator agreement (96.3% identically annotated tokens by the three annotators).

5.3. Overview of the New SSJ Treebank

Finally, the slightly revised original treebank (Section 4) and the two newly available datasets described in Sections 5.1 and 5.2 have been merged into the new–improved and extended–version of the Slovenian SSJ treebank (Table 1), which has been released in UD v2.10.[6]

As shown in Table 1, the SSJ treebank size has increased by 5,435 sentences (+67.9%) and 126,427 tokens (+89.9%) in comparison to the old version and now places as the 30th out of 218 UD treebanks ranked according to the number of words. In the continuation of the paper, we evaluate and discuss the impact of this substantial data increase on the state-of-the-art dependency parsing of Slovenian.

Subset	Sent.	Tokens	Avg.len.
Old SSJ	8,000	140,670	17.58
Ext. 1 (ssj500k)	3,411	95,194	27.91
Ext. 2 (ELEXIS)	2,024	31,233	15.43
Total	13,435	267,097	19.88

Table 1: Overview of the new version of Slovenian SSJ UD treebank.

6. Evaluation

We evaluate the extensions of the SSJ Universal Dependencies treebank by training the Bi-LSTM based biaffine parser (Dozat and Manning, 2016) available in the classla-stanza pipeline (Ljubešić and Dobrovoljc, 2019), a fork of the Stanza pipeline (Qi et al., 2020), the fork containing many improvements primarily on the level of tokenization, part-of-speech tagging and lemmatization.

Besides the parsing training data, we use the CLARIN.SI-embed.sl embedding collection (Ljubešić and Erjavec, 2018) trained on a 3.5 billion tokens collection of Slovenian texts.

In the following subsections we address the decisions of the new SSJ data splits in light of the newly available data, our experimental setup, and, finally, the results of our experiments.

6.1. Data splits

While constructing the new data split, a prerequisite for the official data release, we mostly followed the decisions from the old SSJ dataset, which was a consecutive split, i.e., the first part of the dataset was used as a training dataset, with the two latter parts being the dev and the test datasets, in a rough 8:1:1 sentence-based ratio. Given that Extension 1 of the SSJ dataset, coming from the same text source as the original SSJ (ssj500k), consists of sentences roughly uniformly distributed across the whole dataset, it was possible to keep a similar divide of the newly added ssj500k data, with minor deviations due to the fact that in the new split document

[6]This paper reports work on a penultimate release version (commit fa057316b79779893659bdc007cdc7f6465e58f3), which has been slightly changed for the official UD v2.10 release due to stricter validation rules. Namely, approximately 50 annotations were changed, equally distributed across various morphological and syntactic categories.

boundaries were respected, which was previously not the case. The large majority of the original SSJ sentences was thus preserved in the same (data, dev or test) portion of the dataset.
Given the specificities of each of the two data extensions (the first extension adding significantly longer and syntactically more complex sentences, the second extension adding shorter translated sentences from Wikipedia), Extension 2 data was added to all three data splits as well, again in a 8:1:1 ratio. This decision also allows for a more diverse evaluation, which will prove to be rather useful for identifying potential biases in our data.
The final size of the split, measured in number of sentences, is given in Table 2. The split shows for all three splits of the extended SSJ dataset to consist of 85% of sentences from the ssj500k dataset and the remainder from the ELEXIS dataset.

Subset	Train	Dev	Test
Old SSJ	6,478	734	788
Extension 1	2,807	313	291
Extension 2	1,618	203	203
New SSJ	10,903	1,250	1,282

Table 2: Comparison (in number of sentences) of the old SSJ dataset split and the new SSJ dataset split, by each data extension.

6.2. Experimental setup

To perform an automatic investigation of the potential gains obtained by the SSJ data extension described in Section 5 in comparison to the original SSJ data, we have trained two parsers:

1. The SSJ_old model based on the original SSJ dataset (as described in Section 4)
2. The SSJ_new model based on the original SSJ dataset with both extensions, from the ssj500k (5.1) and the ELEXIS datasets (Section 5.2).

Both during training, development and testing, we use gold-annotated upstream data (tokenization, sentence splitting, morphosyntactic tagging, lemmatization) as we are primarily interested in the improvements in the dependency parsing performance, and not the interplay of automatic upstream and dependency syntax annotations. Using automatically annotated upstream layers with different taggers and lemmatizers (based on the specific training data) would have blurred the impact our data interventions had on the dependency syntax layer, especially given that classla-stanza tagging and lemmatization depend also on additional external processes and data such as rule-based tokenizers that partially perform tagging, inflectional lexicons, and additional training data.
We evaluate both parsers on the new SSJ test set (Table 2, 1,282 sentences) using the standard label attachment score (LAS) that gives the percentage of nodes with correctly assigned parent node and the type of relation between them. To explore the scalability of the new model to different data types, as well as the potential differences in the three main SSJ subsets, the evaluation results are also reported for each test subset individually, i.e. the old SSJ test data (788 sentences), the Extension 1 test data (291 sentences) and the Extension 2 test data (203 sentences).
We report both on the overall parsing performance (Section 6.3) and the performance for individual relations (Section 6.4).

6.3. Overall Performance

The overall parsing performance, reported in Table 3, confirms the general benefits of our data extensions, with the improvement of 1.85 LAS on the whole new SSJ test set (21% relative error reduction).[7] As expected, the biggest increases are observed for the two newly added subsets, that is +4.41 LAS (29% error reduction) for Ext-1 ssj500k data and +2.11 LAS (39% relative error reduction) for Ext-2 ELEXIS data, while the benefits of the new model are much less pronounced when evaluated on the old SSJ data alone (+0.3, 5.5% relative error reduction).

Models	Test datasets			
	New SSJ	Old	Ext-1	Ext-2
SSJ_old	91.36	94.53	84.67	94.60
SSJ_new	93.21	94.83	89.09	96.71

Table 3: Results of the automatic evaluation of the old and new SSJ model, measured through labeled attachment score (LAS) F1 on the new SSJ test set and its subsets.

This confirms the distinct nature of the original and the two newly added datasets, which, as already reported above, differ in terms of data source, sentence length, tree complexity and source of annotations. The higher parsing scores on the old SSJ and the Ext-2 ELEXIS test data in Table 3 for both models suggest that the old SSJ and the Ext-2 ELEXIS data are more similar and easier to parse in general, which is line with the shorter average sentence length reported in Table 1. On the other hand, the newly added Ext-1 ssj500k data is definitely the hardest test set of the three, which is expected given it mostly includes sentences that were too complex to be covered by the automatic rule-based conversion at the time of the original SSJ treebank creation (Section 2).
The original SSJ dataset was therefore potentially biased towards simpler sentences, which is not only illustrated by the seeming drop in performance when com-

[7]We calculate the relative error reduction as the percentage of the difference of the LAS score between the new and the old system in the difference between a perfect LAS score and the old LAS score, i.e. $(LAS_{new} - LAS_{old})/(100 - LAS_{old}) * 100$.

paring the evaluation of the old model on the old test set (94.53 LAS) and the new model on the new test set (93.21 LAS), but has also been suggested by the results of the CoNLL 2018 Shared Task (Zeman et al., 2018)[8] and the official Stanza evaluations,[9] which list the (old) SSJ treebank as one of the highest-ranking treebanks according to LAS score.

6.4. Relation-Based Performance

To better understand which specific constructions benefit from the newly available data and what can be expected from the new model when used for specific parsing tasks in downstream applications, we extend the overall evaluation on the new SSJ test set described in Section 6.3 above to individual dependency relations as well.

As shown in Table 4,[10] with the exception of *vocative* and *dep*,[11] all relations demonstrate an increase of LAS F1 in comparison to the baseline old SSJ. Specifically, the biggest improvements are gained for relations pertaining to constructions which were rare or under-represented in the old SSJ treebank, but are frequent in the newly added data (ssj500k in particular), such as lists (*list*, +75.86 F1), elliptical structures (*orphan*, +68.24 F1), appositional modifiers (*appos*, +13.40 F1) and discourse particles (*discourse*, +9.97 F1), with a significant error reduction also observed for fixed multi-word expressions (*fixed*, 52%) and numeric modifiers (*nummod*, 43%).

On the other hand, the smallest gains are observed for adjectival modifiers (*amod*, +0.10pp, 8% relative error reduction), clausal complements (*ccomp*, +0.23pp, 2% relative error reduction) and expletives (*expl*, +0.40pp, 11% relative error reduction), suggesting that increasing the size of the training data and making it more diverse is less significant for some of the relations.

In absolute terms, the new model is most successful in parsing function words, such as prepositions (*case*), auxiliary verbs (*aux*), determiners (*det*) and subordinating conjunctions (*mark*), as well as adjectival modifiers of nominals (*amod*), which all exhibit LAS above 98 F1. For core semantic phenomena, which are typically the most relevant relations for various downstream applications, above average performance is observed for nominal subjects (*nsubj*) and objects (*obj*). On the other hand, indirect objects (*iobj*, adjuncts (*obl, advmod*) and their clausal counterparts (*ccomp, csubj, advcl*) still exhibit below-average performance despite some important improvements based on the newly available data (e.g. +5.80 LAS and 29% error reduction for *csubj* clausal subjects).

7. Conclusion

We have presented a new version of the reference SSJ Universal Dependencies Treebank for Slovenian, which has been revised and extended to almost double the original size. The process was based on the initial revision and exhaustive documentation of the language-specific UD annotation guidelines for Slovenian, followed by a systematic multi-stage annotation campaign, in which the original SSJ data has been slightly revised and substantially extended by new sentences coming from the ssj500k and ELEXIS corpora. After proposing the official UD data splits for the extended SSJ treebank, the data was used to train a new dependency parsing model in the classla-stanza NLP tool,[12] and compare its performance to the model trained on the old, un-extended SSJ data.

At first glance, the results seem very unimpressive given the labour-intensive data annotation campaign, with only marginal performance gains when the two models are evaluated on the old test data. However, when evaluated on the new, extended and diversified data, the parsing performance improvements are substantially more pronounced, especially for previously under-represented syntactic phenomena, which have mostly been left out of the original SSJ due to the limitations of its rule-based creation.

The new diversified SSJ dataset might therefore introduce some new challenges to the parsing systems, but will also make them much more accurate with respect to naturally occurring language data. This is especially important for under-resourced languages like Slovenian, where large-scale development of domain-specific treebanks and parsing systems cannot be realistically expected.

Nevertheless, given the now empirically confirmed distinct nature of the three SSJ subsets, future work should be dedicated to a systematic in-depth investigation of the possible points of divergence between the datasets with respect to parsing performance, such as text source, sentence length, tree complexity and possible annotation inconsistencies, which could potentially lead to new insights for further SSJ treebank consolidation and extension on the one hand, and parsing system modifications on the other.

Last but not least, although our evaluation was deliberately focused on dependency parsing only, the new SSJ dataset represents an equally important contribution to the development of lemmatization, part-of-speech tagging and other models for morphological processing of

[8] https://universaldependencies.org/conll18/results-treebanks-las.html

[9] https://stanfordnlp.github.io/stanza/performance.html

[10] Relations not occurring in the test set (*dislocated, goeswith, reparandum*) are excluded, while extensions (e.g. *flat:name*) are truncated to their universal counterparts (e.g. *flat*).

[11] The zero increase of performance for *vocative* and *dep* is expected, given that the former only has a single occurrence in the test set, while the latter is used for labelling irregular, marginal phenomena.

[12] The new parsing model is planned to be released on the CLARIN.SI repository and integrated into the classla-stanza pipeline: https://github.com/clarinsi/classla.

Relation	Description	SSJ_old	SSJ_new	F1 diff	RER
acl	clausal modifier of noun	80.76	81.73	0.97	5%
advcl	adverbial clause modifier	71.37	75.86	4.49	16%
advmod	adverbial modifier	87.01	89.95	2.94	23%
amod	adjectival modifier	98.8	98.9	0.1	8%
appos	appositional modifier	50	63.4	13.4	27%
aux	auxiliary verb	98.45	98.93	0.48	31%
case	case marking preposition	98.72	99.17	0.45	35%
cc	coordinating conjunction	94.94	96.27	1.33	26%
ccomp	clausal complement	90.44	90.67	0.23	2%
conj	conjunct	81.52	85.91	4.39	24%
cop	copula verb	93.4	95.43	2.03	31%
csubj	clausal subject	79.73	85.53	5.8	29%
dep	unspecified dependency	54.55	54.55	0	0%
det	determiner	98.31	98.79	0.48	28%
discourse	discourse element	59.26	69.23	9.97	25%
expl	expletive	96.31	96.71	0.4	11%
fixed	fixed multi-word expression	86.03	93.33	7.3	52%
flat	flat multi word-expression	87.97	92.12	4.15	35%
iobj	indirect object	78.57	81.66	3.09	14%
list	list	0	75.86	75.86	76%
mark	marker (subordinating conjunction)	97.88	98.69	0.81	38%
nmod	nominal modifier	85.72	87.44	1.72	12%
nsubj	nominal subject	93.69	95.28	1.59	25%
nummod	numeric modifier	89.95	94.23	4.28	43%
obj	(direct) object	95.08	95.53	0.45	9%
obl	oblique nominal (adjunct)	89.59	91.14	1.55	15%
orphan	dependent of missing parent	0	68.24	68.24	68%
parataxis	parataxis	63.32	70.35	7.03	19%
punct	punctuation symbol	90.3	93.08	2.78	29%
root	root element	95.09	96.26	1.17	24%
vocative	vocative	0	0	0	0%
xcomp	open clausal complement	91.71	92.87	1.16	14%
ALL	all relations	91.36	93.21	1.85	21%

Table 4: Relation-based comparison of LAS F1 performance of the parsing model trained on the old and the new SSJ data with relations listed alphabetically. The last two columns give the absolute F1 difference and the relative error reduction (RER).

Slovenian, especially for systems trained on UD treebanks alone.

8. Acknowledgements

The work described in this paper was supported by the project Development of Slovene in a Digital Environment co-financed by the Republic of Slovenia and the European Union from the European Regional Development Fund, and the research program "Language Resources and Technologies for Slovene" (P6-0411) funded by the Slovene Research Agency. A special acknowledgment goes to the data annotation team (Tina Munda, Ina Poteko, Rebeka Roblek, Luka Terčon and Karolina Zgaga).

9. Bibliographical References

Arhar Holdt, Š. (2007). Korpus FidaPLUS: nova generacija slovenskega referenčnega korpusa. *Jezik in slovstvo*, 52(2).

Brank, J. (2022). Q-CAT corpus annotation tool 1.3. Slovenian language resource repository CLARIN.SI.

De Marneffe, M.-C., Manning, C. D., Nivre, J., and Zeman, D. (2021). Universal Dependencies. *Computational linguistics*, 47(2):255–308.

Dobrovoljc, K., Erjavec, T., and Krek, S. (2017). The Universal Dependencies Treebank for Slovenian. In *Proceedings of the 6th Workshop on Balto-Slavic Natural Language Processing, BSNLP@EACL 2017*, pages 33–38.

Dobrovoljc, K., Erjavec, T., and Ljubešić, N. (2019). Improving UD processing via satellite resources for morphology. In *Proceedings of the Third Workshop on Universal Dependencies (UDW, SyntaxFest 2019)*, pages 24–34, Paris, France, August. Association for Computational Linguistics.

Dozat, T. and Manning, C. D. (2016). Deep biaffine attention for neural dependency parsing. *CoRR*, abs/1611.01734.

Eckart de Castilho, R., Mújdricza-Maydt, É., Yimam, S. M., Hartmann, S., Gurevych, I., Frank, A., and Biemann, C. (2016). A web-based tool for the integrated annotation of semantic and syntactic structures. In *Proceedings of the Workshop on Language Technology Resources and Tools for Digital Humanities (LT4DH)*, pages 76–84, Osaka, Japan, December. The COLING 2016 Organizing Committee.

Erjavec, T., Fišer, D., Krek, S., and Ledinek, N. (2010). The JOS Linguistically Tagged Corpus of Slovene. In *Proceedings of the Seventh conference on International Language Resources and Evaluation (LREC'10)*, Valletta, Malta, May. European Language Resources Association (ELRA).

Krek, S., Arhar Holdt, Š., Erjavec, T., Čibej, J., Repar, A., Gantar, P., Ljubešić, N., Kosem, I., and Dobrovoljc, K. (2020a). Gigafida 2.0: The reference corpus of written standard Slovene. In *Proceedings of the 12th Language Resources and Evaluation Conference*, pages 3340–3345, Marseille, France, May. European Language Resources Association.

Krek, S., Erjavec, T., Dobrovoljc, K., Gantar, P., Arhar Holdt, , Čibej, J., and Brank, J. (2020b). The ssj500k training corpus for Slovene language processing. In *Proceedings of the Conference on Language Technologies and Digital Humanities*, pages 24–33, Ljubljana, Slovenia, September. Institute of Contemporary History.

Ljubešić, N. and Dobrovoljc, K. (2019). What does neural bring? Analysing improvements in morphosyntactic annotation and lemmatisation of Slovenian, Croatian and Serbian. In *Proceedings of the 7th Workshop on Balto-Slavic Natural Language Processing*, pages 29–34, Florence, Italy, August. Association for Computational Linguistics.

Martelli, F., Navigli, R., Krek, S., Tiberius, C., Kallas, J., Gantar, P., Koeva, S., Nimb, S., Pedersen, B., Olsen, S., Langements, M., Koppel, K., Üksik, T., Dobrovolijc, K., Ureña-Ruiz, R.-J., Sancho-Sánchez, J.-L., Lipp, V., Varadi, T., Györffy, A., László, S., Quochi, V., Monachini, M., Frontini, F., Tempelaars, R., Costa, R., Salgado, A., Čibej, J., and Munda, T. (2021). Designing the ELEXIS parallel sense-annotated dataset in 10 european languages. In *eLex 2021 Proceedings*, eLex Conference. Proceedings. Lexical Computing CZ. null ; Conference date: 05-07-2021 Through 07-07-2021.

Nivre, J., de Marneffe, M.-C., Ginter, F., Goldberg, Y., Hajic, J., Manning, C. D., McDonald, R., Petrov, S., Pyysalo, S., Silveira, N., Tsarfaty, R., and Zeman, D. (2016). Universal Dependencies v1: A multilingual treebank collection. In Nicoletta Calzolari (Conference Chair), et al., editors, *Proceedings of the Tenth International Conference on Language Resources and Evaluation (LREC 2016)*, Paris, France, may. European Language Resources Association (ELRA).

Qi, P., Zhang, Y., Zhang, Y., Bolton, J., and Manning, C. D. (2020). Stanza: A python natural language processing toolkit for many human languages. *arXiv preprint arXiv:2003.07082*.

Schwenk, H., Chaudhary, V., Sun, S., Gong, H., and Guzmán, F. (2021). WikiMatrix: Mining 135M parallel sentences in 1620 language pairs from Wikipedia. In *Proceedings of the 16th Conference of the European Chapter of the Association for Computational Linguistics: Main Volume*, pages 1351–1361, Online, April. Association for Computational Linguistics.

Zeman, D., Hajič, J., Popel, M., Potthast, M., Straka, M., Ginter, F., Nivre, J., and Petrov, S. (2018). CoNLL 2018 shared task: Multilingual parsing from raw text to Universal Dependencies. In *Proceedings of the CoNLL 2018 Shared Task: Multilingual Parsing from Raw Text to Universal Dependencies*, pages 1–21, Brussels, Belgium, October. Association for Computational Linguistics.

10. Language Resource References

Ljubešić, Nikola and Erjavec, Tomaž. (2018). *Word embeddings CLARIN.SI-embed.sl 1.0.*

Zeman, Daniel and others. (2022). *Universal Dependencies 2.10.*

Proceedings of the 16th Linguistic Annotation Workshop (LAW-XVI) @LREC 2022, pages 23–30
Marseille, 24 June 2022

Converting the Sinica Treebank of Mandarin Chinese to Universal Dependencies

Yu-Ming Hsieh[1], Yueh-Yin Shih[2], Wei-Yun Ma[2]
Research Center for Humanities & Social Sciences, Academia Sinica
Institute of Information Science, Academia Sinica
morris@gate.sinica.edu.tw, {yuehyin, ma}@iis.sinica.edu.tw

Abstract

This paper describes the conversion of the Sinica Treebank, one of the major Mandarin Chinese treebanks, to Universal Dependencies. The conversion is rule-based and the process involves POS tag mapping, head adjusting in line with the UD scheme and the dependency conversion. Linguistic insights into Mandarin Chinese alongwith the conversion are also discussed. The resulting corpus is the UD Chinese Sinica Treebank which contains more than fifty thousand tree structures according to the UD scheme. The dataset can be downloaded at https://github.com/ckiplab/ud.

Keywords: Sinica Treebank, Universal Dependencies, conversion.

1. Introduction

The recent surge of interest in using a unified tagset and annotation guideline for treebanks of many languages has led to the speedy growing of the Universal Dependencies (UD) Project (Nivre et al., 2016). The project aims to facilitate the development of parsing technologies, enabling the use of techniques such as cross-lingual transfer. The UD version 2.9 consists of 217 treebanks in 122 languages with contributions from 477 researchers around the world.

Apart from developing treebanks by manual parsing or manual correction of automatic parsing, a UD treebank can also be automatically converted from an existing treebank, which uses a different annotation scheme (Arnardóttir et al., 2020). The present work is to convert the Sinica Treebank, in which the thematic relation between a predicate and an argument is marked in addition to grammatical category, to a UD approach treebank.

There are already 5 Mandarin Chinese UD corpora on the UD website. However, compared to other major languages, the data size for Chinese is quite small. The Sinica TreeBank has been a major Traditional Chinese Treebank developed in Taiwan and has made contribution to many NLP tasks. We hope to enlarge the usage of the Sinica treebank by converting it to the UD format and also gain some insights along with the conversion to share with the community.

The paper is structured as follows. Section 2 introduces the design and contents of the Sinica TreeBank. Section 3 describes the conversion process. The resulting corpus and the comparison with other UD Chinese treebanks are presented in Section 4. Section 5 is the conclusion and future work.

2. Sinica Treebank

The Sinica Treebank[1] has been developed and released to public since 2000 by the Chinese Knowledge Information Processing (CKIP) group at Academia Sinica. It is one of the first structurally annotated corpora in Mandarin Chinese. Current version 3.0 (6 files) contains 61,087 structural trees and 361,934 words in Chinese. The textual material is extracted from the tagged Sinica Corpus[2] so the issues of word segmentation and category assignment are previously resolved. Based on ICG grammar (Information-based Case Grammar), the contexts are parsed by an automatic parser (Chen 1996) before human post-editing.

The structural frame of the Sinica Treebank is based on the Head-Driven Principle ; that is, a sentence or phrase is composed of a core Head and its arguments, or adjuncts. The Head defines its phrasal category and relations with other constituents. Each structural tree is annotated with words, part-of-speech of words, syntactic structure brackets, and thematic roles. The POS tagset and themantic roles are defined and explained in the CKIP technical report 93-05 (CKIP 1993) and 13-01 (CKIP 2013) respectively. An example Sinica Tree annotation and the strutural tree are presented below.

(1) 書生用顫抖的手接過銀子

"The scholar took the money with trembling hands"

S(agent:NP(Head:Nab:書生)|instrument:PP(Head:P39:用|DUMMY:NP(predication:V·的(head:VA2:顫抖|Head:DE:的)|Head:Nab:手))|Head:VC2:接過|goal:NP(Head:Nab:銀子))

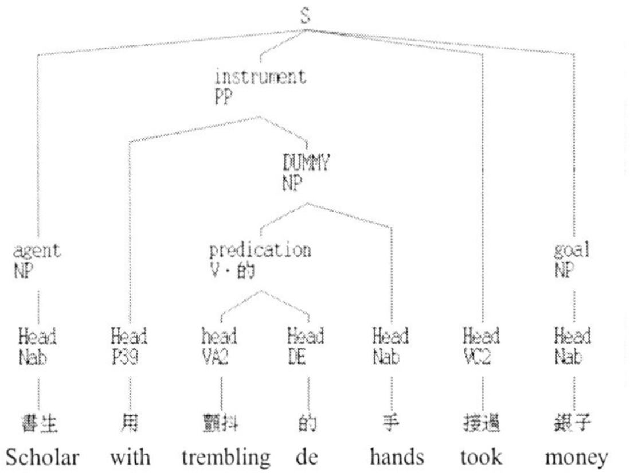

In (1), the Head of the sentence is 接過 "take over" which is a transitive verb classified as VC2 in the CKIP tagset. It

[1] http://turing.iis.sinica.edu.tw/treesearch/

[2] http://asbc.iis.sinica.edu.tw/

takes two core arguments *agent* (scholar) and *goal* (silver, used as money) and an ajunct *instrument* (hand) in this case.

There are six primary phrasal categories annotated in the Sinica Treebank. S is a complete tree headed by a predicate. VP, NP and PP are phrases headed by verb (V), noun (N) and preposition (P) respectively. GP is a phrase headed by locational noun (Nc) or locational adjunct (Ng). XP is a conjunctive phrase headed by a conjunction (C) but the actual category depends on the conjoined elements.

Other non-terminal categories are phrases including structural DE, represented as {A, N, V, S, DM, GP, NP, PP, VP, ADV}·{的, 地} or 得·{V, VP, S}. In (1), for example, the phrase V·的 is the modifier of the DUMMY NP.

DUMMY is the semantic role marked on the locally undecidable categories. It is the semantic head so inherits the semantic role from the upper level. The syntactic head (Head) is distinguishable from the semantic head (head) by the first letter capitalization.

3. The Conversion

Our method of converting the Sinica Treebank to a UD corpus consists of three steps. First, we map the original POS tags of the Sinica Treebank to the UD tags. Some dependency relations also correspond to Parts of speech. Then we examine and adjust the head marking before transferring the dependencies. Finally, we replace the semantic relations with the UD dependencies by transferring rules.

3.1 POS Tag Conversion

To obtain the UD tags, a word's original tag from the Sinica Treebank is used along with transferring rules, which map each original tag to a corresponding UD tag. The correspondent POS tags between two systems are shown in Table 1. There are 15 out of 17 UD tags adopted in our system. Two UD tags, SYM (symbol) and PUNCT (punctuation), are excluded due to the design of the Sinica TreeBank. Texts were cleaned up by removing non-word symbols before annotating. Foreign words do exist but are annotated according to their actual usage. For example, CNN (Cable News Network) gets a "Nba" POS tag. As a result, SYM is useless in our system. As for PUNCT, the discussion is in the subsection below.

3.1.1 Punctuation

In the Sinica Treebank, texts are segmented not only by period, question marks and exclamation marks, but also commas, colons and semicolons, resulting the possible incompleteness of sentences. That is, there are sentence trees as well as phrase trees in the corpus. Most punctuations are not included in our system except "、" Dun Hao, a special Chinese punctuation which is also translated as comma, just like the ",". To avoid the confusion between the two distinct punctuations in Chinese texts, we use "Dun Hao" instead of "comma" in this paper. Dun Hao is indeed a punctuation but functions as coordinating words like "and" and "or". Therefore, the Sinica POS category for Dun Hao is "Caa" (coordinating conjunctions) and be transferred to CCONJ in the resulting UD corpus.

3.1.2 POS and Dependency Correspondence

As shown in Table 1, some dependencies are also available according to their lexical categories. The direct mapping conducts mainly for modifier words and function words. Words which belong to the lexical categories A (adjective), C (conjunction), D (adverbial), P(preposition), I (interjection), T (sentence -final particle), and some sorts of Nouns in the CKIP 93-05 yield direct dependencies according to their POS. For example, conjunction words (Caa) such as 和 "and" and 或 "or" always have the dependency *cc* to their governors/heads and copula 是 (VH_11) is always marked as a *cop*.

SINICA POS	UPOS	Dependency
A	ADJ	amod
Caa	CCONJ	cc
Cab (等、等等、之類)	X	conj
Cbaa, Cbab, Cbba, Cbbb, Cbca, Cbcb	SCONJ	mark
Da, Dbb,Dbc, Dc, Dd Dfa,Dfb, Dg,Dh,Dj,Dk,	ADV	advmod
Dbaa, Dbab	AUX	aux
Di		aux:aspect
P02 (in short BEI construction)		aux :pass
Naa, Nab, Nac, Nad, Naea, Naeb, Ncb, Ncc, Ncda, Ncdb, Ndaaa, Ndaad, Ndaba, Ndabb, Ndabc, Ndabe, Ndabf, Ndca, Ndcb, Ndcc Nv1, Nv2, Nv3, Nv4	NOUN	
DM		det/nummod
Nfa, Nfb, …, Nfi		clf
Nba, Nbc, Nca, Ndaab, Ndaac	PROPN	
Nep, Nes	DET	det
Neqa, Neu	NUM	nummod
Neqb	NUM	nummod:post
Ng	ADP	case:post
Nhaa,Nhab, Nhac,Nhb,Nhc	PRON	
I	INTJ	discourse
P01, P02, P03, ...P66	ADP	case
VA*,VB*, VC*, VD*, VE*, VF*, VG*, VH*, VI*, VJ*, VK*, VL* (* =1 or 2 digit numbers) V_12, V_2	VERB	
V_11	AUX	cop
Ta, Tb, Tc, Td	PART	discourse:sp
DE (的、地、之、得)	PART	case:de mark:adv mark:relcl mark:comp

Table 1: The mapping table of UPOS and Dependencies

Both interjection (I) and sentence-final particle (T) are discourse elements and the dependency relation is *discourse*. The difference between the two categories is that sentence-final particle (T) has an extra feature *sp* to distinguish it from interjection. That is, (I) maps to *discourse* and (T) to *discourse:sp*.

DM is the determiner measurement compound and its dependency varies according to different conditions. For the detailed discussion, please refer to section 4.2.

3.2 Head Adjustment

As mentioned in Section 2, the head of each phrase is already marked in the Sinica structural trees. However, the principles for determining the heads of phrases in the UD project are somewhat different from the Sinica Treebank. Some adjustments have to be made before converting. The different aspects are described below.

3.2.1 Content over Function

In the UD, function words attach to the content words they further specify (Nivre et.al 2016). In the Sinica Treebank, this principle also fits for the NP or VP clauses but diverges in other grammatical structures. There are two kinds of head markers in Sinica. "Head" indicates a syntactic head and "head" reveals a semantic head. In an endocentric phrasal category like NP or VP, the syntactic head and the semantic head are identical. However, in PP, GP, XP or "VP-de" constructions, the syntactic Head doesn't carry sufficient semantic information so the original Sinica annotations violate the UD principles. The conversion from Sinica to UD need to reversely choose the semantic heads as the governors of these structures. We use a PP phrase 為 整 頓 國 內 交 通 'for rectifying the domestic transportation'to illustrate the head ajustment.

In (2a), the original Sinica corpus marked the preposition 為 'for' to be the head. However, the UD version should reversely choose the DUMMY VP and find the VP head 整頓 'rectify' as the head.

(2a)

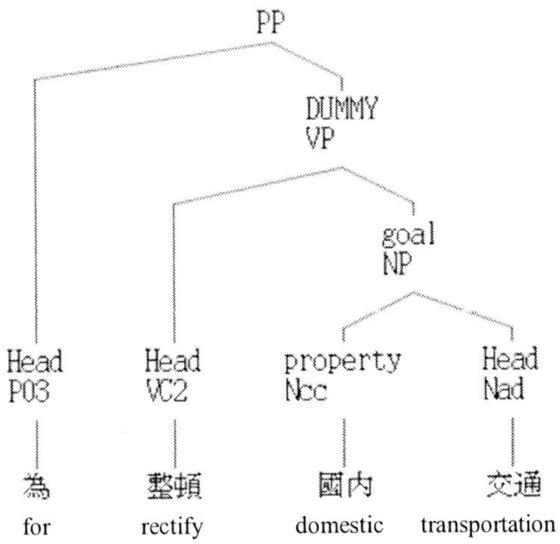

(2b)

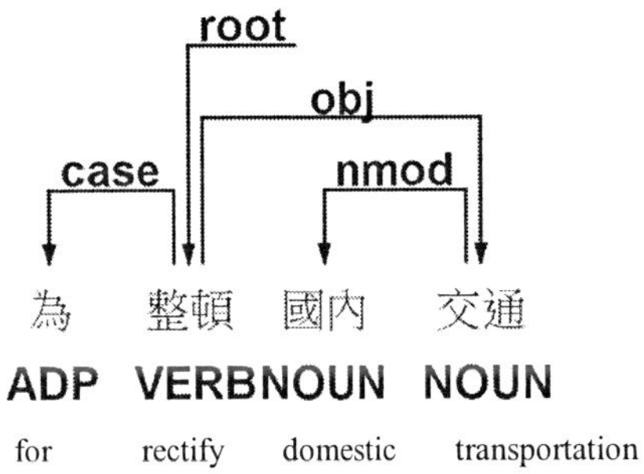

3.2.2 First Head is the Parent in Parallel-Head Constructions

The UD in principle assumes conjuncts of the coordinate structure have equal status as syntactic heads. However, the dependency tree format does not allow this analysis to be encoded directly, so the first conjunct in the linear order is by convention always treated as the parent of all other conjuncts. On the other hand, two conjuncts in Sinica are conjoined by means of a conjunction to form a new DUMMY and continue to conjoin with the right-side conjunct until achieving the rightmost one. The rightmost conjunction word is the head of the whole coordinating structure. An example demostrate in (3a) and the conversion involving both content-oriented and leftmost-dominated is shown in (3b).

(3a) 自私、猜忌和怨恨 'selfishness, suspicion, and resentment'

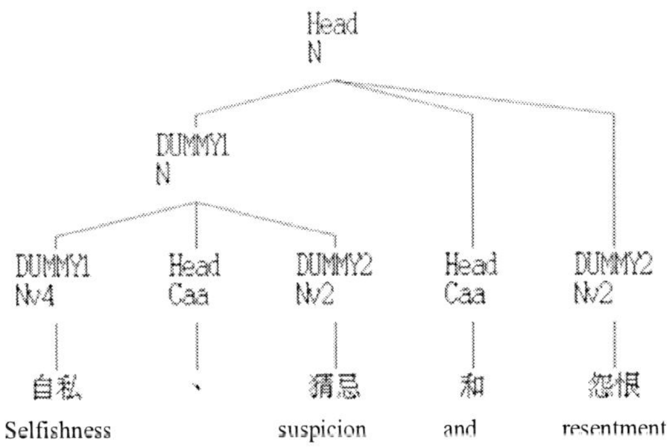

(3b)

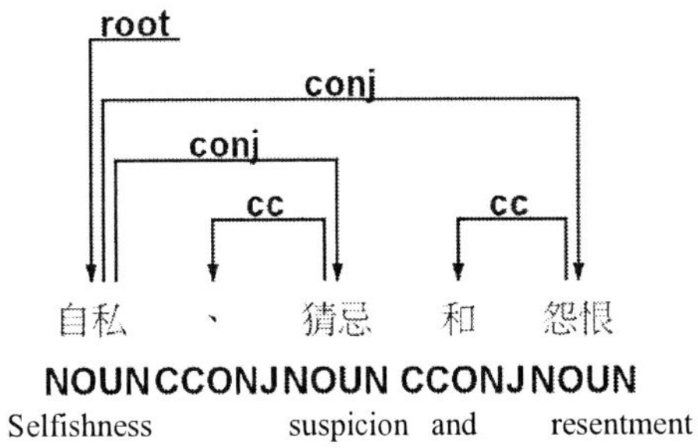

Apposition is another case of parallel-head constructions. In UD, the *appos* relation is also strictly left to right, meaning the first nominal is treated as the head. However, in Sinica, the apposition relation represents as head-final formalism and needs to reverse the head selection. The Sinica tree for the NP phrase 美國總統拜登 "U. S. President Biden" presents in (4a) and the UD version with reversed head is shown (4b).

(4a)

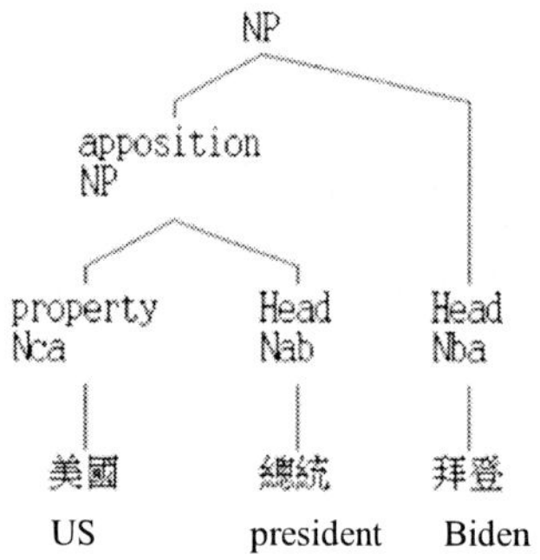

(4b)

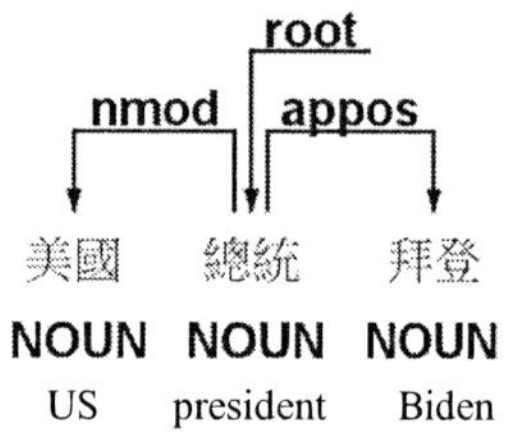

3.2.3 Copula

In the Sinica Treebank, the copula word 是 'SHI' is classified as a verb and its POS tag is "V_11". It functions as the head of a clause just like other verbal predicates and takes two arguments which are "theme" and "range". An example is shown in (5). In the UD scheme, however, the head shifts to the range NP.

(5a)

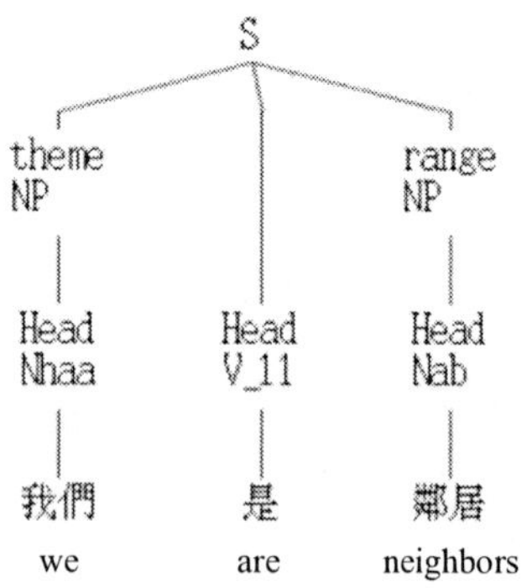

(5b)

3.3 Dependency Conversion

Since the dependent relations, which are semantic roles, have already existed in the Sinica treebank, our challenge is to convert semantic-based relations to syntactic-based UD dependencies. As stated in section 3.1.2 and shown in Table 1, for most function words and modifiers, assigning dependecies according to the lexical categories shows a better result than a direct relation-dependency mapping. For example, "quantifier" sometimes transfers to *det* but sometimes to *nummod.* By mapping Nep, Nes, and DM to *det* and Neu and Neqa to *nummod*, the ambiguilty is solved.

As for the core arguments, it depends on the root of a tree to assign the proper dependencies. For example, in (1) the root is 接過 "take over" and the arguments a*gent* and *goal* should be converted to *nsubj* and *obj* respectively, as shown in (6).

(6)

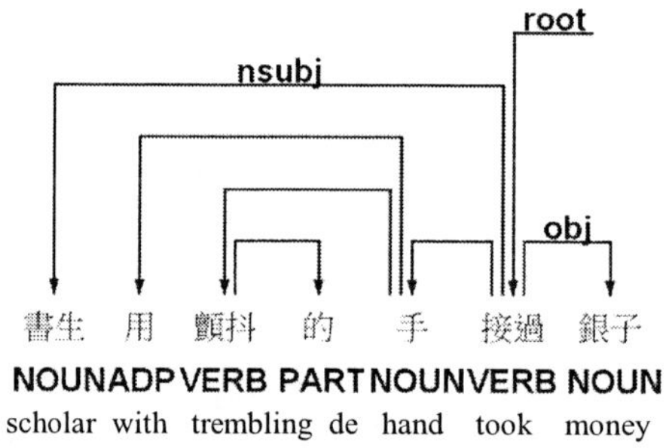

3.3.1 Conversion According to the Sentence Patterns of Each Category

However, it is possible to convey a concept with different surface structures. Consider the sentences (7) and (8) below:

(7) 老師罵學生們 'The teacher scolded students'

(8) 學生們被老師罵 'Students are scolded by the teacher'

They both convey the same meaning and 老師 'teacher'is the *agent* and 學生們'students' is the *goal* of the scolding event. Clause (8) is the passive way of saying clause (7) and the object (*goal*) of the active clause becomes the subject (*goal*) of the passive clause. As a result, we also need rules to deal with such situation and a dependency *nsubj:pass* is introduced to mark the subjects of passive clauses. Thanks to the earlier work that has been done and recorded in CKIP 93-05, the possible sentence patterns for each verb category have been analysized in detail and we can make use of the analysis to produce the transferring rules. We take VC2 for example to demostrate the conversion.

There are five sentence patterns for VC2. The first is the active sentence pattern in which *agent* is in the subject position and *goal* is in the object position. The second is the BA (把) construction of Chinese in which the *goal* is led by a preposition and be put right after the subject. In other word, the BA construction turns the word order from SVO to SOV. The third is BEI (被) construction with the reverse order of *agen*t and *goal.* The last two can be seen as the special cases of BA/BEI constructions (把/被句) with an extra argument *theme* which is a part of arguemnt *goal*. The sentence patterns and corresponding UD dependencies are listed below:

1. AGENT[{NP,PP}]〈 *〈GOAL[NP]
   → (case) nsubj 〈 root 〈 obj
2. AGENT [NP,PP]〈GOAL [PP]〈 *
   → (case) nsubj 〈 case obl:patient 〈 root
3. GOAL[NP]〈 AGENT [{PP,P}]〈 *
   → nsubj:pass〈case obl:agent / aux〈root
4. GOAL[NP]〈AGENT[{PP,P]〈 *〈 THEME [NP]
   →nsubj:pass〈 case obl:agent / aux〈root 〈obj
5. AGENT [NP,PP]〈 GOAL [PP]〈 * 〈 THEME [NP]
   → (case) nsubj 〈 case obl:patient 〈 * 〈 obj

3.3.2 Conversion of Phrases including Structural Particle DE

The structural particle {的、地、得}DE are widely used and can be classified as four types:

1. possessive DE : 她的作品 'her works'
2. attributive DE :美妙 的 聲音 'beautiful sound'
3. adverbial DE 大聲地叫 'shout loudly'
4. complement DE :踩得水花四濺 'stamp one's feet to make water splashes'

By analysing the sinica tree structures of DE phrases, we can gain the following converting rules.

- possessor:{N,NP}·的
  → nmod :poss < case:de
- property:{N,NP, GP, PP, DM}·DE
  → nmod < case :de
- {property,predication}:{A, V, VP, S, VP, ADV}·DE
  → acl < mark:relcl
- manner:{A, ADV, DM, V,VP}·DE}
  → advcl < mark:adv
- complement:得·{V, VP, S}
  → mark:comp <xcomp (if V orVP)
  → mark:comp <ccomp (if S)

Examples of possessive DE 她的作品 'her works' shows the orginal Sinica Tree in (9a) and the converted UD tree in (9b). Similarly, complement DE 踩得水花四濺 'stamp one's feet to make water splashes' also presented in (10a) and (10b) below.

(9a)

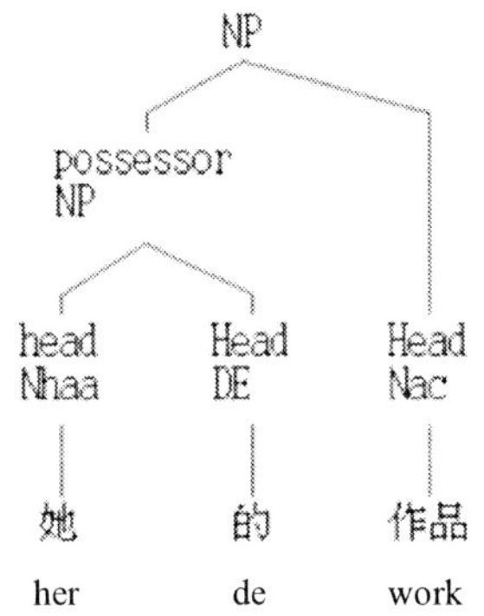

(9b)

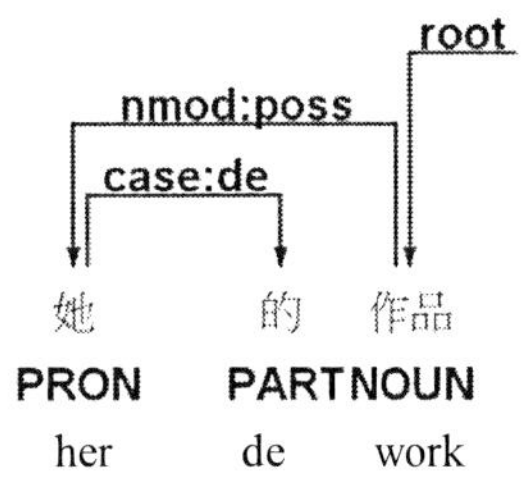

(10a)

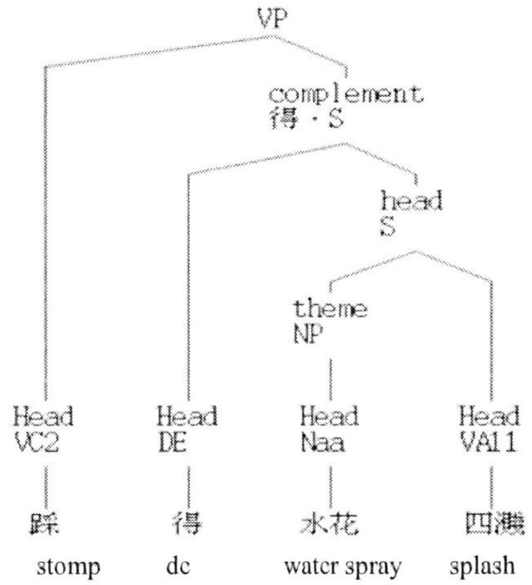

(10b)

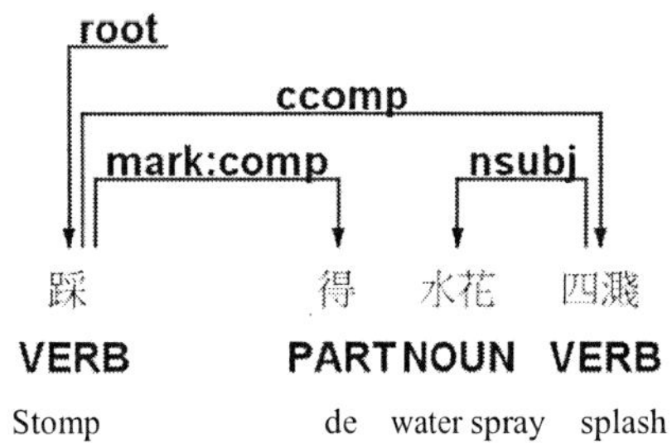

3.4 Evaluation

To evaluate accuracy of the automatic conversion, we manually annotated a selection of 183 trees from the Sinica Treebank. There are 62 sentences manually selected to cover a wide range of syntactic categories which yield different constructions. The remaing 121 trees which have consecutive id numbers in our corpus are also selected to check the accuracy of the conversion. In total, the selection includes 966 tokens and the average tokens per tree is 5.28.

The evaluation results are showed in Table 2. The 121 trees with a lower average tree length (4.66 tokens per tree) reach 92.55% accuracy. However, the result of the 62 hand-picked sentences drops down to 83.83% accuracy because of the longer tree length (6.48 tokens per tree) and more complex sentence structures. The overall accuracy is 0.89 for all 966 tokens. Since the average tree length for the Sinica Treebank is 6.28 tokens per tree (shown in Table 3), which is lower than the hand-picked trees in the evaluation, we expect the accuracy of the whole converted corpus might be slightly higher than 83.83%.

	121 sentences	62 hand-picked	all selected sentences
Aver. tree length	4.66	6.48	5.28
All token numbers	564	402	966
Right-converted	522	337	859
Accuracy	92.55%	83.83%	89.93%

Table 2 : The evaluation results for 183 selected trees

4. The UD Chinese Sinica Treebank

After the conversion process mentioned above has done, the output of resulting corpus in the CoNLL-U format is illustrated in (11).

(11) The scholar took the money with trembling hands.

```
1  書生  _  N   Nab  _  NOUN  6  _  nsubj      _
2  用    _  P   P39  _  ADP   5  _  case       _
3  顫抖  _  V   VA2  _  VERB  5  _  acl        _
4  的    _  DE  DE   _  PART  3  _  mark:relcl _
5  手    _  N   Nab  _  NOUN  6  _  obl        _
6  接過  _  V   VC2  _  VERB  0  _  root       _
7  銀子  _  N   Nab  _  NOUN  6  _  obj        _
```

While the UD POS tags we adopt is similar to other UD Chinese corpora, we have a smaller set of dependencies. The reason is that the textual material of the Sinica treebank is extracted from the tagged Sinica Corpus which has undergone post-editing and compound words and multiword expressions are in principle treated as a unit before trees are drawn, regardless the internal structure of these elements. Also, shorter sentence length results in simpler dependency relations. Currently, there are 23 UD main dependencies as well as 13 subtypes. The alphabetical list of Sinica UD dependency relations explains as follows.

- acl (clausal modifier of noun)
- advcl (adverbial clause modifier)
- advmod (adverbial modifier)
- amod (adjectival modifier)
- appos (appositional modifier)
- aux (auxiliary)
- aux:aspect (aspect auxiliary)
- aux:pass (passive auxiliary)
- case (case marker)
- case:de (case marker for possessive DE)
- case:post (localizer)
- cc (coordinating conjunction)
- ccomp (clausal complement)
- clf (classifier)
- conj (conjuct)
- cop (copula)
- csubj (clausal subject)
- csubj:pass (passive clausal subject)
- det (determiner)
- discourse (discourse element)
- discourse:sp (sentence-final particle)
- dislocated (dislocated/topicalized element)
- iobj (indirect object)
- mark (subordinating marker)
- mark:relcl (mark relative clause)
- mark:adv (mark adverbial)
- mark:comp (mark complement caluse)
- nmod (nominal modifier)
- nmod:poss (possessive nominal modifier)
- nmod:tmod (temporal modifier)
- nummod (numeric modifier)
- nummod:post (post quantifier)
- obj (object)
- obl (oblique)
- obl:agent (agent modifier)
- obl:patient (patient modifier)
- root (root)
- xcomp (open clausal complement)

Because of the complexity of language phenomena, it is impossible to have rules covering all the circumstances of linguistic expression. About 2% of Sinica trees cannot be fully transferred to the UD style annotation. Post-editing is needed for these unsuccessful trees. The list of dependency relations still keeps on updating.

Although this is still an ongoing work, we have found some aspects worth discussing. In comparison with two other UD Chinese research teams, namely Google and City University of Hong Kong, the following issues are described below.

4.1 Tree Length

Due to the phrase/sentence segmentation principle of the Sinica Treebank, some trees have one word only so just have the root without any branches (dependencies). We, therefore, remove the one-word trees and the remaining tree number is 53,548. The sentence length is 6.28 tokens on average, which is a lot shorter than other UD Chinese treebanks.

Table 3 is the comparison of tree length (tokens per tree) among UD Chinese corpora. .Obviously, the sentence segmentation principle of the Sinica Treebank is the main reason to gain shorter sentences. However, for the sake of natural language understanding, shorter sentences are easier to process both for humans and for machines. By looking into the existing UD corpora, the annotations for super long sentences are quite often questionable.

Moreover, the punctuation usage in Chinese is not so strict, resulting in the misuse between comma and period in texts. Some relations should be treated in the discourse level rather than in the syntactic level.

Corpus	Sentences	Tokens	Average Sentence Length
GSD	4,997	123,291	24.67
PUD	1,000	21,415	21.41
CFL	451	7,256	11.09
HK	1,004	9,874	9.83
Sinica	53,548	336,281	6.28

Table 3 : The comparison of tree length among UD Chinese corpora

4.2 Classifier

Classifiers are a special lexical category in Chinese. They are often obligatory in a noun phrase with a numeral modifier and optional with a demonstrative. The two UD Chinese research teams treat classifiers differently. We consider both approaches and make our own choice to fit the tree structures of the Sinica Treebank in which DM is the determiner measure compound/phrase. For the simple (a numeral/demostrative and a classifier) construction, the two elements are grouped together to form a DM. The whole DM depends on the Head of an NP it belongs to. The relation is either *det* or *nummod*, decided by the determiner types. However, if there are more than one numerals as in (12) or zero numeral as in (13), the classifier itself has a *clf* relation to its head Noun.

(12)

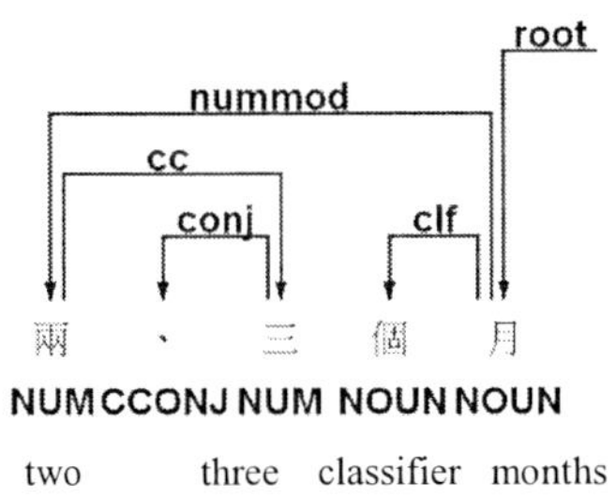

(13)

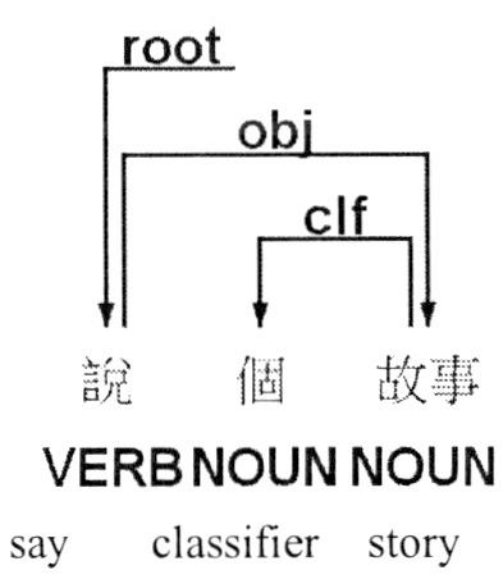

Differences in marking the relation of classifiers and its surrounding elements between each reseach team are shown in Table 4.

Team	condition	Determiner	Classfier
Google	1(+)determiner	H: classfier R:nummod/det	H: head of NP R: clf
	0 determiner	n/a	H: head of NP R: clf
HK	1(+)determiner	H: head of NP R:nummod/det	H: determiner R: clf
	0 determiner	n/a	H: head of NP R : det
Sinica	DM	H : head of NP R :nummod or det	
	2(+)determiners	H : head of NP R :nummod	H : head of NP R :clf
	0 determiner	n/a	H : head of NP R :clf

Table 4: The comparison of classifiers between 3 research teams

5. Conclusion and Future Work

We have presented the process of converting the Sinica Treebank to the UD annotation scheme. It is an attemp to create the Chinese language resource in a universally accepted format so that the long-standing Sinica Treebank can be more usable for a variety of multiligual NLP tasks. The conversion was a challenging task and there is still quite a few works to be done.

More complete converting rules have to be discovered and added to the current system. Features are not included in this version of converting corpus. We will consider the necessity of adding features and make this corpus more compatible to other UD corpora. Finally, to make this corpus more competitive to others, more complete sentences are required. Since sentences are composed of phrases, the methods of finding adjacent phrases and the replacement of some dependency relations due to the composition are worth investigating.

6. Bibliographical References

Chen, K.-J., Huang C.-R, Chang, L.-P. Hsu, H.-L. (1996). Sinica Corpus: Design Methodology for Balanced Corpora. Proceedings of the 11th Pacific Asia Conference on Language, Information, and Computation (PACLIC II), Seoul Korea. p. 167–176.

Chen, K.-J., Luo, C.-C. Chang, M.-C., Chen, F.-Y., Chen, C.-J., Huang, C.-R., Gao. Z.-M. "Sinica Treebank: Design Criteria, Representational Issues and Implementation". In Book "Treebanks — Building and Using Parsed Corpora", Ch. 13, pp. 231–248, 2003.

CKIP (1993). Lexical Category Analysis of Mandarin Chinese. CKIP Technical Report 93-05

CKIP (2013). Semantic roles of Sinica Treebank. CKIP Technical Report 13-01.

Nivre, J., de Marneffe, M.-C., Ginter, F., Goldberg, Y., Hajič, J., Manning, C., McDonald, R., Petrov, S., Pyysalo, S., Silveira, N., Tsarfaty, R., and Zeman, D. (2016). Universal Dependencies v1: A Multilingual Treebank Collection. Proceedings of the Tenth International Conference on Language Resources and Evaluation (LREC 2016): 1659-1666.

Nivre, J., M.-C. de Marneffe, Ginter, F., Hajič, Manning, C., Pyysalo, S., Schuster, S., Tyers, F., and Zeman, D.

(2020). Universal dependencies v2: An evergrowing multilingual treebank collection. In Proceedings of the 12th International Conference on Language Resources and Evaluation. (LREC 2020)

Poiret, R., Wong, T S., Lee, J. et al. Universal Dependencies for Mandarin Chinese. Lang Resources & Evaluation (2021). https://doi.org/10.1007/s10579-021-09564-2

Arnardóttir, Þ., Hafsteinsson, H., Sigurðsson, E., Bjarnadóttir, K., Ingason, A., Jónsdóttir, H., Steingrímsson, S. (2020). A Universal Dependencies Conversion Pipeline for a Penn-format Constituency Treebank. In Proceedings of the Fourth Workshop on Universal Depencies. (UDW 2020)

Proceedings of the 16th Linguistic Annotation Workshop (LAW-XVI) @LREC 2022, pages 31–43
Marseille, 24 June 2022

Desiderata for the Annotation of Information Structure in Complex Sentences

Hannah Booth
Ghent University
Department of Linguistics, Blandijnberg 2, 9000 Gent, Belgium
hannah.booth@ugent.be

Abstract

Many annotation schemes for information structure have been developed in recent years (Calhoun et al., 2005; Paggio, 2006; Götze et al., 2007; Bohnet et al., 2013; Riester et al., 2018), in line with increased attention on the interaction between discourse and other linguistic dimensions (e.g. syntax, semantics, prosody). However, a crucial issue which existing schemes either gloss over, or propose only crude guidelines for, is how to annotate information structure in complex sentences. This unsatisfactory treatment is unsurprising given that theoretical work on information structure has traditionally neglected its status in dependent clauses. In this paper, I evaluate the status of pre-existing annotation schemes in relation to this vexed issue, and outline certain desiderata as a foundation for novel, more nuanced approaches, informed by state-of-the art theoretical insights (Erteschik-Shir, 2007; Bianchi and Frascarelli, 2010; Lahousse, 2010; Ebert et al., 2014; Matić et al., 2014; Lahousse, 2022). These desiderata relate both to annotation formats and the annotation process. The practical implications of these desiderata are illustrated via a test case using the Corpus of Historical Low German (Booth et al., 2020). The paper overall showcases the benefits which result from a free exchange between linguistic annotation models and theoretical research.

Keywords: annotation, information structure, complex sentences, subordination, historical data, Middle Low German

1. Introduction

Recent years have seen a boom in language resources which contain some form of information-structural (IS) annotation, for which various schemes and guidelines have been developed (Calhoun et al., 2005; Paggio, 2006; Götze et al., 2007; Bohnet et al., 2013; Riester et al., 2018). However, the issue of dependent clauses for IS annotation has been largely neglected; many have acknowledged complex sentences as an annotation challenge for IS (Bohnet et al., 2013; Cook and Bildhauer, 2013; Stede and Mamprin, 2016), but few efforts have been made to get to grips with the issue in a concrete and nuanced way. Moreover, theoretical work has highlighted the special status of dependent clauses with respect to IS and related interface phenomena, and thus suggests that we disregard this aspect of IS annotation at our peril (Hooper and Thompson, 1973; Haiman, 1978; Bybee, 2002; Bianchi and Frascarelli, 2010; Lahousse, 2010; Ebert et al., 2014; Matić et al., 2014; Lahousse, 2022).

Neglect of this issue can result in inaccurate and/or conflicting annotations, or even unannotated data. Such outcomes are unsatisfactory and hold back research progress, both theoretical and computational. Without a proper treatment of IS in dependent clauses, theoretical research into the discourse properties of complex sentences and how this interacts with e.g. morphosyntactic and prosodic phenomena cannot rely on the types of corpus-based, quantitative and reproducible investigations which have proven so fruitful in other domains of linguistics. Computational research is also disadvantaged in this context, as inaccurate, conflicting or absent IS annotations, even if confined to a subset of contexts, will inevitably impact NLP downstream tasks.

In this paper, I respond to this challenge by outlining desiderata for the annotation of IS in complex sentences, which can serve as a foundation for novel and nuanced approaches in future. These proposals are underpinned by theoretical insights and are also informed by previous IS annotation schemes which have highlighted specific problems concerning complex sentences. The desiderata relate to aspects of both the annotation format and the annotation process, and are tested in relation to the IS annotation of Middle Low German texts (*c.* 1200–1650) in the Corpus of Historical Low German (Booth et al., 2020), which are known to exhibit highly complex sentence structures (Tophinke, 2012).

2. Theoretical Insights

The IS properties of complex sentences constitute a highly relevant though understudied domain (Matić et al., 2014). Moreover, even from the existing literature on the matter, it is hard to establish a general consensus on even essential questions. This lack of consensus is particularly problematic in the context of linguistic annotation, where schemes which are as theoretically neutral as possible and compatible with different approaches are seen as the gold standard (Bird and Liberman, 2001; Ide and Romary, 2004). In this section, I discuss to what extent some common ground can be established from previous discussions of IS in complex sentences, highlighting crosslinguistic generalisations as well as matters which require nuanced treatment.

2.1. Information-Structural Primitives

A range of theoretical approaches to IS have emerged over recent decades and views differ as to the precise primitives involved and their diagnostic criteria; for useful overviews see e.g. Vallduví (1992); von Heusinger (1999); Büring (2007); de Swart and de Hoop (2014). This paper mainly discusses topic and focus. I follow approaches where topichood is understood as comprising (i) A(BOUTNESS)-TOPIC, (cf. "sentence topic", Reinhart (1981; Krifka (2007)) and (ii) F(RAME)-TOPIC (Krifka, 2007), as defined in (1). Focus is understood as covering (i) I(NFORMATIONAL)-FOCUS (Reinhart, 1981; Vallduví, 1992) and (ii) C(ONTRASTIVE)-FOCUS (Neeleman et al., 2009), cf. (2).[1]

(1) **Topic**
- A(BOUTNESS)-TOPIC: entity/proposition about which a main clause predicates
- F(RAME)-TOPIC: frame within which the main clause predication is interpreted

(2) **Focus**
- I(NFORMATIONAL)-FOCUS: new info which is most relevant to current discourse
- C(ONTRASTIVE)-FOCUS: element/proposition which evokes alternatives

Additionally, I discuss COMMENT, i.e. what is said about the topic, and BACKGROUND, which is material which is neither topic nor focus.

2.2. The Domain(s) of Information Structure

A central issue on which views differ concerns what the precise domain(s) of IS is/are, or more specifically, to what extent dependent clauses can be considered to have IS articulation(s) in their own right. The traditional view is that the domain of IS is the overall utterance, i.e. that even a complex sentence has IS articulation(s) only at the matrix level (Mathesius, 1975; Vallduví, 1992; Vallduví and Zacharski, 1994; Steedman, 2000; Komagata, 2003). However, more recent work assumes that IS can operate within a single utterance at different levels, allowing for dependent clauses to be considered as a potential IS domain. In particular, the notion of recursive IS has been adopted by many (Koktová, 1996; Partee, 1996; Hajicová et al., 1998; Erteschik-Shir, 2007; Matić et al., 2014), with a distinction between (i) "external IS", i.e. the IS status of a dependent clause in the overall matrix clause and (ii) "internal IS", i.e. the IS status of individual constituents within a dependent clause (Erteschik-Shir, 2007; Matić et al., 2014). These two perspectives are illustrated in (3) and (4) respectively (Matić et al., 2014, 9-10). In (3) (external IS), the whole matrix sentence is considered as the relevant IS domain, in which the clefted adverbial clause *after I arrived home* is assigned focus. In (4) (internal IS), the complement clause is viewed as an IS domain its own right, within which *this book* receives a topical interpretation.

(3) [It was only $\underbrace{\textbf{after I arrived home}}_{\text{FOCUS}}$ that I saw them].

(4) I believe [that $\underbrace{\textbf{this book}}_{\text{TOPIC}}$ Mary gave to Paul].

Combining these two perspectives yields recursion, whereby a dependent clause can be a topic/focus with respect to external IS, but can also contain an internal topic/focus, e.g. (5) and (6) (Partee, 1996, 79, 82).

(5) [**What convinced Susan that [our arrest]$_{\text{TOPIC}}$ was caused by Harry**]$_{\text{TOPIC}}$ was a rumour that someone had witnessed Harry's confession.

(6) What convinced Susan that our arrest was caused by Harry was [**a rumour that someone had [witnessed Harry's confession.**]$_{\text{FOCUS}}$]$_{\text{FOCUS}}$

In line with the majority of recent work, I assume that dependent clauses can in principle have internal IS articulation(s) under certain conditions, as I discuss next.

2.3. Assertion and Clause Class

It is widely recognised that the possibility of a clause having internal IS is connected with assertion; clauses which are asserted are more likely to have internal IS than clauses which are presupposed (Bybee, 2002; Lahousse and Borremans, 2014; Matić et al., 2014). Dependent clauses are traditionally understood as being presupposed rather than asserted (Quirk et al., 1985; Hooper and Thompson, 1973; Matsuda, 1998), and thus less susceptible to internal IS permutations (Lehmann, 1988; Bybee, 2002). However, general distinctions can be drawn between different classes of dependent clause, and indeed even within some classes. Complement clauses, for instance, are more likely to have internal IS than adverbial and relative clauses, since the former are often asserted and the latter typically presupposed (Matić et al., 2014).

At the same time, a long-standing body of research has shown that the internal IS of complement clauses is conditioned by the type of embedding predicate in the matrix clause. Only complement clauses which represent the main assertive point, i.e. are embedded under nonfactive predicates, can have an articulated internal IS (Matić et al., 2014), in line with observations that phenomena connected with topicality are restricted to such contexts (Hooper and Thompson, 1973; Boye and Harder, 2007; Dehé and Wichmann, 2010; Matić et al., 2014). For instance, English topic marking via fronting is permitted in the complement of the nonfactive predicate *explain* in (7) (Hooper and Thompson, 1973, 474) but ruled out under a factive predicate like *regret*, e.g. (8) (Maki et al., 1999, 3).

(7) The inspector explained [that **each part** he had examined very carefully].

[1] In principle also topics can be contrastive, but I do not discuss contrastive topics here.

(8) *John regrets [that **this book** Mary read].

The type of embedding predicate also interacts with the external IS of complement clauses; complements of factive verbs are usually discourse-given and generally unfocable, unless they are contrasted with a competing presupposition (Matić et al., 2014). Complements of nonfactive verbs can however carry the main assertion, and in such cases it has been claimed that the matrix clause is informationally demoted to a parenthetical clause (Dehé and Wichmann, 2010).

Likewise, adverbial clauses do not exhibit consistent IS properties. An important distinction here is between "central" (i.e. event-structuring) and "peripheral" (i.e. discourse-structuring) adverbial clauses (Haegeman, 2007). Central adverbial clauses are more syntactically and prosodically integrated into their host clause than their peripheral counterparts, but they also differ in terms of assertion; the central class is generally assumed to be presupposed, and the peripheral class asserted (Lahousse and Borremans, 2014), which has been used to argue for the peripheral type having internal IS and to explain the occurrence of root-like phenomena in such environments (De Cat, 2012).

Relative clauses also exhibit diverse IS properties, in particular, between nonrestrictive, e.g. (9) and restrictive relative clauses, e.g. (10) (Fabb, 1990, 57).[2]

(9) The swans, **which are white**, are in that part of the lake

(10) The swans **which are white** are in that part of the lake.

With respect to external IS, nonrestrictive relative clauses have been argued to be neither focus nor topic but rather backgrounded (Umbach, 2006; Song, 2014), since they provide extra information about a referent already determined on independent grounds (Riester, 2009). Restrictive relatives provide a description which uniquely identifies a referent, and show many similarities with classic focus constructions such as clefts (Schachter, 1973). With respect to internal IS, restrictive relatives are assumed to lack internal IS (Depraetere, 1996; Matić et al., 2014), since they provide a description which uniquely identifies a referent and must thus contain material which is already part of the "common ground" (Stalnaker, 2002). Nonrestrictive relatives contain new, asserted information and are thus more likely constitute an independent IS domain in their own right (Depraetere, 1996; Bybee, 2002).

2.4. Clause Ordering

The relative ordering of a main clause and its dependent clause(s) often affects their IS relations with each other and the wider discourse (Lehmann, 1988; Diessel, 2001; Schilder and Tenbrink, 2002; Komagata, 2003). In terms of external IS, it has been observed for many languages that dependent clauses which occur before their host clause are often topical (Marchese, 1977; Lehmann, 1984; Thompson, 1985; Chafe, 1984; Lehmann, 1988; Diessel, 2001). Conditional clauses, for instance, which typically occur before the host clause, have been observed to be often topics (Schiffrin, 1992; Ebert et al., 2014), to the extent that this has been claimed to be a universal (Haiman, 1978). Further evidence for the correlation between initial dependent clauses and topicality comes from various languages where initial adverbial clauses are marked by the same morpheme as clause-internal topics (Thompson and Longacre, 1985). An example is Lisu (Tibeto-Burman), where initial adverbial clauses are marked by *nya*, which can also mark a topic in the following main clause, e.g. (11) (Thompson and Longacre, 1985, 232).

(11) [ame thæ nwu patsɨ-a dye-a̪ ŋu
yesterday TIME you plain-to go-DECL FACT
bæ̪-a̪ **nya**] nwu **nya** asa ma mu-a.
say-DECL TOPIC you TOPIC Asa not see-Q
'When you went to the plain yesterday, didn't you see Asa?'

Clause ordering has also been shown to be relevant for the internal IS of dependent clauses. Komagata (2003), for instance, claims for English that dependent clauses with their own internal IS only appear after the main clause; dependent clauses which precede a main clause are expected to lack internal IS, in line with the fact that they do not involve assertion but instead relay information already part of the common ground (Lelandais and Ferré, 2017).

3. Previous IS Annotation Schemes

With respect to the treatment of complex sentences, reports on previous IS annotation schemes typically sidestep the issue or propose only a few crude guidelines. For instance, in Buráňová et al. (2000), Baumann et al. (2004) and Calhoun et al. (2005) there are no specific comments regarding the annotation of complex sentences. Elsewhere, a certain amount of attention is given to whether dependent clauses should be treated as having their own internal IS. The guidelines by Paggio (2006), for example, allow dependent clauses to be treated either as an independent IS domain with its own focus and potentially topic, or as simply serving an IS role in the matrix sentence, either as background or part of the focus domain. This is a heuristic used to guide annotation which largely "relies on the coder's intuition" (Paggio, 2006, 1606).

Likewise, in the (otherwise detailed) scheme outlined by Götze et al. (2007), relatively scant detail is provided regarding complex sentences. In terms of topic annotation, they suggest a strategy whereby one first checks whether the whole matrix sentence has an aboutness and/or frame topic. One then examines each finite clause within the complex sentence – with the

[2]In (9), the implication is that all swans under discussion are white; (10) instead implies that the white swans are distinguished from some other swans under discussion.

exception of restrictive relative clauses – to check for whether it has its own aboutness/frame topic. Thus, apart from sidelining restrictive relative clauses, which can be assumed to lack internal IS (see Section 2), no further distinction is made between different classes of dependent clause.

In subsequent tests of Götze et al.'s guidelines for topic annotation (Cook and Bildhauer, 2011; Cook and Bildhauer, 2013), complex sentences were found to be a problematic area for annotation consistency. A particular challenge was whether to annotate dependent clauses for internal IS, and whether different embedding predicates/clause classes merit different approaches. On this point, Stede and Mamprin (2016) include some revisions to Götze et al.'s guidelines, limiting topic annotation to adverbial clauses and excluding complement clauses. This though is an oversimplistic generalisation, which does not acknowledge that internal topics are possible in complement clauses embedded under certain predicates, cf. (7) above.

Bohnet et al. (2013), who assume a tripartite IS articulation ("Theme-Rheme-Specifier"), allow for recursive IS; if a dependent clause constitutes its own proposition, it can be annotated in terms of both external and internal IS.[3] An example is shown in (12) (Bohnet et al., 2013, 1251), where the relative clause belongs both to the R(heme) of the matrix sentence but is itself segmented into T(heme) and (R)heme.

(12) [Years ago]$_{SP}$, [he]$_{T}$ [collaborated with the new music gurus Peter Serkin and Fred Sherry in the very countercultural chamber group Tashi, [**which**]$_{T}$ [**won audiences over to dreaded contemporary scores like Messiaen's Quartet for the End of Time**]$_{R}$]$_{R}$.

Nonetheless, Bohnet et al. (2013) acknowledge that in highly complex sentences, their parser for automatic thematicity annotation suffers errors arising from the incorrect detection of the propositions involved.

Riester et al. (2018) also address the question of what constitutes an IS domain in their Question-Under-Discussion (QUD) approach to IS annotation (von Stutterheim and Klein, 1989; van Kuppevelt, 1995) . With respect to dependent clauses, they rely on *at-issueness* as a diagnostic. Non-at-issue content, i.e. content which does not answer the current QUD, expressed by adverbial and nonrestrictive relative clauses, is treated as lacking internal IS.

In sum, the main challenges highlighted within pre-existing IS annotation schemes include (i) to what extent dependent clauses should be annotated for internal IS, and (ii) whether generalisations can be assumed and employed for the IS properties of different classes of dependent clause.

[3]Theme and Rheme are roughly equivalent with (aboutness) topic and comment,; the Specifier sets of the context of the utterance (≈ frame topic).

4. Desiderata for IS Annotation in Complex Sentences

In this section, I outline certain desiderata which can inform future, more nuanced schemes for the annotation of IS in complex sentences, in line with the theoretical insights discussed in Section 2 and the practical issues identified for previous schemes in Section 3. Some of these desiderata derive from the general nature of IS itself, but many are motivated by the specific issues which complex sentences raise. Language-specific concerns are expected, but here I concentrate on the crosslinguistic generalisations which can be drawn. I distinguish between desiderata which relate to (i) annotation format and (ii) the annotation process.

4.1. Annotation Format

While IS annotation can in principle span a range of different formats, one can nevertheless identify certain key features which any chosen format should be able to handle, in order to achieve a theoretically sound and practically sensible IS annotation: (i) multiplicity, (ii) recursion, (iii) discontinuity, (iv) supra-clausality, (v) uncertainty and (vi) meta-annotation.

4.1.1. Multiplicity

Even at the matrix level alone, any IS annotation scheme needs to be able to handle multiplicity, i.e. multiple, potentially cross-cutting IS articulations within a single clause/sentence. Firstly, it is generally acknowledged that topic and focus are not evaluated on the same basis, and as such cannot be considered complements of one another (Vallduví, 1992; von Heusinger, 1999; de Swart and de Hoop, 2014). As such, topic-comment and focus-background articulations cross-cut each other in various ways. A classic example is provided by Dahl (1974), repeated here in (13) (as discussed by Vallduví (1992, 55)).

(13) Q: What does John drink?

A_1: $\underbrace{\text{John}}_{\text{TOPIC}}$ $\underbrace{\text{drinks beer}}_{\text{COMMENT}}$

A_2: $\underbrace{\text{John drinks}}_{\text{BACKGROUND}}$ $\underbrace{\text{beer}}_{\text{FOCUS}}$

Multiplicity can also surface in clauses which contain multiple topics/foci, although this is a controversial area (Erteschik-Shir, 2007). Some have argued that a clause can contain more than one aboutness topic (Nikolaeva, 2001; Erteschik-Shir, 2007; Krifka and Musan, 2012; Dalrymple and Nikolaeva, 2011), in particular when a relation between two entities is expressed and commented on, e.g. (14) (Krifka and Musan, 2012, 29). Many languages have also been argued to exhibit multiple foci (Krifka, 2007; Surányi, 2007; Hedberg, 2013), e.g. (15) (Krifka, 2007, 258).

(14) As for **Jack**$_{TOPIC}$ and **Jill**$_{TOPIC}$, they married last year.

(15) John only introduced **Bill**$_{FOCUS}$ only to **Sue**$_{FOCUS}$.

4.1.2. Recursion

The issue of recursion presented in particular by dependent clauses is a different type of challenge, cf. (12) above. This ultimately requires some level of hierarchisisation in a single annotation layer. Hierarchical structure is no stranger to linguistic annotation, being widely employed in e.g. syntactic annotation schemes which encode constituency (Brants et al., 2002; Taylor et al., 2003). However, the majority of the previous IS annotation schemes encode IS via flat spans. Moreover, since many IS annotation contexts involve adding IS annotations to a syntactically annotated resource, further hierarchical IS annotations must be carefully designed so as not to result in conflicting hierarchies.

4.1.3. Discontinuity

Many languages exhibit discontinuous IS fields, i.e. when a single IS status is assigned to multiple non-adjacent segments, e.g. (16) (German), which shows a discontinuous focus (Gussenhoven, 1999, 50), and (17) (Serbian), which shows a discontinuous topic (Milićev and Milićević, 2012, 207).[4]

(16) *What happened to the child?*
Karl hat dem Kind **einen Füller** **geschenkt**
Karl has the child a fountain-pen given
'Karl gave the child a fountain pen'

(17) **Marija** sutra, **profesorica latinskog**, odlazi u penziju.
Mary tomorrow professor of-Latin goes to retirement
'Mary, professor of Latin, retires tomorrow.'

Discontinuous phenomena are of course not limited to IS; at the syntactic level, for instance, much work has focused on the representation of discontinuous constituents in linguistic annotation (Boyd, 2007; Maier and Lichte, 2011), but the issue has generally not been addressed in relation to IS annotation.

4.1.4. Supra-clausality

Another issue which arises in particular in relation to the annotation of complex sentences is the need to encode IS fields which are supra-clausal, i.e. span across clause boundaries. Examples of this were already provided in (5) and (12). This issue is particularly pertinent in contexts where IS annotation is combined with some form of syntactic annotation. The format must allow for IS annotations to cross-cut syntactic clause boundaries. In other words, IS annotation cannot simply be parasitic on syntactic annotation; it must have sufficient autonomy.

4.1.5. Uncertainty

Any IS annotation scheme should also be able to encode some level of uncertainty in contexts where a clear-cut identification of IS domains and/or classification of IS articulations cannot be made. The annotation of uncertainty has attracted attention in recent years (Barteld et al., 2014; Merten and Seemann, 2018; Andresen et al., 2020; Beck et al., 2020), and is particularly critical for IS annotation across complex sentences where our theoretical knowledge is still underdeveloped. In particular, whereas much of the theoretical understanding of IS is formulated on the basis of isolated question-answer pairs, the identification and classification of IS in long stretches of natural linguistic data, where non-directly questionable dependent clauses are commonplace, is less straightforward (Lüdeling et al., 2016).

Uncertainty with respect to IS annotation can arise in relation to two different aspects: (i) whether a particular segment constitutes an independent IS domain with its own internal IS articulation(s) and (ii) how and where the IS articulation(s) in a given IS domain should be drawn. The former is particularly relevant in the context of complex sentences where, as discussed in Section 2, views differ as to whether dependent clauses can be IS domains in their own right. As such, some mechanism for capturing (different types of) uncertainty, ideally based on a relatively sophisticated propagation model like that envisaged by Beck et al. (2020), should be a crucial component of any IS annotation scheme.

4.1.6. Meta-annotation

IS annotation schemes should also have the capability of encoding some form of meta-annotation, i.e. information about a given IS annotation, which explains/justifies the choices made. Meta-annotation is generally recognised as an important enhancement to linguistic annotations (Leech, 2005; Smith et al., 2008) and has been implemented in various resources and schemes (Laprun et al., 2002; Romary et al., 2010). It is particularly relevant in the context of IS, which lacks consensus on key concepts and definitions, in particular in relation to complex sentences. As a result, judgements involved are often less clear-cut and more subjective than at other linguistic levels, even with a carefully operationalised set of diagnostic criteria. The use of meta-annotations here can promote the usability of the resources for theoretical studies, making the decision behind the annotation transparent and allowing the user to reclassify the data if desired. In cases where the annotator is uncertain, as discussed above, meta-annotation can also be an important enhancement, setting out the locus of the uncertainty and allowing it to be potentially resolved at a later date.

4.1.7. Summary

Four of the six requirements discussed here (multiplicity, supra-clausality, uncertainty and meta-annotation) can be easily satisfied by employing a stand-off, multi-dimensional annotation format. Such a format in principle allows for independent, linked annotation lay-

[4]On the distinction between multiple foci and discontinuous focus, see Gussenhoven (1999, 49–50).

ers for modelling (i) multiple cross-cutting IS articulations (ii) IS annotations which are autonomous and not structurally dependent on syntactic annotations, (iii) conflicting annotations for a particular IS articulation across co-existing layers in cases of uncertainty or differing theoretical assumptions, and (iv) meta-annotations to aid transparency and usability. At present, the best possibility is to use some stand-off XML format. This is indeed already recommended by e.g. CLARIN-D,[5] and many others have advocated for this format in recent years (Dipper, 2005; Lüdeling et al., 2016) and employed it specifically for IS annotation (Stede and Mamprin, 2016; Celano, 2019). Moreover, purpose-built infrastructures, such as the interoperable *corpus-tools.org* toolchain (Druskat et al., 2016) which caters for the creation, annotation, query and analysis of multidimensional corpora, mean that such projects are relatively achievable. Yet the full potential on offer for capturing the nuances of IS in complex sentences has yet to be exploited.

At the same time, the issues discussed (in particular multiplicity, discontinuity and recursion) also impose demands on the format of individual annotation layers. For any layer which encodes a certain IS articulation, the structural representation of the annotation needs to go beyond labelled spans over continuous segments of text and must be able to capture the distinction between (i) multiple topics/foci in a single clause and (ii) non-adjacent segments which are assigned a single topic/focus value, potentially via some form of coindexation or linking mechanism. Additionally, in order to allow for recursion in complex sentences, IS annotation layers need to allow for hierarchical relations.

4.2. Annotation Process

Manual IS annotation based on pragmatic context-based judgements alone is a relatively subjective and time-intensive process, especially in relation to complex sentences where, as mentioned, our understanding of IS is generally underdeveloped. Overall, various models for the automatic annotation of IS have been trialed (Hempelmann et al., 2005; Nissim, 2006; Cahill and Riester, 2012; Markert et al., 2012; Rahman and Ng, 2012; Ziai and Meurers, 2018), but automatic annotation for IS is not as reliable as for other tasks (Lüdeling et al., 2016). It generally exploits pre-existing annotations for morphosyntactic and lexical features which approximately correlate with IS properties. Most developments in automatic IS annotation focus on the discourse status of referents (e.g. old/new) (Hempelmann et al., 2005; Nissim, 2006; Cahill and Riester, 2012; Markert et al., 2012; Rahman and Ng, 2012), and these approaches thus exploit nominal features, e.g. weight (pronoun/noun), position (sentence-initial/-final), grammatical function (subject/object) and whether the referent has been previously mentioned or not.

To my knowledge, the possibilities for automatic annotation of IS specifically in relation to complex sentences remain as yet unexplored. Given the fact that certain crosslinguistic syntax-IS correspondences can be identified for dependent clauses (see Section 2), it seems sensible to test to what extent these correspondences can be useful in informing a (potentially automated) rule-based approach to the IS annotation of complex sentences, especially since many contexts for IS annotation involve adding additional annotations on top of pre-existing syntactic annotations. In this section, I outline the basis for such an approach, before testing it in Section 5.

The IS annotation process can be broken down into two key tasks: (i) the identification of IS domains and (ii) the classification of IS articulations within those domains. With respect to complex sentences, I argue that adopting an approach whereby each dependent clause is annotated in two separate stages, with respect to (i) external IS and (ii) internal IS (see Section 2), is most efficient. This is because the classification of a dependent clause in terms of its external IS role, and the decision as to whether it has internal IS, are largely independent of each other and informed by different considerations. In particular, it should be borne in mind that identification of an external IS role for a given dependent clause does not necessarily imply that it has internal IS.

4.2.1. Stage I (External IS)

In terms of the external IS of dependent clauses, the most robust crosslinguistic generalisations which can be identified in the literature are those in (18), where *D* stands for dependent clause, RRC for restrictive relative and NRRC for nonrestrictive relative clause.

(18) **Crosslinguistic syntax-IS correspondences**
- *D* occurs before host clause ≈ TOPIC
- *D* is conditional clause ≈ TOPIC
- *D* is clefted ≈ FOCUS
- *D* is nonfactive complement ≈ FOCUS
- *D* is factive complement ≈ BACKGROUND
- *D* is RRC ≈ FOCUS
- *D* is NRRC ≈ BACKGROUND

The correspondences in (18) are general correlations rather than hard and fast constraints. On the basis of these correspondences, I propose the rule-based algorithm in Figure 1 for the assignment of external IS to dependent clauses (*D*), which exploits syntactic/semantic properties. The top split concerns clause ordering, i.e. whether *D* is before the host clause or in another position. If *D* is before the host clause, it is straightforwardly annotated as topic; if *D* occurs in a different position, a range of annotations are possible, subject to clause class and syntactic/semantic properties (clefting/non-restrictiveness). With respect to the (non)factivity of complement clauses, I refer to the predicate classes in Hooper and Thompson (1973).

[5] https://media.dwds.de/clarin/userguide/text/annotation_aspects.xhtml

```
case  D is before host clause
      external IS := TOPIC
case  D is not before host clause
      if    D is conditional clause then
            external IS := TOPIC
      elif  D is clefted then
            external IS := FOCUS
      elif  D is complement clause then
            if    D is nonfactive then
                  external IS := FOCUS
            else
                  external IS := BACKGROUND
      elif  D is relative clause then
            if    D is RRC then
                  external IS := FOCUS
            else
                  external IS := BACKGROUND
      else
            external IS := BACKGROUND
```

Figure 1: Hand-crafted rule-based algorithm for assigning external IS to dependent clauses

```
case  D is before host clause
      status := no internal IS
case  D is not before host clause
      if    D is adverbial clause then
            if    D is central adverbial clause then
                  status := no internal IS
            else
                  status := internal IS
      elif  D is complement clause then
            if    D is factive then
                  status := no internal IS
            else
                  status := internal IS
      elif  D is relative clause
            if    D is RRC then
                  status := no internal IS
            else
                  status := internal IS
      else
            status := unknown
```

Figure 2: Hand-crafted rule-based algorithm for deciding whether to assign internal IS to dependent clauses

4.2.2. Stage II (Internal IS)

Stage II represents a more complex set of tasks, involving the decision as to whether a dependent clause constitutes an IS domain with its own internal IS and, if yes, then classifying any relevant IS articulation(s) within that domain. As discussed in Section 3, the correct identification of IS domains in relation to complex sentences has challenged previous approaches to IS annotation and so I focus on this aspect of the internal IS annotation of dependent clauses.

On the basis of the crosslinguistic tendencies discussed in Section 2, I propose the rule-based algorithm in Figure 2 as a heuristic to aid the decision as to whether a given dependent clause constitutes an IS domain with its own internal IS. Again, this exploits clause ordering as the top split, and then clause classes and subclasses at lower levels. This algorithm can also in principle be combined with information as to whether the dependent clause is asserted or presupposed, as assertive status generally indicates internal IS, and presupposed status lack of internal IS. Here, semantic tests for assertion/presupposition are recommended, of which there are a range in the literature, e.g. the denial and question tests (Hooper and Thompson, 1973; Wiklund et al., 2009) for identifying assertions and the negation test (Kiparsky and Kiparsky, 1970; Hooper, 1975) and the *Hey, wait a minute* test (von Fintel, 2004) for identifying presuppositions. Such tests, however, typically rely on time-intensive judgements and should be considered as a potential supplement to the primarily syntactic-based algorithm in Figure 2, which is designed to exploit pre-annotated morphosyntactic and lexical features as far as possible.

5. Test Case: Middle Low German

The approaches outlined in Section 4.2 were tested in the IS annotation of dependent clauses in a Middle Low German text from the Corpus of Historical Low German (CHLG) (Booth et al., 2020) specifically the text *Engelhus*, which is a Low German version of Dietrich Engelhus' *Chronica Nova*. The text is an historical chronicle from 1435 CE, and contains 709 clauses annotated as dependent clauses (`IP-SUB`) in the syntactic Penn-style annotation, although some of this number will be embedded conjuncts within a larger coordination structure which can likely be assigned a single external IS tag. Moreover, some of the clauses tagged `IP-SUB` will be dependent clauses which themselves are embedded in dependent clauses, which I do not consider for external or internal IS annotation for the purposes of this paper. Whether such multiply embedded dependent clauses should be annotated for their external IS role in the local dependent clause, or exhibit their own internal IS articulations, I leave open for future consideration.

5.1. Annotation of External IS

All dependent clauses in *Engelhus* were manually annotated for external IS on the basis of contextual pragmatic judgements alone (i.e. irrespective of syntactic and lexical features), using the annotation tool Annotald (Beck et al., 2015). The categories which were annotated were as in (19), largely following the diagnostics provided in Götze et al. (2007) (cf. also (1) and (2) in Section 2.1).

(19) **IS tags**

- TOPIC, which includes:
  - A(BOUTNESS)-TOPIC
  - F(RAME)-TOPIC
- FOCUS, which includes:
  - I(NFORMATIONAL)-FOCUS
  - C(ONTRASTIVE)-FOCUS
- BACKGROUND

A fresh round of (manual) annotation was then performed relying exclusively on the rule-based algorithm in Figure 1 as annotation guidelines, without consideration of the pragmatic context. The result was then compared against the first round of annotations in order to assess the algorithm's accuracy. The overall accuracy of the algorithm, i.e. the number of correctly classified instances of all assignments is 81.6%. The precision and recall for each tag is provided in Table 1.

	P	R	F
TOPIC	.849	.753	.798
FOCUS	.860	.636	.731
BACKGROUND	.704	.884	.783

Table 1: Per tag performance of hand-crafted rule-based algorithm for annotation of external IS

A particularly high number of assignments of the BACKGROUND tag were false positives, the majority of which were in fact foci. The over-assignment of the BACKGROUND tag is not surprising, given that this was used as a catch-all for remaining instances of non-initial dependent clauses, cf. Figure 1. As such, future refinements of the algorithm could include finding extra classes/contexts which are likely to coincide with focus for non-initial dependent clauses.

The algorithm in Figure 1 does not distinguish between different types of topic/focus, cf. (19), as it is designed to be crosslinguistically applicable and was thus informed by only the most robust crosslinguistic generalisations. However, with respect to at least Middle Low German, some further language-specific correlations between syntax and specific types of topic/focus can be observed from the first round of pragmatic, context-based annotations, which may perhaps turn out to be more general correlations. For instance, of the 70 dependent clauses which occur before the host clause in *Engelhus*, 67 of these are topics. However, only two of these qualify as aboutness topics, both free relatives in a left-dislocation/resumption structure, e.g. (20).

(20) [**wor auer Noe henkeyme**]$_i$ **dat**$_i$ vindest u
where however Noah comes-to that find you
hir na ffalech
here after Falech
'Wherever Noah comes to though, that you find hereafter, Falech'

The other sentence-initial clauses which qualify as topics (*n*=65) are frame-topics. These were most commonly adverbial clauses, again in a left-dislocation/resumption structure, e.g. (21), or conditional clauses, e.g. (22).

(21) [**Do lamech was clxxii iar** olt]$_i$ **do**$_i$ ghewan
when Lamech was 172 years old then had
he Noe
he Noah
'When Lamech was 172 years old, then he had Noah'

(22) [**wolde eymant eyn belde nomen myner**] de
wanted someone a picture take my.GEN he
nome ok eyn belde mir pyne
take also a picture my.GEN pain.GEN
'If someone wanted to one of my pictures, they would take also a picture of my pain'

With respect to types of focus (information/contrastive), some additional patterns were observed. The (typically nonfactive) complement clauses annotated as focus were all assigned specifically information focus in terms of their external IS, e.g. (23), whereas restrictive relative clauses were typically annotated as contrastive focus, since their function to uniquely identify a referent implies the presence of alternatives, e.g. (24).

(23) Me schrift von eme [**dat he lachede do**...]
one writes of him that he laughed when
'One write of him he laughed when...'

(24) it wore de [**de ore gode vorstoren scholde**]
it be.SBJV DEM REL her god destroy should
'unless it were she who was to destroy her god (and not someone else)'

As such, it seems that, for MLG at least, one should acknowledge extra syntax-IS correlations for dependent clauses, which pertain to specific types of topic/focus. Further crosslinguistic research would however need to be conducted before these could be included in the algorithm in Figure 1, which is intended to be crosslinguistically applicable.

5.2. Annotation of Internal IS

In a separate task, each dependent clause in *Engelhus* was manually annotated on the basis of pragmatic judgements alone for the presence/absence of internal IS, on the basis of whether internal IS articulations could be identified given the context, again largely following the guidelines in Götze et al. (2007) for the identification of aboutness/frame topics, information/contrastive foci, cf. (19). Dependent clauses were also explicitly annotated if they lacked internal IS.

A fresh round of (manual) annotation was then performed using the rule-based algorithm in Figure 2 as guidelines to classify each dependent clause as either having or lacking internal IS, without paying attention to the pragmatic context. The results of the algorithm were then compared with the first round of annotations to assess the algorithm's accuracy at identifying internal IS contexts, which is known to be a challenging area in the IS annotation of complex sentences (see Section 3).

Overall the accuracy of the algorithm, i.e. the number of correctly classified instances of all assignments is 88.3%, indicating that the exploitation of pre-annotated morphosyntactic and lexical features can play a useful role in informing the annotation of complex sentences for internal IS. In particular, the algorithm assigned a relatively large number of false positives for the class NO INTERNAL IS in places where it is in fact present in the form of clause-internal contrastive focus, suggesting that contrast as an IS notion merits special attention with respect to annotation.

6. Conclusion

This paper responded to the challenge of annotating information structure in complex sentences by outlining certain desiderata with respect to both annotation format and the annotation process, informed by state-of-the-art theoretical knowledge, as well as practical issues identified for previous IS annotation schemes. In particular, the specific demands imposed by the IS properties of complex sentences were shown to add further weight to the importance of multidimensional, standoff annotation formats. With respect to the annotation process, a two-stage process was advocated for the IS annotation of dependent clauses (external IS, internal IS); for both stages, it was shown that rule-based algorithms which exploit pre-annotated non-IS features have the potential to play a useful role in the IS annotation of complex sentences in future.

7. Acknowledgements

This research was funded by the Research Foundation Flanders (FWO) via a postdoctoral fellowship awarded to the author [2021–2024, Grant no. 12ZL522N]. The author kindly thanks Anne Breitbarth for her valuable feedback on earlier versions of this paper, as well as two anonymous reviewers for their constructive comments.

8. Bibliographical References

Andresen, M., Vauth, M., and Zinsmeister, H. (2020). Modeling ambiguity with many annotators and self-assessments of annotator certainty. In *Proceedings of the 14th Linguistic Annotation Workshop*, pages 48–59, Barcelona, Spain, December. Association for Computational Linguistics.

Barteld, F., Ihden, S., Schröder, I., and Zinsmeister, H. (2014). Annotating descriptively incomplete language phenomena. In *Proceedings of LAW VIII - The 8th Linguistic Annotation Workshop*, pages 99–104, Dublin, Ireland, August. Association for Computational Linguistics and Dublin City University.

Baumann, S., Brinckmann, C., Hansen-Schirra, S., Kruijff, G.-J., Kruijff-Korbayová, I., Neumann, S., Steiner, E., Teich, E., and Uszkoreit, H. (2004). The MULI project: Annotation and analysis of information structure in German and English. In *Proceedings of the Fourth International Conference on Language Resources and Evaluation (LREC'04)*, Lisbon, Portugal, May. European Language Resources Association (ELRA).

Beck, C., Booth, H., El-Assady, M., and Butt, M. (2020). Representation problems in linguistic annotations: Ambiguity, variation, uncertainty, error and bias. In *Proceedings of the 14th Linguistic Annotation Workshop*, pages 60–73, Barcelona, Spain, December. Association for Computational Linguistics.

Bianchi, V. and Frascarelli, M. (2010). Is topic a root phenomenon? *Iberia: An International Journal of Theoretical Linguistics*, 2(1):43–88.

Bird, S. and Liberman, M. (2001). A formal framework for linguistic annotation. *Speech communication*, 33(1-2):23–60.

Bohnet, B., Burga, A., and Wanner, L. (2013). Towards the annotation of Penn TreeBank with information structure. In Ruslan Mitkov et al., editors, *Proceedings of the Sixth International Joint Conference on Natural Language Processing*, pages 1250–1256, Nagoya. Asian Federation of Natural Language Processing.

Boyd, A. (2007). Discontinuity revisited: An improved conversion to context-free representations. In *Proceedings of the Linguistic Annotation Workshop*, pages 41–44, Prague, Czech Republic, June. Association for Computational Linguistics.

Boye, K. and Harder, P. (2007). Complement-taking predicates: usage and linguistic structure. *Studies in Language*, 31(3):569–606.

Brants, S., Dipper, S., Hansen, S., Lezius, W., and Smith, G. (2002). The TIGER treebank. In *Proceedings of the workshop on Treebanks and Linguistic theories*, pages 24–41, Sozopol, Bulgaria.

Buráňová, E., Hajičová, E., and Sgall, P. (2000). Tagging of very large corpora: Topic-Focus articulation. In *Proceedings of the 18th Conference on Computational Linguistics (COLING)*, pages 139–144, Saarbrücken, Germany, Universität des Saarlandes. Association for Computational Linguistics.

Büring, D. (2007). Semantics, intonation and information structure. In Gillian Ramchand et al., editors, *The Oxford handbook of linguistic interfaces*, pages 445–473. Oxford University Press, Oxford.

Bybee, J. (2002). Main clauses are innovative, subordinate clauses are conservative: consequences for the nature of constructions. In Joan Bybee et al., editors, *Complex sentences in grammar and discourse: Essays in honor of Sandra A. Thompson*, pages 1–17. John Benjamins, Amsterdam.

Cahill, A. and Riester, A. (2012). Automatically acquiring fine-grained information status distinctions in German. In *Proceedings of the 13th Annual Meeting of the Special Interest Group on Discourse and Dialogue*, SIGDIAL '12, pages 232–236, USA. Association for Computational Linguistics.

Calhoun, S., Nissim, M., Steedman, M., and Brenier, J. (2005). A framework for annotating information structure in discourse. In Adam Meyers, editor, *Frontiers in Corpus Annotation II: Pie in the Sky, ACL2005 Conference Workshop*, pages 45–52, Ann Arbor, Michigan, June 2005.

Celano, G. G. A. (2019). Standoff annotation for the Ancient Greek and Latin Dependency Treebank. In *Proceedings of the 3rd International Conference on Digital Access to Textual Cultural Heritage, Brussels, Belgium*, pages 149–153, New York. Association for Computing Machinery.

Chafe, W. (1984). How people use adverbial clauses. In *Proceedings of the Tenth Annual Meeting of the Berkeley Linguistics Society*, pages 437–449, Berkeley, CA. Berkeley Linguistics Society.

Cook, P. and Bildhauer, F. (2011). Annotating information structure: the case of topic. In Stefanie Dipper et al., editors, *Beyond semantics: Corpus-based investigations of pragmatic and discourse phenomena*, Bochumer Linguistische Arbeitsberichte 3, pages 45–56. Ruhr-Universität Bochum, Sprachwissenschaftliches Institut, Bochum.

Cook, P. and Bildhauer, F. (2013). Identifying "aboutness topics": two annotation experiments. *Dialogue & Discourse*, 4(2):118–141.

Dahl, Ö. (1974). *Topic, comment, contextual boundedness and focus*. Buske, Hamburg.

Dalrymple, M. and Nikolaeva, I. (2011). *Objects and information structure*. Cambridge University Press, Cambridge.

De Cat, C. (2012). Towards an interface definition of root phenomena. In Lobke Aelbrecht, et al., editors, *Main Clause Phenomena: New Horizons*, pages 135–158. John Benjamins, Amsterdam.

de Swart, H. and de Hoop, H. (2014). Topic and focus. In Lisa Cheng et al., editors, *The First Glot International State-of-the-Article Book: The Latest in Linguistics*, pages 105–130. de Gruyter, Berlin.

Dehé, N. and Wichmann, A. (2010). Sentence-initial *I think (that)* and *I believe (that)*: prosodic evidence for uses as main clause, comment clause and discourse marker. *Studies in Language*, 34(1):36–74.

Depraetere, I. (1996). Foregrounding in English relative clauses. *Linguistics*, 34:699–731.

Diessel, H. (2001). The ordering distribution of main and adverbial clauses: A typological study. *Language*, 77:433–455.

Dipper, S. (2005). Xml-based stand-off representation and exploitation of multi-level linguistic annotation. In *Proceedings of the Berliner XML Tage 2005 (BXML 2005)*, pages 39–50. Berlin, Germany.

Ebert, C., Ebert, C., and Hinterwimmer, S. (2014). A unified analysis of conditionals as topics. *Linguistics and Philosophy*, 37(5):353–408.

Erteschik-Shir, N. (2007). *Information structure: the syntax-discourse interface*. Oxford University Press, Oxford.

Fabb, N. (1990). The difference between English restrictive and nonrestrictive relative clauses. *Journal of Linguistics*, 26(1):57–77.

Götze, M., Weskott, T., Endriss, C., Fiedler, I., Hinterwimmer, S., Petrova, S., Schwarz, A., Skopeteas, S., and Stoel, R. (2007). Information structure. In Steffi Dipper, et al., editors, *Information Structure in Cross-Linguistic Corpora: Annotation Guidelines for Phonology, Morphology, Syntax, Semantics, and Information Structure*, pages 147–187. Universitätsverlag Potsdam, Potsdam.

Gussenhoven, C. (1999). On the limits of focus projection in English. In Peter Bosch et al., editors, *Focus: linguistic, cognitive, and computational perspectives*, pages 43–55. Cambridge University Press, Cambridge.

Haegeman, L. (2007). Operator movement and topicalisation in adverbial clauses. *Folia Linguistica*, 41(3/4):279–325.

Haiman, J. (1978). Conditionals are topics. *Language*, 54(3):564–589.

Hajicová, E., Partee, B. B. H., and Sgall, P. (1998). *Topic-focus articulation, tripartite structures, and semantic content*. Kluwer, Dordrecht.

Hedberg, N. (2013). Multiple focus and cleft sentences. In Katharina Hartmann et al., editors, *Cleft structures*, pages 227–250. John Benjamins, Amsterdam.

Hempelmann, C. F., Dufty, D., McCarthy, P. M., Graesser, A. C., Cai, Z., and McNamara, D. S. (2005). Using LSA to automatically identify givenness and newness of noun phrases in written discourse. In Bruno Bara, et al., editors, *Proceedings of the 27th Annual Meeting of the Cognitive Science Society*, pages 941–946, Mahwah, NJ. Erlbaum.

Hooper, J. B. and Thompson, S. A. (1973). On the applicability of root transformations. *Linguistic Inquiry*, 4(4):465–497.

Hooper, J. B. (1975). On assertive predicates. In John P. Kimball, editor, *Syntax and Semantics*, volume 4, pages 91–124. Academic Press, San Diego, CA.

Ide, N. and Romary, L. (2004). International standard for a linguistic annotation framework. *Natural Language Engineering*, 10(3-4):211–225.

Kiparsky, P. and Kiparsky, C. (1970). Fact. In M Bierwisch et al., editors, *Progress in linguistics*, pages 143–147. Mouton, The Hague.

Koktová, E. (1996). Wh-extraction and the topic-focus articulation of the sentence. In Barbara H. Partee et al., editors, *Discourse and Meaning: Papers in Honor of Eva Hajičová*, pages 255–271. John Benjamins, Amsterdam.

Komagata, N. (2003). Information structure in subordinate and subordinate-like clauses. *Journal of Logic, Language and Information*, 12(3):301–318.

Krifka, M. and Musan, R. (2012). Information structure: overview and linguistic issues. In Manfred Krifka et al., editors, *The expression of information structure*, pages 1–44. de Gruyter, Berlin.

Krifka, M. (2007). Basic notions of information structure. In Caroline Féry et al., editors, *Interdisciplinary Studies on Information Structure*, pages 13–56. Universitätsverlag, Potsdam.

Lahousse, K. and Borremans, M. (2014). The distribution of functional-pragmatic types of clefts in adverbial clauses. *Linguistics*, 52(3):793–836.

Lahousse, K. (2010). Information structure and epistemic modality in adverbial clauses in French. *Studies in Language*, 34(2):298–326.

Lahousse, K. (2022). Is focus a root phenomenon? In Davide Garassino et al., editors, *When data challenges theory: unexpected and paradoxical evidence in information structure*, pages 148–182. John Benjamins, Amsterdam.

Laprun, C., Fiscus, J., Garofolo, J., and Pajot, S. (2002). Recent improvements to the ATLAS architecture. In *Proceedings of the Second International Conference on Human Language Technology (HLT'02)*, pages 263–268.

Leech, G. (2005). Adding linguistic annotation. In Martin Wynne, editor, *Developing linguistic corpora: a guide to good practice*, pages 17–29. Oxbow Books, Oxford.

Lehmann, C. (1984). *Der Relativsatz: Typologie seiner Strukturen, Theorie seiner Funktionen, Kompendium seiner Grammatik*. John Benjamins, Amsterdam.

Lehmann, C. (1988). Towards a typology of clause linkage. In John Haiman et al., editors, *Clause combining in grammar and discourse*, pages 181–225. John Benjamins, Amsterdam.

Lelandais, M. and Ferré, G. (2017). How are three syntactic types of subordinate clauses different in terms of informational weight? *Anglophonia*, 23. http://journals.openedition.org/anglophonia/1200.

Lüdeling, A., Ritz, J., Stede, M., and Zeldes, A. (2016). Corpus linguistics and information structure research. In Caroline Féry et al., editors, *The Oxford handbook of information structure*, pages 599–620. Oxford University Press, Oxford.

Maier, W. and Lichte, T. (2011). Characterizing discontinuity in constituent treebanks. In Philippe de Groote, et al., editors, *Formal Grammar*, pages 167–182, Berlin, Heidelberg. Springer.

Maki, H., Kaiser, L., and Ochi, M. (1999). Embedded topicalization in English and Japanese. *Lingua*, 1(109):1–14.

Marchese, L. (1977). Subordinate clauses as topics in Godie. In Matin Mould et al., editors, *Papers from the 8th Conference on African Linguistics*, pages 157–164, Los Angeles, CA. Department of Linguistics, University of California.

Markert, K., Hou, Y., and Strube, M. (2012). Collective classification for fine-grained information status. In *Proceedings of the 50th Annual Meeting of the Association for Computational Linguistics: Long Papers - Volume 1*, ACL '12, page 795–804, USA. Association for Computational Linguistics.

Mathesius, V. (1975). *A functional analysis of present day English on a general linguistic basis*. Mouton, The Hague.

Matić, D., Van Gijn, R., and Van Valin Jr, R. D. (2014). Information structure and reference tracking in complex sentences. In Rik van Gijn, et al., editors, *Information structure and reference tracking in complex sentences*, pages 1–42. John Benjamins, Amsterdam.

Matsuda, K. (1998). On the conservatism of embedded clauses. In Monika S. Schmid, et al., editors, *Historical Linguistics 1997: Selected papers from the 13th International Conference on Historical Linguistics, Düsseldorf, 10–17 August 1997*, pages 255–268. John Benjamins, Amsterdam.

Merten, M.-L. and Seemann, N. (2018). Analyzing constructional change: Linguistic annotation and sources of uncertainty. In *Proceedings of the Sixth International Conference on Technological Ecosystems for Enhancing Multiculturality*, TEEM'18, page 819–825, New York, NY, USA. Association for Computing Machinery.

Milićev, T. and Milićević, N. (2012). Leftward movement with discontinuous appositive constructions. *Acta Linguistica Hungarica*, 59(1-2):205–220.

Neeleman, A., Titov, E., Van de Koot, H., and Vermeulen, R. (2009). A syntactic typology of topic, focus and contrast. In Jeroen van Craenenbroeck, editor, *Alternatives to cartography*, pages 15–52. de Gruyter, Berlin.

Nikolaeva, I. (2001). Secondary topic as a relation in information structure. *Linguistics*, 39(1):1–49.

Nissim, M. (2006). Learning information status of discourse entities. In *Proceedings of the 2006 Conference on Empirical Methods in Natural Language Processing*, EMNLP '06, page 94–102, USA. Association for Computational Linguistics.

Paggio, P. (2006). Annotating information structure in a corpus of spoken Danish. In *Proceedings of the 5th international conference on Language Resources and Evaluation (LREC2006)*, pages 1606–1609, Genova, Italy.

Partee, B. H. (1996). Allegation and local accommodation. In Barbara H. Partee et al., editors, *Discourse and meaning: papers in honor of Eva Hajicová*, pages 65–86. John Benjamins, Amsterdam.

Quirk, R., Greenbaum, S., Leech, G., and Svartvik, J. (1985). *A comprehensive grammar of the English language*. Longman, London.

Rahman, A. and Ng, V. (2012). Learning the fine-grained information status of discourse entities. In *Proceedings of the 13th Conference of the European Chapter of the Association for Computational Linguistics*, EACL '12, page 798–807, USA. Association for Computational Linguistics.

Reinhart, T. (1981). Pragmatics and linguistics: An analysis of sentence topics. *Philosophica*, 27(1):53–94.

Riester, A., Brunetti, L., and De Kuthy, K. (2018). Annotation guidelines for Questions under Discussion and information structure. In Evangelia Adamou, et al., editors, *Information structure in lesser-described languages: studies in prosody and syntax*, pages 403–443. John Benjamins, Amsterdam.

Riester, A. (2009). Stress test for relative clauses. In Arndt Riester et al., editors, *Focus at the syntax-semantics interface*, pages 69–86. University of Stuttgart, Stuttgart.

Romary, L., Zeldes, A., and Zipser, F. (2010). [Tiger2/] documentation [Technical Report]. inria-00593903v2.

Schachter, P. (1973). Focus and relativization. *Language*, 41(1):19–46.

Schiffrin, D. (1992). Conditionals as topics in discourse. *Linguistics*, 30:165–197.

Schilder, F. and Tenbrink, T. (2002). The interplay of information structure and the placement of *after* and *before*. In *Proceedings of the Workshop on Information Structure in Context*, Stuttgart. University of Stuttgart.

Smith, N., Hoffmann, S., and Rayson, P. (2008). Corpus tools and methods, today and tomorrow: Incorporating linguists' manual annotations. *Literary and Linguistic Computing*, 23(2):163–180.

Song, S. (2014). Information structure of relative clauses in English: a flexible and computationally tractable model. *Language and Information*, 18(2):1–29.

Stalnaker, R. (2002). Common ground. *Linguistics and Philosophy*, 25(5–6):701–721.

Stede, M. and Mamprin, S. (2016). Information structure in the Potsdam commentary corpus: topics. In *Proceedings of the Tenth International Conference on Language Resources and Evaluation (LREC'16)*, pages 1718–1723, Portorož, Slovenia, May. European Language Resources Association (ELRA).

Steedman, M. (2000). Information structure and the syntax-phonology interface. *Linguistic Inquiry*, 31(4):649–689.

Surányi, B. (2007). Focus structure and the interpretation of multiple questions. In Kerstin Schwabe et al., editors, *On information structure, meaning and form*, pages 229–253. John Benjamins, Amsterdam.

Taylor, A., Marcus, M., and Santorini, B. (2003). The Penn Treebank: an overview. In Anne Abeillé, editor, *Treebanks: building and using parsed corpora*, pages 5–22. Kluwer, Dordrecht.

Thompson, S. A. and Longacre, R. E. (1985). Adverbial clauses. In Timothy Shopen, editor, *Language typology and syntactic description*, volume 2, pages 171–234. Cambridge University Press, Cambridge.

Thompson, S. A. (1985). Grammar and written discourse: Initial vs. final purpose clauses in English. *Text-Interdisciplinary Journal for the Study of Discourse*, 5(1-2):55–84.

Tophinke, D. (2012). Syntaktischer Ausbau im Mittelniederdeutschen: Theoretisch-methodische Überlegungen und kursorische Analysen. *Niederdeutsches Wort*, 52:19–46.

Umbach, C. (2006). Non-restrictive modification and backgrounding. In *Proceedings of the Ninth Symposium on Logic and Language*, pages 152–159, Budapest. Hungarian Academy of Sciences.

Vallduví, E. and Zacharski, R. (1994). Accenting phenomena, association with focus, and the recursiveness of focus-ground. In P. Dekker et al., editors, *Proceedings of the 9th Amsterdam Colloquium*, pages 683–702. ILLC (Institute for Logic, Language and Computation)/Department of Philosophy, Amsterdam.

Vallduví, E. (1992). *The informational component*. Garland Press, New York.

van Kuppevelt, J. (1995). Discourse structure, topicality and questioning. *Journal of Linguistics*, 31(1):109–147.

von Fintel, K. (2004). Would you believe it? The King of France is back! (presuppositions and truth-value intuitions). In Marga Reimer et al., editors, *Descriptions and beyond*, pages 315–341. Oxford University Press, Oxford.

von Heusinger, K. (1999). Intonation and information structure. University of Konstanz. Habilitationsschrift.

von Stutterheim, C. and Klein, W. (1989). Referential movement in descriptive and narrative discourse. In Rainer Dietrich et al., editors, *Language processing in social context*, pages 39–76. North-Holland, Amsterdam.

Wiklund, A.-L., Bentzen, K., Hrafnbjargarson, G. H., and Hróarsdóttir, Þ. (2009). On the distribution and illocution of V2 in Scandinavian *that*-clauses. *Lingua*, 119(12):1914–1938.

Ziai, R. and Meurers, D. (2018). Automatic focus annotation: Bringing formal pragmatics alive in analyzing the information structure of authentic data. In *Proceedings of the 2018 Conference of the North American Chapter of the Association for Computational Linguistics: Human Language Technologies, Volume 1 (Long Papers)*, pages 117–128, New Orleans, Louisiana, June. Association for Computational Linguistics.

9. Language Resource References

Beck, J., Ecay, A., and Ingason, A. K. (2015). Annotald. version 1.3. 7.

Booth, H., Breitbarth, A., Ecay, A., and Farasyn, M. (2020). A Penn-style treebank of Middle Low German. In *Proceedings of The 12th Language Resources and Evaluation Conference*, pages 766–775, Marseille, France, May. European Language Resources Association.

Druskat, S., Gast, V., Krause, T., and Zipser, F. (2016). corpus-tools.org: An interoperable generic software tool set for multi-layer linguistic corpora. In *Proceedings of the Tenth International Conference on Language Resources and Evaluation (LREC'16)*, pages 4492–4499.

Proceedings of the 16th Linguistic Annotation Workshop (LAW-XVI) @LREC 2022, pages 44–61
Marseille, 24 June 2022

The Sensitivity of Annotator Bias to Task Definitions in Argument Mining

Terne Sasha Thorn Jakobsen[1], Maria Barrett[2], Anders Søgaard[3], David Dreyer Lassen[4]
[1,4]Copenhagen Center for Social Data Science, University of Copenhagen
[2]Department of Computer Science, IT University of Copenhagen
[3]Department of Computer Science, University of Copenhagen
{terne.thorn, david.dreyer.lassen}@sodas.ku.dk, mbarrett@itu.dk, soegaard@di.ku.dk

Abstract

NLP models are dependent on the data they are trained on, including how this data is annotated. NLP research increasingly examines the *social biases* of models, but often in the light of their training data and specific social biases that can be identified in the text itself. In this paper, we present an annotation experiment that is the first to examine the extent to which social bias is *sensitive to how data is annotated.* We do so by collecting annotations of arguments in the same documents following *four different guidelines* and from *four different demographic annotator backgrounds.* We show that annotations exhibit widely different levels of group disparity depending on which guidelines annotators follow. The differences are *not* explained by task complexity, but rather by characteristics of these demographic groups, as previously identified by sociological studies. We release a dataset that is small in the number of instances but large in the number of annotations with demographic information, and our results encourage an increased awareness of annotator bias.

Keywords: Annotation, bias, argument mining

1. Introduction

Argument mining is one of the most important and popular tasks at the intersection of natural language processing and the social sciences. Still, it suffers from "a lack of a standardized methodology for annotation" (Lawrence and Reed, 2019). Approaches to argument mining are diverse, i.e. there are various definitions of what constitutes an argument, how to assess its quality (Vecchi et al., 2021), how to model arguments, the granularity of both the input and the target, and hence how arguments are annotated for training (Lippi and Torroni, 2016)[1]. Simultaneously, what constitutes an argument may be sensitive to social biases among annotators. Such social biases have already been documented for related tasks such as fake news identification (Rampersad and Althiyabi, 2020; van der Linden et al., 2020) and stance detection (Joseph et al., 2017). One way in which annotation guidelines differ is how much evidence they require for something to be an argument, from guidelines that essentially equate *claims* with arguments (Morante et al., 2020) to guidelines in which evidence is a necessary component of an argument (Shnarch et al., 2020). In addition to fairness, annotation guidelines must be applicable across topics or domains (Stab et al., 2018).

This paper compares how annotators from different demographic backgrounds interpret annotation guidelines of varying complexity and to what extent they subsequently agree on how to annotate for arguments. To this end, we crowd-source an argument annotation task in conjunction with demographic attributes, as visualized in Figure 1, creating a dataset of sentences with multiple annotations balanced across four argument annotation guidelines, gender, and political alignment. We show that the agreement *cross-group* is much lower than the agreement reported in previous work, suggesting social group differences in how guidelines are interpreted. We further demonstrate clear differences in how much group annotations vary when annotating with different guidelines, and we demonstrate the annotator bias effect on model performance, observing significant differences in performance across some groups and guidelines. We stress that bias – not disagreement – is what has to be mitigated. We need to recruit a diverse set of annotators if we are interested in a defini-

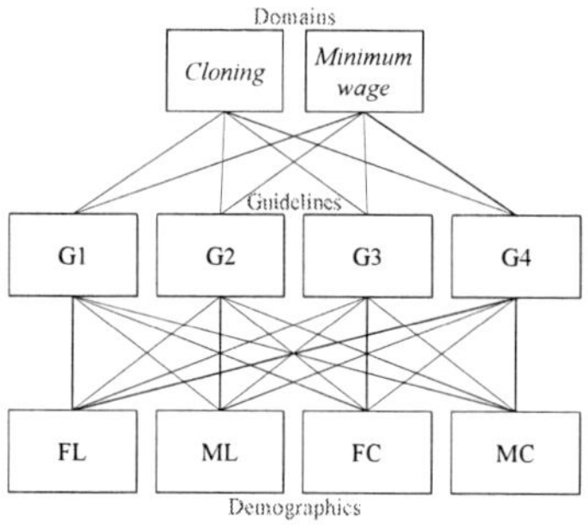

Figure 1: We re-annotate data in two *domains* across four annotation *guidelines* and four *demographics* (participant groups), as defined by binary gender (F/M) and political alignment (L/C) – to study the interaction of these three variables. We show that some guidelines promote cross-group differences and that this effect does not depend on task complexity.

[1]Lippi and Torroni (2016) identify three steps in a full argumentation mining pipeline: argumentative sentence detection, argument component boundary detection, and argument structure prediction. In this work, we focus on annotation schemes used for *argumentative sentence detection.*

tion of arguments that promote cross-group differences. All our annotations with demographic information will be publicly available along with IDs for corresponding sentences, but the sentences must be retrieved from Stab et al. (2018).[2]

2. Task Definitions in Argument Mining

2.1. What is an Argument?

An argument consists of propositions, which are statements that are either true or false. Such statements are also commonly known as claims. An argument needs to have at least two claims, one being the conclusion, also sometimes referred to as the major claim, and at least one reason backing up the conclusion, often called the premise. Arguments are used to justify or explain claims, and argumentation is usually connected to the task of convincing or persuading others, but that need not be the purpose of any argument (Sinnott-Armstrong and Fogelin, 2014). According to Palau and Moens (2009), there are several definitions of an argument, but the (minimal) definition given above – namely that an argument is formed by premises and a conclusion made up of propositions – is common to all. The definition given here deals with explicit arguments. However, *implicit arguments* can be inferred from less than two propositions (i.e. only one proposition from where both the conclusion and premise can be inferred) and from sentences that are not propositions (e.g. questions and imperatives). Such implicit arguments are naturally more complex (and ambiguous) and, therefore, rarely touched in argument mining (Jo et al., 2020).

2.2. Task Definitions

NLP papers are not always explicit about what they mean by *claim*. Sometimes *claim* means conclusion, while at other times it seems to indicate either the premise or both the conclusion and premises (as both parts are formally claims/propositions). The lack of explicitness can make it difficult to compare data and systems. This section describes the definitions used in four argument mining papers and their respective guidelines that we will explore further in this study. The four papers have been chosen based on the availability of annotation guidelines, the extent to which they have been cited, and, most importantly, on the *goals* of the annotations being very similar, although formulated in different ways. In the following, we will underline how their definitions fit with the definition given above and each other.

Morante et al. (2020) use the term *claim* to refer to the conclusion and the term *premise* for the rest of the argument. They use the term "claim-like" to describe sentences that are either claims or premises which resemble claims and focus the annotation task on finding such claim-like sentences. They furthermore define claims as *opinionated statements* wrt some topic, but do not require annotators to distinguish between supporting or opposing claims.

Levy et al. (2018) define the term *claim* as "the assertion the argument aims to prove". Hence, they similarly use this term to describe the conclusion. They do not mention the argument's premises, but they use a simple annotation guideline that focuses on finding statements that clearly support or contest a given topic. In their guideline, they put forward a rule of thumb for correctly identifying such statements: "If it is natural to say 'I (don't) think that <topic>, because <marked statement>', then you should probably select 'Accept'. Otherwise, you should probably select 'Reject'". For this rule of thumb, the example topic is "We should ban the sale of violent video games to minors". The example seems to contradict the earlier definition of a claim because the topic itself is a proposition (claim) that functions as a conclusion. In contrast, the statement functions as the premise of the argument. However, they work with claims under the definition of "context-dependent claims", which explains the seeming contradiction. They define context-dependent claims as "a general, concise statement that directly supports or contests the given Topic" and require annotators to distinguish whether the claim is *pro* or *con*tra a topic.

Stab et al. (2018) likewise use a context-dependent approach. Still, while Levy et al. (2018) use topics that resemble the conclusions of arguments, Stab et al. (2018) use more general topics such as "minimum wage", that does not reflect a conclusion in itself. Unlike both Morante et al. (2020) and Levy et al. (2018) who use the word *claim* as the subject of interest, Stab et al. (2018) do explicitly use the word *argument*. They also use an additional explicit requirement in their definition of an argument: it must provide evidence or reasoning that can be used to support or contest the topic (which essentially says that there should be a claim or premise backing up another claim or conclusion). Like Levy et al. (2018), they require annotators to distinguish between *supporting* and *opposing* arguments.

Shnarch et al. (2018) use the term *claim* as meaning the conclusion and define the *premise* as a type of *evidence*. They work specifically with what they call *evidence sentences* and try to detect sentences that contain evidence that can be used to clearly support or contest a given topic. The topics are the same conclusion-like topics as Levy et al. (2018). Although detecting evidence might sound like a different task, it very much resembles the approach of Stab et al. (2018) who say that a sentence should not be accepted if it only contains a claim – some evidence must back up the claim. Since Stab et al. (2018) also accepts *reasoning* as sufficient backing of a claim, Shnarch et al. (2018) are a bit more strict concerning this requirement.

[2]Annotations, annotation guidelines and code is available on `www.github.com/terne/Annotator-Bias-in-Argmin`

	Authors	Task focus	Guidelines	IAA
G1	Morante et al. (2020)	context-independent claim-like sentence detection	https://git.io/J1OKR	F-score = 42.4 (between token-level annotations)
G2	Levy et al. (2018)	context-dependent claim detection	See Figure 8, Appendix A	Cohen's $\kappa = 0.58$
G3	Stab et al. (2018)	context-dependent claim+premise detection	See Table 6, Appendix A	Cohen's $\kappa = 0.721$ for two expert annotators over 200 sents. For two non-experts $\kappa \approx 0.4$
G4	Shnarch et al. (2018)	context-dependent claim+premise detection	See Figure 9, Appendix A	Fleiss' $\kappa = 0.45$

Table 1: Overview of annotation guidelines used in our experiments. Descriptions of the unmodified guidelines and inter-annotator agreement (IAA) are those reported in the respective papers. We describe G2-4 as context-dependent because the topic in connection to the sentence is an integral part of the argument and evaluating stance. We call G1 context-*in*dependent because, even though the topic is provided, it does not ask annotators to take the topic nor stance towards it into account for recognizing a claim.

2.3. Complexity

In Table 1, we give an overview of the four studies just described and directions to their guidelines. We enumerate them and refer to their guidelines as G(uideline)1-4. The order reflects the level of requirements that must be fulfilled before a sentence can be marked as a claim/argument – which we may also refer to as *complexity* – with G4 requiring most. While G3 and G4 require backing (premises) for claims, G2 and G1 only require claims to be present and opinionated. Before using these annotation guidelines for re-annotating data, we make some important modifications which we explain in section 4.1. Most importantly, the exact role of the context-dependency is modified such that all guidelines may work with non-conclusive topics. In Table 1, we show the agreement between annotators in the original studies, further indicating the complexity of the respective tasks.

3. Bias

In this paper, we study bias in the annotations of arguments in online debates. The ability to mine arguments for and against positions in online debates is critical in monitoring public sentiment and combating misinformation. Often such debates are controversial, associated with high engagement, and susceptible to bias. We define bias as an inclination or prejudice for or against *something*, e.g. groups, individuals, concepts and behaviors. The term *social* bias can be used in two senses: an individual's bias which is explained by the (social) group the individual belongs to, and bias against (social) groups. The latter is typically the focus of bias studies in NLP (as in e.g. Sap et al. (2019; Rudinger et al. (2018); see also Garrido-Muñoz et al. (2021) for more bias definitions).

Men and women are known to exhibit different behavior in online communities (Sun et al., 2020), with men being more active than women (Tsai et al., 2015). There is some evidence of gender differences in both the formulation of and reasoning about arguments (Preiss et al., 2013), and overwhelming evidence of gender differences in perception and attention in general (Halpern, 2012). Similar differences in online debate behavior have been found for conservatives and liberals (Feinberg and Willer, 2015; Chen et al., 2021), as well as differences in how arguments are perceived (Lakoff, 2006; Gampa et al., 2019). Based on this, we hypothesize that the subjective nature of the task, as well as these observations, lead to demographic differences in how arguments are annotated. Being unaware of such differences may lead to biased models. Of course, the extent to which argument annotation is subjective and susceptible to bias depends on how arguments are defined in the task definitions or annotation guidelines. Different definitions may be more or less sensitive to disparate interpretations. We expect that political alignment is likely to produce biased annotations in the annotation of arguments, partially because of what is known as the *affect heuristic* (Slovic et al., 2007). The affect heuristic can be described as a cognitive shortcut whereby a decision is made based on an emotional response, such as evaluating the quality of an argument based on your attitude towards it and will be predominant when the task involves a high degree of uncertainty (ambiguity).

Disparate interpretations may also result from *framing effects* (Tversky and Kahneman, 1981). Something that could potentially affect annotators in different ways is the degree to which a task is defined by what you *should do* versus what you *should not do*.[3] Investigating such framing effects in detail is outside the scope of this paper and would require meticulous experiments with subtle changes in the languages. Some studies show gender differences in framing effects (Huang and Wang, 2010). Finally, Clarkson et al. (2015) found that conservatives exhibit greater self-control relative

[3]Examples of the former can be found in G1, e.g., *if the text is [. . .] you should select Reject*, while G4 contains examples of the latter, e.g., *a candidate that [. . .] should not be accepted*.

	GUIDELINE 1				GUIDELINE 2				GUIDELINE 3				GUIDELINE 4				TOTAL
	LIB		CONS		LIB		CONS		LIB		CONS		LIB		CONS		
	♀	♂	♀	♂	♀	♂	♀	♂	♀	♂	♀	♂	♀	♂	♀	♂	
n	65	66	61	62	66	62	62	61	65	66	62	64	61	64	63	63	1013
AVG SENTS	9.2	9.1	9.8	9.7	9.1	9.7	9.7	9.8	9.2	9.1	9.7	9.4	9.8	9.4	9.5	9.5	–

Table 2: The first row shows the distribution of the 1013 unique annotators of this study, and the second row shows the average number of sentences, out of 600, annotated by each individual in each annotator group.

to liberals due to their enhanced endorsement of free will. This potentially makes conservatives more prone to confirmation bias (Baron and Jost, 2019), more reluctant to follow complex guidelines, and more reluctant to change (Salvi et al., 2016). This may partly explain our observation below that (male) conservatives disagree the most with other groups.

Bias and fairness Our study of bias in annotations is closely related to the concept of fairness because annotator biases could skew the representation of certain phenomena in data, which would, in turn, result in unfair treatment for some users. E.g. while an image gender classification system may struggle with classifying dark-skinned females (Buolamwini and Gebru, 2018) due to lack of representation in the data, a text classifier could struggle with potential arguments that would be treated systematically different by annotators with different backgrounds if people of *both or all* backgrounds are not represented among the annotators. In argument mining, this could lead to discrimination against certain ways of formulating an argument and against arguments expressing certain political viewpoints. What it actually means for a system to be *fair* is purely value-based, and some notions of fairness can be completely contradictory (Friedler et al., 2021). Hence, what attributes are important when investigating annotator bias depends on which aspects we value as important to be fair towards, and our beliefs about how to successfully be fair, and hence it is crucial that researchers and developers are explicit about the values their work embodies. In this study, we operationalize fairness as demographic parity wrt protected attributes that are sensitive to bias in the context of argumentation.

4. Experiments

4.1. Modifications of guidelines

To be able to compare annotations resulting from different guidelines, some modifications of the guidelines were necessary: Firstly, G1 was changed from token-level (marking spans of claims in documents) to sentence-level annotation, and an extra task of identifying claim source was omitted. Secondly, the topics used in G2 and G4 are different from those in G3 (as described in section 2.2). The data we are using in this study is from Stab et al. (2018) (G3), where topics are short and without stance, and therefore we changed the wording of the topics in G2 and G4, such that they could work with the topics "cloning" and "minimum wage". Furthermore, in G2, we changed the wording of a rule-of-thumb and removed the underlining of claims/statements in example sentences. Thirdly, the guideline of Stab et al. (2018) is not public. Therefore we constructed a guideline based on the description in their paper and sent it to the authors who confirmed the similarity.

4.2. Data collection

From the corpus created by Stab et al. (2018) for cross-topic argument mining, we re-annotated 600 sentences. The source is web documents and a wide range of text types within eight controversial topics. Of the 600 sentences we extracted from their corpus, half is from the *cloning* topic half from the *minimum wage* topic, i.e. two distant topics; one from the medical domain and one from the political domain. Each sentence was annotated following G1–4 and, within each guideline, by individuals with different demographic backgrounds.

Demographics We defined demographic backgrounds by gender identifications (female or male) and political alignments (liberal or conservative). Binary genders were chosen due to the lower frequency of non-binary individuals and the need for having balanced sets of annotators in this study – but when asked about their gender, respondents could choose "other". The political alignments chosen are well suited for the dataset, which seems to consist of instances mostly discussing topics from a US perspective. Only annotators with a US nationality were invited to participate in the study. It is standard to study liberals and conservatives as opposing ideologies in a US political scene, where the large majority of the population identifies as either liberal or conservative, though with a larger part conservative.[4]

Process Importantly, a meticulous process was used to balance the number of annotators and the number of sentences each annotator was given, to ensure reliable statistical tests of differences: Firstly, annotators were recruited through Prolific[5][6] with the relevant demographic backgrounds and a US nationality as prescreening conditions, and they performed the annota-

[4]According to a recent Gallup poll https://tinyurl.com/45nadh6z

[5]https://www.prolific.co/

[6]mTurk does not enable balanced recruitment across participant groups. We include an mTurk replication of our study *without balanced groups*, which served as a pilot study, in Appendix C for interested readers.

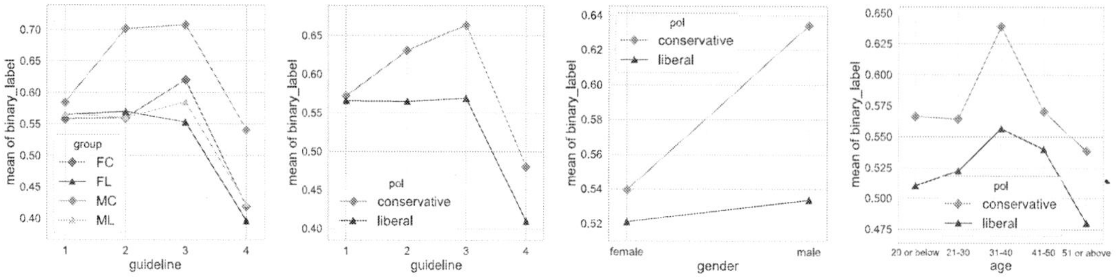

Figure 2: Interaction plots showing the interaction between variables (guideline, political alignment, gender and age) in terms of positive rate (the mean of binary labels). The plots furthermore illustrate the distribution of binary labels within demographic groups and guidelines.

tion task in a Qualtrics[7] survey. Annotators who passed the pre-screening were directed to the Qualtrics survey designated to annotators with their background, and here they were firstly met with a few questions on their background to confirm the pre-screening conditions and to get further information that could be confounding factors: age, ethnicity, and education. Survey question formulations followed standards from European Social Survey and US Census. Secondly, when an annotator had passed the pre-screening conditions and the confirmation of these, one of the four guidelines was presented, at random, to the annotator, followed by a set of 10 random sentences. The randomization in Qualtrics made sure each element (guideline and sentences) was presented evenly. However, when annotators left the survey without finishing, a count of the presented items would still be added and, therefore, some manual checks and new recruiting had to be done to make sure all sentences where annotated with each guideline and by an annotator of each demographic background.

End-result Table 2 shows that the number of annotators, and the number of sentences each annotator received, were *balanced across groups and guidelines*. In our final dataset, the individuals representing different demographic backgrounds are composed of between 61-66 annotators within each guideline, giving a total of **1013 annotators** used in this study, as there are 4(guidelines)×4(backgrounds) set of annotations. With this process, each sentence was re-annotated a total of 16 times (and by 16 individuals).

To be able to compare the annotations across both guidelines and demographics, we binarized all non-binary annotations before later model training and analysis, such that 1 equals a claim/accept/supporting argument/opposing argument, and 0 equals no claim/reject/no argument.

4.3. Models

We fine-tuned BERT-base on one topic and evaluated on the other using each of the 16 sets of re-annotated sentences. We used a batch size of 5, learning rate of 5e-5 and fine-tuned each model over 5 epochs and 10 random seeds (of which we took the majority label). The models were fine-tuned and tested with binarized labels.

We then fine-tuned another BERT-base and a model for multi-task learning on the *entire corpus* of Stab et al. (2018), the source of the re-annotated sentences, but those 600 sentences were removed from the training and validation set of the corpus before fine-tuning, leaving approx. 17,000 sentences, herein approx. 3,500 sentences from the *cloning* and *minimum wage* topics. We used Huggingface's BertForSequenceClassification for the single-task setup, and for multi-task learning, we used Microsoft's MT-DNN (Liu et al., 2019; Liu et al., 2020) with a pre-trained BERT-base as the main (shared) layer and eight classification heads, i.e. for each topic. Using 5 epochs, a batch size of 8, cross-entropy loss for MT-DNN, and otherwise default hyperparameters, we trained and tested each model over 10 random seeds and collected the majority predictions for analysis.

5. Analysis

5.1. Demographic (dis)parity

We analyze the interaction between the positive rate of binarized annotations and four variables of interest: the guideline and three demographic attributes of the annotator: gender, political alignment, and age. Expectantly, positive rates differ between guidelines: the guideline containing most requirements for detecting a claim (G4) also exhibits the lowest positive rates. This holds for all annotators, but there are notable gaps between the positive rates of female/male and liberal/conservative annotations with G2–4: males and conservatives – and especially male conservatives – annotate more sentences as claims or arguments than other annotators. The following will explore the differences across demographic groups of the annotators. We analyze the per guideline difference in positive rates between all groups: female liberal (FL), male liberal (ML), female conservative (FC) and male conservative (MC), shown in Figure 3. The differences vary greatly between groups, and most importantly, they vary in

[7] https://www.qualtrics.com

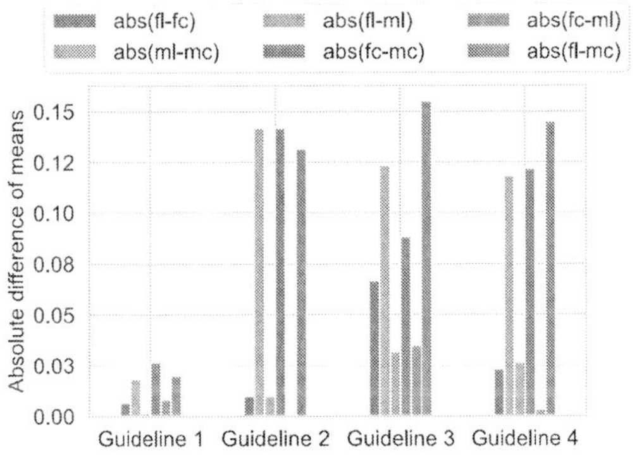

Figure 3: Absolute difference of positive rates of binarized annotations, i.e., the difference between annotator groups using the same guideline.

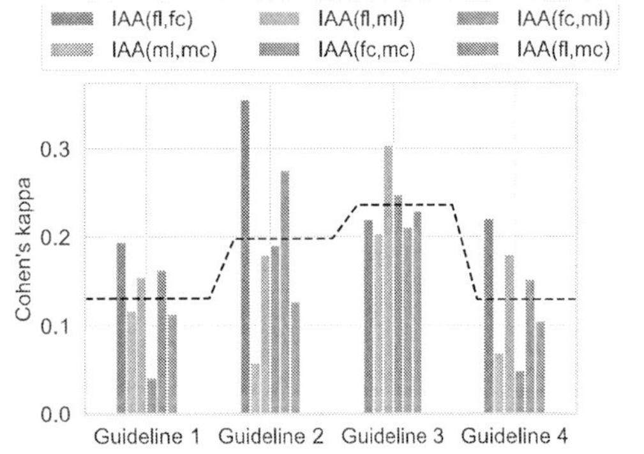

Figure 4: Agreement by Cohen's κ between the 600 (binarized) annotations from each group. The line indicates guideline means.

a meaningful way; we observe minor differences between groups that are, from a social science empirical perspective, also more similar: female conservatives are more similar to male liberals than to male conservatives and female liberals; all groups are distant from male conservatives; male conservatives are in particular distant from female liberals. Table 3 summarizes where significant differences were found using a χ^2-test. G2–4 exhibit significant differences across political spectrum and gender, and annotations with G3 and G4 also show significant differences across ages. Only G1 exhibits no significant proportional differences in labels across these three attributes. The positive rate is higher for middle-aged (31–40) annotators, and this is a bit more pronounced for conservatives. See Figure 2. Since the group of male conservative annotators are on average older than the other groups, it is reasonable to question whether age may be a mediator for the relationship between this group and its higher fraction of positive annotations. We performed a mediation analysis[8], and we found that there is *no mediation effect* of age.

	G1	G2	G3	G4
Political spectrum	ns	$\leq$0.01	$\leq$0.0001	$\leq$0.001
Gender	ns	$\leq$0.01	$\leq$0.01	$\leq$0.001
Age	ns	ns	$\leq$0.01	$\leq$0.0001

Table 3: p-values from χ^2-tests of differences of label frequencies given different backgrounds across the four guidelines. χ^2-tests were made over contingency tables of non-binarised labels.

5.2. Agreement

We measure the inter-annotator agreement with Cohen's κ between each set of annotations from each guideline, and for all guidelines, we find the highest agreement within genders and political alignments (Figure 4). The lowest agreements are found between male conservatives and all other groups, even female conservatives. This aligns with findings in social science that female conservatives are more liberal than male conservatives (Welch, 1985; Bonica et al., 2015). We note that when measuring the agreement between females–males and liberal–conservatives (both at approx. 0.2 highest κ-score), i.e. of higher-level groups, there is a lot of information loss, including insight to considerable disagreements between female and male conservatives. *We emphasize that more fine-grained knowledge of background (including more attributes) expose such hidden patterns.* We also see, in Figure 4, that the agreement varies depending on guidelines. G3, based on Stab et al. (2018), has low differences in agreement. Counterintuitively, the guideline exhibiting the lowest difference in label distributions (and positive rates), i.e. G1, also shows low agreement. We include examples of sentences that were easiest to agree on (Table 7) and more difficult to agree on (Table 8-11) in Appendix B. In general, it seems easier to agree on sentences that clearly state a thought outcome (e.g. of raising the minimum wage). Agreeing on the stance of the argument is of course more difficult than agreeing on whether it is an argument at all. More difficult sentences to agree on seem to include factual statements, and statements with unclear stance relations, but also statements with a clear political narrative such as, "And, of course, you can also expect to hear conservatives shout back that the idea is a job killer."

We compare our annotations to the original from Stab et al. (2018) in Figure 5. For three out of four guidelines, annotations by liberals match the original annotations best. The min-max difference in agreement is fairly equal across G2–3, with a difference of 0.2. Even though Figure 4 show that G3 has the most stable cross-group agreement, when we compare them to the original annotations, there is a clear hierarchy in the

[8]Performed with `statsmodels.stats.mediation.Mediation`.

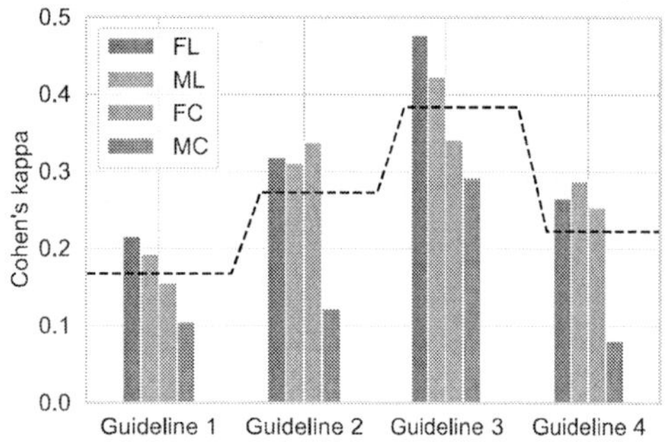

Figure 5: Agreement between the original annotations from the Stab et al. (2018) dataset and each set of our new annotations. Note that our κ-scores for G3 is higher than those reported for non-experts in Stab et al. (2018), see Table 1. This indicates that our annotation setup is generally of high quality and that low levels of agreement across groups reflect group differences rather than poor annotation conditions. We also compared our annotations to those gathered in a pilot study on mTurk, likewise finding the highest agreement with G3, with a κ-score of .34.

		Mean diff.	p-value
FC	FL	0.02	ns
FC	MC	0.16	$\leq$0.001
FC	ML	0.08	ns
FL	MC	0.14	$\leq$0.001
FL	ML	0.06	ns
MC	ML	-0.08	ns
G1	G2	-0.11	$\leq$0.01
G1	G3	0.03	ns
G1	G4	-0.21	$\leq$0.001
G2	G3	0.14	$\leq$0.001
G2	G4	-0.09	$\leq$0.01
G3	G4	-0.24	$\leq$0.001

Table 4: We test the cross-topic performance of all pairs of annotations and perform pairwise, two-tailed student's t-test of F_1-scores, with Tukey's post hoc correction. The top half shows results from models evaluated on annotations from different guidelines (than train data), but by annotators with the same demographic attributes as train data and comparing these cross-guideline results to those of other demographic groups. The bottom half shows results from cross-group evaluations, evaluating models on annotations from a different demographic group (than train data) but using the same guideline as train data. All cross-group and cross-guideline scores are visualized in heatmaps in Figure 6.

agreements, indicating that the original annotators were likely liberal and also mostly female. The higher mean Cohen's kappa scores may also be explained by using female, liberal annotators, as they agree most with other groups, as we saw in Figure 4.

5.3. Algorithmic bias

We have shown that annotator bias exists in the annotation of arguments. We now investigate the consequence of guideline differences and annotator bias on model performance. As described in §4.3, we firstly trained and tested models, cross-topic, on each combination of the 16 sets of annotations. Figure 6 shows the results, but here we focus on the cross-group and cross-guideline differences. We, therefore, perform student's t-tests between the sets of F_1-scores (i.e. between each map in fig. 6). Models trained on data annotated using different guidelines produce significantly different cross-group performances. The bottom half of Table 4 shows that *cross-group* F_1-scores differ significantly when comparing all guidelines except G1 and G3. The top half of Table 4 shows that *cross-guideline* F_1-scores are significantly different when comparing the scores of models trained by annotations by male conservatives to models trained on both annotations by female conservatives as well as by female liberals. This aligns with the findings above, that male conservatives disagree more with other groups.

We then fine-tuned BERT and MT-DNN on the entire original dataset. From Figure 5, we infer that annotations from male conservatives are most likely underrepresented in the dataset of Stab et al. (2018). In effect, the large models systematically perform worse when evaluated on this group's annotations. With BERT, we see that the min-max difference between groups is more pronounced when data is annotated using G1 and G3 (Figure 7b). G1 also stands out with MT-DNN. (See scores of both models in Table 5.) However, χ^2-tests with proportions of correct and incorrect predictions of MT-DNN tell us that group differences within each guideline are only significant when including MC. I.e. differences in performance between FL, ML and FC are not significant given the same guideline. Differences between guidelines for each group are significant at the 95% significance level for all *except* MC.

Based on the above analysis, it seems that differences in annotator bias, depending on task definitions, cannot be simply explained by differences in guideline complexity. If this was the case, we would expect that more complex tasks, given by G3 and G4, contain more instances of ambiguity where intuition will play are larger role in the annotations. Vice versa, we would expect less intuition-lead annotations with G1 and G2. This may hold true when comparing positive rates, but when comparing agreement and model performance, differences seem to derive from annotator characteristics, with especially one demographic group standing out.

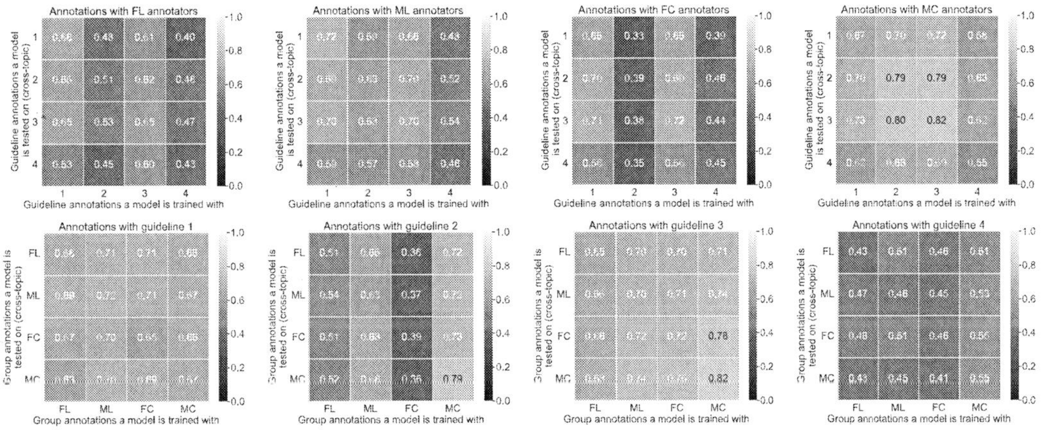

Figure 6: Cross-topic performance with binary F_1. **Top row**: evaluating models on annotations from different guidelines (than train data) but by annotators with the same demographic attributes as train data. Means from left to right: 0.55, 0.61, 0.53, 0.69. **Bottom row**: evaluating models on annotations from annotators with different demographic attributes (than train data) but from the same annotation guideline as train data. Means from left to right: 0.68, 0.57, 0.71, 0.48.

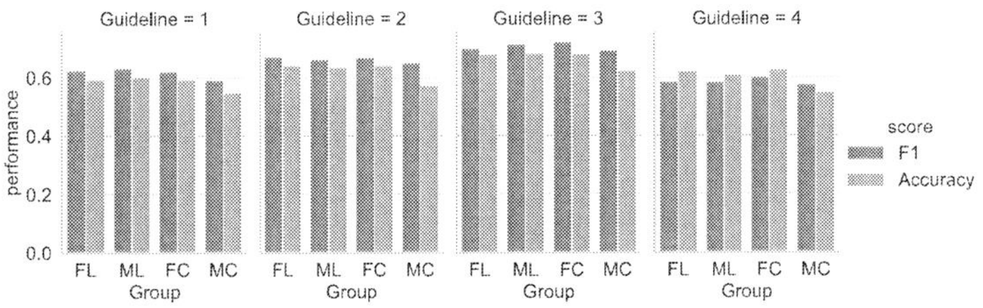

(a) Fine-tuned BERT. Baseline on original annotations F_1 = .8, accuracy = .802.

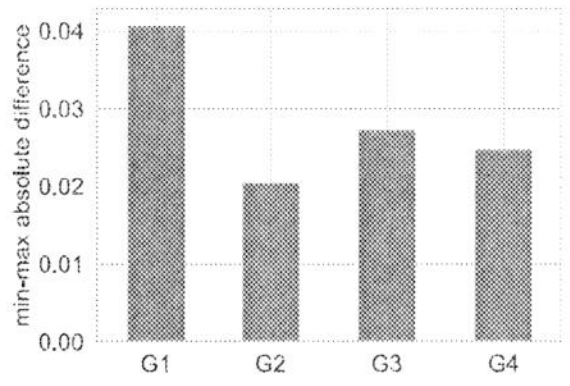

(b) BERT min-max absolute difference in F_1-scores.

Figure 7: These models are trained on all 8 topics of the dataset of Stab et al. (2018) and tested on our 300 sentences from the topics cloning and minimum wage, which we have re-annotated and removed from the training data. MT-DNN shows similar results, see Table 5.

6. Related Work

6.1. Evaluating argument annotation schemes

Argument annotation schemes (and specifically *argument schemes* that define the annotation of relations between argumentative discourse units) have been *theoretically* compared and evaluated extensively (Bentahar et al., 2010; Lippi and Torroni, 2016; Lawrence and Reed, 2019; Visser et al., 2021), and to a lesser degree practically or *directly*, by annotating the same data with different guidelines (Habernal et al., 2014). Most related to ours, wrt practically comparing annotations deriving from different annotation guidelines, is the work of Lindahl et al. (2019) who investigate annotations of *argument schemes*, following the schemes by Walton et al. (2008). Here, an argument – consisting of a conclusion and a set of premises – is given an additional label reflecting the type (scheme) of the argument, such as *argument from analogy*, *practical reasoning*, or *argument from consequences*. They find low inter-annotator agreement in both the selected schemes and the selected conclusion and premises and observe that annotators may recognize and annotate argument conclusions, premises and types very differently, even when having expert (linguistic) knowledge[9].

6.2. Annotator bias

Geva et al. (2019) show that conditioning on annotator ID leads to better performance in question answering and natural language inference (NLI). Al Kuwatly et al. (2020) investigate annotator bias in hate speech classification, focusing on the role of gender, first language, age and education on annotators' ability to identify personal attacks and on model performance and find all variables except gender to affect the annotation of hate speech. A different approach is taken by Gururangan et al. (2018) who investigate what they call *annotation artifacts* in NLI datasets, and they find that simple classifiers perform well when only observing the hypothe-

[9]The challenges in identifying argument schemes and ways of improving schemes and annotation guidelines have also previously been identified by Musi et al. (2016).

	GUIDELINE 1				GUIDELINE 2				GUIDELINE 3				GUIDELINE 4			
	LIB		CONS		LIB		CONS		LIB		CONS		LIB		CONS	
	♀	♂	♀	♂	♀	♂	♀	♂	♀	♂	♀	♂	♀	♂	♀	♂
BERT	.62	.63	.62	.59	.67	.66	.67	.65	.70	.71	.72	.69	.59	.58	.60	.58
MT-DNN	.62	.63	.60	.58	.67	.66	.66	.64	.70	.71	.69	.68	.60	.59	.60	.57

Table 5: F_1 scores of fined-tuned BERT and the multi-task learning model MT-DNN. MT-DNN is trained with the 8 topics as separate tasks, and predictions are made with the classification heads for the two topics of interest. BERT results are visualized in Figure 7.

sis without the premise, likely due to the framing of the annotation task. Recently, Prabhakaran et al. (2021) investigated the impact of label aggregation (e.g. majority vote) on demographic biases, showing that aggregation under-represents, or ignores, a substantial number of annotators, and they encourage to release more information about annotators and transparency of selection biases. Davani et al. (2021) further tests the effectiveness of using individuals' annotations in a multi-task learning scheme and find it outperforms majority voting.

6.3. Fairness

The paper contributes to the fairness literature by pointing out how group-level biases may have a severe influence on our gold standards. In our point-of-view, models should be insensitive to protected attributes such as gender and political leaning. How fairness is defined varies, with some seeing fairness as (approximately) equal positive class rates (or *equal odds*) (Hardt et al., 2016; Ghassami et al., 2018), and others are seeing fairness as (approximately) equal risk (Donini et al., 2018) or equal error (Zafar et al., 2017). Our study has been focused on fairness defined by *demographic parity*. See Williamson and Menon (2019) and Mehrabi et al. (2021) for surveys of fairness definitions.

7. Conclusion

We have shown that annotator bias *is* sensitive to task definitions. By re-annotating data from two domains of online debate, using four guidelines and four groups of annotators with distinctly different demographic backgrounds known to affect argumentation (political leaning and gender), we find significant differences in demographic disparity, agreement and algorithmic bias depending on both the guideline and the background of the annotators. Differences in group disparity are not explained by task complexity; instead they seem to be driven by social characteristics from the differences in demographic backgrounds.

Acknowledgments

Many thanks to Anna Rogers and Carsten Eriksen for their insightful comments.

Maria Barrett is supported by a research grant (34437) from VILLUM FONDEN.

Impact Statement

Broader impact Our work shows the importance of recruiting a balanced set of annotators and considering the impact of guideline biases across different demographics. We hope this work will contribute to pushing for a more fair dataset and model development.

Informed consent Annotators were informed of the overall aim of the study, to study demographics and natural language understanding, and they consented to the sharing and use of their responses for research purposes.

Sensitive and personal information Responses were anonymous and voluntary. We did not ask for any information that could be reasonably linked to any individual. We present experiments with annotators that are grouped by their gender and political leaning. Annotators were also asked about their level of education and ethnicity, but since we did not balance based on these attributes, we did not include further analysis based on them. Most annotators identified as white (75%) and were college-educated (86%), which is important to keep in mind for the interpretation of our results.

Remuneration Annotators were paid an average of \$10.7 hourly wage.

Intended use The collected annotations and demographic information will be publicly available for research purposes.

Institutional approval The study is exempt from IRB approval at the authors' institutions because it deals with anonymous responses.

8. Bibliographical References

Al Kuwatly, H., Wich, M., and Groh, G. (2020). Identifying and measuring annotator bias based on annotators' demographic characteristics. In *Proceedings of the Fourth Workshop on Online Abuse and Harms*, pages 184–190, Online, November. Association for Computational Linguistics.

Baron, J. and Jost, J. T. (2019). False equivalence: Are liberals and conservatives in the united states equally biased? *Perspectives on Psychological Science*, 14(2):292–303. PMID: 30836901.

Bentahar, J., Moulin, B., and Bélanger, M. (2010). A taxonomy of argumentation models used for knowledge representation. *Artificial Intelligence Review*, 33:211–259.

Bonica, A., Chilton, A. S., and Sen, M. (2015). The political ideologies of american lawyers. *Journal of Legal Analysis*, 8(2):277–335, 10.

Buolamwini, J. and Gebru, T. (2018). Gender shades: Intersectional accuracy disparities in commercial gender classification. In *FAT*.

Chen, W., Pacheco, D., Yang, K.-C., and Menczer, F. (2021). Neutral bots probe political bias on social media. *Nature Communications*, 12(5580).

Clarkson, J. J., Chambers, J. R., Hirt, E. R., Otto, A. S., Kardes, F. R., and Leone, C. (2015). The self-control consequences of political ideology. *Proceedings of the National Academy of Sciences*, 112(27):8250–8253.

Davani, A. M., D'iaz, M., and Prabhakaran, V. (2021). Dealing with disagreements: Looking beyond the majority vote in subjective annotations. *ArXiv*, abs/2110.05719.

Donini, M., Oneto, L., Ben-David, S., Shawe-Taylor, J. S., and Pontil, M. (2018). Empirical risk minimization under fairness constraints. In S. Bengio, et al., editors, *Advances in Neural Information Processing Systems*, volume 31. Curran Associates, Inc.

Feinberg, M. and Willer, R. (2015). From gulf to bridge: When do moral arguments facilitate political influence? *Personality and Social Psychology Bulletin*, 41(12):1665–1681. PMID: 26445854.

Friedler, S. A., Scheidegger, C., and Venkatasubramanian, S. (2021). The (im)possibility of fairness: Different value systems require different mechanisms for fair decision making. *Commun. ACM*, 64(4):136–143, mar.

Gampa, A., Wojcik, S. P., Motyl, M., Nosek, B. A., and Ditto, P. H. (2019). (ideo)logical reasoning: Ideology impairs sound reasoning. *Social Psychological and Personality Science*, 10(8):1075–1083.

Garrido-Muñoz, I., Montejo-Ráez, A., Martínez-Santiago, F., and Ureña-López, L. A. (2021). A survey on bias in deep nlp. *Applied Sciences*, 11:3184.

Geva, M., Goldberg, Y., and Berant, J. (2019). Are we modeling the task or the annotator? an investigation of annotator bias in natural language understanding datasets. In *Proceedings of the 2019 Conference on Empirical Methods in Natural Language Processing and the 9th International Joint Conference on Natural Language Processing (EMNLP-IJCNLP)*, pages 1161–1166, Hong Kong, China, November. Association for Computational Linguistics.

Ghassami, A., Khodadadian, S., and Kiyavash, N. (2018). Fairness in supervised learning: An information theoretic approach.

Gururangan, S., Swayamdipta, S., Levy, O., Schwartz, R., Bowman, S., and Smith, N. A. (2018). Annotation artifacts in natural language inference data. In *Proceedings of the 2018 Conference of the North American Chapter of the Association for Computational Linguistics: Human Language Technologies, Volume 2 (Short Papers)*, pages 107–112, New Orleans, Louisiana, June. Association for Computational Linguistics.

Habernal, I., Eckle-Kohler, J., and Gurevych, I. (2014). Argumentation mining on the web from information seeking perspective. In *ArgNLP*.

Halpern, D. F. (2012). *Sex differences in cognitive abilities*. Psychology press, 4 edition.

Hardt, M., Price, E., Price, E., and Srebro, N. (2016). Equality of opportunity in supervised learning. In D. Lee, et al., editors, *Advances in Neural Information Processing Systems*, volume 29. Curran Associates, Inc.

Huang, Y. and Wang, L. (2010). Sex differences in framing effects across task domain. *Personality and Individual Differences*, 48(5):649–653.

Jo, Y., Visser, J., Reed, C., and Hovy, E. (2020). Extracting implicitly asserted propositions in argumentation. In *Proceedings of the 2020 Conference on Empirical Methods in Natural Language Processing (EMNLP)*, pages 24–38, Online, November. Association for Computational Linguistics.

Joseph, K., Friedland, L., Hobbs, W., Lazer, D., and Tsur, O. (2017). ConStance: Modeling annotation contexts to improve stance classification. In *Proceedings of the 2017 Conference on Empirical Methods in Natural Language Processing*, pages 1115–1124, Copenhagen, Denmark, September. Association for Computational Linguistics.

Lakoff, G. (2006). *Moral Politics : How Liberals and Conservatives Think*. University of Chicago Press.

Lawrence, J. and Reed, C. (2019). Argument mining: A survey. *Computational Linguistics*, pages 765–818.

Levy, R., Bogin, B., Gretz, S., Aharonov, R., and Slonim, N. (2018). Towards an argumentative content search engine using weak supervision. In *Proceedings of the 27th International Conference on Computational Linguistics*, pages 2066–2081.

Lindahl, A., Borin, L., and Rouces, J. (2019). Towards assessing argumentation annotation - a first step. In *Proceedings of the 6th Workshop on Argument Mining*, pages 177–186, Florence, Italy, August. Association for Computational Linguistics.

Lippi, M. and Torroni, P. (2016). Argumentation mining: State of the art and emerging trends. *ACM Transactions on Internet Technology (TOIT)*, 16(2):1–25.

Liu, X., He, P., Chen, W., and Gao, J. (2019). Multi-task deep neural networks for natural language understanding. In *Proceedings of the 57th Annual Meeting of the Association for Computational Linguistics*, pages 4487–4496, Florence, Italy, July. Association for Computational Linguistics.

Liu, X., Wang, Y., Ji, J., Cheng, H., Zhu, X., Awa, E., He, P., Chen, W., Poon, H., Cao, G., and Gao, J. (2020). The Microsoft toolkit of multi-task deep neural networks for natural language understanding. In *Proceedings of the 58th Annual Meeting of the*

Association for Computational Linguistics: System Demonstrations, pages 118–126, Online, July. Association for Computational Linguistics.

Mehrabi, N., Morstatter, F., Saxena, N., Lerman, K., and Galstyan, A. (2021). A survey on bias and fairness in machine learning. *ACM Comput. Surv.*, 54(6), July.

Morante, R., van Son, C., Maks, I., and Vossen, P. (2020). Annotating perspectives on vaccination. In *Proceedings of the 12th Language Resources and Evaluation Conference*, pages 4964–4973, Marseille, France, May. European Language Resources Association.

Musi, E., Ghosh, D., and Muresan, S. (2016). Towards feasible guidelines for the annotation of argument schemes. In *Proceedings of the Third Workshop on Argument Mining (ArgMining2016)*, pages 82–93, Berlin, Germany, August. Association for Computational Linguistics.

Palau, R. and Moens, M.-F. (2009). Argumentation mining: the detection, classification and structure of arguments in text. In *ICAIL*.

Prabhakaran, V., Davani, A. M., and D'iaz, M. (2021). On releasing annotator-level labels and information in datasets. *ArXiv*, abs/2110.05699.

Preiss, D. D., Castillo, J. C., Flotts, P., and San Martín, E. (2013). Assessment of argumentative writing and critical thinking in higher education: Educational correlates and gender differences. *Learning and Individual Differences*, 28:193–203.

Rampersad, G. and Althiyabi, T. (2020). Fake news: Acceptance by demographics and culture on social media. *Journal of Information Technology & Politics*, 17(1):1–11.

Rudinger, R., Naradowsky, J., Leonard, B., and Van Durme, B. (2018). Gender bias in coreference resolution. In *Proceedings of the 2018 Conference of the North American Chapter of the Association for Computational Linguistics: Human Language Technologies, Volume 2 (Short Papers)*, pages 8–14, New Orleans, Louisiana, June. Association for Computational Linguistics.

Salvi, C., Cristofori, I., Grafman, J., and Beeman, M. (2016). The politics of insight. *The Quarterly Journal of Experimental Psychology*, 69(6):1064–1072. PMID: 26810954.

Sap, M., Card, D., Gabriel, S., Choi, Y., and Smith, N. A. (2019). The risk of racial bias in hate speech detection. In *Proceedings of the 57th Annual Meeting of the Association for Computational Linguistics*, pages 1668–1678, Florence, Italy, July. Association for Computational Linguistics.

Shnarch, E., Alzate, C., Dankin, L., Gleize, M., Hou, Y., Choshen, L., Aharonov, R., and Slonim, N. (2018). Will it blend? blending weak and strong labeled data in a neural network for argumentation mining. In *Proceedings of the 56th Annual Meeting of the Association for Computational Linguistics (Volume 2: Short Papers)*, pages 599–605.

Shnarch, E., Choshen, L., Moshkowich, G., Aharonov, R., and Slonim, N. (2020). Unsupervised expressive rules provide explainability and assist human experts grasping new domains. In *Findings of the Association for Computational Linguistics: EMNLP 2020*, pages 2678–2697, Online, November. Association for Computational Linguistics.

Sinnott-Armstrong, W. and Fogelin, R. (2014). *Cengage Advantage Books: Understanding Arguments: An Introduction to Informal Logic*. Cengage Learning.

Slovic, P., Finucane, M. L., Peters, E., and MacGregor, D. G. (2007). The affect heuristic. *European Journal of Operational Research*, 177(3):1333–1352.

Stab, C., Miller, T., Schiller, B., Rai, P., and Gurevych, I. (2018). Cross-topic argument mining from heterogeneous sources. In *Proceedings of the 2018 Conference on Empirical Methods in Natural Language Processing*, pages 3664–3674, Brussels, Belgium, October-November. Association for Computational Linguistics.

Sun, B., Mao, H., and Yin, C. (2020). Male and female users' differences in online technology community based on text mining. *Frontiers in Psychology*, 11:806.

Tsai, M.-J., Liang, J.-C., Hou, H.-T., and Tsai, C.-C. (2015). Males are not as active as females in online discussion: Gender differences in face-to-face and online discussion strategies. *Australasian Journal of Educational Technology*, 2015:263–277, 05.

Tversky, A. and Kahneman, D. (1981). The framing of decisions and the psychology of choice. *Science*, 211(4481):453–458.

van der Linden, S., Panagopoulos, C., and Roozenbeek, J. (2020). You are fake news: political bias in perceptions of fake news. *Media, Culture & Society*, 42(3):460–470.

Vecchi, E. M., Falk, N., Jundi, I., and Lapesa, G. (2021). Towards argument mining for social good: A survey. In *ACL*.

Visser, J., Lawrence, J., Reed, C., Wagemans, J. H. M., and Walton, D. (2021). Annotating argument schemes. *Argumentation*, 35:101 – 139.

Walton, D., Reed, C., and Macagno, F. (2008). *Argumentation schemes*. Cambridge University Press.

Welch, S. (1985). Are women more liberal than men in the U. S. congress? *Legislative Studies Quarterly*, 10(1):125–134.

Williamson, R. and Menon, A. (2019). Fairness risk measures. In Kamalika Chaudhuri et al., editors, *Proceedings of the 36th International Conference on Machine Learning*, volume 97 of *Proceedings of Machine Learning Research*, pages 6786–6797. PMLR, 09–15 Jun.

Zafar, M. B., Valera, I., Gomez Rodriguez, M., and Gummadi, K. P. (2017). Fairness beyond disparate treatment & disparate impact. *Proceedings of the 26th International Conference on World Wide Web*, Apr.

Appendix A: Annotation guidelines

We present the guidelines used for annotating the referenced corpora either as screenshots of the actual guidelines, when these are provided by the authors or as extracts from the articles, describing the annotation rules and process. Our slightly modified guidelines are available on `www.github.com/terne/Annotator-Bias-in-Argmin`.

(Stab et al., 2018)	*We define an argument as a span of text expressing evidence or reasoning that can be used to either support or oppose a given topic. An argument need not be "direct´´ or self-contained – it may presuppose some common or domain knowledge or the application of commonsense reasoning – but it must be unambiguous in its orientation to the topic. (...) unlike (other) models, which are typically used to represent (potentially deep or complex) argument structures at the discourse level, ours is a flat model that considers arguments in isolation from their surrounding context. A great advantage of this approach is that it allows annotators to classify text spans without reading large amounts of context and without considering relations to other topics or arguments. (...) Annotators classified the sentences using a browser-based interface that presents a set of instructions, a topic, a list of sentences, and a multiple-choice form for specifying whether each sentence is a supporting argument, an opposing argument, or not an argument with respect to the topic.*

Table 6: Extracts from Stab et al. (2018) describing the rules and process of annotation.

Assessing the value of potential claims

In this task you are given a topic and possibly-related statements, each marked within a particular sentence.

For each candidate, you should select "**Accept**", if you think that the marked statement can be used "as is" during discourse, to directly support or contest the given topic. Otherwise, you should select "**Reject**".

If you selected "Accept", you should further indicate whether the marked text supports the topic ("Pro") or contests it ("Con").

Note, that if the marked text is non-coherent, hence cannot be used "as is" during a discussion about the topic, you should select "Reject".

Similarly, if the marked text supports/contests a *different* topic, even if it is somewhat related to the examined topic, you should typically select "Reject".

As a rule of thumb, if it is natural to say "I (don't) think that <topic>, because <marked statement>", then you should probably select "Accept". Otherwise, you should probably select "Reject".

Finally, if you are unfamiliar with the examined topic, please briefly read about it in a relevant data source like Wikipedia.

Examples for the topic "We should ban the sale of violent video games to minors" -

1. "The researchers found that adolescents that play violent video games are most at-risk for violent behavior (but without statistical significance)." -- **Accept / Pro.**

2. "Previous reports suggested that kids playing Doom are not at a greater risk for violent behavior." -- **Accept / Con.**

3. "The researchers found that adolescents that play violent video games are at no risk for violent behavior." -- **Reject.** Due to the prefix "found that", the marked text is not coherent and cannot be used "as is" while discussing the topic.

4. "While violent video games are often associated with aggressive behavior, recent studies are starting to suggest otherwise". - **Reject.** Due to the prefix "While", the marked text is not coherent and cannot be used "as is" while discussing the topic.

5. "Many people believe that some TV shows increase youth violence." -- **Reject**. The marked text is not *directly* supporting/contesting the topic.

Figure 8: Annotation guidelines of Levy et al. (2018)

1. General instruction

In this task you are given a topic and evidence candidates for the topic. Consider each candidate independently. For each candidate please select **Accept** if and only if it satisfies ALL the following criteria:

1. The candidate ***clearly supports*** or ***clearly contests*** the given topic. A candidate that merely provides neutral information related to the topic should not be accepted.
2. The candidate represents a ***coherent***, ***stand-alone*** statement, that one can articulate (nearly) "as is" while discussing the topic, with no need to change/remove/add more than two words.
3. The candidate represents valuable evidence to ***convince one*** to support or contest the topic. Namely, it is not merely a belief or merely a claim, rather it provides an indication whether a belief or a claim is true.

Note, if you are unfamiliar with the topic, please briefly read about it in a relevant data source like Wikipedia.

Figure 9: Annotation guidelines of Shnarch et al. (2018). Besides the general instructions shown here, the guideline also includes some examples.

Appendix B: Annotation examples

topic	sentence	label1	label2	label3	label4
Cloning	God Bless you man.	NO CLAIM	Reject	Non-argument	Reject
Minimum wage	Regular increases allow workers' wages to keep pace with inflation.	CLAIM	Accept/Con	Supporting argument[1]	Accept
Minimum wage	Scarda says that the downside to a $15 minimum wage is that some minimum wage earners will lose their jobs or have their hours cut.	CLAIM	Accept/Con[2]	Opposing argument	Accept
Minimum wage	Proponents of minimum wages argue that giving workers more disposable income puts money back into the economy, which in turn creates jobs.	CLAIM	Accept/Pro	Supporting argument	Accept
Minimum wage	Despite the inevitable negative outcomes that will surely result from a $ 15 minimum wage – we've already seen negative effects in Seattle's restaurant industry – politicians and unions seem intent on engaging in an activity that could be described as an "economic death wish.	CLAIM	Accept/Con[3]	Opposing argument	Accept
Minimum wage	Raising the wage will make it more expensive to hire younger and low-skill workers.	CLAIM	Accept/Pro	Opposing argument[4]	Accept

Table 7: Examples of sentences that were easy to annotate with all guidelines, based on all annotators agreeing on whether the sentence contained a claim/argument or not. Numbering signifies instances with one disagreement wrt stance: [1]MC disagreed and chose *Opposing argument*; [2]FL disagreed and chose *Accept/Pro*; [3]MC disagreed and chose *Accept/Pro*; [4]FC disagreed and chose *Supporting argument*. Agreeing on the stance of the argument is more difficult than agreeing on whether it is an argument at all.

guideline	group	label
1	FL	CLAIM
	ML	CLAIM
	FC	CLAIM
	MC	CLAIM
2	FL	Reject
	ML	Reject
	FC	Accept / Con
	MC	Accept / Pro
3	FL	Non-argument
	ML	Non-argument
	FC	Non-argument
	MC	Supporting argument
4	FL	Reject
	ML	Reject
	FC	Reject
	MC	Accept

Table 8: *Lebowski-isms aside, among academics, the minimum wage debate really has become a war over arcane methodological differences.*

guideline	group	label
1	FL	NO CLAIM
	ML	CLAIM
	FC	NO CLAIM
	MC	CLAIM
2	FL	Reject
	ML	Reject
	FC	Accept / Pro
	MC	Accept / Pro
3	FL	Supporting argument
	ML	Non-argument
	FC	Non-argument
	MC	Supporting argument
4	FL	Reject
	ML	Accept
	FC	Reject
	MC	Accept

Table 9: *In cloning, the nucleus of an ordinary cell, such as skin or muscle, is placed in an egg from which the nucleus has been removed.*

guideline	group	label
1	FL	CLAIM
	ML	CLAIM
	FC	NO CLAIM
	MC	CLAIM
2	FL	Accept / Pro
	ML	Reject
	FC	Accept / Pro
	MC	Accept / Pro
3	FL	Non-argument
	ML	Non-argument
	FC	Supporting argument
	MC	Supporting argument
4	FL	Reject
	ML	Reject
	FC	Reject
	MC	Reject

Table 10: *The White House proposed to increase minimum wages to $10.10.*

guideline	group	label
1	FL	CLAIM
	ML	NO CLAIM
	FC	CLAIM
	MC	NO CLAIM
2	FL	Accept / Con
	ML	Accept / Pro
	FC	Reject
	MC	Accept / Pro
3	FL	Supporting argument
	ML	Supporting argument
	FC	Non-argument
	MC	Opposing argument
4	FL	Reject
	ML	Reject
	FC	Reject
	MC	Reject

Table 11: *And, of course, you can also expect to hear conservatives shout back that the idea is a job killer.*

Appendix C: Mechanical Turk pilot study

In this appendix we describe the method and results of a pilot study on Amazon Mechanical Turk (mTurk), for the interested reader. In this pilot study, we learned that mTurk does not, at the time of writing, facilitate complex data collection and experiments with options to balance across attributes (demographics and guideline), randomize presented items and present them evenly among participants. When collecting annotations in a standard fashion, i.e. with none on the balancing and randomization methods, the resulting distribution of annotators is very unbalanced and there are large differences in how many items (HITs) each annotator choose to work on. This pilot motivated us to use the platforms Prolific and Qualtrics[10] for our data collection for the main study.

Data collection

We designed an MTurk survey in which annotators could self-report demographic information and express interest in a text annotation task. Based on this survey, we recruited annotators that were then presented with different annotation guidelines (the same as in the main study) and asked to annotate texts for arguments according to these guidelines across the two different domains, cloning and minimum wage.

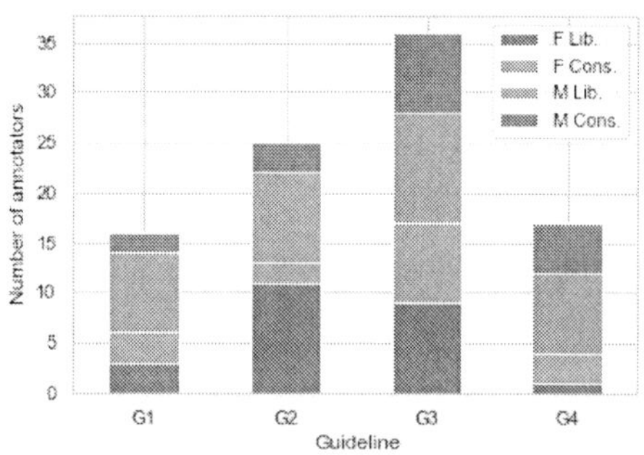

Figure 10: On the x-axis are the four guidelines and on the y-axis are the number of annotators who annotated following a given guideline. All 600 sentences were annotated once per guideline and demographic group. Annotator demographics are *not* balanced per guideline, and the total number of annotators also varies across guidelines.

Figure 10 shows the number of annotators involved with annotating the 600 sentences within each guideline and demographic group. The varying number of annotators across these dimensions reflect that in some groups, more individuals were involved in annotating

	LIBERAL		CONSERVATIVE		μ
	♀	♂	♀	♂	
G1	0.650	0.517	0.690	0.363	0.555
G2	**0.805**	0.382	0.700	<u>0.342</u>	0.557
G3	0.733	0.487	0.683	0.653	0.639
G4	0.668	0.432	0.383	0.480	0.496
μ	0.714	0.454	0.638	0.460	–

Table 12: Positive rate, i.e., the fraction of sentences labeled as claims or arguments across guidelines (G1–4) and demographics, averaged over both topics. The highest value is boldfaced, lowest is underlined.

the 600 sentences; hence they annotated fewer sentences each, while in other groups, only a few (as little as one individual with Guideline 4 with the Female and Liberal background) participated, and hence annotated more sentences each. Annotations with Guideline 3 is the most balanced wrt. the number of annotators with backgrounds who participated. Annotators could annotate using another guideline if at least one day passed from their last annotation task using another guideline. Furthermore, they were given instructions saying it was essential that they only considered the new instructions given in the new guideline and followed these closely.

Model training

We trained a model on one topic and tested it on the other using each of the 16 sets of re-annotated sentences. We used Microsoft's MT-DNN (Liu et al., 2019; Liu et al., 2020) with a pre-trained bert-base as the main (shared) layer but trained the model with the *single* classification task.[11]. Using 5 epochs, a batch size of 5, cross-entropy loss, and otherwise default hyperparameters, we trained and tested each model over 10 random seeds and collected the majority predictions for analysis. Table 13 show the positive rate of all predictions and Table 15 show F1 scores between the predictions and the matching guideline-group annotations.

Results

We briefly outline some of the main results from the pilot. Due to attributes not being balanced, we caution against too much interpretation of the results.

Female liberals and male conservatives disagree the most The agreement between two different groups can be calculated from our data as pairwise F1 scores and can be seen in Table 14. The agreement is generally highest within genders and political leanings. The macro-averaged agreement across the four guidelines is 0.734 between female conservatives and female liberals, but only 0.641 between male conservatives and female liberals. The agreement is 0.677 between female conservatives and male liberals.

[10]We note that Qualtrics is a fairly costly platform and we therefore see the development of open-source JavaScripts for controlled data collection as a direction for future research which many could benefit from.

[11]Meaning the model is comparable to simply fine-tuning bert-base.

	LIBERAL ♀	LIBERAL ♂	CONSERVATIVE ♀	CONSERVATIVE ♂	μ
CLONING→MINIMUM WAGES					
G1	0.683	0.243	0.710	0.133	0.442
G2	0.950	0.217	0.753	0.073	0.498
G3	**0.963**	0.297	0.713	0.693	0.667
G4	0.670	0.000	0.133	0.217	0.255
μ	0.817	0.189	0.577	0.279	–
MINIMUM WAGES→CLONING					
G1	0.760	0.503	0.680	0.143	0.522
G2	0.783	0.183	0.543	0.137	0.412
G3	**0.977**	0.277	0.637	0.603	0.623
G4	0.603	0.057	0.127	0.233	0.255
μ	0.781	0.255	0.497	0.279	–

Table 13: Positive rate of cross-topic predictions of fine-tuned argument mining models. To understand how to read the table, take this example: the first value, 0.683, is the mean of the predictions over the minimum wage sentences by a model trained with the cloning sentences that were annotated by liberal females using Guideline 1. Highest value is boldfaced, lowest is underlined.

Cross-group argument mining is hard From Table 14, we immediately see that cross-group argument mining is hard. This follows directly from the low agreement rates. We also see clear performance drops when evaluating our models across different groups. Training a model on one domain with annotations from liberal females following Guideline 1, for example, lead to an F1 score of 0.86 on the other domain (on average, across both directions), when the test data is also annotated by liberal females; for the other three groups, F1 scores drop to 0.85, 0.76, and 0.66. Similar results are observed across the other group combinations.

			LIBERAL ♀	LIBERAL ♂	CONSERVATIVE ♀	CONSERVATIVE ♂
G1	LIB.	♀	1.000	–	–	
	LIB.	♂	0.703	1.000	–	–
	CON.	♀	0.759	0.707	1.000	–
	CON.	♂	0.615	0.617	0.644	1.000
G2	LIB.	♀	1.000	–	–	–
	LIB.	♂	0.612	1.000	–	–
	CON.	♀	0.855	0.647	1.000	–
	CON.	♂	0.570	0.624	0.608	1.000
G3	LIB.	♀	1.000	–	–	–
	LIB.	♂	0.601	1.000	–	–
	CON.	♀	0.744	0.721	1.000	–
	CON.	♂	0.714	0.800	0.696	1.000
G4	LIB.	♀	1.000	–	–	–
	LIB.	♂	0.639	1.000	–	–
	CON.	♀	0.577	0.634	1.000	–
	CON.	♂	0.665	0.687	0.651	1.000

Table 14: Agreement between groups within guidelines calculated with F1 for the positive class. These align well with the reported inter-annotator agreement scores in the literature; see Table 1. Average agreement for Guideline 1-4 is .67, .65, .71 and .64, respectively.

	LIBERAL ♀	LIBERAL ♂	CONSERVATIVE ♀	CONSERVATIVE ♂	μ
CLONING→MINIMUM WAGES					
G1	0.833	0.498	0.850	0.426	0.651
G2	**0.871**	0.451	0.846	0.262	0.608
G3	0.833	0.579	0.818	0.785	0.754
G4	0.798	0.000	0.438	0.507	0.436
μ	0.832	0.382	0.738	0.495	–
MINIMUM WAGES→CLONING					
G1	0.862	0.656	0.825	0.413	0.689
G2	0.859	0.432	0.772	0.397	0.615
G3	0.846	0.449	0.797	0.736	0.707
G4	0.704	0.169	0.419	0.495	0.507
μ	0.818	0.427	0.703	0.510	–

Table 15: Cross-topic F1 score of fine-tuned argument mining models across different guidelines. F1-scores are for the positive class between predictions and annotations of same guideline-group combination, e.g. cross-topic predictions over the minimum wage sentences from a model trained on cloning sentences annotated by liberal females using guideline 1 are compared to the annotations for the minimum wage sentences by liberal females. Highest value is boldfaced, lowest is underlined.

Proceedings of the 16th Linguistic Annotation Workshop (LAW-XVI) @LREC 2022, pages 62–69
Marseille, 24 June 2022

NLP in Human Rights Research: Extracting Knowledge Graphs About Police and Army Units and Their Commanders

Daniel Bauer[‡*], Tom Longley [†*], Yueen Ma[‡*], Tony Wilson[†*]
[‡]Computer Science Department
Columbia University
{db2711, ym2745}@columbia.edu

[†] Security Force Monitor
Human Rights Institute
Columbia Law School
{tom,tony}@securityforcemonitor.com

[*] All authors contributed equally.

Abstract

In this paper we explore the use of an NLP system to assist the work of Security Force Monitor (SFM). SFM creates data about the organizational structure, command personnel and operations of police, army and other security forces, which assists human rights researchers, journalists and litigators in their work to help identify and bring to account specific units and personnel alleged to have committed abuses of human rights and international criminal law. This paper presents an NLP system that extracts from English language news reports the names of security force units and the biographical details of their personnel, and infers the formal relationship between them. Published alongside this paper are the system's code and training dataset. We find that the experimental NLP system performs the task at a fair to good level. Its performance is sufficient to justify further development into a live workflow that will give insight into whether its performance translates into savings in time and resource that would make it an effective technical intervention.

Keywords: Ethics and Legal Issues; Information Extraction, Information Retrieval; Knowledge Discovery, Representation; Named Entity Recognition; Tools, Systems, Applications

1. Introduction

Human rights organizations around the world gather large amounts of information for the purposes of promoting and protecting human rights. The promise offered by automated information extraction and processing technologies is of making these rivers of information easier to comprehend and take action on. This promise is much touted; it also feels like such capacities might be more accessible to everyone in a world where software can drive cars or defeat a 9 *dan* ranked Go master. What, however, does this promise mean in practice for the basic daily work of human rights researchers, rather than their counterparts in commercial, scientific and industrial domains? In this paper we try to provide some insight into this question by reporting the initial outcomes of a multi-disciplinary collaboration to explore the value of Natural Language Processing (NLP) methods as components of information extraction systems used to gather detailed data about state security and defense forces implicated in human rights abuses.

Security Force Monitor[1] (SFM) (Wilson, 2017) is a human rights research project that compiles and analyzes public information to create detailed data on the organizational structure, command personnel and operations of police, army and other security forces. They provide this data to other human rights researchers, investigative journalists and litigators to help them identify and bring to account specific units and command personnel alleged to have committed abuses of human rights and international criminal law. SFM's research has been used in the investigation of drug-related killings by police in the Philippines (Security Force Monitor, 2019), allegations of war crimes committed by the army in Mexico (Longley, 2018), and the use of lethal force by the Nigerian military against protesters in Nigeria (Searcey and E., 2018).

SFM's approach[2] is to identify salient material ("sources") through targeted web searches, extract up to 80 specific pieces of information about people, locations and organizations from these sources, and arrange them into a graph-like data structure. These data are transformed into hierarchical organograms or other visualizations of security force structures, showing additional information about personnel (name, rank, role, title), geographic footprint (facilities, bases, camps) and areas of operation. For example, figures 1 and 2 show the command structure and areas of operation of the Western Regional Military Command of the Myan-

[1] Security Force Monitor is part of the Columbia Law School Human Rights Institute (`https://securityforcemonitor.org`).

[2] See "Research Handbook for Security Force Monitor", `https://help.securityforcemonitor.org/`

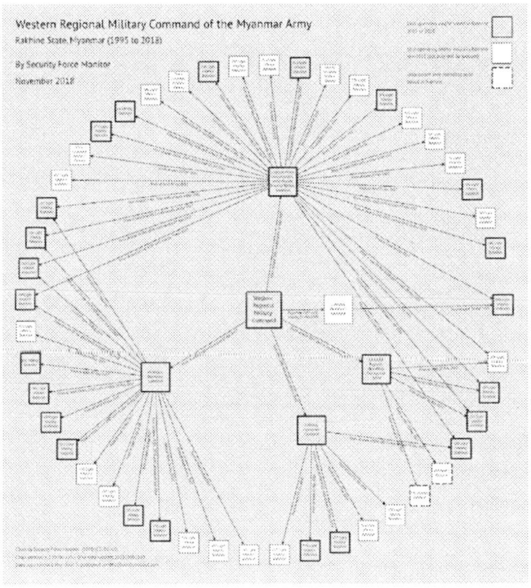

Figure 1: Western Regional Military Command of the Myanmar Army – Rakhine State (1995 to 2018) – a chart by Security Force Monitor (CC-BY-4.0) (Security Force Monitor, 2018)

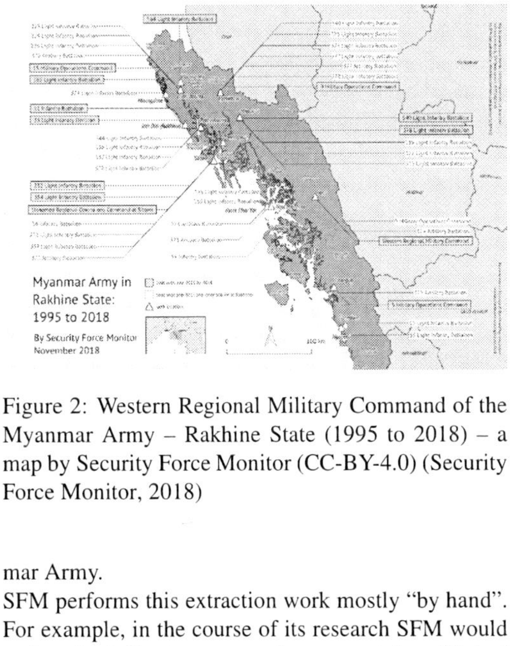

Figure 2: Western Regional Military Command of the Myanmar Army – Rakhine State (1995 to 2018) – a map by Security Force Monitor (CC-BY-4.0) (Security Force Monitor, 2018)

mar Army.
SFM performs this extraction work mostly "by hand". For example, in the course of its research SFM would review the following extract from an article published in Nigeria's *Vanguard* newspaper in 2012 (Obateru, 2012):

> General Officer Commanding 3 Armoured Division of the Nigerian Army, Major General Jack Nwaogbo, has again re-assured Nigerians that the Boko Haram insurgency would soon be contained.

From this, SFM would extract the following pieces of information and enter them into a database:

- Name of person: "Jack Nwaogbo"
- Rank of person: "Major General"
- Title of person: "General Officer Commanding"
- Organization/unit: "3 Armoured Division"
- Role of person in unit: "Commander"

SFM also applies a number of integrity measures to every data point: they are specifically evidenced by one or more sources, are time-bound (valid from, valid until) and are rated for confidence in their accuracy (from low to high). SFM also extracts and encodes geographical information about the emplacements and operations of specific units. The resulting datasets are made public by SFM, and can be searched through a public website[3]. At the time of writing, SFM has manually analyzed over 8,000 documents (of which 130 have been annotated for use in this experiment), assembling data on 10,900 specific units, 2,700 command personnel and over 200 alleged human rights violations in 19 countries, going back a decade. Already faced with managing a rich and complicated dataset, SFM faces challenges of scale on numerous fronts: extending coverage to include new force branches and new countries, updating existing data as relevant new material appears online, and working in a number of different languages.
Given the centrality of this type of text analysis to SFM's research process, NLP would seem to hold potential in automating - partly, or fully - time-consuming tasks like identifying and relating a specific person to a specific unit, and extracting contextual biographical data such as rank and official title. The value to SFM is in picking out common named entities (like Persons and Organizations), and in establishing and extracting the relationships between them in a format that can be quickly appraised for accuracy.
This paper explores this potential in the form of a pilot study and is organized as follows. Section 2 describes the research task and an annotated dataset of 130 news reports about the defense and security forces of Nigeria, which is released with this paper. Section 3 presents initial results of a pilot/baseline system implemented by the authors. We show the system's results with respect to both named entity recognition and relation extraction tasks. Finally, in Section 4 we look at some of the limitations of the system and the experimental results.

2. Data and task description

SFM identified 130 of the most information-rich text documents from which it has extracted material to create its data on the Nigerian Army and Nigerian Police Force. This document corpus contains 4,711 lines. A single, expert annotator annotated the text of these articles to create a gold standard dataset for use in the

[3] `https://WhoWasInCommand.com`

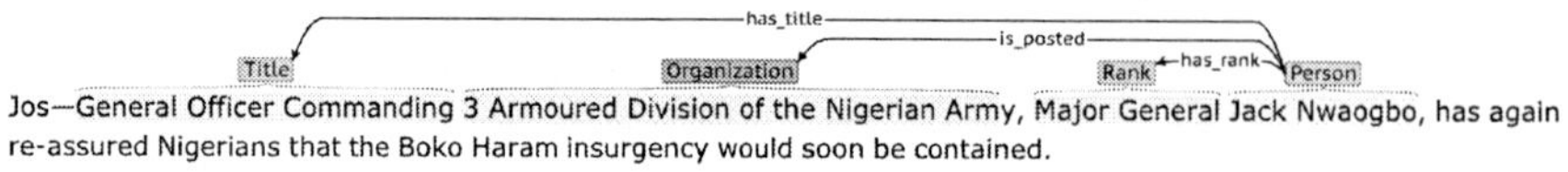

Figure 3: An example from our dataset

development of an NLP system. A single expert annotator annotated the 130 documents in the corpus. In the future we plan to develop this dataset by introducing additional annotators and monitoring inter-rater agreement to assure quality. The annotations describe the relationships between persons and the units to which they are posted, which is one of the main information extraction tasks done by hand by SFM. SFM have published the corpus of annotated texts online, along with extensive documentation on the document selection, processing and annotation process .[4]

The SFM expert annotator created the annotations using the Berkeley Rapid Annotation Tool (BRAT) (bra, 2020a), which has a graphical interface that the annotator can use to highlight and connect different information contained in the text. The types of information that can be annotated are described in a BRAT configuration file:

```
[entities]
Person
Organization
Rank
Title
Role
[relations]
is_posted    Arg1:Person, Arg2:Organization
has_title    Arg1:Person, Arg2:Title
has_role     Arg1:Person, Arg2:Role
has_rank     Arg1:Person, Arg2:Rank
<OVERLAP>    Arg1:Role, Arg2:Rank, <OVL-TYPE>:<ANY>
<OVERLAP>    Arg1:Title, Arg2:Role, <OVL-TYPE>:<ANY>
```

The "entities" section above shows us that an annotator can decide a particular word or extract describes a "Person" or an "Organization", as well as biographical information like the "Title", "Rank" or "Role" the person may have within that organization. The "relations" section shows how these building blocks can be connected to each other: a "Person" can be "Posted" to an "Organization", and a "Person" can have a "Role" and a "Rank" during the course of that posting.

Each document in the annotated corpus has two corresponding files: the first stores the raw text, the second the annotations made to that text. A third file contains the document title, date, and other metadata and is not used in the research. The text and annotation files share the same file name (a 36-character UUID) while the suffixes are '.txt' and '.ann', respectively.

Annotations follow the BRAT Standoff format (bra, 2020b). Named entities are identified by text-bounds, which use two numbers to locate the first character and the last character of a name entity. Relations are identified with two arguments, which are the ID's of the two

Class	Unique	Mentions
Person	409	531
Rank	103	513
Organization	320	735
Title	151	360
Role	44	167
All Classes	1028	2307

Table 1: Annotations - Unique Named Entities and mentions

Class	Occurrence
has_rank	507
has_title	450
has_role	168
is_posted	391
All Relations	1416

Table 2: Annotations - Relationships between Named Entities

name entities involved in the relation. Relations are directed. The following is an example of the annotations for the sentence mentioned above:

```
T1  Title_Role 35 38      GOC
T2  Title_Role 52 70      Officer Commanding
T3  Organization 71 90    3 Armoured Division
T4  Organization 98 111 Nigerian Army
R1 has_rank Arg1:T1 Arg2:T2
R2 is_posted Arg1:T1 Arg2:T3
R3 has_title Arg1:T1 Arg2:T4
```

The annotations can be also be visualized in the BRAT tool, an example of which is shown in Figure 3. Summaries of the occurrence of Named Entities in the corpus, and the relationships between them, are included in Table 1 and Table 2.

In addition to this dataset of annotated documents, SFM also provided lists of known names of Nigerian military and police units.[5] These additional datasets were extracted from SFM's own research into the Nigerian security forces, as well as from lists of named Nigerian military units that the United States government has provided with assistance and training since 2000.

Our research task is to automate the extraction of such annotations from a raw-text input, and gain insight into way in which this capability could replace, substantially augment or otherwise assist researchers in performing this task. The experimental system is not required to reconcile entities across documents or with

[4]https://github.com/security-force-monitor/nlp_starter_dataset

[5]Available at https://github.com/security-force-monitor/nlp_starter_dataset/tree/master/other_training_data

Class	True Positives	False Positives	False Negatives	Precision	Recall	F1 Score
Person	87	13	6	0.87	0.94	0.90
Rank	80	14	11	0.85	0.88	0.86
Organization	103	33	31	0.76	0.77	0.76
Title/Role	85	20	23	0.81	0.79	0.80
All Classes	355	80	71	0.82	0.83	0.82

Table 3: NER model evaluation

an external dataset (entity linking). Even though our pilot system is basic, our aim is to quantify the system's performance and identify the key factors that affect this performance, sufficiently to say whether or not the task can be accomplished in a way that would make it worth implementing as part of SFM's research workflow. The following section discusses some of these factors.

3. Pilot System

Our pilot system[6] addresses only two sub-tasks of the full knowledge graph extraction task: Named Entity recognition, and relation extraction. We aim to address entity linking in a future paper.

3.1. Named Entity Recognition (NER)

To extract name entities, we use BiLSTM-CNN-CRF model (Ma and Hovy, 2016) in the traditional inside–outside–beginning (IOB) tagging framework (Sang and Veenstra, 1999). Here is an example of the IOB tagging for the sentence in Figure 3:

```
General Officer Commanding 3     Armoured Division
B-TTL   I-TTL   I-TTL      B-ORG I-ORG    I-ORG

of    the   Nigerian Army  , Major General Jack
I-ORG I-ORG I-ORG    I-ORG   B-RNK I-RNK   B-PER

Nwaogbo, has again re-assured Nigerians that the
I-PER    O   O     O          O         O    O

Boko Haram insurgency would soon be contained.
O    O     O          O     O    O  O
```

We first compute input representations for each token by applying a convolutional neural network (CNN) to compute character-level representations. CNNs have been shown to be effective at extracting morphological information (Dos Santos and Zadrozny, 2014; Chiu and Nichols, 2016). The output of the CNN layer is concatenated with pre-trained GloVe word embedding (Pennington et al., 2014) to represent each token.

Next, we compute context representations from the word-level representations by encoding the context using a BiLSTM (Hochreiter and Schmidhuber, 1997; Pascanu et al., 2012). Because we are using the IOB tagging format (Sang and Veenstra, 1999), the label sequence follows certain rules. For instance, I-ORG cannot follow I-PER. Therefore, label sequences are modeled jointly using a conditional random field (CRF) (Lafferty et al., 2001).

[6]Available at https://github.com/security-force-monitor/sfm-graph-extractor

Because the data created by SFM for this task is relatively small (Security Force Monitor, 2020), and part of it is needed for testing, we retrained the model with two additional datasets. First, we added part of the CoNLL-2003 dataset (Tjong Kim Sang and De Meulder, 2003). The CoNLL-2003 dataset has two classes which also appears in our dataset: 'Person' and 'Organization'. In addition, as mentioned above, SFM provided a a list of known organizations that could be added our dataset. Since it is hard to draw a clear line between the class 'Title' and the class 'Role', which were specified as distinct in SFM's knowledge graph, we decided to collapse them into a single class.

The performance of the named entity model is shown in Table 3.

3.2. Relation Extraction

In our pilot system, we experiment with three approaches to relation extraction: nearest person, shortest dependency path, and a neural network based approach. These approaches all share the same underlying idea: starting at each non-Person named entity e, our system tries to identify an entity of type Person in the same sentence that stands in a relation with e, and then tries to predict the type of this relation. We will look at each approach in turn.

3.2.1. Nearest Person

This baseline algorithm is based on the simple idea that a non-Person named entity is often related to a Person named entity nearby. For example, one could say "General Lamidi Adeosun" where "'Lamidi Adeosun" has the rank "General", as in one of the documents in our corpus. The algorithm, therefore, merely relates a non-Person named entity to the Person named entity immediately to the right; if there is no Person named entity to its right, then the algorithm relates it to the nearest Person entity no matter which side the Person entity is on. Although we did not expect performance of this system to be competitive, an immediate advantage of this simple technique is that its decisions are transparent.

3.2.2. Shortest Dependency Path

Instead of using the distances between named entities in raw text, we can take syntactic information into account. This method relates a non-Person named entity to the person named entity to which the dependency path is shortest. This relies largely on how well the de-

Method	True Positives	False Positives	False Negatives	Precision	Recall	F1 score
Nearest Person (Baseline)	993	759	423	0.567	0.701	0.627
Shortest Dep. Path (No constraint)	1083	651	333	0.625	0.765	0.687
Shortest Dep. Path (With constraint)	**1180***	559	**236***	0.679	**0.833***	**0.748***
Neural Network (No constraint)	1086	667	330	0.620	0.767	0.685
Neural Network (With constraint)	1103	**450***	313	**0.710***	0.779	0.743

Table 4: RE algorithms evaluation

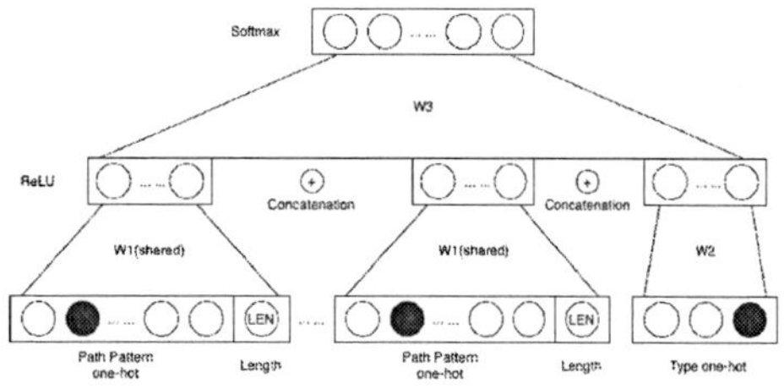

Figure 4: The architecture of the neural network: The weight matrix W_1 for path pattern information is shared across all path pattern one-hot vectors, but it is distinct from the weight matrix W_2 for type one-hot vector. The softmax-activated output vector represents the probability of potential Person name entities.

pendency parser performs, so we used a state-of-the-art dependency parser (Nguyen and Verspoor, 2018). Since one named entity could span multiple tokens, we only use the shortest path among the various possible paths between the tokens of two named entities.

We find that constraining the algorithm to only choose between the two Persons that appear immediately to the left and to the right increases performance, at least on our data set. We use this constraint in the final version of our system.

Assuming reasonable performance by the dependency parser, decisions of this heuristic dependency based approach are easy to trace.

3.2.3. Neural Network

In this approach, we use machine learning to predict relations based on dependency paths and named entity types. We use the phrase "path pattern" to refer to the list of edge types along a dependency path. The path patterns are encoded into one-hot vectors. Uncommon path patterns are treated as a single "unknown" category. Since there are multiple possible persons in a sentence, there will be a one-hot vector for each Person. We pass these multiple vectors as input to the network, so that it makes a joint decision over multiple candidate entities of type Person.

In addition, the path length is concatenated to the one-hot vector to compensate for the loss of information when we replace the less frequent path patterns. Multiple one-hot + length vectors of different persons are concatenated together along with a small one-hot vector which encodes the type of the non-person name entity, which makes up the input of the neural network. The network architecture is shown in Figure 4 and its performance is shown in Table 4. The first layer has a set of shared weights for those one-hot + length vectors and a separate set of weights for the name entity type vector. The second layer is a dense layer whose output is activated by a softmax layer. The softmax layer outputs a vector where the largest element corresponds to the target Person.

The number of persons that the model could process within a sentence is limited to 7. If there are more than 7 persons in a sentence, we set the target to an all-zero vector. If a prediction does not correspond to any person, such as when there are only 3 persons in a sentence while the model predicts the fourth person, then we do not build any relations for the name entity.

To include the constraint mentioned in Section 3.2.2, we made the target a 3-element vector. If the first element is the largest, then the Person on the left side is the predicted person; if the second element is the largest, then the Person on the right side is the predicted Person; if the third element is the largest, then the model predicts that the correct Person should be some Person other than the two nearest Persons. When the model predicts that the Person is not nearby, we select the Person that has shortest dependency path excluding the two nearest Persons.

4. Experimental results

For sentences with relatively few named entities (for example, a sentence has only 1 Person named entity), both Shortest Dependency Path and Neural Network perform very well since there are not many choices to make. When there are more named entities in a sentence, it becomes harder to make a correct choice and that is where the two methods make different predictions.

The neural network method looks at the path length, its pattern and the named entity type, so it sees more information than the shortest dependency path method, which only looks at path length. These two additional pieces of information sometimes do help make a better prediction, but they can confuse the neural network as well. In Figure 5, the shortest dependency path method falsely related the name entity "Chief of Logistics" to the person "M. T. Ibrahim". "Chief of Logistics" is closer to "M. T. Ibrahim" than to "Emmanuel Atewe"

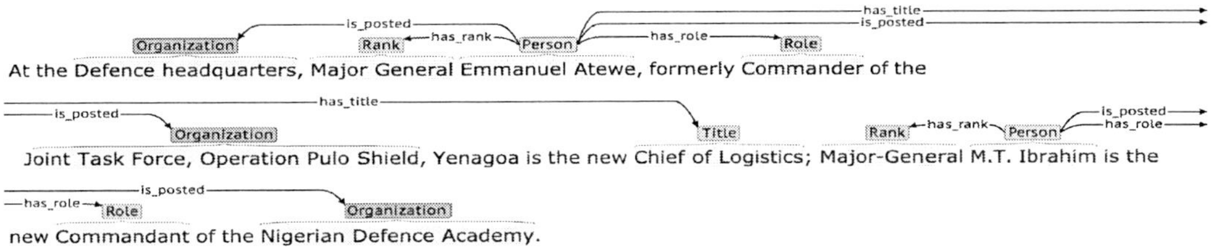

(a) True Annotations

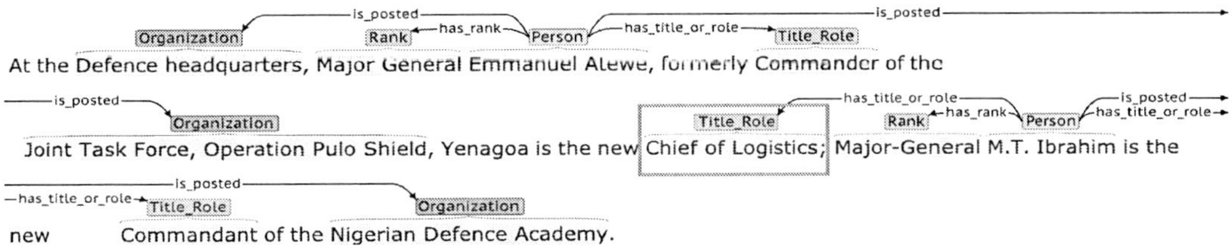

(b) Shortest Dependency Path

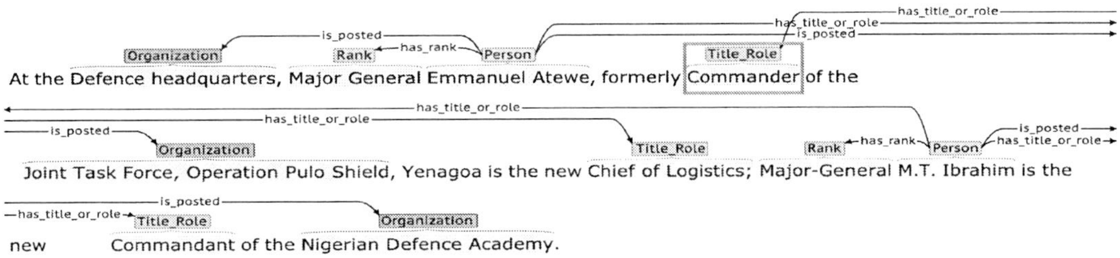

(c) Neural Network

Figure 5: Two methods make different mistakes

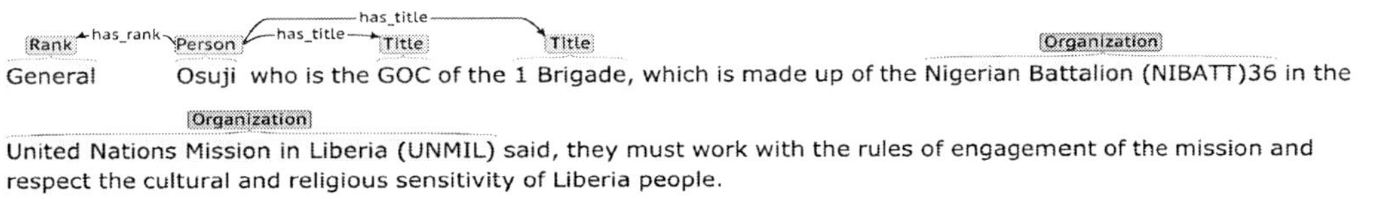

(a) True Annotations

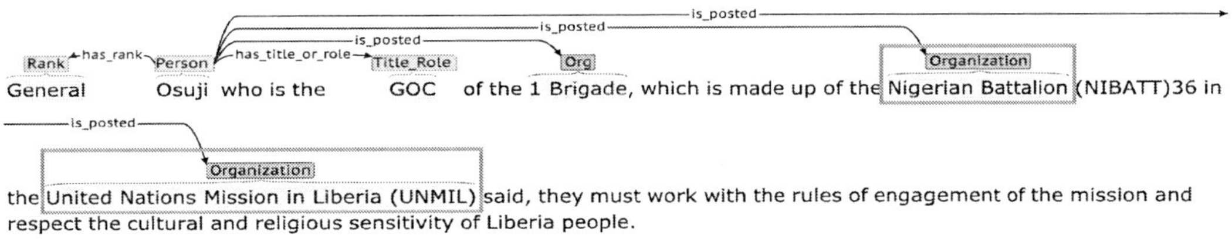

(b) Shortest Dependency Path

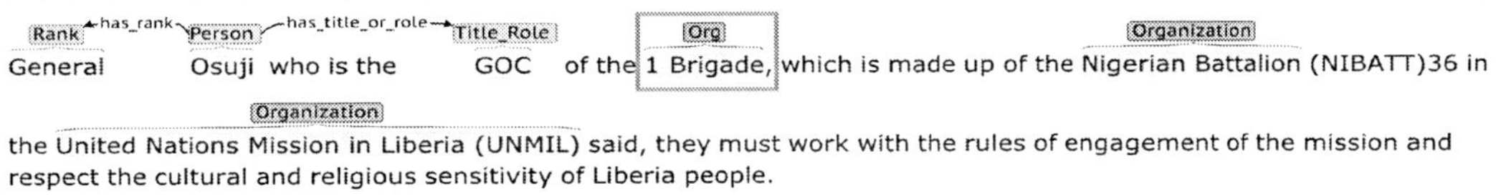

(c) Neural Network

Figure 6: Neural Network is more conservative

Component	Time (Seconds)	Model Size (Parameters)
NER	1.54	6153100
Dep. Parsing	0.70	8791858
Shortest Dep. Path	0.0039	N/A
Neural Network	0.051	294

Table 5: Average processing time per line and model sizes

in the dependency tree, but the additional information helped the neural network method make the correct choice. But when predicting "Commander", simply using the length of the dependency path yields the right relation.

The neural network method has fewer false positives, since the shortest dependency path method is forced to build a relation for every non-Person name entity while the neural network has the option not to build a relation. Therefore, the neural network has fewer false positives and more false negatives. This indicates that the neural network is slightly too conservative when deciding whether there exists a correct relation for a given non-Person name entity. One example is shown in Figure 6.

There are some obvious limitations of our algorithms. First, all three algorithms only relate two named entities when they are in the same sentence. When there are relations that cross sentences, our algorithms will not be able to capture them. Second, sometimes, one named entity can be related to multiple other entities. Our algorithms only relate one non-Person name entity to a single Person name entity. Third, we have not implemented the functionality to collect and reconcile the information of Person named entities that exist in different documents.

We also measured the average processing time of different components in the pipeline, as shown in Table 5. The results are based on three independent but identical measurements of the processing time on our entire dataset. The numbers are obtained by averaging the measured time after discarding obvious outliers. The measurements are conducted on a MacBook Pro with a quad-core CPU @ 4.1GHz Max. It is worth noting that the processing time of NER and dependency parsing is dependent on the length of the sentences and the processing time of the shortest dependency parsing algorithm or the neural network is dependent on the amount of named entities in a line.

5. Discussion and conclusion

The results show that an NLP system can perform the research task with a *fair to good* degree of accuracy, albeit with some clear limitations that we must acknowledge.

Our experiment was conducted in an unusual domain in which attention to NLP is in its infancy and there are no pre-existing, domain-specific systems against which we could compare our results . That said, our experiment would have benefited from the inclusion of a comparison between the system designed and trained to perform the present task and a different, off-the-shelf NER system. Though we saw some improvement to the system's performance in identifying Organizations by including items from CoNLL-2003 and SFM unit lists, bench-marking against a distinct, untrained system would have provided us with an additional insight.

The size of the material available for training, even if it were not further restricted to the context of the Nigerian security forces, also poses a challenge. The annotated documents were drawn from English-language news sources in Nigeria, and as such are similar to the news-wire material used to train many English language NER models. There are three points worth making, however. First, the approach that we took to annotation could be strengthened in future work with the inclusion of additional annotators and monitoring interrater agreement. Second, we did not tune the NER model to better identify Nigerian given and patronymic names, which could have helped boost the system's performance in detecting Persons. Finally, the names of security force units are often generic and contain numbers ("4 Motorized Regiment", "25th Division"). It is an open question about whether there is, in the universe of military naming, sufficient material to identify and distinguish these from non-military entities.

The system skews a little towards recall, which is preferable where a subsequent human review is intended. Demonstrating this capability meets the first objective of this collaboration. However, the results alone do not tell us whether its performance is tolerable within SFM's research workflow (and by extension that of other human rights researchers). Understanding this requires implementing the system in a way that enables SFM to accept, reject or quickly update the proposals it makes, and assessing whether this creates savings in time and resource as compared to doing the work wholly "by hand". Subsequent work will focus on this next, implementation step.

Although the present paper is mostly technical and focused on practical application, throughout the authors' collaboration we have ranged across the wider matters of NLP and the challenges of technology implementation within the human rights domain. The potential that NLP represents is set against the sector's considerable financial and technical capacity constraints and a dearth in transparent examples of successful NLP use within it. Surrounding this are concerns about the human rights implications of NLP methods themselves: the discriminatory potential of the datasets used to train them; the dominance of government and corporate actors in their technical development; and, implementations that infringe human rights directly. In future papers drawn from our research, we aim to assess how these affect the desirability and feasibility of NLP use within the wider non-profit domain.

6. References

brat, (2020a). *BRAT Rapid Annotation Tool.*

brat, (2020b). *BRAT Standoff Format.*

Chiu, J. P. and Nichols, E. (2016). Named entity recognition with bidirectional LSTM-CNNs. *Transactions of the Association for Computational Linguistics*, 4:357–370.

Dos Santos, C. N. and Zadrozny, B. (2014). Learning character-level representations for part-of-speech tagging. In *Proceedings of the 31st International Conference on International Conference on Machine Learning - Volume 32*, ICML'14, pages II–1818–II–1826. JMLR.org.

Hochreiter, S. and Schmidhuber, J. (1997). Long short-term memory. *Neural Comput.*, 9(8):1735–1780, November.

Lafferty, J. D., McCallum, A., and Pereira, F. C. N. (2001). Conditional random fields: Probabilistic models for segmenting and labeling sequence data. In *Proceedings of the Eighteenth International Conference on Machine Learning*, ICML '01, pages 282–289, San Francisco, CA, USA. Morgan Kaufmann Publishers Inc.

Longley, T. (2018). Prosecutor of the international criminal court receives complaint of crimes against humanity by the mexican army. `https://securityforcemonitor.org/2018/06/11/prosecutor-of-the-international-criminal-court-receives-complaint-of-crimes-against-humanity-by-the-mexican-army/`.

Ma, X. and Hovy, E. (2016). End-to-end sequence labeling via bi-directional lstm-cnns-crf.

Nguyen, D. Q. and Verspoor, K. (2018). An improved neural network model for joint POS tagging and dependency parsing. In *Proceedings of the CoNLL 2018 Shared Task: Multilingual Parsing from Raw Text to Universal Dependencies*, pages 81–91, Brussels, Belgium, October. Association for Computational Linguistics.

Obateru, T. (2012). Boko haram 'll soon be contained – goc. `http://www.vanguardngr.com/2012/07/boko-haram-ll-soon-be-contained-goc/`, 7.

Pascanu, R., Mikolov, T., and Bengio, Y. (2012). On the difficulty of training recurrent neural networks.

Pennington, J., Socher, R., and Manning, C. (2014). Glove: Global vectors for word representation. In *Proceedings of the 2014 Conference on Empirical Methods in Natural Language Processing (EMNLP)*, pages 1532–1543, Doha, Qatar, October. Association for Computational Linguistics.

Sang, E. F. T. K. and Veenstra, J. (1999). Representing text chunks. In *Proceedings of the Ninth Conference on European Chapter of the Association for Computational Linguistics*, EACL '99, pages 173–179, Stroudsburg, PA, USA. Association for Computational Linguistics.

Searcey, D. and E., A. (2018). Nigeria says soldiers who killed marchers were provoked. video shows otherwise. *New York Times*, 12.

Security Force Monitor. (2018). The structure and operations of the myanmar army in rakhine state: a review of open source evidence. `https://securityforcemonitor.org/2018/11/20/myanmar-army-in-rakhine-state-structure-and-operations/`.

Security Force Monitor. (2019). Investigating drug related killings in the philippines. `https://securityforcemonitor.org/2019/08/19/investigating-drug-related-killings-in-the-philippines/`.

Security Force Monitor. (2020). WhoWasInCommand. https://whowasincommand.com/.

Tjong Kim Sang, E. F. and De Meulder, F. (2003). Introduction to the CoNLL-2003 shared task: Language-independent named entity recognition. In *Proceedings of the Seventh Conference on Natural Language Learning at HLT-NAACL 2003*, pages 142–147.

Wilson, T. (2017). Why I Started The Security Force Monitor. `https://securityforcemonitor.org/2017/04/11/why-i-started-the-security-force-monitor/`, 4.

Proceedings of the 16th Linguistic Annotation Workshop (LAW-XVI) @LREC 2022, pages 70–78
Marseille, 24 June 2022

Advantages of a complex multilayer annotation scheme: The case of the Prague Dependency Treebank

Eva Hajičová, Marie Mikulová, Barbora Štěpánková, Jiří Mírovský
Institute of Formal and Applied Linguistics
Computer Science School, Faculty of Mathematics and Physics, Charles University, Prague
{hajicova,mikulova,stepankova,mirovsky}@ufal.mff.cuni.cz

Abstract

Recently, many corpora have been developed that contain multiple annotations of various linguistic phenomena, from morphological categories of words through the syntactic structure of sentences to discourse and coreference relations in texts. Discussions are ongoing on an appropriate annotation scheme for a large amount of diverse information. In our contribution we express our conviction that a multilayer annotation scheme offers to view the language system in its complexity and in the interaction of individual phenomena and that there are at least two aspects that support such a scheme: (i) A multilayer annotation scheme makes it possible to use the annotation of one layer to design the annotation of another layer(s) both conceptually and in a form of a pre-annotation procedure or annotation checking rules. (ii) A multilayer annotation scheme presents a reliable ground for corpus studies based on features across the layers. These aspects are demonstrated on the case of the Prague Dependency Treebank. Its multilayer annotation scheme withstood the test of time and serves well also for complex textual annotations, in which earlier morpho-syntactic annotations are advantageously used. In addition to a reference to the previous projects that utilise its annotation scheme, we present several current investigations.

Keywords: complex language description, multilayer annotation scheme, linguistically-based pre-annotation, linguistically-based checks, corpus-based study

1. Introduction

One of the aims of modern linguistic studies is to describe and explain the collection of language phenomena as a structured whole and at the same time to understand this structured whole as a functioning means of communication. In this context, several concepts of function should be distinguished; in one of these interpretations, function is opposed to form, which comes close to Saussure's binary understanding of sign (Saussure, 1916). This interpretation offers a basis for understanding language as a set of levels, which gave rise to several descriptive frameworks, from the original stratificational grammar of Lamb and Newell (1966) through Halliday's systemic grammar (Halliday, 1970) to Sgall's Functional Generative Description (Sgall, 1967; Sgall et al., 1986) or Mel'chukovian Meaning-Text Model (Mel'chuk, 1988), to name just a few that refer to strata or levels explicitly, and leaving aside those which acknowledge the existence of units with different status without giving them specific names (as is e.g. the case of the so-called construction grammar).

Following the multistratal descriptions of the language, various multilayer annotation schemes have been proposed, the purpose of which is to take into account multifarious linguistic phenomena from morphological categories of words through the syntactic structure of sentences to discourse and coreference relations in texts and other semantic features (such as temporal or spatial annotation), which allow for an assignment of labels to tokens, groups of tokens, sentences and entire sections of the raw texts.

In the present paper, we want to substantiate our conviction that such a complex annotation scheme offers to view the language system in its complexity, in the interaction of individual phenomena and thus contributes to the theoretical studies of this system. All aspects supporting a multilayer annotation scheme are demonstrated on the case of the Prague Dependency Treebank based on the language description framework known as Functional Generative Description. The annotation scheme of the Prague Dependency Treebank is described in Sect 3. In Sect. 4, annotation related aspects of a multilayer annotation scheme are demonstrated. The possibility to base linguistic research on a corpus search on more than a single layer of annotation has led to a series of studies which are introduced in Sect. 5.

2. Related Work

Recently, there has been an increased interest in the development of multilayer corpora, e.g. Groningen Meaning Bank (Bos et al., 2017) based on Discourse Representation Theory (Kamp, 1984; Kamp and Reyle, 1993) and Combinatory Categorial Grammar (Steedman, 2001), Manually Annotated Sub-Corpus (Ide, 2017) based on Linguistics Annotation Framework (Ide and Romary, 2004), Georgetown University Multilayer Corpus (Zeldes, 2017), OntoNotes (Hovy et al., 2006; Pradhan and Ramshaw, 2017), AnCora-UPF corpus (Mille et al., 2013), which is based on the Meaning-Text Model mentioned above. An overview of recently developed multilayer corpora with a proposal of a multilayer semantic annotation scheme is most recently presented by Silvano et al. (2021).

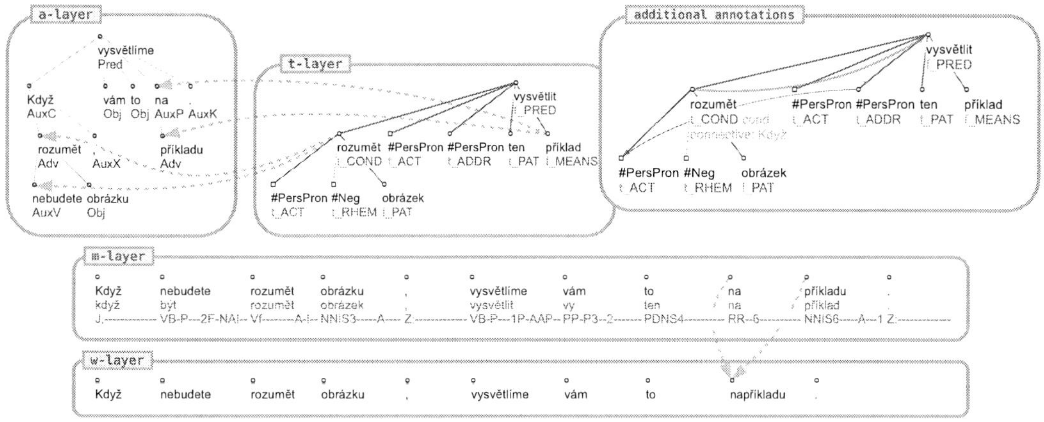

Figure 1: Multilayer annotation scheme of the PDT-treebank

In principle, a multilayer corpus is such a corpus that "contains mutually independent forms of information, which cannot be derived from one another reliably" (Zeldes, 2018). However, Ide et al. (2017) note that there are different types of multilayer annotation schemes. The layers may be defined in an independent way or a single scheme may be used that integrates all the layers; each layer may point directly into raw data, or each layer may define independently its units by referring to tokens in raw text, or to other units on some other annotation layer. The decision to represent annotation layers in this way does not automatically lead to a distribution of layers in separate data files or to a visualization of layers in separate graphs, etc.

3. The case of a complex multilayer annotation scheme: Prague Dependency Treebank

In the paper, we outline and illustrate the advantages of a multilayer corpus based on the hierarchical architecture of several annotation layers as applied in the family of the Prague Dependency Treebank (PDT). In order not to lose any piece of the original information, units (tokens, nodes) at a lower layer are explicitly referred to from the corresponding closest (immediately higher) layer. These links allow for tracing every unit of annotation all the way down to the original raw text. Thus, an annotation layer can provide information both about raw data and also about other annotations.

The annotation scheme of the PDT is inspired by and theoretically rooted in the stratificationally and dependency-based Functional Generative Description of language as proposed by Petr Sgall in the sixties (Sgall, 1967) and then developed and enriched by his students and followers up to the present time. The annotation scheme was first introduced at the end of the nineties of the last century (cf. (Hajič, 1998), more recently (Hajič et al., 2017; Hajič et al., 2020a) and the annotation manuals presented on the project web site[1]). The hierarchical multilayer architecture of PDT-annotation scheme is schematically illustrated in Fig. 1 on the example of the Czech sentence:

Když nebudete rozumět obrázku, vysvětlíme vám to napříkladu.
When you-will-not understand picture we-will-explain you it onexample.
'If you do not understand the picture, we will explain it to you on an example.'

In Fig. 1, each layer of the system is indicated by a separate box. The links between the layers are indicated by the red arrows. In fact, all nodes/tokens are linked. The original raw text is stored at the lowest layer of the system (**w-layer** box in Fig. 1). At this **raw text layer**, the text is segmented into documents and paragraphs and individual tokens are assigned unique identifiers.
Above the raw text layer, there are the following layers of annotations:

- **morphological layer** (**m-layer** box in Fig. 1): all tokens from the raw text (including punctuation marks) get a lemma and a (disambiguated) morphological tag and they are linearly structured. Also, typos and similar errors are corrected here. As we can see in Fig. 1, there is a typo in the original sentence: the preposition *na* 'on' is not separated – as it should be – from the following noun *příkladu* 'example' and at the m-layer, a correction is realized.
- **analytical layer** (**a-layer**) capturing surface syntactic dependency structure in the shape of a tree with the specification of the head for each node and the assignment of a syntactic function (so-called *afun*) that denotes the relation between the dependent node and its head (e.g. subject (`Sb`),

[1] `https//ufal.mff.cuni.cz/pdt-c/documentation`

object (Obj), adverbial (Adv)). In the PDT-style surface syntactic annotation, every token from the raw text of a sentence (including punctuation marks – cf. nodes for comma (AuxX) and terminal symbol of the sentence (AuxK) in Fig. 1) is represented by a node of the tree and at the same time, no additional nodes are allowed. The linear ordering of nodes corresponds to the word order of the tokens in the sentence.

- **tectogrammatical layer (t-layer)** representing the deep syntactic structure. The deep syntactic relations are captured by the so-called *functors*; cf. the value PRED for predicate, ACT for actor, PAT for patient, COND for adverbial with condition meaning, etc. in Fig. 1. The tectogrammatical dependency structure of a sentence consists of nodes only for the content (lexical) words; function words such as prepositions, subordinating conjunctions, auxiliary verbs, etc. are not present as separate nodes, their contribution to the meaning of the sentence is captured within the complex labels of the content words. Thus, there is for example only one node for the prepositional phrase *na příkladu* 'on example' in the tectogrammatical tree in Fig. 1. The red arrows indicate the links between the nodes at the tectogrammatical layer and corresponding nodes at the analytical layer. At the tectogrammatical layer, new nodes are also established for semantic units deleted on the surface; in Fig. 1 the restoration of deletions is illustrated by the *#PersPron* nodes for the Actors of the predicates in the main and dependent clause.

  The green values t and f (in front of the functor values) stand for topic-focus articulation: t is for contextually bound nodes and f for contextually non-bound nodes. The ordering of nodes corresponds to the information structure of a sentence (cf. different position of pronouns *vám* 'you' and *to* 'it' at the analytical and tectogrammatical layer in Fig. 1.)

- The last box attached to the t-layer box in Fig. 1 indicates **additional annotations** such as textual coreference, bridging and discourse relations and other properties of the sentence such as genre specification, name entities which are technically also captured at the tectogrammatical layer of annotation. However, these phenomena are not a part of the tectogrammatical layer in the sense of the theoretical framework of Functional Generative Description. The additional annotation is exemplified here by the orange link between the predicates of the main and the dependent clause and is labelled as a discourse relation of condition, and by the blue coreferential link between the actor of the predicate *rozumět* 'understand' and the addressee of the predicate *vysvětlit* 'explain'.

In the paper, we use the data of the Prague Dependency Treebank (PDT) sub-corpus published within the consolidated release of the PDT-treebanks of Czech texts PDT-C 1.0 (Hajič et al., 2020),[2] and the Prague Czech-English Dependency Treebank PCEDT 2.0 (Hajič et al., 2012).[3] The whole Prague Dependency Treebank - Consolidated consists of over 2.2 million tokens, or 175 thousand sentences. The PDT sub-corpus consists of 675 thousand tokens, or 49 thousand sentences annotated at all annotation layers. The parallel corpus PCEDT sized over 1.2 million tokens in almost 50 thousand sentences for each part.
The corpora are encoded in the Prague Markup Language data format, PML (Pajas and Štěpánek, 2008), and the research was performed in the PML application framework: tree editor TrEd[4] for browsing and editing the PML data, btred for applying Perl scripts to the data and Prague Markup Language - Tree Query, PML-TQ (Pajas and Štěpánek, 2009), as a powerful graphically oriented query system.[5]

4. Annotation related aspects of a multilayer annotation scheme

A multilayer annotation scheme makes it possible to use relevant features of the existing annotation of a given layer to design a scheme for the annotation of other (not necessarily neighbouring) layers both conceptually and in a form of an automatic pre-annotation procedure (Sect. 4.1) or in a form of annotation checking rules (Sect. 4.2).

4.1. Automatic pre-annotation based on cross-layer relations

In the theoretical framework we subscribe to, information structure is considered to be a semantically relevant phenomenon and as such it should be represented at the layer of sentence meaning (tectogrammatical, in our terms). However, it has its reflection in the surface shape of the sentence, be it word order, prosody or similar means. This approach has led us to the idea to formulate and test a **pre-annotation module of information structure** in the PCEDT treebank assigning the features of contextual boundness (*t* for contextually bound nodes and *f* for contextually non-bound nodes) from which the global division of the sentence into its Topic and Focus can be derived based on several features present in the annotation of sentences on some of the lower layers (Mírovský et al., 2013). The pre-annotation procedure was able to mark over 40% of the text and the results of the application of such a pre-annotation procedure were evaluated face-to-face a sample of manually annotated sentences and the results were very encouraging: the average success rate was over 96%.

[2] https://ufal.mff.cuni.cz/pdt-c
[3] https://ufal.mff.cuni.cz/pcedt2.0/
[4] https://ufal.mff.cuni.cz/tred/
[5] http://ufal.mff.cuni.cz/pmltq

The benefits of tectogrammatical dependency structure used in the PDT for annotating language phenomena that cross the sentence boundary, namely coreference and bridging relations were also studied, described and applied by Nedoluzhko and Mírovský (2013). The authors use the detailed representation of deletions (important esp. in pro-drop languages), information on the deep syntactic relations (functors), and syntactic decisions for coordination and apposition structures at the tectogrammatical layer. These features make possible **to code basic coreference relations** in cases that are not so easy when annotating on the raw texts.

In distinction to methods based on raw texts, (Jínová et al., 2012a; Jínová et al., 2012b) formulated an automatic pre-annotation **procedure determining discourse relations, connectives and their arguments** directly on tectogrammatical trees, based on the assumption that certain syntactic features of a sentence analysis correspond to certain discourse-layer features. Hence, the authors looked for a possible analogy between intra-sentential syntactic relations already annotated in the corpus and intra-sentential discourse relations. An ideal case for the automatic detection based on tectogrammatical functors were those that directly correspond to some discourse type; this was the case e.g. of the functors of `REAS` (reason), `CSQ` (consequence), and `CAUS` (cause) all indicating the discourse relation reason-result; also the temporal functors were used as signals of a certain discourse relation. The scope of the discourse arguments was identified on the basis of the tectogrammatical tree structures. As a result, 9,991 tectogrammatical dependencies were converted into discourse relations, along with all properties of the relations (i.e. the position of arguments, the discourse type and the connective).

4.2. Automatic annotation checking rules based on cross-layer relations

Currently, the Prague team is in the process of extending the fully manual mid-layer syntax annotation to all parts of the PDT-C. To get a higher quality and a greater consistency of annotated data, a set of automatic checking procedures has been proposed and created in accordance with the annotation guidelines and incorporated into the annotation process to prevent the annotators from making accidental mistakes. When building the annotation rules, we also utilize the multilayer structure of PDT and use relevant information from the finished manual annotation of the lower morphological layer.

There are two main groups of rules which exploit the already established morphological tagging. The first group includes rules that take advantage of the fact that some surface syntactic functions (afuns) strictly correspond to the word-type of the word or token (part of speech (abbreviated POS), or type of punctuation), which is contained in the morphological tag of the corresponding node at the morphological layer, cf. the following examples:

- Prepositions are assigned afun `AuxP`: a node with the afun `AuxP` corresponds to a node with the tag for preposition at the morphological layer (the tag has the letter `R` in the first position).
- Subordinate conjunctions are assigned afun `AuxC`: a node with the afun `AuxC` corresponds to a node with the tag for subordinate conjunction at the morphological layer (the tag has the letters `J,` in the first two positions).
- Auxiliary verbs are assigned afun `AuxV`: a node with the afun `AuxV` corresponds to a node with the tag for verb at the morphological layer (the tag has the letter `V` in the first position).
- Punctuation marks are assigned afun `AuxX` (in case of comma), `AuxG` (in case of colon, slash, bracket, etc.), or `AuxK` (in case of final punctuation mark): a node with the afun `AuxX`, `AuxG` or `AuxK` corresponds to a node with the tag for a non-alphanumeric character at the morphological layer (the tag has the letter `Z` in the first position).

The second group of rules is based on the fact that dependency relations are defined with respect to the POS characteristics of the head node (e.g. attribute depends on a noun), see the following examples:

- Attribute (afun `Atr`) never depends on a verb, i.e. the corresponding node at the morphological layer does not have a tag for a verb (the tag with the letter `V` in the first position).
- Adverb (afun `Adv`) never depends on a noun, i.e. the corresponding node at the morphological layer does not have a tag for a noun (the tag with the letter `N` in the first position),
- Nominal part of a predicate (`Pnom`) depends on the verb *být* 'to be', i.e. the corresponding node at the morphological layer has the lemma *být*.

Annotators run the checking procedure after annotation of every single tree and consequently check and fix possible errors.[6] The experiment we performed at the beginning of the annotation project (Mikulová et al., 2022) showed that the control rules considerably contribute to the quality of the resulting annotation. Moreover, the rules formulated on the basis of current knowledge about language not only contribute to the improvement of annotation, but also point to insufficiently described phenomena and refine knowledge of language.

[6] A similar automatic linguistically-based (rule-formulated) checks have been used with advantage also in previous annotation projects (for example, the annotation at the tectogrammatical layer of PCEDT corpus; (Mikulová and Štěpánek, 2010)).

5. Corpus studies based on features across the layers

The possibility to base linguistic research on a corpus search on more than a single layer of annotation has led to a number of findings that take advantage of the multilayer annotation scheme in PDT-corpora to more accurately describe language phenomena. E.g., a valency dictionary of Czech (Urešová et al., 2021) is based on the relation between tectogrammatical, morphological and analytical annotation. It not only describes the participants of predicates, but also provides a detailed list of their formal realizations including surface syntactic structure. A lexicon of Czech discourse connectives (Mírovský et al., 2021) also draws on information from multiple layers. Similarly, a detailed description of the forms and functions of adverbials of place (Mikulová et al., 2017) and time (Panevová and Mikulová, 2020) exploit the cross-layer information of the adverbials. Different principles of annotation at the syntactic layers (see Sect. 3) are also an invaluable basis for examining the surface deletion (Hajičová et al., 2015). A monograph devoted to the syntax of Czech was also created on the basis of the PDT (Panevová et al., 2014).

A substantial part of the cross-layer studies examines the information structure and discourse structure in relation to the form of its expression at the analytical layer and at the tectogrammatical layer, also in comparison of Czech and English (in the PCEDT). There belongs e.g. our study on the variability of the position of adverbials of time and place in Czech and English word order and their function in the information structure of the sentence (Hajičová et al., 2019).

The annotation of Czech and English at the analytical and tectogrammatical layers has also allowed us to examine the morpho-syntactic properties of three representatives of the class of the so-called focalizers, namely *only*, *also* and *even*, and their word order position in English compared with Czech and their semantic scope vis-à-vis the information structure (Hajičová and Mírovský, prep).

The corpus served as a basis for another study of the contribution of expressions having the functor of focalizers at the tectogrammatical layer to the discourse structure as discourse connectors and for determination which kinds of discourse relations they indicate (Hajičová et al., 2020).

In the following two sections, we present two recent case studies as an illustration of the use of a multilayer annotation for a comprehensive description of a linguistic phenomenon performed on the data presented in Sect. 3. In the first study (Sect. 5.1), the syntactic annotations are used for a more precise part-of-speech determination of uninflected word types. Sect. 5.2 contains a comparative corpus study of Czech and English with regard to the relation between the analytical syntactic functions, the surface word order and the information structure as captured at the tectogrammatical layer.

5.1. Case study I: Distinguishing homonymous uninflected words

One of the traditional language phenomenon that combines morphological, syntactic and semantic features is the part of speech category (POS). In our study, we focussed primarily on uninflected word types and tried to show how sentence representation at the different layers can be useful for their better description, classification and annotation.

At the morphological layer, all tokens of a sentence are traditionally assigned the part of speech value within the morphological tag (e.g. `Dg` for adverbs forming negation and degrees of comparison, `Db` for the other adverbs, `J` for conjunctions, `R` for prepositions, `T` for particles). We are aware that from the strictly morphological point of view a subcategorization of uninflected words might be considered questionable because in case of uninflected words the morphological criterion is rather irrelevant; moreover, together with the frequent homonymy of these words such a subcategorization leads to issues concerning disambiguation. However, there are several practical reasons for POS tagging of uninflected words: The most important one is that the structure and also the content of the PDT-C morphological layer is unified with the MorfFlex - the Morphological Dictionary of Czech (Hajič et al., 2020b). MorfFlex, among other things, serves for tagging and lemmatization of other synchronic corpora of Czech, which have a one-layer structure and therefore the morphological tag is their main/only source of linguistic information.

Thanks to the fact that each syntactic layer of the PDT scheme captures different aspects of syntactic behaviour of a word, we postulated a hypothesis that the annotation of values of an afun (at the analytical layer) and of a functor (at the tectogrammatical layer) might be helpful in the disambiguation of homonymous uninflected words at the morphological layer.

We identified 12 types of homonymous uninflected POS combinations at the morphological layer. The most frequent are homonyms used as a preposition and an adverb (30 different words; e.g. *kolem*: *šel kolem domu* 'he walked *around* the house' (preposition) vs. *šel kolem* 'he walked *by*' (adverb)), then a non-graded adverb and a particle (25 words; e.g. *hned*: *přijď hned* 'come *immediately*' (adverb) vs. *hned ze dvou důvodů* '*even* for two reasons' (particle)), graded adverb and particle (14 words; e.g. *prostě*: *oblékl se prostě* 'he dressed *plainly*' (adverb) vs. *prostě to udělej* '*just* do it' (particle)), and a conjunction and a particle (11 words; e.g. *přece*: *prší, a přece šli* 'it's raining and *yet* they did go' (conjunction) vs. *tomu přece nevěříš* '*surely* you don't believe that' (particle)). Due to the lack of distinctive features, the most problematic are the words used as adverbs and particles, in contrast to prepositions and adverbs, which differ in the presence of a valency potential, or in contrast to particles and conjunctions, which usually differ in the position in a sentence.

Functor	Afun	Tag	Freq
RHEM	AuxZ	TT-------------	247
CM	AuxZ	TT-------------	63
CM	Apos	TT-------------	3
CM	Adv	TT-------------	1
ATT	AuxZ	TT-------------	1
RHEM	Adv	TT-------------	1

Table 1: Annotation of the homonymous particle *zejména* 'particularly' at the three layers of PDT

Functor	Afun	Tag	Freq
ATT	AuxY	Dg-------1A----	33
ATT	Adv	Dg-------1A----	18
ATT	AuxY	TT-------------	15
ATT	Adv	TT-------------	3
MANN	Adv	Dg-------1A----	3
ATT	AuxZ	Dg-------1A----	1

Table 2: Annotation of the homonymous particle *prostě* 'plainly, just, simply' at the three layers of PDT

At the analytical layer, particles are assigned the afun AuxY (for modifying words) or the afun AuxZ (for emphasizing words) and at the tectogrammatical layer, these words are assigned the functor RHEM or CM (for words with a rhematizing function), PREC (for words linking the sentence to its preceding context), MOD (for words expressing modality), and ATT (for words expressing attitude). Thus we expect that a co-occurrence of a "particle" afun and a "particle" functor with a single word in a text indicates also the particle value of the POS at the morphological layer (T). Cf. the results of annotation of a non-homonymous particle *zejména* 'particularly' in Tab. 1. We can observe that with the exception of two errors (the combination of "particle" functors RHEM or CM with "adverb" afun Adv), the tectogrammatical functor, analytical afun, and morphological tag are consistent.

As an example of homonymous particle annotation see the analysis of the words *prostě* and *hned*. The word *prostě* is understood as a graded adverb Dg (plainly) or a particle T (just). According to the annotated data, the frequency of the particle *prostě* is quite higher, there are only 3 examples of the adverb *prostě* in the annotated dataset (cf. Tab. 2). The combination of the tectogrammatical functor ATT (attitude) and the analytical afun AuxY (modifying word) seems to be annotated correctly (ex. (1)), as well as the combination of functor MANN (adverbial of manner) and afun Adv (adverbial) function (2).

(1) ATT+AuxY: Padělek chtěl mladík *prostě* vyměnit.
'The boy *just* wanted to exchange the fake.'

(2) MANN+Adv: Veronique, *prostě* oblečena, típla cigaretu.
'Veronique, *plainly* dressed, lit the cigarette.'

These two cases represent two main meanings of the word *prostě* (its particle and adverb function). However, in Tab. 2, we can observe that the POS annotation at the morphological layer is not consistent with the annotation at the syntactic layers. The combination of the functor ATT (attitude) and the afun Adv (adverbial) represents transitional cases (3); combination of functor ATT and afun AuxZ is a mistake made by an annotator at the analytical layer. (Mistakes of this kind should be detected using the automatic checking rules described above in Sect. 4.2.)

(3) ATT+Adv: Roku 1981 předvedla světu svůj první osobní počítač, nazvaný *prostě* IBM PC.
'In 1981, it introduced to the world first personal computer, called *simply/just* IBM PC.'

From this, we can deduce: if a word *prostě* is annotated at the syntactic layers by a combination of the functions ATT and AuxY, then the word *prostě* belongs to the POS of the particle (T) at the morphological layer; if a word *prostě* is annotated at the syntactic layers by a combination of functions MANN and Adv, then the word *prostě* belongs to the POS of the adverb (Dg) at the morphological layer.

Functor	Afun	Tag	Freq
RHEM	AuxZ	Db-------------	58
TWHEN	Adv	Db-------------	36
RHEM	Adv	Db-------------	13
TWHEN	AuxZ	Db-------------	9
RHEM	AuxZ	TT-------------	2

Table 3: Annotation of the homonymous word *hned* 'immediately, even' at the three layers of the PDT

Similarly, the word *hned* is considered an adverb Db with a temporal or spatial meaning (immediately, soon) and an emphasizing particle T (even, right). The PDT data show that in most cases there is a match between the assignment of the given functor and the assignment of the afun (cf. Tab. 3) with 60 matches of the particle combination of functor RHEM (rhematizer) and afun AuxZ (emphasizing word; (4)), and 36 matches of the combination of functor TWHEN (temporal adverbial answering the question "when?") and the afun Adv (adverbial; (5)). The other combinations point again to questionable cases.

(4) RHEM+AuxZ: Spolupráce pediatra s obchodníkem je výhodná *hned* z několika důvodů.
'The cooperation of a pediatrician with a businessman is beneficial *even* for several reasons.'

(5) TWHEN+Adv: Přináší blaho *hned*, hoře z něj později.
'It brings happiness *immediately*, grief later.'

The analysis of words *prostě* and *hned* shows that manual annotation at the two syntactic layers can be relevant for the tagging of the POS information at the morphological layer. While the annotation at the morphological layer appears to be quite inconsistent, in most cases there is an agreement in the annotation of functions at the syntactic layers. A minority of cases where there is no consistence between functions at the two syntactic layers points to a transitional area between the two possible POS values. In these cases, the determination of the POS is always questionable.

5.2. Case study II: Information structure and its expression in Czech and English

At present, our attention is focussed on a comparative corpus study of Czech and English with regard to the relation between the analytical syntactic functions, the surface word order and the information structure as captured at the tectogrammatical layer. It is commonly assumed by traditional comparative grammars of Czech and English (see e.g. Dušková et al. (1971) following up Mathesius (1947) pioneering observations) that if the information structure of sentences in Czech and English is to be preserved (which is a precondition consistent with the assumption of the semantic relevance of information structure we subscribe to), the grammatically fixed English word order (the preverbal position of subject, in our case) and the relatively free word order in Czech (the subject may principally occur in any word order position) makes it necessary to use some means other than word order to express information structure in English.

For our study, we used the part of the parallel English-Czech corpus PCEDT containing 267 documents with 4,826 sentences annotated also for information structure. We searched for Czech sentences in which the noun with the afun `Sb` (subject) at the analytical layer was placed after the governing predicate and at the tectogrammatical layer it was annotated as belonging to the Focus. There were 328 cases fulfilling these conditions. We then searched in the English part of the corpus for corresponding (i.e. aligned) English sentences and we have found 133 cases in which the noun corresponding to the subject in the search in the Czech part was also placed after the predicate though in any syntactic function and at the tectogrammatical layer annotated as belonging to the Focus.

Based on this search, we have found that there were three most frequent English constructions corresponding to the Czech subject in Focus: (i) the use of passive voice (6), (ii) the use of a *there*-construction (7), and (iii) the use of a different verb allowing for a change of the Czech subject into another analytical afun that can be placed in English after the predicate (8). In addition, our material has allowed us to identify some special contexts where the subject was placed after the verb in English. This was the case of structures in which the predicate is the verb *to be* ((9) and (10)).

(6) Most of the picture *is taken up* with endless *scenes* of many people.
Většinu filmu *zabírají* nekonečné *scény* velkého množství lidí.

(7) Moreover, *there have been* no *orders* for the Cray-3 so far.
Kromě toho *nepřišly* dosud na Cray-3 žádné *objednávky*.

(8) Besides Messrs. Cray and Barnum, other management at the company *includes* Neil Davenport.
Kromě pánů Craye a Barnuma *je* hlavní řídící pracovník ve společnosti Neil Davenport.

(9) Behind all the hoople *is* some heavy-duty competition.
Za vším tímto nadšením *je* velmi tvrdá soutěž.

(10) The one *character* at least somewhat interesting *was* Irving Louis *Lobsenz*.
Jednou alespoň trochu zajímavou *postavou je* Irving Louis *Lobsenz*.

It is important to note that besides these special contexts we have found no case in which the two languages would differ in the information structure with regard to the postverbal placement of the nominal subject in Czech at the analytical layer and its functioning as (a member of) Focus at the tectogrammatical layer.

The observation presented in this case study offers an additional support for our thesis that information structure is a semantically relevant phenomenon, which may be expressed on the surface structure of sentences by different means such as word order (esp. in the so-called free word order languages), prosody (the position of the intonation centre or the intonational contour), or special constructions (such as the particles *wa* and *ga* in Japanese, or the above mentioned *there*-construction in English). The nature and the extent of the use of these means depend largely on the type of language concerned.

6. Conclusion

In our contribution, we argue that a complex multi-layer annotation of a corpus provides an invaluable resource for both an in-depth study of different language phenomena in their relationships as well as for the automatic pre-annotation and checking procedures. We have supported these claims by several case studies based on the multilayer annotation scheme of the Prague Dependency Treebank.

This scheme is a hierarchical architecture of several annotation layers where units (tokens, nodes) at a lower layer are explicitly referred to from the corresponding higher layer. These links allow for tracing every unit of annotation all the way down to the original raw text. The annotation scheme was introduced at the end of the nineties of the last century, and to this day, the annotation scheme has proven to withstand the test of time: it can serve very well for complex annotations of discourse and coreference relations over whole texts, in which earlier morpho-syntactic annotations are advantageously used.

7. Acknowledgements

The research and language resources reported in the paper have been supported by the LINDAT/CLARIAH-CZ project funded by Ministry of Education, Youth and Sports of the Czech Republic (project LM2018101) and by the project No. GX20-16819X funded by the Grant Agency of the Czech Republic.

8. Bibliographical References

Bos, J., Basile, V., Evang, K., Venhuizen, N. J., and Bjerva, J. (2017). The Groningen Meaning Bank. In N. Ide et al., editors, *Handbook of linguistic annotation*, pages 463–496. Springer, Dordrecht.

Dušková, L., Caha, J., and Bubeníková, L. (1971). *Stručná mluvnice angličtiny [A concise grammar of English]*. Academia, Praha.

Hajič, J., Hajičová, E., Mikulová, M., and Mírovský, J. (2017). Prague Dependency Treebank. In N. Ide et al., editors, *Handbook of linguistic annotation*, pages 555–594. Springer, Dordrecht.

Hajič, J., Bejček, E., Hlaváčová, J., Mikulová, M., Straka, M., Štěpánek, J., and Štěpánková, B. (2020a). Prague Dependency Treebank - Consolidated 1.0. In *Proceedings of the 12th Language Resources and Evaluation Conference*, pages 5208–5218, Marseille, France, May. European Language Resources Association.

Hajič, J., Hlaváčová, J., Mikulová, M., Straka, M., and Štěpánková, B. (2020b). *MorfFlex CZ*. LINDAT/CLARIAH-CZ, Prague, URL: http://hdl.handle.net/11234/1-3186.

Hajič, J. (1998). Building a syntactically annotated corpus: The Prague Dependency Treebank. In E. Hajičová, editor, *Issues of Valency and Meaning. Studies in Honour of Jarmila Panevová*. Karolinum, Prague.

Hajičová, E. and Mírovský, J. (prep). Focalizers through the lens of a parallel english–czech corpus. a case study.

Hajičová, E., Mikulová, M., and Panevová, J. (2015). Reconstruction of deletions in a dependency-based description of czech: Selected issues. In Eva Hajičová et al., editors, *Proceedings of the Third International Conference on Dependency Linguistics (Depling 2015)*, pages 131–140, Uppsala, Sweden. Uppsala University, Uppsala University.

Hajičová, E., Mírovský, J., and Rysová, K. (2019). Ordering of adverbials of time and place in grammars and in an annotated english–czech parallel corpus. In *Proceedings of the 18th International Workshop on Treebanks and Linguistic Theories (TLT, SyntaxFest 2019)*, pages 51–60, Paris, France. Université Paris Sorbonne Nouvelle, Association for Computational Linguistics.

Hajičová, E., Mírovský, J., and Štěpánková, B. (2020). Focalizers and discourse relations. *The Prague Bulletin of Mathematical Linguistics*, (115):187–197.

Halliday, M. A. (1970). Language structure and language function. *New horizons in linguistics*, 1:140–165.

Hovy, E., Marcus, M., Palmer, M., Ramshaw, L., and Weischedel, R. (2006). Ontonotes: The 90% solution. In *Proceedings of the Human Language Technology Conference of the NAACL, Companion Volume: Short Papers*, pages 57–60. Association for Computational Linguistics, Stroudsburg.

Ide, N. and Romary, L. (2004). International standard for a linguistic annotation framework. *Natural Language Engineering*, 10(3-4):211–225.

Ide, N., Chiarcos, C., Stede, M., and Cassidy, S. (2017). Designing annotation schemes: From model to representation. In N. Ide et al., editors, *Handbook of linguistic annotation*, pages 73–111. Springer, Dordrecht.

Ide, N. (2017). Case study: The manually annotated sub-corpus. In N. Ide et al., editors, *Handbook of Linguistic Annotation*, pages 497–519. Springer, Dordrecht.

Jínová, P., Mírovský, J., and Poláková, L. (2012a). Analyzing the most common errors in the discourse annotation of the Prague Dependency Treebank. In *Proceedings of the 11th International Workshop on Treebanks and Linguistic Theories*, pages 127–132. Edicoes Colibri, Lisboa.

Jínová, P., Mírovský, J., and Poláková, L. (2012b). Semi-automatic annotation of intra-sentential discourse relations in PDT. In *Proceedings of the Workshop on Advances in Discourse Analysis and its Computational Aspects (ADACA) at Coling 2012*, pages 43–58. Coling 2012 Organizing Committee, Mumbai.

Kamp, H. and Reyle, U. (1993). Tense and aspect. In *From Discourse to Logic*, pages 483–689. Springer, Dordrecht.

Kamp, H. (1984). A theory of truth and semantic representation. In J. Groenendijk, et al., editors, *Truth, interpretation and information*, pages 1–41. Foris, Dordrecht.

Lamb, S. M. and Newell, L. E. (1966). *Outline of Stratificational Grammar: With an Appendix by LE Newell*. Georgetown University Press, Georgetown.

Mathesius, V., (1947). *Čeština a obecný jazykozpyt*, chapter O funkci podmětu [On the Function of Subject], pages 277–285. Melantrich, Praha.

Mel'chuk, I. A. (1988). *Dependency syntax: theory and practice*. SUNY press, New York.

Mikulová, M. and Štěpánek, J. (2010). Ways of evaluation of the annotators in building the Prague Czech-English Dependency Treebank. In *Proceedings of the 7th International Conference on Language Resources and Evaluation (LREC 2010)*, pages 1836–1839. European Language Resources Association, Valletta.

Mikulová, M., Bejček, E., Kolářová, V., and Panevová, J. (2017). Subcategorization of adverbial meanings based on corpus data. *Jazykovedný časopis / Journal of Linguistics*, 68(2):268–277.

Mikulová, M., Straka, M., Štěpánek, J., Štěpánková, B., and Hajič, J. (2022). Quality and efficiency of manual annotation: Pre-annotation bias. In *Proceedings of the 13th International Conference on Language Resources and Evaluation (LREC 2022)*. European Language Resources Association, Marseille.

Mille, S., Burga, A., and Wanner, L. (2013). AnCora-UPF: A multi-level annotation of Spanish. In *Proceedings of the Second International Conference on Dependency Linguistics (DepLing 2013)*, pages 217–226. Charles University, Prague.

Mírovský, J., Rysová, K., Rysová, M., and Hajičová, E. (2013). (Pre-)Annotation of Topic-Focus Articulation in Prague Czech-English Dependency Treebank. In *Proceedings of the 6th International Joint Conference on Natural Language Processing*, pages 55–63. Asian Federation of Natural Language Processing, Nagoya.

Mírovský, J., Synková, P., Poláková, L., Kloudová, V., and Rysová, M. (2021). *CzeDLex 1.0*. LINDAT/CLARIAH-CZ, Prague, URL: http://hdl.handle.net/11234/1-4595.

Nedoluzhko, A. and Mírovský, J. (2013). How dependency trees and tectogrammatics help annotating coreference and bridging relations in Prague Dependency Treebank. In *Proceedings of the Second International Conference on Dependency Linguistics, Depling 2013*, pages 244–251. Charles University, Prague.

Pajas, P. and Štěpánek, J. (2008). Recent Advances in a Feature-rich Framework for Treebank Annotation. In Donia Scott et al., editors, *Proceedings of the 22nd International Conference on Computational Linguistics*, pages 673–680, Manchester. The Coling 2008 Organizing Committee.

Pajas, P. and Štěpánek, J. (2009). System for Querying Syntactically Annotated Corpora. In *Proceedings of the ACL–IJCNLP 2009 Software Demonstrations*, pages 33–36, Suntec. Association for Computational Linguistics.

Panevová, J. and Mikulová, M. (2020). Subcategorization of adverbials (the case of temporal meanings). *Korpus – gramatika – axiologie*, (22):16–30.

Panevová, J., Hajičová, E., Kettnerová, V., Lopatková, M., Mikulová, M., and Ševčíková, M. (2014). *Mluvnice současné češtiny 2, Syntax na základě anotovaného korpusu*, volume 2. Karolinum, Praha.

Pradhan, S. and Ramshaw, L. (2017). Ontonotes: Large scale multi-layer, multi-lingual, distributed annotation. In N. Ide et al., editors, *Handbook of linguistic annotation*, pages 521–554. Springer, Dordrecht.

Saussure, F. d. (1916). *Cours de linguistique générale*. C. Bally and A. Sechehaye, with the collaboration of A. Riedlinger (eds.), Payot, Lausanne and Paris.

Sgall, P., Hajičová, E., and Panevová, J. (1986). *The Meaning of the Sentence and Its Semantic and Pragmatic Aspects*. Academia/Reidel Publishing Company, Prague/Dordrecht.

Sgall, P. (1967). *Generativní popis jazyka a česká deklinace*. Academia, Praha.

Silvano, P., Leal, A., Silva, F., Cantante, I., Oliveira, F., and Mario Jorge, A. (2021). Developing a multilayer semantic annotation scheme based on ISO standards for the visualization of a newswire corpus. In *Proceedings of the 17th Joint ACL - ISO Workshop on Interoperable Semantic Annotation*, pages 1–13. Association for Computational Linguistics, Groningen.

Steedman, M. (2001). *The Syntactic Process*. The MIT Press, Cambridge.

Urešová, Z., Bémová, A., Fučíková, E., Hajič, J., Kolářová, V., Mikulová, M., Pajas, P., Panevová, J., and Štěpánek, J. (2021). *PDT-Vallex: Valenční slovník češtiny propojený s korpusy 4.0*. LINDAT/CLARIAH-CZ, Charles University, Prague, URL: http://hdl.handle.net/11858/00-097C-0000-0015-8DAF-4.

Zeldes, A. (2017). The Gum corpus: Creating multilayer resources in the classroom. *Language Resources and Evaluation*, 51(3):581–612.

Zeldes, A. (2018). *Multilayer corpus studies*. Routledge, New York and London.

9. Language Resource References

Hajič, J. and Bejček, E. and Bémová, A. and Buráňová, E. and Fučíková, E. and Hajičová, E. and Havelka, J. and Hlaváčová, J. and Homola, P. and Ircing, P. and Kárník, J. and Kettnerová, V. and Klyueva, N. and Kolářová, V. and Kučová, L. and Lopatková, M. and Mareček, D. and Mikulová, M. and Mírovský, J. and Nedoluzhko, A. and Novák, M. and Pajas, P. and Panevová, J. and Peterek, N. and Poláková, L. and Popel, M. and Popelka, J. and Romportl, J. and Rysová, M. and Semecký, J. and Sgall, P. and Spoustová, J. and Straka, M. and Straňák, P. and Synková, P. and Ševčíková, M. and Šindlerová, J. and Štěpánek, J. and Štěpánková, B. and Toman, J. and Urešová, Z. and Vidová Hladká, B. and Zeman, D. and Zikánová, Š. and Žabokrtský, Z. (2020). *Prague Dependency Treebank - Consolidated 1.0 (PDT-C 1.0)*. LINDAT/CLARIAH-CZ digital library, Charles University, Prague, http://hdl.handle.net/11234/1-3185.

Hajič, J. and Hajičová, E. and Panevová, J. and Sgall, P. and Cinková, S. and Fučíková, E. and Mikulová, M. and Pajas, P. and Popelka, J. and Semecký, J. and Šindlerová, J. and Štěpánek, J. and Toman, J. and Urešová, Z. and Žabokrtský, Z. (2012). *Prague Czech-English Dependency Treebank 2.0*. LINDAT/CLARIAH-CZ digital library, Charles University, Prague, http://hdl.handle.net/11858/00-097C-0000-0015-8DAF-4.

Proceedings of the 16th Linguistic Annotation Workshop (LAW-XVI) @LREC 2022, pages 79–84
Marseille, 24 June 2022

Introducing StarDust: A UD-based Dependency Annotation Tool

Arife Betül Yenice♡, Neslihan Cesur♡, Aslı Kuzgun♡, Olcay Taner Yıldız◇
Starlang Yazılım Danışmanlık♡, Özyeğin University◇
Istanbul, Turkey
{arife, neslihan, asli}@starlangyazilim.com, olcay.yildiz@ozyegin.edu.tr

Abstract

This paper aims to introduce StarDust, a new, open-source annotation tool designed for NLP studies. StarDust is designed specifically to be intuitive and simple for the annotators while also supporting the annotation of multiple languages with different morphological typologies, e.g. Turkish and English. This demonstration will mainly focus on our UD-based annotation tool for dependency syntax. Linked to a morphological analyzer, the tool can detect certain annotator mistakes and limit undesired dependency relations as well as offering annotators a quick and effective annotation process thanks to its new simple interface. Our tool can be downloaded from the Github.

Keywords: Dependency parsing, Annotation tool, Turkish

1. Introduction

With recent developments in Natural Language Processing (NLP) studies and tools such as parsers, the demand for datasets is constantly increasing. The quality of these corpora, which are used to train and evaluate parsers, mostly lies in an efficient annotation process. User-friendly and effective annotation tools enable human annotators to have a better and easier experience.
Our aim in creating StarDust is to develop a simple and easy-to-learn interface, which can be used by anyone with minimal instruction and regardless of prior experience. Our interface offers a multi-layered structure with many different tools for different purposes. These include tools for semantic and morphological analysis, dependency annotation and verb frame annotation.We also seek to minimize annotator errors and increase inter-annotator agreement by embedding the rules of Universal Dependencies (UD) (Nivre et al., 2016) annotation scheme as a restriction for possible head-dependent relations. In this paper we will firstly introduce related work and our motivation for a new tool and elaborate on the features of our interface and how it is used. Then, we will briefly talk about its implementation and some technical details. Finally, we will refer to the treebanks annotated using this tool.

2. Related Work and Motivation

There are currently several annotation tools for dependency annotation, all of which promise different advantages for different tasks. Before introducing StarDust, it is useful to give an overview of some of these tools and explain why they did not suffice to use for our goals personally. The one which is used for the UD documentation system is BRAT (Stenetorp et al., 2012), which is a web-based tool that requires user log in to do annotations. It has a good range of features; however, it was not ideal for us to opt for a web-based tool and it does not support word tokenization. The most recent one is Palmyra (Habash and D.Taji, 2020). It is suitable for morphologically rich languages and its ability to annotate various linguistic features are attractive. However, its dependency tree representation is not ideal for our purposes. Other annotation tools include Prodigy (Montani and Honnibal, 2018) which is a great tool for those who are experienced in the field and it is a desktop tool which is what we desire; however our aim in creating a new tool was to provide a beginner friendly, easy annotation process, therefore it did not suit our needs. ConlluEditor (Heinecke, 2019), WebAnno (de Castilho et al., 2016) , UD Annotatrix (Tyers et al., 2017), and Arborator (Gerdes, 2013) are some of the other tools used for annotations. WebAnno, UD Annotatrix and Arborator permit collaborative work and they are web-based tools. A full list of tools can be found on UD's website. [1] For the functions we needed and our desire for simplicity, we needed another tool.
We need an annotation tool that is both multifaceted and user-friendly for precise annotations in languages of different typologies such as Turkish, an agglutinative language with rich morphology and free word order. For this reason, we present StarDust, an open source annotation tool that aims to simplify the main editing window while only keeping the main information such as POS-tags and dependency relations. In doing so, we still made sure to offer some crucial functions such as editing and deleting tokens, finding and grouping tokens based on their initializer tags, and preventing invalid tags or tree structures. We have opted for a linear representation of the sentences instead of using tree representations to make the annotation more intuitive for inexperienced or first-time annotators. By linking a semi-automatic disambiguation tool to our dependency annotator, we wanted to make sure that human annotators can immediately correct the morphological analysis of tokens. Overall, this has increased the accuracy of the annotations and reduced the time spent for cor-

[1] `https://universaldependencies.org/tools.html`

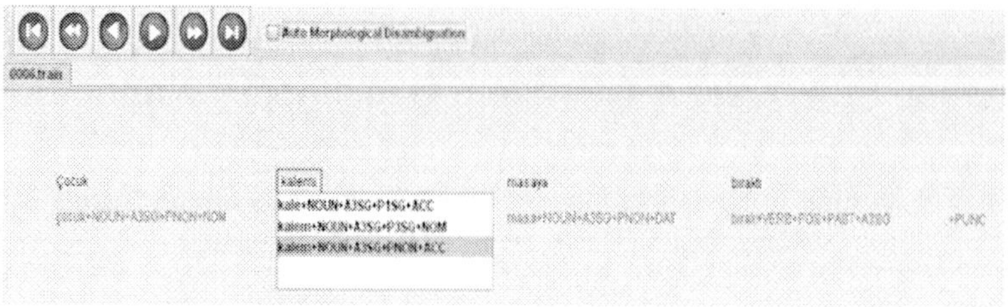

Figure 1: A screenshot of the StarDust's morphological disambiguation layer

rection considerably. StarDust is efficient in annotating compounding languages like English as well as morphologically rich languages like Turkish. It can also be adapted to annotate other languages, if there is a morphological analyzer for the language we can intergrate.

3. Features

StarDust is a desktop annotation tool which can be used offline. To keep the interface clean, we have opted for a linear representation and used a layered architecture where only two layers are necessary for dependency annotation purposes. Nonetheless, extra layers could be implemented for more in-depth annotations. For dependency annotations, the first layer of the tool is for the morphological disambiguation layer and the second layer is dependency annotation layer .

The annotators navigate between layers freely during the annotation process while keeping both layers uncluttered yet functional. Even though morphological features cannot be edited in dependency annotation layer, switching back to morphological disambiguation layer to fix the errors is possible. This prevents any errors from accumulating and yield higher accuracy in annotations. Opting for a desktop tool rather than a web based tool comes with a few challenges such as collaboration issues and ensuring inter-annotator agreement. These can be easily overcome if the annotators are working online. They can easily see other annotators working on the data and check with their annotations. However, when working offline, the annotator can only see the last synchronised version, which can still be helpful with their decisions but it would require them to check their annotations when everything is synchronised. In the future versions, we can optimize it for web platforms to make collaborative work easier.

Changes are saved automatically for each token; however, the change history can be seen in Dropbox and the token can be reverted back to its original form. This might be useful for those who wish to see the original token for any reason. A change history feature that is internal to the tool might be added in the future. If there are changes made to a specific word form - POS tag combination at any level, you can go back to morphological analyzer and list all the annotations from View Annotations tab (See Figure 2) to apply the changes to all of the same word form - POS Tag combination in the dataset consistently. The features of both layers will be demonstrated in the following sections.

4. Pos Tagging

Typically, the burden of annotating each word, its root, its features, and its POS-tag and falls on the dependency annotator. Thanks to our multi-layered interface, all this information is provided by the morphological analyzer. All words are parsed automatically, and to enable alternations, all possible features that might constitute their internal morphology are listed for annotators to choose from. It uses a rule-based method to parse the words and their features.

Figure 1 shows a screenshot of our interface. The automatic annotation checkbox on the top of the program automatically parses the word in all possible derivations. The annotators can also select the relevant derivation manually. This configuration leads to a consistent annotation for the morphological analyses and saves time. For the morphological annotation, our current editor makes use of the format introduced by (Oflazer, 1994). However, we are working on converting this format into the CoNLL-U format. Each sentence is stored as a different file, therefore, the annotators can work on different files simultaneously. The arrows on the control panel allows the annotators to go back and forth between files in different distances.

Our morphological analyzer tool is suited for the analysis of languages with different morphological typologies such as English, an analytic language, and Turkish, an agglutinative language. Agglutinative languages need more in-depth analyses in morphology for dependency parsing because the grammar of such languages is encoded at the word level rather than at sentence level. Also, in agglutinating derivation systems the same word forms can have multiple different meanings depending on their internal morphology. Previous dependency tools developed for agglutinative languages such as Hungarian and Turkish address this fact (Zsibrita et al., 2013); (Türk et al., 2020). At this layer of StarDust, morphological disambiguation for Turkish and Pos tagging for English are automatically derived.

4.1. Turkish Morphological Disambiguation

Due to its high reliance on affixation, Turkish word forms bear great complexity; thus, Turkish morphology needs to be analyzed and disambiguated before

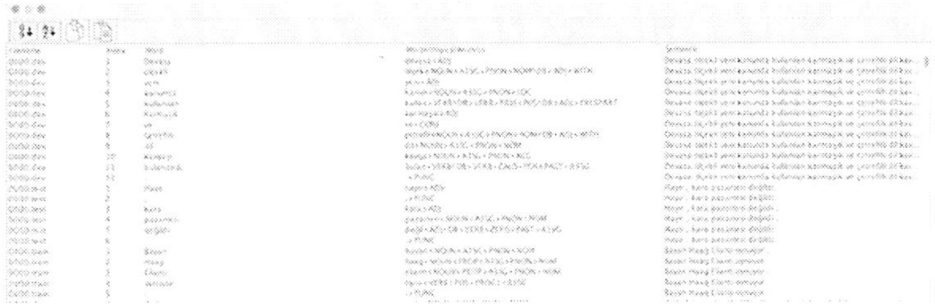

Figure 2: Viewing All Annotations in Morphological Analyzer

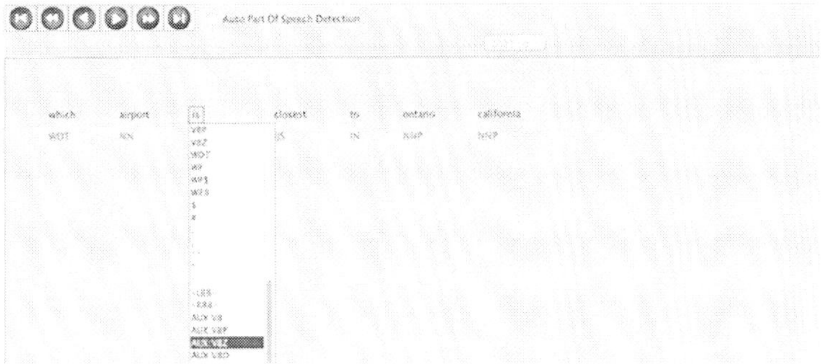

Figure 3: A screenshot of the StarDust's Pos-tagging layer for English

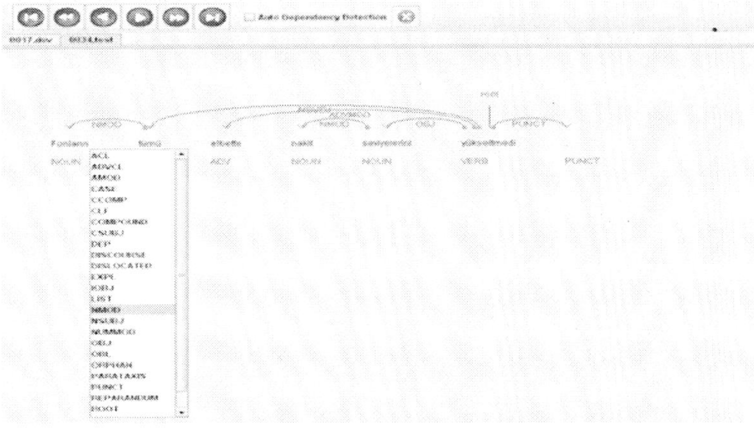

Figure 4: Dependency Layer of StarDust's Interface

dependency relations can be established. Our method for automatic annotation of words finds the roots of the words and annotates their POS-tags and features. For each word, it takes the word with its annotation layers and sets the corresponding morphological layers. For each annotation layer, the method divides the layers and derives all possible internal morphologies layer by layer. If the language is Turkish, it directly calls Universal Dependency POS tags of the parse. Next, it returns the features of the Universal Dependency relations of the word. For instance all possible derivations of "kalemi" are shown in Figure 1. As can be seen, the internal morphology of Turkish is so complicated that one word form with minimal affixation can have three different meanings encoded in it, and our method can derive them automatically and successfully.

4.2. English Pos Tagging

English is an analytical language; therefore, internal morphologies of the words in English are simpler. English mostly depends on functional words instead of multiple suffixes on words. Thus, our method follows different rules for English words. Our method takes the word and returns its annotation layers and sets corresponding layers. When setting the dependency layer of the word, If the language is English, it returns Universal Dependency POS tags based on the Penn tag of the word from Penn Treebank Project. For instance, if the Penn tag of the word is "VB", "VBD" or "VBN", it returns the POS tag "VERB". There is not always a one-to-one mapping between POS tags and Penn tags, in these cases, extended versions of POS tags are used. Then, it returns the features of the UD relations of the word. After this, dependency features are established based on the Penn tag of the word (Figure 3)

5. The Dependency Annotation Layer

The front-end of our dependency editor helps the annotators to visualize the head-dependent relationships between the words. Its simplistic structure has enabled some untrained annotators to make annotations by only watching basic annotation videos [2] created by our team. Figure 4 shows our interface. The buttons on the top left corner in here make it possible to browse the data by skipping different amounts of files. The most embedded arrows skip one file, the two headed arrows skip 10 files, and the ones with a vertical stroke skip 100 files at once. Each word token has its POS tag shown below. This information comes from the previous layer. The annotators click on a word and drag the cursor from the dependent to its head. Upon this, a box pops up displaying all possible dependency tags between those two words based on the UD annotation framework. Possible dependency tags are listed for annotators to choose according to the frequency rate of their use with the chosen dependent and head. Another feature is displaying examples for each dependency tag listed. (See Figure 5) When the annotator holds the cursor on the tag, a few example sentences highlighting the words between which the tag is used appear. These features are available for both Turkish and English tags. Once the relevant dependency tag is chosen, the relation is shown with arrows. The little circle on the tail of the arrow marks the head word of the constituent while the head of the arrow indicates the dependent word. The Automatic Dependency Annotation checkbox automatically annotates some certain structures by using the information that comes from the previous layer. In the most basic two layered structure, nominal modifiers, punctuations, and the root nodes can be annotated automatically with the information provided from the morphological analyzer. It is possible to edit the word tokens during the annotation. Ctrl+click to the word token enables the annotators to edit or delete the words individually. Whenever a change is made for a token during the dependency annotation, the changed token is also updated on the other levels of the editor. However, the annotator should make sure to check and if needed update the morphological analysis of the token. Since the tool was designed to be used with a translated corpus, the annotators are able to see the original sentence that corresponds to the sentence being annotated as represented in the bottom left corner of the Figure 4 . StarDust allows the users to see all the annotations sorted as in Figure 7. The annotations can be sorted according to the alphabetical order of the word tokens, or they can be sorted according to the number of the data types. This function mainly helps the annotators to check the annotations. Another feature of the StarDust is the error warnings. It has been mentioned that this editor is designed for UD style annotations. The editor prevents the annotators from doing any annotation that conflicts with the UD annotation framework by giving an error as shown in Figure 6. In Figure 6 the black cautions shows the earlier mistakes made in the annotation by stating which node causes the error.

6. Implementation

Our tool is compatible with all platforms on Desktop (Windows, OS, Linux) with its implementation in Java. We have not opted for a browser-based system to ensure that annotators can work offline, when needed. For the projects which were carried out so far, the edited files and .jar editors were all kept in Dropbox, ensuring immediate synchronization of the data. The back-end is supported in many other languages such as Python, Cython, C#, Swift, Javascript, and C++. The back-end of the morphological analyzer has been discussed briefly in Section 4. Our morphological analyzer follows different methods for Turkish and English. It creates the roots, the features and POS tags of each token following from rules written specific for the specific language. There are rules and methods for the morphological analysis; for example, methods for possesives, plurality etc. For inter-annotator agreement and gold standard annotations, we implemented rule-based methods of restrictions and controls that are independent of the language and follow rules of Universal Dependencies (UD). These controls can check the dependency relations and rule out the impossible ones.

The front-end is currently only available in Java but it can be adapted to any desired language. Before dependency annotations are done, all other annotated layers are stored on each token within a .txt file. Each text file contains one sentence or phrase. In order to store dependency annotations, these .txt files are processed by Annotated Sentence Library and transformed into CoNLL-u format. This library also contains information from Turkish WordNet and FrameNet, which can provide automatic annotation for certain compounds.

7. Annotated Corpora

So far, our tool has been used in five different Turkish Treebanks, and one English Treebank project. The annotated sentences of the Turkish FrameNet Project are already available on Github.[3] **English Atis** : This treebank is taken from English ATIS corpus[4]. It con-

[2]The videos are available here (in Turkish): `https://tinyurl.com/y2jq5lrw`

[3]`https://github.com/UniversalDependencies/UD_Turkish-FrameNet`

[4]`https://github.com/howl-anderson/ATIS_dataset/blob/master/README.en-US.md`

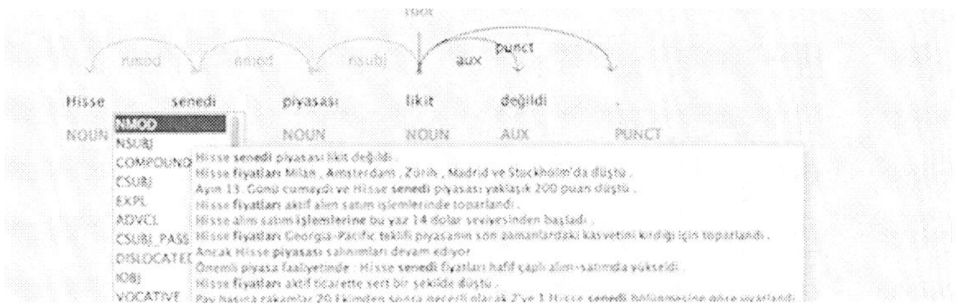

Figure 5: Example sentences feature in dependency layer

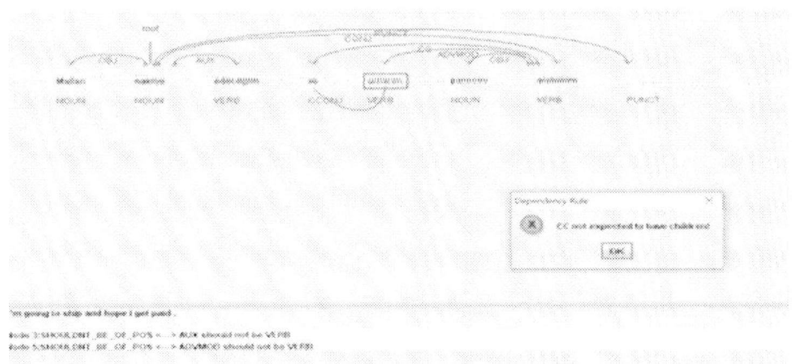

Figure 6: UD-based errors and limitations

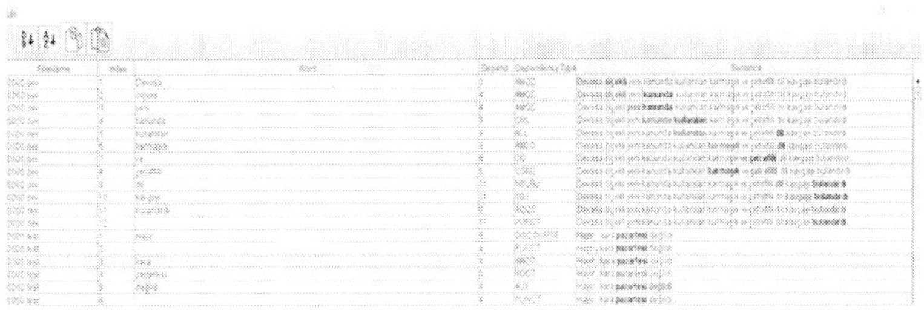

Figure 7: Show Annotations feature of dependency layer

sists of 5,432 sentences[5]. **Turkish Atis** : This treebank is a translation of English ATIS corpus. It consists of 5,432 sentences[6]. **Turkish FrameNet Project**: In this project, about 2,500 example sentences were manually annotated with the help of our annotation tool (Marsan et al., 2021). **Turkish WordNet** : This project contains 18,700 example sentences from the Turkish Wordnet (Bakay et al., 2021). **Turkish Penn TreeBank** : The Turkish version of Penn Treebank (Kuzgun et al., 2020) includes the translation of 17,000 sentences retrieved from the original Penn Treebank (Marcus et al., 1993). **Tourism** : This is a domain-specific corpus that contains around 20,000 sentences. (Arıcan et al., 2021).

[5]https://github.com/UniversalDependencies/UD_English-Atis

[6]https://github.com/UniversalDependencies/UD_Turkish-Atis

8. Conclusion and Future Work

Overall, the convenience of our annotation tool lies in its approachable interface with the basic functions. Its easy-to-learn and easy-to-use interface makes it usable by anyone without lengthy instructions or learning periods. The tool could be improved by embedding the morphological layer into the dependency annotator to facilitate any necessary changes in POS tags, without navigating back to morphological analyzer. Currently, any mistake done during the annotation process can be arranged simply by rearranging the arrows. So far, there has been no reported problems about this but an "undo" button could also be implemented in the future. For more feedback from the annotators, we plan to conduct user studies in the future. Moreover, even though we have used a linear representation for the sentences to make the annotation more intuitive, an option to view the sentences as tree representations could be added. This would allow different annotators with different preferences to choose the view that suits them.

9. Bibliographical References

Arıcan, B. N., Ozçelik, M., Aslan, D. B., Sarmıs, E., Parlar, S., and Yıldız, O. T. (2021). Creating domain dependent turkish wordnet and sentinet.

Bakay, O., Ergelen, O., Sarmis, E., Yildirim, S., Kocabalcioglu, A., Arican, B., Ozcelik, M., Saniyar, E., Kuyrukcu, O., Avar, B., et al. (2021). Turkish wordnet kenet. In *Proceedings of GWC 2021*.

de Castilho, R. E., Mujdricza-Maydt, E., Yimam, S. M., Hartmann, S., Gurevych, I., Frank, A., and Biemann, C. (2016). A web-based tool for the integrated annotation of semantic and syntactic structures. In *Proceedings of the Workshop on Language Technology Resources and Tools for Digital Humanities (LT4DH)*, pages 76–84.

Gerdes, K. (2013). Collaborative dependency annotation. In *Proceedings of the second international conference on dependency linguistics (DepLing 2013)*, pages 88–97.

Habash, N. and D.Taji. (2020). Palmyra 2.0: A configurable multilingual platform independent tool for morphology and syntax annotation. In *In Proceedings of Universal Dependencies Workshop (UDW) 2020*.

Heinecke, J. (2019). Conllueditor: a fully graphical editor for universal dependencies treebank files. In *Proceedings of the Third Workshop on Universal Dependencies (UDW, SyntaxFest 2019)*, pages 87–93.

Kuzgun, A., Cesur, N., Arıcan, B. N., Özçelik, M., Marşan, B., Kara, N., Aslan, D. B., and Yıldız, O. T. (2020). On building the largest and cross-linguistic turkish dependency corpus. In *2020 Innovations in Intelligent Systems and Applications Conference (ASYU)*, pages 1–6. IEEE.

Marcus, M., Santorini, B., and Marcinkiewicz, M. A. (1993). Building a large annotated corpus of english: The penn treebank.

Marsan, B., Kara, N., Ozcelik, M., Arican, B. N., Cesur, N., Kuzgun, A., Saniyar, E., Kuyrukcu, O., and Yıldız, O. T. (2021). Building the Turkish FrameNet. In *Proceedings of GWC 2021*.

Montani, I. and Honnibal, M. (2018). Prodigy:a new annotation tool for radically efficient machineteaching. Artificial Intelligence.

Nivre, J., De Marneffe, M.-C., Ginter, F., Goldberg, Y., Hajic, J., Manning, C. D., McDonald, R., Petrov, S., Pyysalo, S., Silveira, N., et al. (2016). Universal dependencies v1: A multilingual treebank collection. In *Proceedings of the Tenth International Conference on Language Resources and Evaluation (LREC'16)*, pages 1659–1666.

Oflazer, K. (1994). Two-level description of turkish morphology. *Literary and linguistic computing*, 9(2):137–148.

Stenetorp, P., Pyysalo, S., Topić, G., Ohta, T., Ananiadou, S., and Tsujii, J. (2012). Brat: a web-based tool for nlp-assisted text annotation. In *Proceedings of the Demonstrations at the 13th Conference of the European Chapter of the Association for Computational Linguistics*, pages 102–107.

Türk, U., Atmaca, F., Özateş, Ş. B., Berk, G., Bedir, S. T., Köksal, A., Başaran, B. Ö., Güngör, T., and Özgür, A. (2020). Resources for turkish dependency parsing: Introducing the boun treebank and the boat annotation tool. *arXiv preprint arXiv:2002.10416*.

Tyers, F., Sheyanova, M., and Washington, J. (2017). Ud annotatrix: An annotation tool for universal dependencies. In *Proceedings of the 16th International Workshop on Treebanks and Linguistic Theories*, pages 10–17.

Zsibrita, J., Vincze, V., and Farkas, R. (2013). magyarlanc: A tool for morphological and dependency parsing of hungarian. In *Proceedings of the International Conference Recent Advances in Natural Language Processing RANLP 2013*, pages 763–771.

Proceedings of the 16th Linguistic Annotation Workshop (LAW-XVI) @LREC 2022, pages 85–90
Marseille, 24 June 2022

Annotation of Messages from Social Media for Influencer Detection

Kévin Deturck, Damien Nouvel, Namrata Patel, Frédérique Segond
Inalco Ertim, Inalco Ertim, Université Montpellier 3, Inria Minatec – Inalco Ertim
2 r. de Lille 75007 Paris, 2 r. de Lille 75007 Paris, Rte de Mende 34090 Montpellier, 17 av. des Martyrs 38000 Grenoble
{kevin.deturck, damien.nouvel, frederique.segond}@inalco.fr
namrata.patel@univ-montp3.fr

Abstract

To develop an influencer detection system, we designed an influence model based on the analysis of conversations in the "Change My View" debate forum. This led us to identify enunciative features (argumentation, emotion expression, view change, ...) related to influence between participants. In this paper, we present the annotation campaign we conducted to build up a reference corpus on these enunciative features. The annotation task was to identify in social media posts the text segments that corresponded to each enunciative feature. The posts to be annotated were extracted from two social media: the "Change My View" debate forum, with discussions on various topics, and Twitter, with posts from users identified as supporters of ISIS (Islamic State of Iraq and Syria). Over a thousand posts have been double or triple annotated throughout five annotation sessions gathering a total of 27 annotators. Some of the sessions involved the same annotators, which allowed us to analyse the evolution of their annotation work. Most of the sessions resulted in a reconciliation phase between the annotators, allowing for discussion and iterative improvement of the guidelines. We measured and analysed inter-annotator agreements over the course of the sessions, which allowed us to validate our iterative approach.

Keywords: annotation, influencer, social media

1. Introduction

1.1 Research problem: influencer detection

An influencer is defined in sociology as a person having the power to change peoples' views or behaviour simply by interacting with them (Katz and Lazarsfeld, 2017). Social psychology analyses such an impact by describing interpersonal interactions as a set of stimuli that can lead to a psychological change in everyone involved (Turner and Oakes, 1986). We define the process of influence by interactions initiated by an influencer, leading to the production of new opinions or actions among the targeted individuals.

Recent years have seen an increasing interest in influencer detection as it helps identify key users within a large inter-personal network. Influential users are likely to express their ideas with a greater impact than other individuals, as seen in political (Katz, 1957), commercial (Trusov et al., 2010) or terrorist recruitment contexts (Fernandez et al., 2018).

Interpersonal interactions being the vehicle of influence, we choose social media as a ripe field of observation as they are inherent to its very structure. The development of social media has boosted research on many issues pertaining to artificial intelligence and its impact on society; the detection of influence being one of them.

1.2 Annotation requirements: development of an influencer detection system

Our study is centred around an influence model designed to characterise the process of influence (Deturck, 2021). As computational linguists, we follow our predisposition to analyse the textual content of conversations. Our goal is to detect the linguistic markers of influence we identified by analysing conversations in the "Change My View" debate forum[1]. The markers reflect the specific discourse of both (1) the influencers, initiating the influence process, and (2) the individuals reacting to the influencers.

To develop an influencer detection system based on our model, we needed reference data to (1) develop linguistic rules, train models by learning and (2) evaluate the different modules of the system. As our model features original linguistic markers, we had to produce the corresponding reference data by supervising human annotators through successive annotation sessions.

Our annotation task corresponds to the *unitizing* type (Krippendorff, 1995). A unitizing annotation consists in extracting units by segmenting a text and categorizing the resulting segments. In our case, it is a matter of identifying, in social media messages, the text segments that correspond to one of our linguistic markers of influence.

The task is particularly difficult because annotators must identify both the relevant text boundaries and the corresponding category. In addition to that, the text segments are not necessary nor usually on sentence boundaries, they can be sub-sentence or super-sentence level spans.

The annotation task is also particularly difficult because it requires the identification of linguistic markers which involve interpretation of statements: on the one hand, each annotator must manage to do this interpretation work, which is complex, and, on the other hand, we must achieve consistent annotation across through the interpretations of the different annotators to build a reference corpus.

The rest of the article is organised as follows: in section 2 we introduce our influence model, in section 3 we present the annotation schema, in section 4 we describe the data, in section 5, we present and analyse the results of the annotation campaign, then we conclude in section 7.

[1] https://www.reddit.com/r/changemyview/

2. Influence Model

The model we present in this section is in line with works in social psychology, such as the one by Mason et al. (2007), and communication science, for example the one by Dillard and Wilson (2014). It describes influence as a process with source individuals impacting the minds of target individuals through the exchange of messages.

Our model contains three components: the *stimulus* and *stimulation* components correspond to a theoretical framework in social psychology, described by Turner and Oakes (1986), which gives an individual's social environment as a carrier of *stimuli* that can *stimulate* (or modify) the psychological state of the individuals in it. The *decision* component relates to the decision-making process, particularly studied in social psychology, as in the work by Ajzen (1996); the impact on decision-making is the conclusion of the influence process in our model.

3. Annotation Schema

3.1 *Stimulus* Linguistic Markers

3.1.1 Claim

A claim is a type of expression by which an individual delivers a description as factual, i.e. an assertion of what is allegedly a fact in the world (Saurí and Pustejovsky, 2012). A claim can be factual only in appearance, i.e. it can make a concrete description with certainty without it being true.

Example: "*#ISIS has showered Ayn al-Asad airbase*", in a tweet from the "pro-Islamic State" dataset used for the annotation campaign (cf. section 4.1).

3.1.2 Pedagogy

The linguistic marker *Pedagogy* is the statement of an individual who guides other individuals in their understanding of the world or their behaviour in the world. This type of discourse is based on advices and explanations. Pedagogy had already been identified by Dillard and Wilson (2014) as having a link to influence.

Example: "*Turn it off so they can stay in the darkness of their misguidance.*", in a tweet from the "pro-Islamic State" dataset.

3.1.3 Argumentation

Argumentation is a type of discourse that consists of supporting the truthfulness of a statement with one or more logically articulated arguments (Eckle-Kohler et al., 2015). Example: "*It appears that ISIS are the best diplomats on Earth since they work for Iran, America, Turkey, Saudi and Israel*", from the "pro-Islamic State" dataset used for the annotation campaign (cf. section 4.1).

3.2 *Stimulation* Linguistic Markers

3.2.1 Understanding

Understanding is manifested in the discourse of an individual reporting on the reasoning they have managed to produce through a message. This type of expression links to research in social psychology which considers the process of understanding a message as an important factor for the impact of communication (Wyer and Shrum, 2015).

Example: "*Yours was the first comment to make me understand how changing the definition would render the word useless*", a participant in the "Change My View" forum

3.2.2 Information

Information acquisition appears in any utterance where the enunciator indicates receiving new information. Information acquisition corresponds to a stimulation of the intellect (Hidi and Baird, 1986).

Example: "*I realised that i was misinformed when it came to Duty to Retreat laws*", a participant in the "Change My View" forum

3.2.3 Affectation

Any reaction relating the experience of a feeling or emotion by the enunciator, in relation to the enunciation situation. The influence of affect on decision making is a research topic (Binali et al., 2010).

Example: "*You gave me some hope for the oils*", a participant in the "Change My View" forum

3.2.4 Agreement

An utterance in which the speaker posits an equivalence between his or her viewpoint or actions and the viewpoint or actions of others, to whatever degree. Agreement is studied in relation to individuals' decision making (Germesin and Wilson, 2009).

Example: "*I do agree that the left has similar issues*", a participant in the "Change My View" forum

3.3 *Decision* Linguistic Marker: Change of Mind

Change of mind is the purpose of an influencing action in the "Change My View" forum. We identify the expression of a change of mind with any statement in which the speaker indicates a questioning or evolution of his or her opinion, to whatever degree.

Example: "*I won't continue with the position I stated I'm my last comment*", a participant in the "Change My View" forum

4. Methodology

4.1 Material

An annotation guide was designed to drive and facilitate the annotation process. It is a 24-page PDF document that provides definitions supplemented with examples and counter-examples for each of the markers (Deturck, 2021). This document was revised after each annotation session, based on post-annotation meetings between and with the annotators, to iteratively refine the marker definitions, an *agile* corpus annotation (Voormann and Gut, 2008).

For the variety of our reference corpus, we used two complementary data sources in English: the "Change My View" debate forum, in which the authors must elaborate on their views, and a corpus of tweets, constrained to a limited number of characters, posted by individuals categorized as supporters of the "Islamic State of Iraq and

Syria" (ISIS) organisation[2]; we used the latter only for the *stimuli* markers as it was not designed to provide reactions to the pro-ISIS' tweets.

We partitioned the data to distribute it among annotator groups and thus maximise the quantity of messages annotated during a session by including several groups. To simplify the annotation and thus promote its quality, we made sure that each dataset contains only one kind of message ("Change My View" or Twitter).

We sized each dataset so that it could be processed by a single annotator in a maximum of two hours, which is the duration imposed for session. We empirically estimated the annotation time for a single message according to its textual genre (a tweet or a forum post): 45 seconds for a tweet and 80 seconds for a forum post. This led us to create "Twitter" datasets containing 100 messages and "Forum" datasets containing 80 messages.

We used Gate software (Cunningham et al., 2013) as an annotation tool. This software provides a graphical interface for selecting portions of text and assigning a label, which allowed us to use it as is for our "unitizing" annotation task.

4.2 Annotators and Sessions

We organised five annotation sessions with non-native English speaking NLP students as annotators (see Table 1). It is not a concern that for all annotators English is not a native language, they can still understand enough the documents to correctly annotate it. In each session, the annotators were divided into groups of two or three and each group was given one dataset to annotate.

Session	Annotators	Datasets	Markers
Session 1	7 duos	5 "Twitter", 2 "Forum"	Claim
Session 2	5 duos, 1 trio	4 "Twitter", 2 "Forum"	Stimuli
Session 3	2 duos	2 "Twitter", 1 "Forum"	Stimuli
Session 4	2 duos	1 "Twitter", 1 "Forum"	Stimuli
Session 5	2 duos	2 "Forum"	Stimulation, Decision

Table 1: Annotation session configurations

The annotators in sessions 1 and 2 were completely different, whereas sessions 3 to 5 were held with four annotators who had already worked in session 2. Each group in a session annotated a different dataset; in session 3, the group that annotated the "Twitter" dataset had time to annotate one more while the other group was annotating a "Forum" dataset.

With the same objective of simplifying the task and thus improving the annotation quality as for the choice of one genre per dataset, we had annotated a subset of the markers per session.

[2] https://www.kaggle.com/datasets/fifthtribe/how-isis-uses-twitter

Most of the sessions are focused on the markers used by influencers, *claims* and more broadly *stimuli*. For these sessions, "forum" datasets contain only messages from participants who are not the initial authors of discussions: in the "Change My View" debate forum, discussions are initiated by participants who expose their point of view on a topic of their choice, then, the other participants have to change the initial participants' mind and be influencers.

Session 1 focuses on *claims* because the annotation guide was written only for this marker at this point in the campaign.

Session 5 is the only session dedicated to *reaction* markers (*Stimulation* and *Decision*). Only forum messages are used for this session as it is the only resource that presents the reactions to the messages. Also, we selected for the datasets only the messages of the initial authors of discussions because, in the "Change my view" forum, they are the ones that must be influenced by other participants in a discussion, what we want to detect in their reactions.

At the end of each annotation session, we organised a *reconciliation* phase: each group of annotators discussed their disagreements (the text segments they did not annotate identically) to reach a single annotation set that could be used in the gold corpus. Finally, the conflicts were discussed together in a final phase, allowing us to update the annotation guide for future sessions.

As our annotation task is particularly subjective, we think that this reconciliation process, as it integrates different judgements, allows to achieve a relative objectivity and thus a better reference (Bonin et al., 2020). We can nevertheless question the limits of this objectivity, which may only be local, reconciliation leading to overtraining (Hovy and Lavid, 2010), limited in our case by the small number of sessions shared by the same annotators.

5. Results

5.1 Quantitative Synthesis

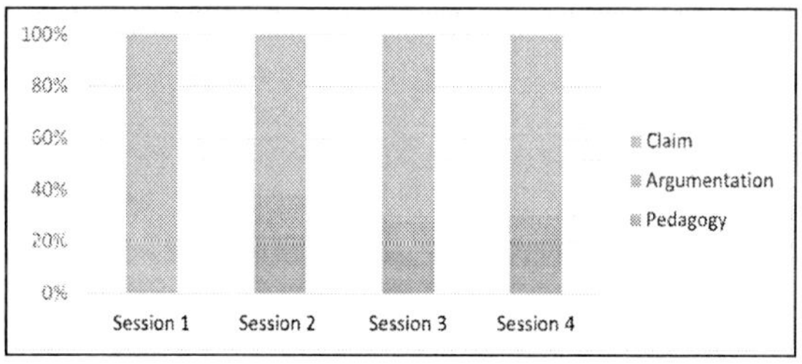

Figure 2: Pro-ISIS tweet annotation distribution

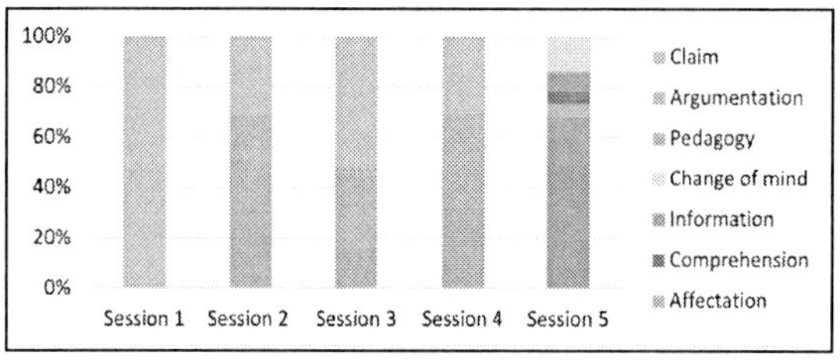

Figure 3: "Change My View" forum annotation distribution

We compare the volumes of annotated marker types between the Twitter and forum datasets, respectively represented in figures 2 and 3.

To characterise the *stimuli* across the two textual genres, we can notice that forum messages contain, for two out of three sessions (sessions 2 and 4), a majority of argumentation. This shows a reasonable characterization of the authors' attempts to influence the debate forum and thus defend one's opinions. Tweets tend to contain more claims than forum messages, which corresponds well to the particularly brief nature of tweets.

The distribution of *stimulation* markers (Figure 3) shows a large predominance of *Agreement;* this is a reasonable response to the predominance of *Argumentation* among *stimuli* markers because agreement is an alignment of opinions while argumentation is used to support an opinion. The predominance of *stimuli* markers over the *decision* ones (see Figure 3) shows that it is rare for an influence process to reach its conclusion.

A gold dataset was created only for the *stimuli* markers, on the one hand because we did not have time to develop for *stimulation* detection and on the other hand because we performed *change of mind* (*decision*) detection by using as reference the "delta" system in the "Change My View" forum (Deturck, 2021): when initial authors of discussions change their mind because of messages, they have to cite them with a new message including a "delta" symbol and an explanation of their change of mind, then, an automatic moderation validates or not the delta.

We present in Table 2 the number of annotated messages in the gold dataset per marker, with the percentage of these messages that contain at least one occurrence of the marker.

Marker	Number of annotated messages	% of messages containing the marker
Claim	1126	45%
Pedagogy, Argumentation	716	14% for *pedagogy*, 7% for *argumentation*

Table 2: Message volumes by marker in the gold dataset

Quantity differences among markers are directly related to the session configurations (see Table 1): one more session was dedicated to *claim* annotation, also, tweets are more represented than forum messages, which explains the higher proportion of *pedagogy* compared to *argumentation*.

5.2 Qualitative Synthesis

5.2.1 Inter-annotator Agreement

Since it is argued that an annotation is more reliable if it is reproduced by several annotators (Krippendorff, 2004), we measured inter-annotator agreement. Two measures have been specifically designed for unitizing annotation tasks: the Alpha family (Krippendorff et al., 2016), and the Gamma family (Mathet, 2017). Alpha measures cannot be applied to annotations containing overlapping entities, as may be the case in our annotation task. We will therefore use Gamma measures.

We use two coefficients in the Gamma family: the standard Gamma coefficient, which takes the location and categorisation of annotations into account, and the GammaCat coefficient, which focuses on the categories associated with the selected units. This allows us to distinguish between two forms of disagreement: (1) a confusion between categories or (2) differing boundaries of relevant text.

	Gamma score	GammaCat score
Session 1	0.38	N/A
Session 2	0.35	0.53
Session 3	0.48	0.7
Session 4	0.62	0.88
Session 5	0.71	0.91

Table 3: Average inter-annotator agreement scores

Table 3 shows the Gamma inter-annotator agreement measures for each session. These results were calculated by averaging the scores of all groups in a session. We present sessions 2 to 4 in a different colour because they are fully comparable in terms of the annotated categories (the *stimuli* ones).

We observe an interesting improvement in results between sessions 2 and 4, both for Gamma and GammaCat. These three sessions were specifically designed using the same traits to evaluate the annotation progression. This improvement confirms the relevance of our iterative approach, especially as regards improving the annotation guide.

Overall, we notice that the GammaCat coefficient gives much better results than the Gamma coefficient. We can therefore conclude that the disagreement measured is mainly due to a problem in delimiting the units rather than to a difficulty in identifying the presence of categories in the messages. This is a positive result for the use of annotations since the units found, even not exact in their boundaries, are consistent with the defined categories.

5.2.2 Annotation Mistakes

Error type / Expected	*Claim*	*Pedagogy*	*Argumentation*
Claim confusion	N/A	20%	17%
Pedagogy confusion	25%	N/A	25%
Argumentation confusion	2%	16%	N/A
Delimitation error	49%	36%	32%
Out of the scope	24%	28%	26%

Table 4: Statistics on error types regarding *stimuli*

We manually identified the "mistakes" made by annotators, that is those annotations, among disagreements, that contradict the guidelines. It is a necessary step to determine annotation difficulties and improve the annotation guide.

Besides confusion between markers, we distinguished between two error types that we describe below.

- *Delimitation error*: boundaries incorrect, but semantics are valid, for example, the two claim annotations in "[[Most to all mass shootings in the US are where carrying guns is banned]1 (for the laws abiding)]2,
- *Out of the scope*: semantics are not valid; it is a critical error, for example, *"These types of calculations aren't helpful"* is *out of the scope* because it is a judgement alone, without argumentation

We present the distribution of these error types for *stimuli* markers (see Table 4), which constitute a significant part of the annotations. A large proportion of annotation errors relates only to the delimitation of units. This is a relatively positive observation as regards the quality of the annotations since annotations of this type still contain relevant statements.

Confusion between marker types is important due to similarities: pedagogical discourse may contain claims, pedagogy explains a fact and argumentation explains a point of view. *Out of scope* errors are globally in a minority; they are mainly due to the difficulty of distinguishing factual from viewpoint statements.

6. Conclusion

We have described an annotation campaign organized as part of the development of a system to detect influencers. The annotation schema is composed of linguistic markers corresponding to our influence model.

The annotation task was particularly difficult, on the one hand because the linguistic markers involved the interpretation of statements and on the other hand because it required annotators to precisely identify the text segments that corresponded to each marker. To deal with this difficulty, we chose to design an iterative annotation campaign, involving multiple annotation-revision cycles.

Inter-annotator agreement measures throw different annotation sessions showed that our method allowed to build a relative consensus. It may be a validation of our approach to get reliable annotations, but it may also reflect overtraining due to the reconciliation phases. The resulting *gold* annotations have been used to train models that we applied for influencer detection.

7. Bibliographical References

Ajzen, I. (1996). The social psychology of decision making. Social psychology: Handbook of basic principles, 297-325.

Binali, H., Wu, C., and Potdar, V. (2010). Computational approaches for emotion detection in text. In *4th IEEE international conference on digital ecosystems and technologies* (pp. 172-177). IEEE.

Bonin, F., Finnerty, A., Moore, C., Jochim, C., Norris, E., Hou, Y., ... and Michie, S. (2020). HBCP corpus: A new resource for the analysis of behaviour change intervention reports.

Cunningham, H., Tablan, V., Roberts, A., and Bontcheva, K. (2013). Getting more out of biomedical documents with GATE's full lifecycle open source text analytics. *PLoS computational biology*, *9*(2), e1002854.

Deturck, K. (2021). *Détection des influenceurs dans des médias sociaux* (Doctoral dissertation, Institut National des Langues et Civilisations Orientales-INALCO PARIS-LANGUES O').

Deturck, K. (2021). *Guide d'annotation en discours pour la détection d'influenceurs* (Doctoral dissertation, Institut National des Langues et Civilisations Orientales).

Dillard, J. P. and Wilson, S. R. (2014). Interpersonal influence. *Interpersonal communication*, *6*, 155.

Eckle-Kohler, J., Kluge, R., and Gurevych, I. (2015). On the role of discourse markers for discriminating claims and premises in argumentative discourse. In Proceedings of the 2015 Conference on Empirical Methods in Natural Language Processing (pp. 2236-2242).

Fernandez, M., Asif, M., & Alani, H. (2018). Understanding the roots of radicalisation on twitter. In Proceedings of the 10th ACM conference on web science (pp. 1-10).

Germesin, S. and Wilson, T. (2009). Agreement detection in multiparty conversation. In *Proceedings of the 2009 international conference on Multimodal interfaces* (pp. 7-14).

Hidi, S. and Baird, W. (1986). Interestingness—A neglected variable in discourse processing. *Cognitive science*, *10*(2), 179-194.

Hovy, E. and Lavid, J. (2010). Towards a 'science'of corpus annotation: a new methodological challenge for corpus linguistics. *International journal of translation*, *22*(1), 13-36.

Katz, E. (1957). The two-step flow of communication: An up-to-date report on an hypothesis. *Public opinion quarterly*, *21*(1), 61-78.

Katz, E. and Lazarsfeld, P. F. (2017). *Personal influence: The part played by people in the flow of mass communications*. Routledge.

Krippendorff, K. (1995). On the reliability of unitizing continuous data. *Sociological Methodology*, 47-76.

Krippendorff, K. (2004). Measuring the reliability of qualitative text analysis data. *Quality and quantity*, *38*, 787-800.

Krippendorff, K., Mathet, Y., Bouvry, S., and Widlöcher, A. (2016). On the reliability of unitizing textual continua: Further developments. *Quality & Quantity*, *50*(6), 2347-2364.

Mason, W. A., Conrey, F. R., and Smith, E. R. (2007). Situating social influence processes: Dynamic, multidirectional flows of influence within social networks. *Personality and social psychology review*, *11*(3), 279-300.

Mathet, Y. (2017). The Agreement Measure γ cat a Complement to γ Focused on Categorization of a Continuum. *Computational Linguistics*, *43*(3), 661-681.

Saurí, R. and Pustejovsky, J. (2012). Are you sure that this happened? assessing the factuality degree of events in text. *Computational linguistics*, *38*(2), 261-299.

Strötgen, J. and Gertz, M. (2012). Temporal tagging on different domains: Challenges, strategies, and gold standards. In *Proceedings of the Eight International Conference on Language Resources and Evaluation (LREC 2012)*, pages 3746–3753, Istanbul, Turkey, May. European Language Resource Association (ELRA).

Trusov, M., Bodapati, A. V., and Bucklin, R. E. (2010). Determining influential users in internet social networks. *Journal of marketing research*, *47*(4), 643-658.

Turner, J. C. and Oakes, P. J. (1986). The significance of the social identity concept for social psychology with reference to individualism, interactionism and social influence. *British Journal of Social Psychology*, *25*(3), 237-252.

Voormann, H. and Gut, U. (2008). Agile corpus creation.

Wyer Jr, R. S., and Shrum, L. J. (2015). The role of comprehension processes in communication and persuasion. *Media Psychology*, *18*(2), 163-195.

Proceedings of the 16th Linguistic Annotation Workshop (LAW-XVI) @LREC 2022, pages 91–96
Marseille, 24 June 2022

Charon: a FrameNet Annotation Tool for Multimodal Corpora

Frederico Belcavello[1], Marcelo Viridiano[1], Ely Edison Matos[1], Tiago Timponi Torrent[1,2]
[1] FrameNet Brasil Lab, Graduate Program in Linguistics, Federal University of Juiz de Fora
[2] Brazilian National Council for Scientific and Technological Development – CNPq
{fred.belcavello, ely.matos, tiago.torrent}@ufjf.br, barros.marcelo@estudante.ufjf.br

Abstract

This paper presents Charon, a web tool for annotating multimodal corpora with FrameNet categories. Annotation can be made for corpora containing both static images and video sequences paired – or not – with text sequences. The pipeline features, besides the annotation interface, corpus import and pre-processing tools.

Keywords: FrameNet, Multimodality, Picture Annotation, Video Annotation, Text Annotation

1. Introduction

Multimodality refers to the property of any communication phenomenon where two or more modes – defined as experientially recognized resources for meaning-making shaped by society and culture – are brought into play (Jewitt and Kress, 2003; Kress, 2010; Bateman et al., 2017) . This paper approaches the expansion of FrameNet annotation into the multimodal domain, as proposed in Belcavello et al. (2020), by presenting Charon: a semi-automatic, human-in-the-loop tool for annotating static and dynamic images for semantic frames. Charon was developed to meet the following key requirements: (i) compatibility with existing FrameNet software; (ii) annotation of image with FrameNet categories; (iii) linkage of image and textual annotations.

2. FrameNet Annotation

FrameNet is a curated language model where lexical items have their meaning defined against systems of concepts called frames (Fillmore and Baker, 2009). For instance, words such as *arrive.v* and *arrival.n* have their meanings defined based on a scene where a THEME arrives at a GOAL: the `Arriving` frame (Figure 1). Moreover, frames are connected to one another via a network of typed relations. The `Arriving` frame, for instance, is inherited by the `Vehicle_landing` and preceded by the `Departing` frames.

Annotation plays a key role in FrameNet, to the extent that it provides evidence supporting the analysis in the model. Two text annotation methods are used: lexicographic and full-text. In the former, the focus lies on a specific Lexical Unit (LU), and sentences instantiating that LU are extracted from corpora and annotated for a given frame. The aim is to cover the valence patterns of the LU, i.e. its semantic and syntactic affordances. In the latter, the focus is on the corpus being annotated, and the annotator creates Annotation Sets (AS) for each word for which there is an LU in FrameNet. Figure 2 shows two of the ASs created for the sentence in (1).

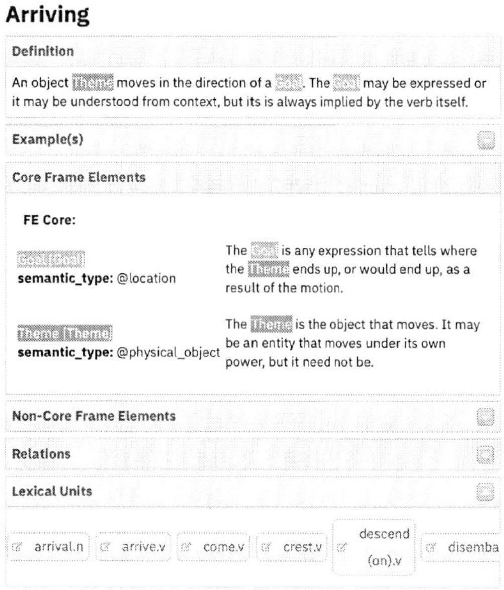

Figure 1: The `Arrival` frame.

(1) Então, acabei de chegar em Reykjavik, na Islândia.
So, I have just arrived in Reykjavik, Iceland.

In (1) the word forms *acabei* and *chegar*, highlighted in black in Figure 2, are the annotation targets. Note that, for each of them, there are three layers of annotation: Frame Element (FE), Grammatical Function (GF) and Phrase Type (PT). The column NI is used for indicating that core FEs are not instantiated in the sentence, but can be inferred.

The idea behind the development of Charon is that other communication modes, namely visual objects, can either evoke frames – similarly to LUs – or complement the valencies of LUs present in text accompanying the images (Belcavello et al., 2020), expanding FrameNet annotation to the multimodal domain. In section 4, we describe the tool, but, first, let us turn to a brief summary of other multimodal annotation tools.

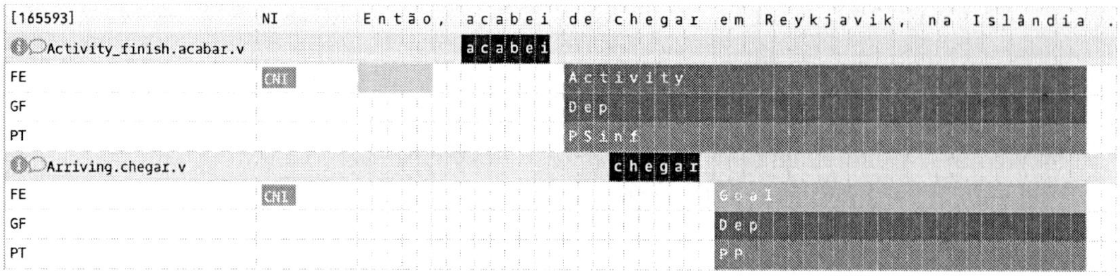

Figure 2: Full-text annotation for sentence (1).

3. Related Work

The past two decades have witnessed accelerated development of data labeling tools for human annotation of monomodal visual corpora – e.g. COCO Annotator (Lin et al., 2014), ImageTagger (Fiedler et al., 2018), and LabelBox (Sharma et al., 2019). Moreover, highly generic and flexible multimodal annotation tools, such as Anvil (Kipp, 2001) and ELAN (Wittenburg et al., 2006), allow users to design their own annotation schemes for timeline-based annotation of both audio and visual phenomena from multiple synchronized streams. Finally, frameworks, like SIDGrid (Levow et al., 2007), extend the functionality of ELAN by allowing the application of user-defined analysis programs to media, time series, and annotations associated with each project.

Nonetheless, none of these tools and annotation clients allows for the combination of data labeling with the extensive semantic granularity offered by the network of frames and frame elements provided by FrameNet. Allowing for such a combination is the main contribution of Charon, which is presented next.

4. Charon: Multimodal Annotation Tool

Charon is a multimodal annotation and database management tool. It was developed to annotate visual objects, correlate them with textual data and label frames and Frame Elements evoked by them. Charon is compatible with the FN-Br WebTool: a database management and annotation software used by both local framenet projects in Brazil, Sweden, Croatia and Japan, and in the Global FrameNet Shared Annotation Task (Torrent et al., 2018).[1] Charon is composed of two modules: a static mode, for annotating picture-text pairings, and a dynamic mode, for annotating video. Both are described next.

4.1. Annotation of Picture-Caption Pairings

Charon's static annotation mode can be used to improve multimodal datasets containing picture-text pairings by adding fine-grained semantic information provided by FrameNet. The version of the tool presented in this paper has been tuned to the requirements of the Flickr 30K Entities dataset (Plummer et al., 2015) – an expansion of Flickr 30K (Young et al., 2014) that adds manually annotated bounding boxes and coreference chains linking entities from each image to their correspondent descriptors in each caption. However, any dataset featuring pictures, captions and bounding boxes identifying parts of the picture can be used. The annotation process is divided into two stages: (i) corpus import and pre-processing, and (ii) annotation.

4.1.1. Picture Corpus Import and Pre-Processing

To upload a new corpus, all related files – a folder with JPEG images, a text file with all the sentences, and a XML with the classes and coordinates for each object's bounding box – must be compressed into a ZIP file. Next, Charon creates a new corpus folder in which documents containing lists of image-sentence pairs are built. Before being presented to the annotator, the sentences in these documents are pre-processed by a disambiguation algorithm – DAISY (Torrent et al., 2022) – that identifies and associates each frame-evoking lemma with a semantic frame in the FrameNet database, resulting in an automated frame annotation for each sentence. Such an automated annotation can be checked during a human-in-the-loop process. Charon also checks the image related files for all objects that might have been previously tagged via data labeling tools or computer vision algorithms, and automatically correlates the classes of these objects – obtained from datasets like COCO (Lin et al., 2014) and Open Images (Kuznetsova et al., 2020) – with existing Lexical Units in FrameNet. After that, images and sentences are loaded into the interface where the human annotation happens.

4.1.2. Picture Annotation Process

Figure 3 presents the static mode interface, used for the annotation of Picture-Caption pairings. This annotation interface is composed of several panels that are loaded depending on the type of corpus or annotation task being developed. The upper left corner of the interface offers a view of the uploaded image. The panel titled Boxes shows the coordinates for the bounding boxes related to each object/entity being annotated in that picture. The Annotations panel shows the correlations between each object/entity in the image, its co-referenced phrase extracted from the sentence in the

[1] The FN-Br WebTool is available at https://github.com/FrameNetBrasil/webtool.

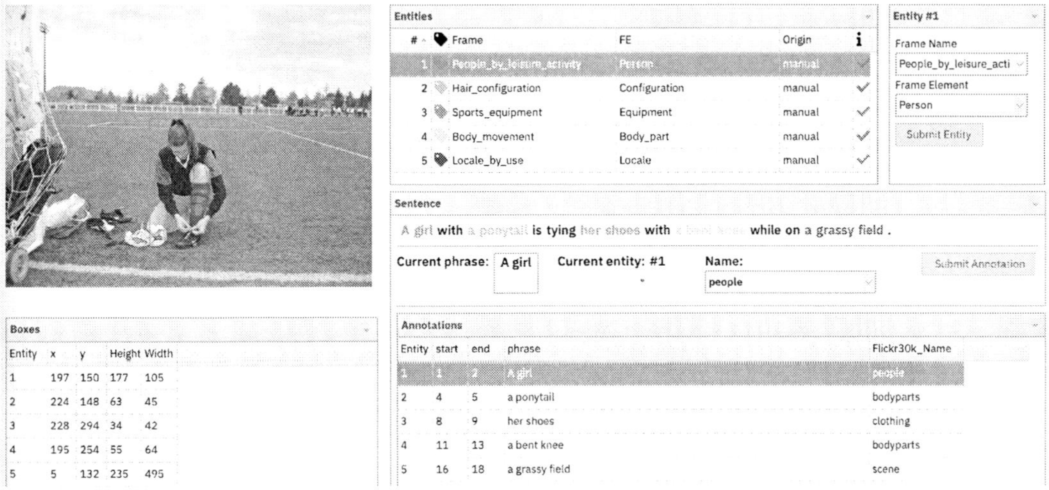

Figure 3: User interface for the annotation of Picture-Caption pairings.

middle panel, and the class used to label this object in the original dataset. Finally, the panels Entities and Object are the ones used by the human annotator to assign a Semantic Frame and a FE to each picture-text pair composed by the object/entity in the bounding box and the highlighted phrase in the sentence.

Example sentence (2) has the phrases "A girl", "a ponytail", "her shoes", "a bent knee", and "a grassy field" correlated with five distinct objects/entities in the image. For the phrase "A girl", corresponding to the Entity 1 in the image, the annotator assigned the frame `People_by_leisure_activity` and the FE PERSON.

(2) A girl in a ponytail is tying her shoes with a bent knee while on a grassy field.

This annotation mode generates an XML file, allowing the output to be used with other multimodal annotation tools and integrated with existing transcriptions and annotations from other modules and databases in the FN-Br Webtool environment.

4.2. Annotation of Videos

Two types of media are involved in the annotation of videos in FrameNet: audio and image. Therefore, this module of Charon was designed to pre-process videos by (i) extracting verbal data from both audio and images (i. e. subtitles) and deliver it for annotation in the FN-Br Webtool; and (ii) submitting image to an external computer vision system that identifies visual objects and make bounding boxes for those objects available for annotation in Charon. In the following subsections we describe the video annotation pipeline.

4.2.1. Video Corpus Import and Pre-Processing

The pipeline designed for corpus import and video pre-processing starts with the selection of the video input, which is imported, pre-processed and separated into two data flows: one for the audio and another for the images.

The next step is the selection of the language of the verbal mode. After the language is selected, the audio data runs through a speech-to-text cloud service, which detects word by word what is said throughout the video.[2] Each word receives time stamps indicating the time span during which they are spoken.

From the image flow, subtitles are extracted using an optical character recognition software. They are time-stamped and then merged to the text corpus with the output of the speech-to-text software.[3] Words and sentences extracted then go through a human-in-the-loop stage, where users can build sentences from the words, edit them, as well as check and adjust time stamps. Finally, the textual part of the corpus is saved and sent to the FN-Br Webtool for annotation.

Charon also processes non-verbal visual data. The images extracted at a 25 frames per second rate are stamped for both time (in seconds) and video frame (in sequential numbers). They run through a computer vision algorithm, which automatically tags objects in each frame, associating a bounding box and a category to them. [4]

At the end of the pipeline, annotators access the video annotation module, where they visualize both the annotated sentences and the automatically detected objects. This module is described next.

[2]For the current implementation, Google Cloud Speech API (`https://cloud.google.com/speech-to-text`) is used.

[3]For the current implementation, Tesseract OCR (`https://github.com/tesseract-ocr/tesseract`) is used.

[4]For the current implementation, YOLOv3 (Redmon and Farhadi, 2018), trained on the COCO dataset (Lin et al., 2014) is used.

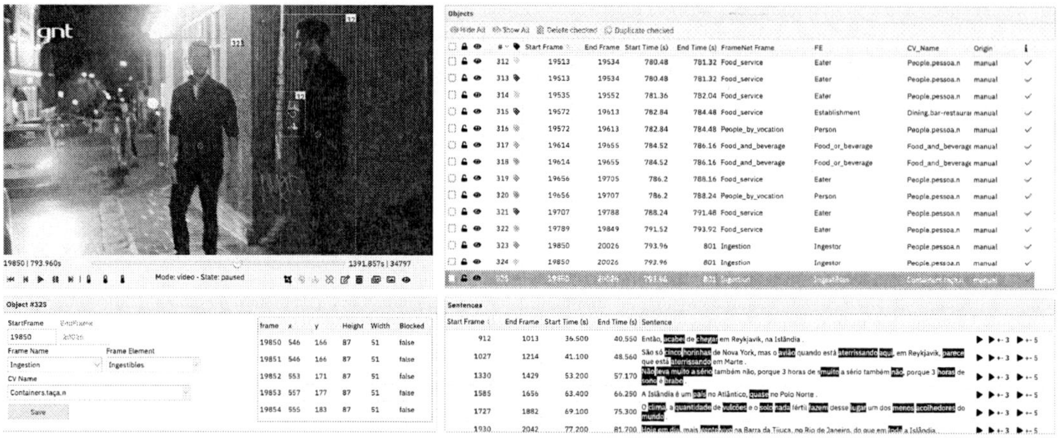

Figure 4: Example of video annotation.

4.2.2. Video Annotation Process

Charon provides a myriad of possibilities for video annotation by human users, in terms of both methodologies and goals. So far, it has been used to annotate and compare semantic frames evoked by visual objects with those evoked by LUs in sentences. This is why the video annotation module features not only the annotation tools for tagging images, but also the visualization of the sentences annotated in the FN-Br WebTool for the same corpus.

Human annotators can start by reviewing the objects automatically detected by the computer vision software. If annotators agree with the bounding box drawn by the CV software, they select the object in the panel, then use the edit tracking button in the player to link the bounding box to the object through the following video frames. Once the object is not visible anymore or there is a cut point, the annotator presses the pause tracking button, and then the end object one. If annotators do not agree with the bounding box drawn, they can select the object in the panel and delete it.

To create new objects, annotators use the new object button, draw the bounding box over the object they want to detect, then start tracking it. Tracking can be executed manually, frame by frame, or automatically, using the start tracking button. In both cases, annotators determine the end point for the bounding box when the object is not visible anymore or there is a cut point. Next, annotators have to manually attribute a Semantic Frame and a FE to the object. They choose the frame from the list under the Frame Name field. Once the frame is chosen, a list of its FEs is loaded in the Frame Element field. Annotators should also attribute a Computer Vision name to the object or confirm the label automatically assigned by the computer vision software. This category associates one LU with the object, considering its value as an entity recognizable by computer vision tools or algorithms. In the CV Name field, users may choose from any LU in the framenet database they are using. Figure 4 shows an example of video annotation. At the moment the image in Figure 4 is seen on screen, viewers listen one of the men speaking the sentence annotated as in (3):

(3) Bom$^{\texttt{Desirability}}$ que aqui$^{\texttt{Locative_relation}}$ a gente bebe$^{\texttt{Ingestion}}$ e vai esquentando$^{\texttt{Change_of_temperature}}$, né?

It's good that here we drink and warm ourselves up, innit?

When looking for correspondences between text and image, objects 323 and 324 were annotated as the INGESTORS for the `Ingestion` frame (Figure 5). On the other hand, as what is visually recognizable are two human figures, the CV Names chosen were person.n in the `People` frame. Object 325 was annotated as the INGESTIBLES in the `Ingestion` frame and as glass.n in the `Container` frame for the CV Name. What is interesting here is that in the sentence there is no mention to the INGESTIBLES FE – it is a null instantiation, – neither to the `Container` Frame. Therefore, this example shows how meaning layers and granularity can be added to the FrameNet semantic representation by annotating visual data in correspondence with textual data in a corpus.

5. Expected Datasets

As demonstrated so far, the addition of other communicative modes to FrameNet annotation allows for building fine-grained semantically annotated multimodal datasets. Two datasets are being currently built by means of Charon's annotation affordances: the Framed Multi 30k and the Frame^2 datasets (Torrent et al., 2022).

The Framed Multi 30k Dataset will consist of an improved version of two datasets: the Multi30k dataset (Elliott et al., 2016) – a multilingual extension of the popular dataset for sentence-based image description

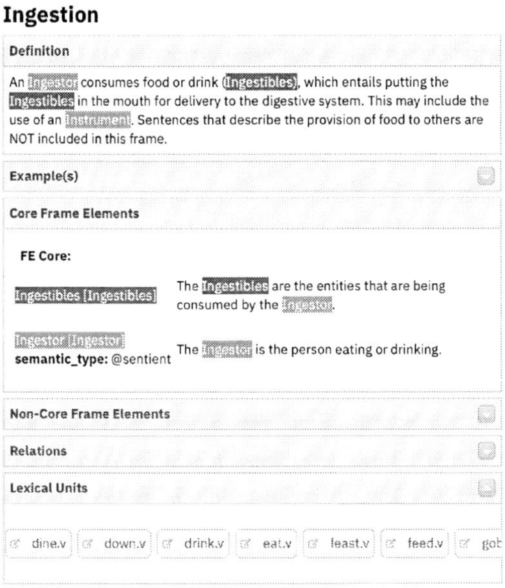

Figure 5: The `Ingestion` frame.

Flickr30k (Young et al., 2014), – and Flickr30k Entities (Plummer et al., 2015). For each of the 276,000 bounding boxes from Flickr30K Entities, our Framed Multi 30k dataset will add five new sets of Entity-Frame-Frame Element relations, 155,070 new Brazilian Portuguese descriptions, and 155,070 new English-Portuguese translated descriptions.

The Frame[2] dataset, in turn, is being built to provide means to analyze the interaction between the frame-based semantic representation of verbal language and that produced by the frame-based annotation of video sequences, i.e. sequences of visual frames related with audio, forming a video. The aim is to make it possible to analyze audio and video combination possibilities in terms of frames, as in the example shown in Figure 4. This dataset is composed by the multimodal objects selected for annotation in the corpus of the TV Travel Series "Pedro pelo Mundo." The first data release of Frame[2] will comprise the annotation of all 10 episodes of the show's first season. This means approximately 12,200 annotation sets for text and 5,000 for image.

6. Conclusion

Charon is a unique and robust tool that provides an user-friendly, web-based interface for fine-grained semantic annotation of both static and dynamic multimodal corpora. The integration with the ever-growing network of semantic frames provided by framenets worldwide allows for large-scale multimodal data analysis. While the current release has already demonstrated its usefulness, many updates and extensions are in the works. A priority is to improve the integration with metadata obtained from machine vision models for automatic object detection.

7. Acknowledgments

Authors acknowledge the support of the Graduate Program in Linguistics at the Federal University of Juiz de Fora , as well as the role of Oliver Czulo and Mark Turner in co-supervising, respectively, the doctoral research by Marcelo Viridiano and Frederico Belcavello, whose contributions are reported in this paper. Research presented in this paper was funded by CAPES PROBRAL grant 88887.144043/2017-00 and CNPq grants 408269/2021-9 and 315749/2021-0. Viridiano's research was funded by CAPES PROBRAL PhD exchange grant 88887.628830/2021-00. Belcavello's research was funded by CAPES PDSE PhD exchange grant 88881.362052/2019-01. Authors also acknowledge the contributions of E. P. Hackett[5] and Prishita Ray[6] to the initial development phase of Charon. Both projects were developed and funded under the Google Summer of Code Program.

8. Bibliographical References

Bateman, J., Wildfeuer, J., and Hiippala, T. (2017). *Multimodality: Foundations, Research and Analysis – A Problem-Oriented Introduction*. Mouton Textbook. De Gruyter.

Belcavello, F., Viridiano, M., Diniz da Costa, A., Matos, E. E. d. S., and Torrent, T. T. (2020). Frame-based annotation of multimodal corpora: Tracking (a)synchronies in meaning construction. In *Proceedings of the International FrameNet Workshop 2020: Towards a Global, Multilingual FrameNet*, pages 23–30, Marseille, France, May. European Language Resources Association.

Elliott, D., Frank, S., Sima'an, K., and Specia, L. (2016). Multi30K: Multilingual English-German image descriptions. In *Proceedings of the 5th Workshop on Vision and Language*, pages 70–74, Berlin, Germany, August. Association for Computational Linguistics.

Fiedler, N., Bestmann, M., and Hendrich, N. (2018). Imagetagger: An open source online platform for collaborative image labeling. In *Robot World Cup*, pages 162–169. Springer.

Fillmore, C. J. and Baker, C. (2009). A frames approach to semantic analysis. In Bernd Heine et al., editors, *The Oxford Handbook of Linguistic Analysis*, pages 791–816. Oxford University Press, Oxford, UK, December.

Jewitt, C. and Kress, G. (2003). *Multimodal Literacy*. New literacies and digital epistemologies. P. Lang.

Kipp, M. (2001). Anvil-a generic annotation tool for multimodal dialogue. In *Seventh European Conference on Speech Communication and Technology*. Citeseer.

[5] `https://summerofcode.withgoogle.com/archive/2019/projects/5902293138931712`

[6] `https://summerofcode.withgoogle.com/archive/2020/projects/4857286331203584`

Kress, G. (2010). *Multimodality: A Social Semiotic Approach to Contemporary Communication*. Multimodality: A Social Semiotic Approach to Contemporary Communication. Routledge.

Kuznetsova, A., Rom, H., Alldrin, N., Uijlings, J., Krasin, I., Pont-Tuset, J., Kamali, S., Popov, S., Malloci, M., Kolesnikov, A., Duerig, T., and Ferrari, V. (2020). The open images dataset v4: Unified image classification, object detection, and visual relationship detection at scale. *IJCV*.

Levow, G.-A., Bertenthal, B., Hereld, M., Kenny, S., McNeill, D., Papka, M., and Waxmonsky, S. (2007). Sidgrid: A framework for distributed and integrated multimodal annotation and archiving and and analysis. In *Proceedings of the 8th SIGdial Workshop on Discourse and Dialogue*, pages 231–234.

Lin, T.-Y., Maire, M., Belongie, S., Hays, J., Perona, P., Ramanan, D., Dollár, P., and Zitnick, C. L. (2014). Microsoft coco: Common objects in context. In David Fleet, et al., editors, *Computer Vision – ECCV 2014*, pages 740–755, Cham. Springer International Publishing.

Plummer, B. A., Wang, L., Cervantes, C. M., Caicedo, J. C., Hockenmaier, J., and Lazebnik, S. (2015). Flickr30k entities: Collecting region-to-phrase correspondences for richer image-to-sentence models. In *2015 IEEE International Conference on Computer Vision (ICCV)*, pages 2641–2649.

Redmon, J. and Farhadi, A. (2018). Yolov3: An incremental improvement. *arXiv preprint arXiv:1804.02767*.

Sharma, M., Rasmuson, D., Rieger, B., Kjelkerud, D., et al. (2019). Labelbox: The best way to create and manage training data. software, labelbox. *Inc, https://www.labelbox.com*.

Torrent, T. T., Ellsworth, M., Baker, C., and Matos, E. E. d. S. (2018). The Multilingual FrameNet Shared Annotation Task: a Preliminary Report. In Tiago Timponi Torrent, et al., editors, *Proceedings of the Eleventh International Conference on Language Resources and Evaluation (LREC 2018)*, Paris, France, may. European Language Resources Association (ELRA).

Torrent, T. T., Matos, E. E. d. S., Belcavello, F., Viridiano, M., Gamonal, M. A., Costa, A. D. d., and Marim, M. C. (2022). Representing context in framenet: A multidimensional, multimodal approach. *Frontiers in Psychology*, 13.

Wittenburg, P., Brugman, H., Russel, A., Klassmann, A., and Sloetjes, H. (2006). ELAN: a professional framework for multimodality research. In *Proceedings of the Fifth International Conference on Language Resources and Evaluation (LREC'06)*, Genoa, Italy, May. European Language Resources Association (ELRA).

Young, P., Lai, A., Hodosh, M., and Hockenmaier, J. (2014). From image descriptions to visual denotations: New similarity metrics for semantic inference over event descriptions. *Transactions of the Association for Computational Linguistics*, 2:67–78.

Proceedings of the 16th Linguistic Annotation Workshop (LAW-XVI) @LREC 2022, pages 97–102
Marseille, 24 June 2022

Effect of Source Language on AMR Structure

Shira Wein, Wai Ching Leung, Yifu Mu, Nathan Schneider
Georgetown University, USA
{sw1158, wl607, ym431, nathan.schneider}@georgetown.edu

Abstract

The Abstract Meaning Representation (AMR) annotation schema was originally designed for English. But the formalism has since been adapted for annotation in a variety of languages. Meanwhile, cross-lingual parsers have been developed to derive English AMR representations for sentences from other languages—implicitly assuming that English AMR can approximate an interlingua. In this work, we investigate the similarity of AMR annotations in parallel data and how much the language matters in terms of the graph structure. We set out to quantify the effect of sentence language on the structure of the parsed AMR. As a case study, we take parallel AMR annotations from Mandarin Chinese and English AMRs, and replace all Chinese concepts with equivalent English tokens. We then compare the two graphs via the Smatch metric as a measure of structural similarity. We find that source language has a dramatic impact on AMR structure, with Smatch scores below 50% between English and Chinese graphs in our sample—an important reference point for interpreting Smatch scores in *cross-lingual* AMR parsing.

Keywords: Abstract Meaning Representation (AMR), Chinese language resources, annotation

1 Introduction

Though the Abstract Meaning Representation (AMR; Banarescu et al., 2013) framework was originally designed for annotating English sentences, and not intended as an interlingua, it has since been adapted to a number of other languages (§2.1), raising the question of how well it abstracts away from the particularities of individual languages. To investigate AMR's ability to serve as an interlingua, previous work has explored methods of characterizing the types of differences between parallel AMR graphs (AMRs annotating parallel sentences in different languages; §2.2). However, there has not yet been an effort to *systematically quantify* the effect on AMR structure of the language of the sentence being parsed (hereafter, the *source language*). We hypothesize that regardless of any language-specific information in the AMR (i.e. if the labels are made to be in the same language), the structure of AMRs across language pairs will likely differ because of the linguistic properties of the source sentence. To better understand the impact of language on AMR structure in the pursuit of effective evaluation of cross-lingual AMR pair similarity, we aim to quantify the amount of impact in parallel AMRs.

Here we explore the effect of source language on AMR structure in the large annotated parallel corpus of Mandarin Chinese and English AMRs (Li et al., 2016). To quantify the impact of source language on the AMR, we eliminate the measurable impact of lexical divergence and focus solely on structural divergences. To do this, we take a pair of parallel English and Chinese AMRs and manually translate every word in the Chinese graph into its English equivalent. Structural elements of the AMR are largely unchanged (§3.2). We then evaluate via Smatch (Cai and Knight, 2013), which is an algorithm to compare AMR graphs and calculate similarity. Ultimately, we have a Smatch score quantifying the effect of source language on AMR structure.

From these Smatch scores, we are able to demonstrate that the source language has a dramatic effect on the structure of an AMR, even if the AMR is a gold annotation with no noise introduced by automatic parsing. This result has important implications for (1) identifying cross-linguistic inconsistencies in the AMR schema, and (2) interpreting scores in cross-lingual AMR parsing evaluations (Damonte, 2019).[1]

Our primary contributions include:

- a novel approach to quantifying effect of source language on AMR structure;
- a small dataset of 120 Chinese AMRs with English concept labels, following our approach;[2] and
- an analysis of the Smatch score differences between our Chinese AMRs with English concept labels and the corresponding gold English AMRs.

2 Related Work

2.1. Abstract Meaning Representation

The Abstract Meaning Representation (AMR) formalism is a graph-based representation of the meaning of a sentence or phrase. In AMR annotations, nodes reflect entities and events, and the edges are labeled with semantic roles. AMR aims to abstract away from surface details of morphology and syntax in favor of core elements of meaning, such as predicate-argument structure and coreference. With that in mind, sentences with the same meaning (and content word vocabulary) should be represented by the same AMR. English AMR annotations are unanchored—the nodes are not explicitly

[1] "Cross-lingual AMR parsing" typically refers to parsing a sentence from a language other than English into a standard English AMR.

[2] Our annotations can be found at `https://github.com/shirawein/effect-language-amr-structure`

mapped to tokens in the sentence—but the concepts (semantic node labels) largely consist of lemmatized words from the sentence.

AMR was designed exclusively for English and was not intended to be an interlingua (Banarescu et al., 2013), but has now been extended to multiple languages. AMR has been adapted to Chinese (Li et al., 2016), Portuguese (Anchiêta and Pardo, 2018; Sobrevilla Cabezudo and Pardo, 2019), Spanish (Migueles-Abraira et al., 2018; Wein et al., 2022), Vietnamese (Linh and Nguyen, 2019), Turkish (Azin and Eryiğit, 2019; Oral et al., 2022), Korean (Choe et al., 2020), and Persian (Takhshid et al., 2022).

A multilingual adaptation of AMR, the Uniform Meaning Representation (Van Gysel et al., 2021), was developed to incorporate linguistic diversity into the AMR annotation process.

2.2. Differences in Cross-lingual AMR Pairs

AMR has been assessed as an interlingua, considering the types of differences which appear across AMR language pairs, for Czech (Hajič et al., 2014), Chinese (Xue et al., 2014), and Spanish (Wein and Schneider, 2021), in comparison to English.

Xue et al. (2014) explore the adaptability of English AMR to Czech and Chinese. They suggest that AMR may be cross-linguistically adaptable because it abstracts away from morpho-syntactic differences. Cross-linguistic comparisons between English/Czech and English/Chinese AMR pairs indicate that most pairs align well. Also, the compatibility is higher for English and Chinese than for English and Czech.

Hajič et al. (2014) describe the types of differences between AMRs for parallel English and Czech sentences, and find that the differences may be either due to convention/surface-level nuances which could be changed in the annotation guidelines, or may be due to inherent facets of the AMR annotation schema. One notable cross-lingual AMR difference is from the appearance of language-specific idioms and phrases.

Wein and Schneider (2021) define the types and causes of divergences between cross-lingual AMR pairs for English-Spanish parallel sentences. The causes of structural differences between parallel AMRs are identified as being due to semantic divergences, syntactic divergences, or annotation choices.

Though previous work has explored methods of characterizing the differences between pairs of cross-lingual AMRs, in this work, we aim to quantify the impact of the source language on AMR structure.

3 Annotation

3.1. Dataset

For our annotation and analysis, we make use of parallel gold Chinese and English AMR annotations of the novel *The Little Prince*—the Chinese AMRs from the CAMR dataset (Li et al., 2016)[3] and their parallel English AMR annotations (Banarescu et al., 2013).[4] We were interested in using this set of parallel data because of the notable divergence in linguistic properties between Chinese and English, as well as the prominence of Chinese sentence–to–English AMR parsing (Damonte and Cohen, 2020). The 100 AMRs used are the first 100 annotations of both development sets, corresponding to the first 100 sentences of *The Little Prince*.[5] The average sentence length is 15.3 tokens for the 100 English sentences and 19.5 tokens for the 100 Chinese sentences. Since the Chinese AMRs do not include `:wiki` tags, we remove all `:wiki` tags from the gold English AMRs.

Note that *The Little Prince* was originally written in French, so both the English and Chinese versions are translations and may exhibit features of translationese and/or may be subject to differences due to French serving as a third pivot language (Koppel and Ordan, 2011).

3.2. Approach

Our broad approach to annotation consists of taking the CAMR annotation and replacing the Chinese concepts with English tokens. We want to replace the Chinese concepts with English tokens so that we do not penalize lexical differences (which are apparent as the words are originally in different languages), but rather, exclusively measure the structural differences between the AMRs. Specifically, this consists of a three-step process:

1. Manually translate the Chinese concepts to equivalent English tokens.
2. Check the parallel gold English AMR to identify synonyms of the manually generated translations of the Chinese concepts.
3. If a synonym (close enough in meaning such that faithfulness to the Chinese sentence is not lost) of the manually generated translation appears in the gold English AMR, the term from the English AMR is used to replace the manually generated translation. Otherwise, the manually generated translation is used.

Additionally, there are some terms that appear in the CAMR annotations which would not appear in English AMR annotations. For example, functional particles such as 就 (a central particle with a multitude of uses) appear in the CAMR annotation schema but prepositions and other morphosyntactic details do not appear in the English AMR annotation schema. We remove these functional particles from the Chinese annotations rather than attempt to translate them into English. No other structural changes are made to the Chinese AMR.

We trained two linguistics students bilingual in English and Chinese in our approach. Approximately 4 hours were spent per annotator to produce the annotations and no annotation tool was used.

[3] `https://www.cs.brandeis.edu/~clp/camr/res/blj_dev.txt`

[4] `https://amr.isi.edu/download/amr-bank-struct-v1.6-dev.txt`

[5] 20 sentences were double-annotated: see §4.

4 Results & Analysis

We collect 60 annotations from each annotator, with 20 sentences overlapping so that we can calculate inter-annotator agreement (120 annotations total, on 100 unique sentences). We calculate the Smatch scores between the annotations (Chinese AMR with English concepts) and the corresponding gold English AMR.

4.1. Inter-Annotator Agreement

English translation: Nothing about him gave any suggestion of a child lost in the middle of the desert, a thousand miles from any human habitation.
Annotation 1:

```
(x0 / look-02
   :polarity  (x2 / -)
   :degree  (x3 / slightest)
   :arg0  (x4 / he)
   :arg1  (x5 / child
      :quant  (x6 / 1)
      :arg0-of  (x7 / lose-02
         :location  (x8 / desert
            :mod  (x9 / large)
            :mod  (x10 / uninhabited)))))
```

Annotation 2:

```
(x0 / seem-01
   :polarity  (x2 / -)
   :degree  (x3 / remote)
   :arg0  (x4 / he)
   :arg1  (x5 / child
      :quant  (x6 / 1)
      :arg0-of  (x7 / lose-02
         :location  (x8 / desert
            :mod  (x9 / huge)
            :mod  (x10 / uninhabited)))))
```

Figure 1: Both annotations (from Annotator 1 and Annotator 2) for one of the sentences in our dataset. Note that the annotators provided the English concepts and the structure of the annotation is derived from the parallel Chinese annotation.

We find that the average inter-annotator agreement (calculated by Smatch) is 0.8645, on a scale from 0 to 1, with 1 being exactly the same. Inter-annotator agreement here measures lexical agreement between the translators. The reason IAA would not be 1 is because translation choices are being made when producing the annotations. For example, in figure 1, one annotator felt that a more faithful translation of 像 is `seem`, while the other annotator decided that a more accurate translation would be `look`. The same is true for the difference between `slightest` and `remote`, as well as between `huge` and `large`. None of those terms (either item of any of the three pairs) are captured in the parallel gold English AMR, so these differences reflect translation choices and not errors in annotation. This pair of annotations received an IAA score of 0.85.

4.2. Annotations versus Gold English AMRs

English sentence: "It has horns."
Gold English annotation:

```
(h / have-03
   :arg0 (i / it)
   :arg1 (h2 / horn))
```

Chinese sentence: "还有犄角呢。"
Annotation (Chinese AMR with English concept labels).

```
(x0 / say
   :arg1  (x2 / have-03
      :manner  (x3 / even)
      :arg1  (x4 / horn)))
```

Figure 2: Gold English AMR and our annotation for parallel sentences.

English sentence: "Boa constrictors swallow their prey whole , without chewing it.
Gold English annotation:

```
(s2 / say-01
   :arg0 (b2 / book)
   :arg1 (s / swallow-01
      :arg0 (b / boa)
      :arg1 (p / prey
         :mod (w / whole)
         :poss b)
      :manner (c2 / chew-01 :polarity -
         :arg0 b
         :arg1 p)))
```

Chinese sentence: 这本书中写道: "这些蟒蛇把它们的猎获物不加咀嚼地囫囵吞下
Annotation (Chinese AMR with English concept labels):

```
(x11 / writes-01
   :arg0  (x13 / book-01)
   :arg1  (x14 / swallow-01
      :arg0  (x15 / boa
         :mod  (x16 / these))
      :arg1  (x17 / prey
         :poss  (x25 / x15))
      :manner  (x19 / whole)
      :manner  (x21 / chew-01 :polarity -))))
```

Figure 3: Gold English AMR and our annotation for parallel sentences (some roles removed for brevity of presentation).

The production of our annotations is motivated by the ability to then quantify the amount of difference between our annotations and the gold English AMRs. We

English sentence: And after some work with a colored pencil I succeeded in making my first drawing.
Chinese sentence: 于是，我也用彩色铅笔画出了我的第一副图画。
Literal English translation of Chinese sentence: So, I also drew my first drawing with colored pencils.

Figure 4: An English and Chinese sentence pair from the dataset, displaying slight variation in the translation.

use Smatch to quantify this difference as the standard similarity evaluation technique for AMR pairs.

The Smatch score for the gold English AMRs in comparison to the annotations is 41% for those produced by Annotator 1 and 44% for those produced by Annotator 2. These Smatch scores are over 60 sentence pairs each. This indicates that there is a sizable effect of source language on the structure of the AMR even with the Chinese labels being replaced, raising questions for how we evaluate cross-lingual AMR parsers.

We expect that some of the differences we capture in our approach are due to translation, and some differences are due to syntactic and semantic properties, as established by previous work comparing more similar languages (Spanish and English) (Wein and Schneider, 2021). One example of a syntactic effect on AMR structure can be seen in figure 2.

This divergence arises out of the ability in Chinese to omit sentence subjects when they can be understood from context, which explains why the Chinese graph is missing an `:arg0` argument. It is likely that there are differences in meaning in parallel sentences as caused by the translation process, though there are also observed syntactic differences as noted in the example in figure 2.

A more subtle effect of source language on AMR structure can be seen in figure 3 relating to the `:arg1 prey`. In English, we have "swallow their prey whole," such that "whole" is a semantic modifier of "prey," denoted by `:mod`. In Chinese, the equivalent is 囫囵 (wholly, possibly barbarically) 吞下 (swallow). Wholly (囫囵) is annotated as `:manner` to the swallowing (吞下), instead of as the `:mod` of `prey`. We consider this a faithful and standard translation reflective of cross-linguistic differences between the "swallow whole" construction in English and the "wholly swallow" construction in Chinese. This difference is reflected in the AMR.

One example of sentences being slight variants of each other rather than literal translations is the sentence pair seen in figure 4. The annotation (same for both annotators) received a Smatch score of 0.43 similarity with the gold English AMR. The majority of the sentences are closely parallel, so we expect that the difference we are quantifying is an effect of syntactic and semantic divergence between Chinese and English.[6]

[6] If Chinese and English gold AMRs are released in different domains in future work, it would be interesting to repeat this analysis on those texts and compare our findings.

4.3. Accounting for Design Differences

A few relatively superficial differences in annotation guidelines between Chinese and English need to be accounted for, as they may impact the Smatch score without being a direct reflection of source language impact. We found four types of differences which have an impact on AMR structure:

- CAMR uses the concept `mean` for elaboration/further explanation of another concept/structure, which is often included in parentheses/colon (present in 3 AMR pairs)
- CAMR uses the concept `cause` instead of `cause-01` to refer to the cause of an event, which is considered a non-core role (in 4 AMR pairs)
- CAMR occasionally uses `:beneficiary` instead of `:arg2` to refer to indirect object (in 5 AMR pairs)
- While English AMR does not account for the sentence being a quotation, CAMR roots all quotations with `say` (in 13 AMR pairs)[7]

Removed Diff.	Anno.1/Gold	Anno.2/Gold
None	41%	44%
Mean	43%	44%
Cause	41%	44%
Beneficiary	41%	43%
Quotation	41%	43%
All	42%	45%

Table 1: Smatch scores without each of the four design differences.

As can be seen in table 1, even when removing all AMR pairs noticeably affected by schema differences, the Smatch score similarity between our annotations and the gold English AMRs only increases incrementally, and a large effect of source language remains. This indicates that the dissimilarity we measure in AMR structure is not due to differences in annotation schema.

5 Conclusion

Our case study between Chinese and English serves as an analysis of the impact of linguistic divergence between those two languages on AMR structure. Through our annotation process of translating Chinese concepts to English, we find that there is a dramatic impact on AMR structures, with Smatch scores between our annotations and the gold English AMRs falling below 50%. For comparison, inter-annotator Smatch scores within a single language (Chinese) in the same domain have been reported at 83% (Li et al., 2016).

This substantive impact on AMR structure motivates further consideration for source language when working with AMR cross-lingually—either in evaluating cross-lingual AMR parsers or when developing and comparing AMR schema in new languages.

[7] In English AMR, only the first sentence in the quotation, starting with open quotes, is rooted with `say`. In Chinese AMR, any sentence containing quotes is rooted with `say`.

As a meaning representation, it is critical that an AMR graph effectively reflect the meaning of the sentence being parsed. Current cross-lingual AMR parsers evaluate accuracy of a parsed non-English sentence by comparing to the corresponding gold English AMR. Our newfound evidence that source language has a sizable effect on AMR structure should be taken into account when interpreting cross-lingual Smatch evaluations. Ideally, gold AMRs should be created in the source language for evaluating cross-lingual parsers (even if sufficient training data is only available in English). Future work might investigate steps to mitigate source language impact when evaluating cross-lingual AMR parsing, or further investigate the effect in other language pairs.

Acknowledgments

We thank anonymous reviewers for their feedback. This work is supported by a Clare Boothe Luce Scholarship.

6 Bibliographical References

References

Anchiêta, Rafael and Pardo, Thiago (2018). Towards AMR-BR: A SemBank for Brazilian Portuguese language. In *Proceedings of the Eleventh International Conference on Language Resources and Evaluation (LREC 2018)*. European Language Resources Association (ELRA), Miyazaki, Japan.

Azin, Zahra and Eryiğit, Gülşen (2019). Towards Turkish Abstract Meaning Representation. In *Proceedings of the 57th Annual Meeting of the Association for Computational Linguistics: Student Research Workshop*, pages 43–47. Association for Computational Linguistics, Florence, Italy. doi: 10.18653/v1/P19-2006.

Banarescu, Laura, Bonial, Claire, Cai, Shu, Georgescu, Madalina, Griffitt, Kira, Hermjakob, Ulf, Knight, Kevin, Koehn, Philipp, Palmer, Martha, and Schneider, Nathan (2013). Abstract Meaning Representation for sembanking. In *Proceedings of the 7th Linguistic Annotation Workshop and Interoperability with Discourse*, pages 178–186. Association for Computational Linguistics, Sofia, Bulgaria.

Cai, Shu and Knight, Kevin (2013). Smatch: an evaluation metric for semantic feature structures. In *Proceedings of the 51st Annual Meeting of the Association for Computational Linguistics (Volume 2: Short Papers)*, pages 748–752. Association for Computational Linguistics, Sofia, Bulgaria.

Choe, Hyonsu, Han, Jiyoon, Park, Hyejin, Oh, Tae Hwan, and Kim, Hansaem (2020). Building Korean Abstract Meaning Representation corpus. In *Proceedings of the Second International Workshop on Designing Meaning Representations*, pages 21–29. Association for Computational Linguistics, Barcelona Spain (online).

Damonte, Marco (2019). *Understanding and Generating Language with Abstract Meaning Representation*. Ph.D. thesis, University of Edinburgh.

Damonte, Marco and Cohen, Shay (2020). Abstract Meaning Representation 2.0 - Four Translations. Technical Report LDC2020T07, Linguistic Data Consortium, Philadelphia, PA.

Hajič, Jan, Bojar, Ondřej, and Urešová, Zdeňka (2014). Comparing Czech and English AMRs. In *Proceedings of Workshop on Lexical and Grammatical Resources for Language Processing*, pages 55–64. Association for Computational Linguistics and Dublin City University, Dublin, Ireland. doi:10.3115/v1/W14-5808.

Koppel, Moshe and Ordan, Noam (2011). Translationese and its dialects. In *Proceedings of the 49th Annual Meeting of the Association for Computational Linguistics: Human Language Technologies*, pages 1318–1326. Association for Computational Linguistics, Portland, Oregon, USA.

Li, Bin, Wen, Yuan, Qu, Weiguang, Bu, Lijun, and Xue, Nianwen (2016). Annotating The Little Prince with Chinese AMRs. In *Proceedings of the 10th Linguistic Annotation Workshop held in conjunction with ACL 2016 (LAW-X 2016)*, pages 7–15. Association for Computational Linguistics, Berlin, Germany. doi: 10.18653/v1/W16-1702.

Linh, Ha and Nguyen, Huyen (2019). A case study on meaning representation for Vietnamese. In *Proceedings of the First International Workshop on Designing Meaning Representations*, pages 148–153. Association for Computational Linguistics, Florence, Italy. doi:10.18653/v1/W19-3317.

Migueles-Abraira, Noelia, Agerri, Rodrigo, and Diaz de Ilarraza, Arantza (2018). Annotating Abstract Meaning Representations for Spanish. In *Proceedings of the Eleventh International Conference on Language Resources and Evaluation (LREC 2018)*. European Language Resources Association (ELRA), Miyazaki, Japan.

Oral, Elif, Acar, Ali, and Eryiğit, Gülşen (2022). Abstract meaning representation of Turkish. *Natural Language Engineering*, pages 1–30. doi:10.1017/S1351324922000183.

Sobrevilla Cabezudo, Marco Antonio and Pardo, Thiago (2019). Towards a general Abstract Meaning Representation corpus for Brazilian Portuguese. In *Proceedings of the 13th Linguistic Annotation Workshop*, pages 236–244. Association for Computational Linguistics, Florence, Italy. doi:10.18653/v1/W19-4028.

Takhshid, Reza, Shojaei, Razieh, Azin, Zahra, and Bahrani, Mohammad (2022). Persian Abstract Meaning Representation. *arXiv preprint arXiv:2205.07712*.

Van Gysel, Jens E. L., Vigus, Meagan, Chun, Jayeol, Lai, Kenneth, Moeller, Sarah, Yao, Jiarui, O'Gorman, Tim, Cowell, Andrew, Croft, William, Huang, Chu-Ren, Hajič, Jan, Martin, James H., Oepen, Stephan, Palmer, Martha, Pustejovsky, James, Vallejos, Rosa, and Xue, Nianwen (2021). Designing a Uniform Meaning Representation for natural language processing. *KI - Künstliche Intelligenz.*

Wein, Shira, Donatelli, Lucia, Ricker, Ethan, Engstrom, Calvin, Nelson, Alex, and Schneider, Nathan (2022). Spanish Abstract Meaning Representation: Annotation of a general corpus. *arXiv preprint arXiv:2204.07663.*

Wein, Shira and Schneider, Nathan (2021). Classifying divergences in cross-lingual AMR pairs. In *Proceedings of The Joint 15th Linguistic Annotation Workshop (LAW) and 3rd Designing Meaning Representations (DMR) Workshop*, pages 56–65. Association for Computational Linguistics, Punta Cana, Dominican Republic.

Xue, Nianwen, Bojar, Ondřej, Hajič, Jan, Palmer, Martha, Urešová, Zdeňka, and Zhang, Xiuhong (2014). Not an interlingua, but close: Comparison of English AMRs to Chinese and Czech. In *Proceedings of the Ninth International Conference on Language Resources and Evaluation (LREC'14)*, pages 1765–1772. European Language Resources Association (ELRA), Reykjavik, Iceland.

Proceedings of the 16th Linguistic Annotation Workshop (LAW-XVI) @LREC 2022, pages 103–110
Marseille, 24 June 2022

Midas Loop: Prioritized Human-in-the-Loop Annotation for Large Scale Multilayer Data

Luke Gessler, Lauren Levine, Amir Zeldes
Georgetown University
Department of Linguistics
{lg876, lel76, amir.zeldes}@georgetown.edu

Abstract

Large scale annotation of rich multilayer corpus data is expensive and time consuming, motivating approaches that integrate high quality automatic tools with active learning in order to prioritize human labeling of hard cases. A related challenge in such scenarios is the concurrent management of automatically annotated data and human annotated data, particularly where different subsets of the data have been corrected for different types of annotation and with different levels of confidence. In this paper we present Midas Loop, a collaborative, version-controlled online annotation environment for multilayer corpus data which includes integrated provenance and confidence metadata for each piece of information at the document, sentence, token and annotation level. We present a case study on improving annotation quality in an existing multilayer parse bank of English called AMALGUM, focusing on active learning in corpus preprocessing, at the level of sentence segmentation, which remains surprisingly challenging for automated systems. Our results show improvements to state-of-the-art sentence segmentation and a promising workflow for getting "silver" data to approach gold standard quality.

Keywords: corpus, annotation, collaborative, active learning, multilayer, sentence segmentation, human in the loop

1. Introduction

Multilayer corpora (Ide et al., 2010; Santos and Mota, 2010; Zeldes, 2018) are richly annotated language resources that contain information about a variety of linguistic phenomena in parallel, such as morpho-syntactic analyses, named entity recognition, semantic role labeling or 'PropBanking' (Palmer et al., 2005), coreference resolution and more. While they are highly valuable for both linguistic studies and computational applications, such datasets can be challenging to maintain: the existence of multiple annotations for each text means that different annotations may be aligned or interconnected, that segmentations such as word tokenization and sentence splitting will often need to match across layers (Krause et al., 2012), and that correcting one part of a corpus may have complex consequences for another (Peng and Zeldes, 2018). These challenges can more easily be overcome for small, hand-curated datasets, but may become unmanageable for larger corpora, especially if iterative improvement and corrections to the data are envisioned.

In this paper we present a new, open-source, production-ready system for iterative correction of large-scale multilayer data. The system, called Midas Loop, integrates with retrainable NLP models to provide confidence metadata for CoNLL-U annotations. This confidence metadata allows for both the targeting of low confidence areas of the data for manual review, as well as harnessing higher confidence areas of the data in order to curate subsets that can be used for tasks that have specific requirements regarding annotation quality.

We use the freely available AMALGUM corpus (Gessler et al., 2020) as a case study, containing 4M tokens in 8 English genres, automatically annotated for high quality Universal Dependencies (UD) parses (incl. enhanced dependencies); document structure using TEI p5 XML tags (Burnard and Bauman, 2008); typed and nested named and non-named entity recognition; normalized time expressions; coreference resolution; and discourse parses in Rhetorical Structure Theory (Mann and Thompson, 1988). Of these tasks, our system currently handles sentence segmentation (at the document level), as well as structural tasks which are edited at the sentence level, including POS tagging, lemmatization, dependency syntax corrections etc. These capabilities thus encompass the standard UD/CoNLL-U format column annotations[1], and in the future we plan to add extensible support for other kinds of annotations expressed in the MISC column or metadata lines of the CoNLL-U format, such as annotations for entities, coreference and discourse parses.

Since the substantial size of the data curated by the system makes comprehensive manual correction unfeasible, we adopt an active learning strategy, which allows users to query the system for likely errors based on NLP model output probabilities, which are then highlighted in context and presented to annotators.

We evaluate the effectiveness of our strategy on the surprisingly tricky task of automated sentence splitting in multiple genres, by iteratively retraining tools on high-priority corrected data in a synergistic cycle of manual and automated correction. The resulting data contains mixed gold and silver quality annotations, which necessitate facilities for keeping track of version controlled annotation provenance, as well as qualitative and quantitative quality estimates at the document, sentence, token and annotation levels.

The main contributions of this paper are:

[1] `https://universaldependencies.org/format.html`; see below for more details

1. We present an open source annotation system for large scale multilayer corpus correction incorporating active learning across a broad range of tasks, which highlights uncertain NLP outputs prioritized for annotator correction and tracks annotation quality through metadata.
2. We also present a new and improved version of this work's test case corpus, AMALGUM, with very high quality automatic and some manually corrected NLP output.
3. We evaluate the effectiveness of active learning for sentence splitting and achieve a substantially improved SOTA score for English sentence splitting on the genre-diverse gold standard GUM dataset, which includes both spoken and written data, as well as challenging unedited user generated content from the Web. (Sanguinetti et al., 2022)

2. Previous work

2.1. Multilayer annotation

Because of their complex structure and potential interdependencies between layers, multilayer corpora can be particularly challenging to annotate and to maintain. While an initial focus on correcting treebanking (Lai and Bird, 2004) allowed the use of single tools without many cross-checks, subsequent work on integrating frame semantics, prosody and pragmatics led to multilayer data with intertwined syntactic, phonological, semantic and pragmatic graphs that pushed single interface tools to their limit, as in the SALSA project (Burchardt et al., 2008) or the NXT Switchboard Corpus (Calhoun et al., 2010). Later corpora such as MASC (Ide et al., 2010) and OntoNotes (Weischedel et al., 2012) added increasingly many levels of annotation, such as concurrent word senses, semantic role labeling, coreference resolution and named entity recognition, in addition to morpho-syntactic analyses, with the result that separate tools were often used for editing each layer.

Many single-task annotation interfaces exist for the layers handled by our system, including Arborator (Gerdes, 2013) and UD Annotatrix (Tyers et al., 2018) for dependency trees, and CorefAnnotator (Reiter, 2018) for coreference annotation. There also exist widely used generic web based tools, such as WebAnno (Eckart de Castilho et al., 2016) and INCEpTION (Klie et al., 2018), which target the annotation of typed spans and relations. Such tools are highly effective for individual annotation types. However, they are not designed to simultaneously handle the full spectrum of annotation types found in multilayer corpora, nor do they interact well with concurrent editing of segmentation and sentence-level annotations, or preserve versioned provenance information during iterative improvements to documents.

There are also a few examples of annotation tools tailored to multilayer editing, including FoLiA (van Gompel and Reynaert, 2014) and Atomic (Druskat et al., 2014), which were built from the ground up to support diverse, possibly interdependent, annotations in a single graph data model. Our approach follows these in that we use a single data model to support multiple layers, though we maintain a closer workflow to annotation of corpora such as OntoNotes, in that each annotation task interface is specialized and separate, exposing only necessary facets of the data and simplifying user interactions by limiting the amount of training required for each task. However, this inevitably means that our API must keep track of single layer changes which have meaningful consequences for other layers, which we manage in a non-destructive and version controlled way during updates (see Section 3).

2.2. Active learning

Active learning (AL), initially called 'uncertainty sampling' (Lewis and Gale, 1994) has a long history in NLP as a technique to reduce the amount of data required to learn a task: by targeting uncertain outputs from a large pool of automatically labeled data, human annotators can focus effort on resolving cases that algorithms find particularly challenging. AL continues to be applied successfully in recent papers for sentence classification (Ein-Dor et al., 2020), Named Entity Recognition (NER) (Shen et al., 2017), paraphrase detection (Bai et al., 2020), sentiment analysis (Ashrafi Asli et al., 2020) and much more.

We observe two trends in previous work on annotation systems for AL: 1. they typically target a single, specific task and/or domain (e.g. NER output for biomedical data) and typically only support relatively simple structures, such as non-overlapping span annotations (Searle et al., 2019; Lin et al., 2019) or document classification (Wiechmann et al., 2021); 2. they often simplify tasks by presenting specific questions to annotators: for example, a system might present a pair of mentions with questionable coreference status to an annotator for validation, substantially simplifying the interaction and interface requirements (Li et al., 2020).

Such systems can be highly valuable for targeted needs, however they fall short when the goal is to iteratively upgrade large-scale, silver-quality data into a gold-standard-near multilayer resource, with comprehensive linguistic annotations. Probably the closest existing tool to Midas Loop in implementing these goals is *prodigy*[2], which allows annotation with AL for customizable spans, as well as some graph annotations; however it is a non-freely available commercial tool, is tied to the SpaCy NLP platform,[3] which does not support some of our annotation workflows, and cannot handle discourse trees, which are relevant to our work with AMALGUM.

Finally, although AL is generally expected to improve NLP tool accuracy, care must be taken to prevent a focus on skewed outlier data, which can result

[2] `https://prodi.gy/`
[3] `https://spacy.io/`

if AL-selected examples outnumber 'normal' common examples, or substantially alter their relative likelihood (Baldridge and Osborne, 2004; Karamcheti et al., 2021). In our experiment in Section 4 we therefore focus on choosing entire documents with high levels of uncertainty (which presumably also contain 'common' cases), rather than just individual sentences from all documents, but the risk of data skewing nevertheless remains. To assess the practical impact of AL in the context of the present project, Section 4.2 evaluates the gains from targeted data selection for one early and very important task in the compilation of multilayer corpora: sentence splitting.

3. System Architecture

Midas Loop can be divided into two parts. The core system is a web server which maintains the state of the data and allows changes to be made to the data via an HTTP API. The frontend system is a web browser application which provides a graphical user interface with multiple annotation components for making changes to data. Guidance from machine learning models on which annotations are most dubious (and therefore most in need of manual review) is stored in order to be visually indicated in the interface.

Our frontend system's functionality enables the human-in-the-loop workflow described in this paper and enables editing of most annotations in the popular CoNLL-U format adopted by UD. However, the core system's API is agnostic regarding the frontend interface, and as such it is also possible to interact with the core system in other ways: for example, another web browser frontend could be created, or a crowdsourcing study on Amazon Mechanical Turk could send updates to the core system, which is an independent component.

3.1. Core System[4]

Overview The core system is a web server implemented in Clojure[5] which provides an HTTP API for clients to create, read, update, and delete CoNLL-U annotations. Token-based authentication restricts access to only authorized users, and it is possible to import and export data both via the HTTP API and the command-line. The core system is distributed as a single standalone .jar file and works on any platform with a Java Virtual Machine implementation. The core system contacts NLP services via HTTP and is therefore completely decoupled from them, allowing services to be implemented ad hoc in another programming language, such as Python. A full description of the API is included in the system's repository.

Data Model Internally, CoNLL-U file strings are deserialized and represented as a graph. Each document, sentence, metadata line, and "token" (i.e., 10-column row) is represented as a node. Additionally, each annotation within a token is represented as a node: for each token, there is a separate node for its FORM column, and for fields with multiple annotations like morphological features (FEATS) and MISC annotations,[6] each key-value pair is represented as a separate node. This proliferation of graph structure is needed in order to easily keep track of which annotations are human-verified "gold" annotations, and which annotations are NLP system-provided "silver" annotations: some tokens may have e.g. a gold part of speech annotation but silver syntactic head and dependency relation annotations.

Database The immutable graph database XTDB[7] is used to store and process this representation. We additionally note that XTDB stores the full history of all past database states. This functionality is not used by the core system at the moment, but it could be used in the future in order to allow access to **all** past versions of a certain document or sentence.

NLP Integration In order for active learning support to be available for a certain kind of annotation, an NLP system must be available which can provide annotation probabilities. This functionality is entirely "opt-in" and may be configured for as many or as few annotation kinds as desired. It is required that NLP systems are reachable via HTTP and can handle a few standardized API calls, and we anticipate that users will find it most convenient to take existing NLP models and wrap them in an implementation of this HTTP protocol using a Python web framework such as Flask.

NLP services are consulted at a sentence-level resolution: every time any element of a sentence changes, all registered NLP services are notified, and have the opportunity to provide new annotations and probability distributions for the layer in that sentence. Annotations from NLP services will overwrite existing annotations, unless an existing annotation is "gold" (i.e. manually added by an annotator), in which case the existing annotation will not be overwritten. For example, if sentence segmentation is altered, we assume that an automatic parser should be called to parse the resulting, newly formed sentences.

Supported Data The core system provides full support for reading, editing, importing, and serializing core datatypes in a standard CoNLL-U file. This includes changes to the 10 standard columns, as well as changes to sentence splits. Multiword and empty tokens as specified in the CoNLL-U format are fully supported. Changes to tokenization, changes to metadata lines, enhanced dependency editing,[8] and creation of new textual data other than via import of a CoNLL-U string are cur-

[4] `https://github.com/gucorpling/midas-loop-ui.git`

[5] `https://clojure.org/`

[6] See `https://universaldependencies.org/format.html`

[7] `https://xtdb.com/`

[8] For English, as in other UD data, we currently propagate corrected enhanced dependencies automatically based on corrected un-enhanced morphosyntax.

rently unsupported, but are planned for future releases.

Future Supported Data Additionally, although our system does not yet support editing of annotations not natively expressed in CoNLL-U, such as those for entities, coreference, and discourse, we plan to support these eventually using a configuration which will tell the system how to read them from the MISC column or metadata lines. We also plan to support representations proposed by the recent Universal Anaphora project (`http://universalanaphora.org/`). These extensions will allow the system to continue working with just CoNLL-U while allowing it to process arbitrary annotations.

3.1.1. Layer Interdependencies

As some annotation layers have dependencies on others, a word on how layer dependencies are handled in our system is warranted. For instance, head attachments in a dependency syntax layer are constrained by token and sentence annotations: in UD, valid heads must be tokens within the same sentence as the child token. This complicates the process of programmatically applying changes to multilayer data: for example, if an existing sentence is split, any head attachments that span the new sentence boundary must be removed, or else some tokens will have invalid heads.

For issues such as this, where a change in a "lower" layer could render existing annotations in "higher" layers ill-formed, our general approach is to perform the smallest number of adjustments necessary in order to arrive at a valid state. For example, in the situation just described where a dependency syntax layer is affected by a sentence split, we choose to nullify any head attachments which span the new sentence boundary, ensuring that the tree will remain valid, albeit incomplete. (Note however that if an NLP service is registered for dependency syntax, the new sentences will soon receive new parses from the service.) Analogous operations are implemented for other layer interactions which ensure that data in the system will avoid invalid states.

3.2. Frontend System[9]

Our frontend system provides a UI for performing our active learning workflow on a subset of CoNLL-U annotation types. Specifically, we support read/write as well as active learning support for sentence boundaries, HEAD/DEPREL, XPOS, and UPOS and currently read/write only support for LEMMA. We also support querying and ordering documents according to the number of probable annotation errors in a document, as identified by proportion of gold annotations (Figure 3) or NLP model output probabilities for a given type of annotation. Specifically, with regard to the output probabilities, given a document D with tokens $t_1, \ldots, t_n$ and annotations $a_1, \ldots, a_n$ for a given layer, and given a probability distribution over possible annotations on

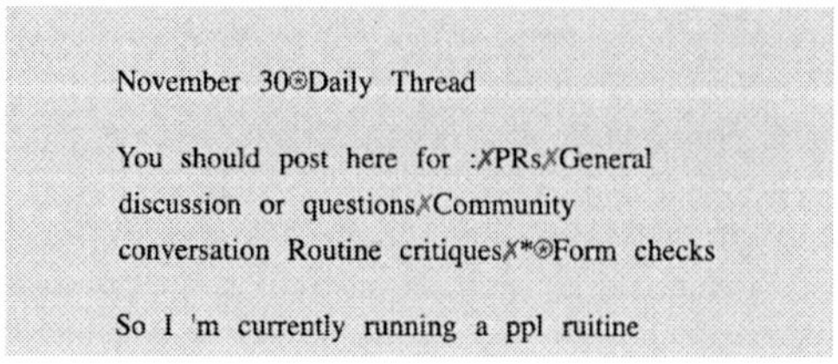

Figure 1: Segmentation interface: ✗ indicates a sentence split; ⊛ indicates that a space is not a sentence split. Red indicate a suspicious position for annotator inspection, while blue indicates edits by the user.

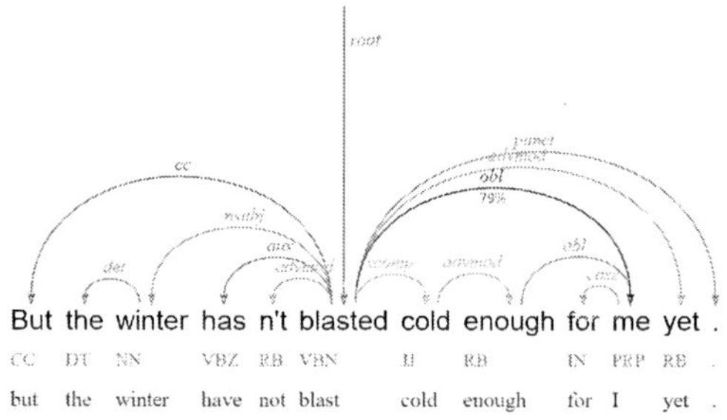

Figure 2: The syntax interface showing a suspicious annotation in red, and a high-confidence corrected annotation in green. Each suspicious annotation is shown to the user, who can determine which annotation to keep.

that layer at each position i, $P(A_i = a_i|D)$, we compute $\frac{1}{n}\sum_1^n \max_{a_i} P(A_i = a_i|D)$, i.e. the average probability of the most likely label at each position for the entire document. This information is used in aggregate, and there is currently no functionality for querying for documents with specific likely error types.

We have two different interfaces at the document level: one interface is for handling segmentation boundaries (Figure 1), and the other handles all remaining supported annotation types, i.e. tree by tree editing of UD data (Figure 2).[10] A third annotation UI for entities and coreference is currently being developed.

4. Evaluation

4.1. Data and setup

In order to evaluate the effectiveness of the prioritized sentence split corrections completed in Midas Loop for this case study, we used data corrected for sentence splits from the AMALGUM corpus to supplement the training data of GUM (Georgetown University Multilayer corpus (Zeldes, 2017)), the smaller human annotated English web corpus on which AMALGUM is based. The auto-annotated AMALGUM corpus itself is considered silver data, while the sentence split corrections completed in Midas Loop are considered gold

[9] `https://github.com/gucorpling/midas-loop`

[10] We would like to credit Gerdes (2013) for the look and feel of the dependencies interface, which re-implements the graphical style of the annotation Arborator tool.

Figure 3: The document selection interface, which is used to query documents for annotation correction.

data. GUM is entirely human annotated and is thus considered to be composed of entirely gold data.

While sentence splitting has not enjoyed as much attention as syntactic or semantic analysis, and is sometimes regarded as an easy or solved task, even recent results on its accuracy in unseen data indicate that it is highly challenging, with f-scores on the GUM test set ranging from 86.35 (Stanza, (Qi et al., 2020)), to 91.60 (Trankit, (Nguyen et al., 2021)) to 93.5 (GumDrop, (Yu et al., 2019)).[11] At the same time, incorrectly split sentences by definition result in incorrect syntax trees, malsegmented discourse parses and potentially cut off entities or mentions for coreference resolution, meaning that it is a high priority to start the multilayer annotation process with high accuracy splitting.

Within the AMALGUM corpus, 10 documents of the highest priority for correction were chosen from each of the 8 genres included in the corpus: academic, biography, fiction, forum, how-to, interview, news, and travel. To determine the documents most in need of correction, each document of the AMALGUM corpus was run through a transformer based, shingled sentence splitter, which applies tokenwise binary classification to overlapping spans of 20 tokens in an attempt to find split points. The splitter is implemented using flair (Akbik et al., 2019) as an LSTM-based sequence tagger fed by transformer word embeddings encoded by the pretrained English `bert-base-cased` model.

The splitter's confidence score (0–1) on whether or not there was a sentence split at the proceeding space was recorded for each token: we say that a space needs to be examined by a human annotator if it precedes a token with a recorded confidence threshold of under 0.9. The document with the highest count of instances in need of human inspection, normalized by the token

[11]These numbers are not perfectly comparable, since different papers have used different release versions of the UD dataset, but they give an idea of the challenging nature of the task.

Metric	ALL	POS.
Raw agreement	0.9965	0.9660
F_1 score	0.9827	0.9827
Cohen's κ	0.9808	—

Table 1: Microaveraged agreement for 8 documents, considering either ALL tokens or only the positive split class (POS., no credit for correct negatives)

length of the document, is designated as the document of highest priority for correction. The 80 AMALGUM documents identified by prioritization, containing approximately 68K tokens, were divided amongst three human annotators and their sentence splits were corrected.

We assess the quality of our gold sentence split annotations by double-annotating one document out of the 10 for each genre, for a total of 8 double-annotated documents. Sentence split annotation is treated as a binary sequence tagging task, where the token at the beginning of each sentence is given the positive label ("B") and all other tokens are given the negative label ("O"). We report our scores in Table 1, including the measures for raw tokenwise agreement (% tokens where both annotators made the sae decision), mutual F1 score (the F1 score, taking one annotator as gold and the other as the prediction), as well as Cohen's Kappa. Overall, our agreement measures indicate very high consistency in our gold sentence split annotations.

4.2. Results

Due to non-deterministic GPU behavior, we report 5-run averages for splitting scores on each genre (as is common practice, we use positive class F1, with no credit for the very common correct negative class), as well as the cross-genre macro average and the instance-based micro average, which can differ since some genres have substantially more splits per document, as well as different distributions of longer or shorter sentences per document. Results are broken down into several scenarios: first, we compare the use of just the gold standard GUM corpus as training data versus adding the AMALGUM data from the active learning corrections to training. Second, because AMALGUM is a multilayer corpus which includes information about TEI XML tags in the source data, such as paragraphs, headings, bulleted lists and more, this information can easily be used to improve sentence splitting accuracy (Gessler et al., 2020) – for example, sentences are usually assumed not to cross paragraph boundaries, or run on from headings into subsequent text. We therefore compare the effect of adding data both 'ex situ' in splitting from plain tokenized text, and 'in situ', with access to the XML tags, which represents a more realistic but also easier scenario for our use case.

Figure 4 shows the results, with boxplots for the spread of scores across genres, without active learning data (red) and with it (teal). We note that in the

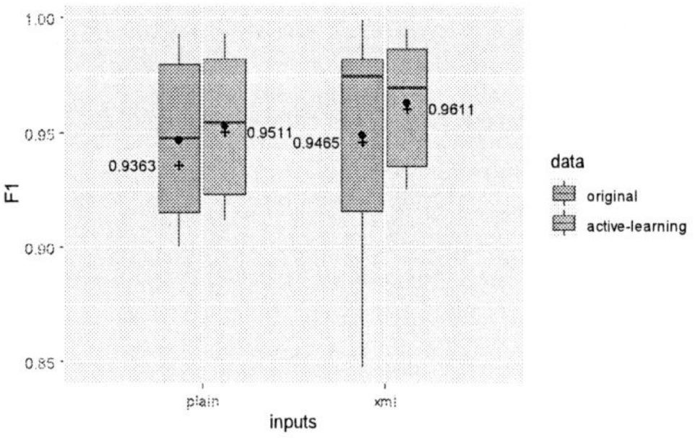

Figure 4: Sentence splitting results for 8 genres in GUM's test set when training on GUM, with and without added AMALGUM data from active learning. In the XML scenario, XML tags are used to prevent sentences crossing paragraphs and other block elements. Crosses and their labels indicate micro-averages and dots mark the 8-genre macro-averages.

plain text scenario, micro-averaged accuracy improves by ~1.5%, which is substantial when scores are already in the mid-90s, corresponding to a 23% reduction in errors. Adding XML block information, which prevents sentences crossing paragraphs, headings, etc., improves both scenarios almost exactly by 1%, leading to a realistic sentence splitting accuracy score of 96.11%, an extremely high score compared to scores reported by systems on past versions of GUM (to the best of our knowledge, the plain text score, too, constitutes a new SOTA result on any version of GUM). Although scores are relatively close, the difference is highly significant for all contrasts ($p < 0.01$) across all 5 runs (the added XML or AL scenarios never underperform scenarios without them, in any of the five runs).

We also note that the active learning-enhanced data leads to increased stability across genres in both scenarios (less variance), with a noticeable instability in the unenhanced XML scenario. Qualitative analysis shows that the instability is caused by unfortunate split decisions across block elements in both Reddit and news data, whose elimination by the XML boundaries creates extremely long unsplit sentences. These contexts result from the noisiness and lack of punctuation in user-generated content on Reddit, and oddities of headline syntax, captions and other 'news-speak', which are common in the news genre (Bostan et al., 2020). It appears that the active learning data, which was selected to reflect contexts that models were uncertain about in each genre, prevents some of these errors and leads to more consistent scores, across the 5 runs on average.

We also review the annotator corrections made to the AMALGUM data in order to determine how effectively we identified documents that were of high priority for annotators to review. Table 2 shows the proportions of token boundaries flagged for review as well as proportions of boundaries that were changed by annotators during review. As 46.78% of flagged sentence splits were identified as false positives by the annotators reviewing the documents, we note that the cases high-

Splits	
Splits flagged	29.85%
Flagged splits merged	46.78%
Non flagged splits merged	1.82%
Spaces	
Spaces flagged	0.89%
Flagged spaces split	24.14%
Non flagged spaces split	0.47%

Table 2: Proportions of token boundaries that were flagged for review and proportions of changes that were made by annotators during review.

lighted for review were truly non-obvious cases that the splitter could not reliably predict and as such needed to be reviewed by a human annotator. We also note that nearly all of the necessary changes in the documents were correctly flagged for review, as only 1.82% of non-flagged sentence splits were additionally identified by annotators as false positives. Looking at Table 2, we see a similar picture on a smaller scale when we look at the non-sentence split spaces flagged as possible false negatives for review.

5. Conclusion

In this paper we presented Midas Loop, a collaborative multilayer corpus annotation system built specifically for active-learning-guided, iterative correction of automatically annotated data analyzed across different and interdependent annotation types representable in the CoNLL-U format. By using the system, we were able to improve annotation quality for the challenging and fundamental task of sentence splitting, whose accuracy is a prerequisite for subsequent annotation layers affected by sentence level decisions, such as dependency annotation, NER, coreference resolution and discourse parsing.

Our results on sentence splitting indicated that the system was effective in suggesting documents which were likely to contain many errors, and that the potential error positions identified by the system were indeed likely to require correction (about half of the time) and contained almost all positions requiring correction (over 98% in this case). Re-training our sentence splitter using the added AL-selected data proved highly effective, resulting in new SOTA scores on sentence splitting with and without XML tag information, and bringing substantial error reductions and cross-genre stability in every scenario tested.

Our future plans for the system include adding more annotation functionality, and especially support for discourse level annotations covered by the AMALGUM corpus, such as coreference resolution and the annotation of associated mentioned entities, as well as support for full document discourse parsing. We plan to leverage the existing, separate annotation tools used to annotate the original GUM corpus, but which do not currently offer good integration for multilayer interactions and active learning. These include the GitDox (Zhang and Zeldes, 2017) editor's Spannotator widget[12] and the discourse annotation interface of rstWeb (Zeldes, 2016).[13]

6. Bibliographical References

Akbik, A., Bergmann, T., Blythe, D., Rasul, K., Schweter, S., and Vollgraf, R. (2019). FLAIR: An easy-to-use framework for state-of-the-art NLP. In *NAACL 2019, 2019 Annual Conference of the North American Chapter of the Association for Computational Linguistics (Demonstrations)*, pages 54–59.

Ashrafi Asli, S. A., Sabeti, B., Majdabadi, Z., Golazizian, P., Fahmi, R., and Momenzadeh, O. (2020). Optimizing annotation effort using active learning strategies: A sentiment analysis case study in Persian. In *Proceedings of the 12th Language Resources and Evaluation Conference*, pages 2855–2861, Marseille, France. European Language Resources Association.

Bai, G., He, S., Liu, K., Zhao, J., and Nie, Z. (2020). Pre-trained language model based active learning for sentence matching. In *Proceedings of the 28th International Conference on Computational Linguistics*, pages 1495–1504, Barcelona, Spain (Online).

Baldridge, J. and Osborne, M. (2004). Active learning and the total cost of annotation. In *Proceedings of the 2004 Conference on Empirical Methods in Natural Language Processing*, pages 9–16, Barcelona, Spain.

Bostan, L. A. M., Kim, E., and Klinger, R. (2020). GoodNewsEveryone: A corpus of news headlines annotated with emotions, semantic roles, and reader perception. In *Proceedings of the 12th Language Resources and Evaluation Conference*, pages 1554–1566, Marseille, France. European Language Resources Association.

Burchardt, A., Padó, S., Spohr, D., Frank, A., and Heid, U. (2008). Formalising multi-layer corpora in OWL DL - lexicon modelling, querying and consistency control. In *Proceedings of the Third International Joint Conference on Natural Language Processing (IJCNLP 2008)*, pages 389–396, Hyderabad, India.

Burnard, L. and Bauman, S., (2008). *TEI P5: Guidelines for Electronic Text Encoding and Interchange*.

Calhoun, S., Carletta, J., Brenier, J., Mayo, N., Jurafsky, D., Steedman, M., and Beaver, D. (2010). The NXT-format Switchboard Corpus: A rich resource for investigating the syntax, semantics, pragmatics and prosody of dialogue. *Language Resources and Evaluation*, 44(4):387–419.

Druskat, S., Bierkandt, L., Gast, V., Rzymski, C., and Zipser, F. (2014). Atomic: An open-source software platform for multi-layer corpus annotation. In Josef Ruppenhofer et al., editors, *Proceedings of KONVENS 2014*, pages 228–234, Hildesheim, Germany.

[12]See https://corpling.uis.georgetown.edu/gitdox/spannotator.html

[13]https://corpling.uis.georgetown.edu/rstweb/info/

Eckart de Castilho, R., Mújdricza-Maydt, É., Yimam, S. M., Hartmann, S., Gurevych, I., Frank, A., and Biemann, C. (2016). A web-based tool for the integrated annotation of semantic and syntactic structures. In *Proceedings of the Workshop on Language Technology Resources and Tools for Digital Humanities (LT4DH)*, pages 76–84, Osaka, Japan, December. The COLING 2016 Organizing Committee.

Ein-Dor, L., Halfon, A., Gera, A., Shnarch, E., Dankin, L., Choshen, L., Danilevsky, M., Aharonov, R., Katz, Y., and Slonim, N. (2020). Active Learning for BERT: An Empirical Study. In *Proceedings of the 2020 Conference on Empirical Methods in Natural Language Processing (EMNLP)*, pages 7949–7962, Online.

Gerdes, K. (2013). Collaborative dependency annotation. In *Proceedings of the Second International Conference on Dependency Linguistics (DepLing 2013)*, pages 88–97, Prague, Czech Republic, August. Charles University in Prague, Matfyzpress, Prague, Czech Republic.

Gessler, L., Peng, S., Liu, Y., Zhu, Y., Behzad, S., and Zeldes, A. (2020). AMALGUM - a free, balanced, multilayer English web corpus. In *Proceedings of LREC 2020*, pages 5267–5275, Marseille, France.

Ide, N., Baker, C., Fellbaum, C., and Passonneau, R. (2010). The Manually Annotated Sub-Corpus: A community resource for and by the people. In *Proceedings of ACL 2010*, pages 68–73, Uppsala, Sweden.

Karamcheti, S., Krishna, R., Fei-Fei, L., and Manning, C. (2021). Mind your outliers! investigating the negative impact of outliers on active learning for visual question answering. In *Proceedings of the 59th Annual Meeting of the Association for Computational Linguistics and the 11th International Joint Conference on Natural Language Processing (Volume 1: Long Papers)*, pages 7265–7281, Online.

Klie, J.-C., Bugert, M., Boullosa, B., de Castilho, R. E., and Gurevych, I. (2018). The inception platform: Machine-assisted and knowledge-oriented interactive annotation. In *Proceedings of the 27th International Conference on Computational Linguistics: System Demonstrations*, pages 5–9. Association for Computational Linguistics, June. Event Title: The 27th International Conference on Computational Linguistics (COLING 2018).

Krause, T., Lüdeling, A., Odebrecht, C., and Zeldes, A. (2012). Multiple tokenizations in a diachronic corpus. In *Exploring Ancient Languages through Corpora*, Oslo.

Lai, C. and Bird, S. (2004). Querying and updating treebanks: A critical survey and requirements analysis. In *Proceedings of the Australasian Language Technology Workshop*, pages 139–146, Sydney.

Lewis, D. D. and Gale, W. A. (1994). A sequential algorithm for training text classifiers. In *Proceedings of SIGIR '94*, Dublin.

Li, B. Z., Stanovsky, G., and Zettlemoyer, L. (2020). Active learning for coreference resolution using discrete annotation. In *Proceedings of the 58th Annual Meeting of the Association for Computational Linguistics*, pages 8320–8331, Online.

Lin, B. Y., Lee, D.-H., Xu, F. F., Lan, O., and Ren, X. (2019). AlpacaTag: An active learning-based crowd annotation framework for sequence tagging. In *Proceedings of the 57th Annual Meeting of the Association for Computational Linguistics: System Demonstrations*, pages 58–63, Florence, Italy.

Mann, W. C. and Thompson, S. A. (1988). Rhetorical Structure Theory: Toward a functional theory of text organization. *Text*, 8(3):243–281.

Nguyen, M. V., Lai, V., Veyseh, A. P. B., and Nguyen, T. H. (2021). Trankit: A light-weight transformer-based toolkit for multilingual natural language processing. In *Proceedings of the 16th Conference of the European Chapter of the Association for Computational Linguistics: System Demonstrations*, pages 80–90.

Palmer, M., Gildea, D., and Kingsbury, P. (2005). The Proposition Bank: A corpus annotated with semantic roles. *Computational Linguistics*, 31(1):71–106.

Peng, S. and Zeldes, A. (2018). Validating and merging a growing multilayer corpus – the case of GUM. In *14th American Association of Corpus Linguistics Conference (AACL 2018)*, Atlanta, GA.

Qi, P., Zhang, Y., Zhang, Y., Bolton, J., and Manning, C. D. (2020). Stanza: A Python natural language processing toolkit for many human languages. In *Proceedings of the 58th Annual Meeting of the Association for Computational Linguistics: System Demonstrations*, pages 101–108.

Reiter, N. (2018). CorefAnnotator - A New Annotation Tool for Entity References. In *Abstracts of EADH: Data in the Digital Humanities*, December.

Sanguinetti, M., Cassidy, L., Bosco, C., Özlem Çetinoğlu, Cignarella, A. T., Lynn, T., Rehbein, I., Ruppenhofer, J., Seddah, D., and Zeldes, A. (2022). Treebanking user-generated content: a UD based overview of guidelines, corpora and unified recommendations. *Language Resources and Evaluation*.

Santos, D. and Mota, C. (2010). Experiments in human-computer cooperation for the semantic annotation of Portuguese corpora. In *Proceedings of LREC 2010*, pages 1437–1444, Valletta, Malta.

Searle, T., Kraljevic, Z., Bendayan, R., Bean, D., and Dobson, R. (2019). MedCATTrainer: A biomedical free text annotation interface with active learning and research use case specific customisation. In *Proceedings of the 2019 Conference on Empirical Methods in Natural Language Processing and the 9th International Joint Conference on Natural Language Processing (EMNLP-IJCNLP): System Demonstrations*, pages 139–144, Hong Kong, China.

Shen, Y., Yun, H., Lipton, Z., Kronrod, Y., and Anandkumar, A. (2017). Deep active learning for named entity recognition. In *Proceedings of the 2nd Workshop on Representation Learning for NLP*, pages 252–256, Vancouver, Canada.

Tyers, F. M., Sheyanova, M., and Washington, J. N. (2018). UD annotatrix: An annotation tool for universal dependencies. In *Proceedings of the 16th International Workshop on Treebanks and Linguistic Theories (TLT16)*, pages 10–17.

van Gompel, M. and Reynaert, M. (2014). Folia: A practical XML format for linguistic annotation - a descriptive and comparative study. In *Proceedings of CLIN 2014*.

Weischedel, R., Pradhan, S., Ramshaw, L., Kaufman, J., Franchini, M., El-Bachouti, M., Xue, N., Palmer, M., Hwang, J. D., Bonial, C., Choi, J., Mansouri, A., Foster, M., aati Hawwary, A., Marcus, M., Taylor, A., Greenberg, C., Hovy, E., Belvin, R., and Houston, A. (2012). OntoNotes release 5.0. Technical report, Linguistic Data Consortium, Philadelphia.

Wiechmann, M., Yimam, S. M., and Biemann, C. (2021). ActiveAnno: General-purpose document-level annotation tool with active learning integration. In *Proceedings of the 2021 Conference of the North American Chapter of the Association for Computational Linguistics: Human Language Technologies: Demonstrations*, pages 99–105, Online.

Yu, Y., Zhu, Y., Liu, Y., Liu, Y., Peng, S., Gong, M., and Zeldes, A. (2019). GumDrop at the DISRPT2019 shared task: A model stacking approach to discourse unit segmentation and connective detection. In *Proceedings of Discourse Relation Treebanking and Parsing (DISRPT 2019)*, pages 133–143, Minneapolis, MN.

Zeldes, A. (2016). rstWeb - a browser-based annotation interface for Rhetorical Structure Theory and discourse relations. In *Proceedings of NAACL-HLT 2016 System Demonstrations*, pages 1–5.

Zeldes, A. (2017). The GUM corpus: Creating multilayer resources in the classroom. *LREC*, 51(3):581–612.

Zeldes, A. (2018). *Multilayer Corpus Studies*. Routledge Advances in Corpus Linguistics 22. Routledge, London.

Zhang, S. and Zeldes, A. (2017). GitDOX: A linked version controlled online XML editor for manuscript transcription. In *Proceedings of FLAIRS-30*, pages 619–623, Marco Island, FL.

Proceedings of the 16th Linguistic Annotation Workshop (LAW-XVI) @LREC 2022, pages 111–119
Marseille, 24 June 2022

How "Loco" is the LOCO Corpus? Annotating the Language of Conspiracy Theories

Ludovic Mompelat[†], Zuoyu Tian[†], Amanda Kessler[†], Matthew Luettgen[†], Aaryana Rajanala[†], Sandra Kübler[†], Michelle Seelig[‡]
[†] Indiana University, [‡] University of Miami
{lmompela,zuoytian,amckess,mluettg,aarajana,skuebler}@iu.edu, mseelig@miami.edu

Abstract

Conspiracy theories have found a new channel on the internet and spread by bringing together like-minded people, thus functioning as an echo chamber. The new 88-million word corpus *Language of Conspiracy* (LOCO) was created with the intention to provide a text collection to study how the language of conspiracy differs from mainstream language. We use this corpus to develop a robust annotation scheme that will allow us to distinguish between documents containing conspiracy language and documents that do not contain any conspiracy content or that propagate conspiracy theories via misinformation (which we explicitly disregard in our work). We find that focusing on indicators of a *belief* in a conspiracy combined with textual cues of conspiracy language allows us to reach a substantial agreement (based on Fleiss' kappa and Krippendorff's alpha). We also find that the automatic retrieval methods used to collect the corpus work well in finding mainstream documents, but include some documents in the conspiracy category that would not belong there based on our definition.

Keywords: corpus, conspiracy theory, annotation scheme

1. Introduction

Conspiracy theories have found a new channel on the internet and spread by bringing together like-minded people, thus functioning as an echo chamber that accelerates the spread of conspiracy theories and contributes to the further polarization of extremes (e.g., (Papacharissi, 2016)). In recent years, researchers have thus become interested in the mechanisms of how conspiracy theories are spread, and which types of people are susceptible to them (Barkum, 2013; Douglas and Sutton, 2018; Samory and Mitra, 2018, a.o.).

Miani et al. (2021) created LOCO, the Language of Conspiracy Corpus. They collected the large-scale corpus from automatically retrieved texts using a seeding approach, one subcorpus focusing on conspiracy theory documents, and the second subcorpus focusing on mainstream documents for each seed. The corpus creators intend this corpus to serve as a basis for investigating the linguistic differences between conspiratorial and mainstream texts.

We use the LOCO corpus as the basis for our work. Ultimately, our goal is to create machine learning approaches that can tell conspiracy content from mainstream content, ideally independent of the individual conspiracy theory. As a first step, we needed to determine how well the retrieval strategies of the LOCO corpus worked, in other words, whether the grouping of documents into conspiracy or mainstream subcorpora was reliable. This led to an annotation project, in which we annotated a considerable number of texts from two different conspiracy theories, and in the process created annotation guidelines. We used documents using the seed "Sandy Hook" as our first set, and documents retrieved using the seed "Coronavirus" to decide whether our annotation guidelines were applicable across different conspiracy theories. Sandy Hook refers to conspiracy theories centered around the Sandy Hook Elementary School shooting in 2012, including claims that the shooting was staged by the US government, potentially to establish tighter gun control regulations; that nobody died in the event; or that there was a second conspirator, etc. The Coronavirus conspiracy theory revolves around claims that the virus was engineered in China; that the virus was spread by elites to gain influence and increase profit; or that the vaccine is more dangerous than the virus, etc.

The paper is structured as follows: Section 2 explains our research questions in more detail and section 3 introduces related work. Section 4 presents the LOCO corpus, and section 5 describes the first round of annotations of Sandy Hook documents. Section 6 explains the adaptation of the annotation guidelines based on the first annotations, section 7 the experiment on annotating documents from a different seed, and section 8 gives an overview of all the annotations. Section 9 concludes and describes future work.

2. Research Questions

The goal of this project is to annotate the texts of the LOCO corpus (Miani et al., 2021) for conspiracy theory language. This is a challenge that has not been addressed in this form before (but see the next section). Similar to abusive language detection (e.g., (Lopez Long et al., 2021)), we assume that this type of annotation is non-trivial, since the categories sound intuitive at first but tend to have soft boundaries, which may depend on personal stance and knowledge of the annotator. In order to develop a robust annotation scheme, we need to answer the following research questions:

1. Can we start with a minimal definition of conspiracy theory, and use the difficulties arising from applying this definition in annotation to develop robust annotation guidelines that will lead to high inter-annotator agreement?
2. Do our guidelines cover both conspiracy theory and mainstream texts? Are there differences in the annotation quality between these two types of texts?
3. If the guidelines are developed based on texts from one specific conspiracy theory, are they robust enough so that they can be applied to texts from other conspiracy theories?

Additionally, we will have a look at the quality of the texts in the LOCO corpus. Since the corpus texts were collected automatically without human supervision, it is important to know how reliable the search criteria are that were chosen to create the corpus, and whether the reliability of the retrieval strategies is dependent on the relevant conspiracy theory.

3. Related Work

Before creating guidelines for annotating the language of conspiracy theories, we first need a working definition of what constitutes a conspiracy theory, and what constitutes a conspiracy theory text. Banas and Miller (2013) define conspiracy theories (CTs) as "causal narratives of an event as a covert plan orchestrated by a secret cabal of people or organizations instead of a random or natural happening." Douglas et al. (2019) define them as "attempts to explain the ultimate causes of significant social and political events and circumstances with claims of secret plots by two or more powerful actors". Miani et al. (2021) define CTs as follows: "Conspiracy theories are narratives that attempt to explain significant social events as being secretly plotted by powerful and malicious elites at the expense of an unwitting population."

Samory and Mitra (2018) identify three key elements of previous CT definitions: agent, action, and target. In the work by Douglas et al. (2019), for example, the agent is "two or more powerful actors'", the target is"significant social and political events and circumstances", and the action is "attempts to explain the ultimate causes ... with claims of secret plots". We can easily identify these three key elements from a theoretical level, and Samory and Mitra (2018) show that such methods work well for conspiratorial statements in real texts. However, Samory and Mitra (2018) also point out that "conspiracy theories are often collages of many smaller scale theories", which makes them a difficult phenomenon to study.

Investigating linguistic characteristics of conspiracy theories, Fong et al. (2021) identify lexical cues that represent "psychological themes" relevant to "conspiracy ideation" identification, for example *ingroup vs. outgroup* language or the "we vs. them" ideology, and *cognitive processes* creating a higher past- and certainty-oriented language that is focused on causal explanations and closure. This distinguishes the language of CT from that of mainstream media, which is more oriented towards the factuality of information. In addition to lexical cues, the authors also identify lexical themes based on power, death, and religion. Introne et al. (2020) use a narrative framework to investigate conspiracy theory texts. They use the following definition: "A conspiracy theory is a narrative explaining an [event or series of events] that involve [deceptive, coordinated actors] working together to achieve [a goal] through [an action or series of actions] that have consequences that intentionally disenfranchise or harm an [individual or population]." They identify six main terms, marked in the square brackets above. Additionally, they distinguish between CTheory (for which annotators need to distinguish actors, actions, consequences, and victims) and CThinking for posts that "implied a conspiracist point of view ... but did not themselves contain identifiable CTheories". For this category, only one of the six categories needed to be present. Introne et al. found that CTheories are very infrequent in their data, CThinking less so. Additionally, CT posts mostly focused on actors and actions.

The next problem to be addressed concerns how to compile a corpus of CT documents. CT researchers have studied texts with potential CT content on different social media platforms such as Twitter, Facebook, and Reddit (Wood, 2018; Smith and Graham, 2019; Samory and Mitra, 2018). However, Miani et al. (2021) argue that texts from discussion threads are not a good resource for investigating CT narratives and tracking how CT beliefs are transmitted, because in most cases, Twitter comments, etc. are short and very contextualized in a (potentially asynchronous) "conversation", and it is difficult to interpret such posts independent of the whole thread.

Instead of extracting potential CT content from social media resources, other efforts focused on building CT corpora using full documents. For example, Uscinski et al. (2011) compiled a corpus of conspiracy documents using letters to the editor of *The New York Times* from 1897 to 2010. This corpus contains 100 000 documents, out of which 800 were manually annotated as conspiracies. Unfortunately, this corpus is no longer available (p.c. J. Uscinski, 2021). The most recent, large-scale corpus of conspiracy documents was released by (Miani et al., 2021), it covers a wide range of different conspiracy theories and was collected automatically using a seeding approach. This is the corpus we will use for our work, for more details see below.

4. The LOCO Corpus

Miani et al. (2021) created the Language Of Conspiracy Corpus (LOCO) (Miani, A. et al., 2021), which contains 23 937 conspiracy and 72 806 mainstream

Topic	Category	Round	5 ann. agree	4+ ann. agree	Fleiss' kappa	Krippendorff's alpha
Sandy Hook	CT	1	9/20	17/20	0.466	0.469
	mainstream	1	18/20	20/20	-0.020	-0.010
Sandy Hook	CT	2	14/20	17/20	0.696	0.699
	mainstream	2	20/20	20/20	1.0	1.0
Coronavirus	CT		12/20	17/20	0.577	0.575
	mainstream		19/20	20/20	-0.010	0

Table 1: Inter-annotator agreement for documents from two CT seeds, when annotating for CT vs. non-CT.

documents, about 88 million words overall. All texts were retrieved based on a set of seeds, following the strategy used for the WaCky corpus (Baroni et al., 2009). The seeds were collected from a national poll[1], a list of 17 items from Douglas and Sutton (2018), plus an additional "20 seeds corresponding to popular (e.g., Illuminati, genetically modified organisms, Pizzagate) and current (e.g., coronavirus, Bill Gates, 5G) CTs" chosen by Miani et al. (2021).

There are two categories used in the corpus, conspiracy and mainstream documents, which are retrieved via different strategies: To gather conspiracy texts, Miani et al. (2021) used a list of conspiracy theory websites based on scores from mediabiasfactcheck[2]. To retrieve mainstream documents, the authors used Google to search for the seeds and extracted website domains, from which they retrieved the texts. The authors acknowledge that not all conspiracy theory (CT) texts will contain conspiracy content. Mainstream documents may contain CT content, but they reflect the mix of CT and non-CT that the general public is exposed to.

Compared to previous corpora on related areas (conspiracy, rumors, fake news (e.g. (Uscinski et al., 2011; Kwon et al., 2017; Castelo et al., 2019)), the LOCO corpus covers a large set of conspiracy texts and a sizable number of different CTs, plus a detailed set of metadata, including date, website, and measures of social media engagement. To determine the accuracy of the CT and mainstream categories, Miani et al. (2021) randomly sampled 60 documents from the conspiracy and mainstream subcorpora each, and manually annotated them. Their annotation results indicate that 85% of the conspiracy documents and 92% of the mainstream documents are correctly labeled.

It is clear that the LOCO corpus is a valuable resource for exploring the narratives of conspiracy theories and their effect on social media. However, in order to use this corpus for creating machine learning models of CT, we need a better understanding of the quality of the corpus, i.e., the degree to which the automatic grouping into the CT and mainstream subcorpora corresponds to human judgments across the different seeds.

[1]https://www.publicpolicypolling.com/polls/democrats-and-republicans-differ-on-conspiracy-theory-beliefs/

[2]https://mediabiasfactcheck.com/conspiracy/

5. Annotating Sandy Hook Documents

5.1. Distinguishing Conspiracy Theory Texts from Mainstream

Our first question concerns the problem of defining the target of our annotations. What do we consider a conspiracy theory (CT) document? Where do we draw the line between conspiracy theory and mainstream / non-conspiracy theory? To answer these questions, we conducted a first round of annotations on a sample of 40 documents from the set of documents in the LOCO corpus on Sandy Hook. We chose 20 documents from the conspiracy subcorpus and 20 from the mainstream subcorpus. The annotations were conducted by 2 undergraduate and 3 graduate students, who had read and discussed relevant literature prior to the annotations.

Our starting definition of CT was the definition by Douglas et al. (2019) (see section 3). However, after our pilot annotation, we found this definition too general for our goal since it does not give any guidance on the distinction between reports of the event, reports of conspiracy theories related to the event, and the propagation of conspiracy theories. Since we are mostly interested in the latter, we decided to incorporate the concept of *conspiracy belief*, as defined by Barkum (2013): "A conspiracy belief is the belief that an organization made up of individuals or groups was or is acting covertly to achieve some malevolent end." We adopted the definition proposed by Seelig et al. (2022), which is based on the definition by Banas and Miller (2013):

(1) A conspiracy belief is the belief that an organization made up of individuals or groups was or is acting covertly to achieve some malevolent end. It depicts causal narratives of an event as a covert plan orchestrated by a secret cabal of people or organizations instead of a random or natural happening.

The results of this first annotation round are shown in the first two rows of Table 1. We found that the mainstream documents from the LOCO corpus were mostly labeled correctly, and our annotators agreed in most cases: Only 2 documents had 1 annotator disagreeing with the majority. Note that the kappa and alpha values for the mainstream subcorpora show either negative numbers or 0 even though the annotators mostly agreed. The reason for this can be found in the very

How Zionist Politicians Brought On Newtown Killings - Part 2
The first half of this analysis of the Connecticut shootings, MK-ULTRA Links to Sandy Hook Assault, examined how the CIA's mind-control program spread like a metastasizing cancer across the Eastern Seaboard, delivering a nightmarish cocktail of synthetic drugs, sexual abuse and lethal violence. The focus of that essay was on the three major players in the New England region - CIA/FBI agents, the pedophile Catholic clergy and the Irish drug-trafficking mob, while giving only passing mention of the Jewish politicians whose salesmanship was needed for the monumental task of social engineering a proud nation into a herd of sheep.
The major political figure in the Newtown tragedy who has once again evaded personal responsibility for the bloody consequences of his idiotic policies, which include the war in Iraq and arms shipments to Israel, is Joseph Isadore Lieberman. The chairman of the Homeland Security Committee and U.S. senator from Tel Aviv and Stamford is the elephant in the schoolroom that nobody seems to notice.
Soon to retire from the senatorial seat he's kept warm for 22 years, Joe Lieberman has been a contemporary of New England gangland boss Whitey Bulger and his CIA controllers. His Senate term has run exactly parallel to the takeover and transformation of once-puritanical Connecticut into a sleazy hub of underage prostitution, child porn, drug peddling and gambling.
Without the powerful senator's protection and nurturing of unsavory characters and corporate criminals over the decades, the Sandy Hook school massacre probably would never have happened. Here, in Part 2, the role of Jewish politicians in first promoting and later suppressing child prostitution, kiddie porn and drug use is explored, along with the blowback from that policy reversal provoking the school attack and subsequent cover-up.

Figure 1: Example of a clear CT document [LOCO ID: C006b9].

Trial Date Set in Sandy Hook Families' Lawsuit Against Remington – Infinite Unknown
A lawsuit by families of Sandy Hook victims is proceeding against Remington, manufacturer of the AR-15, in the new push to hold gun manufacturers responsible for what is done by people who purchase their products and use them illegally.
The New York Times is pretty excited about it: The legal challenge faces long odds, and a key hearing next week will determine its future.
Question: Do you think it's a bit hypocritical of the system to applaud the Sandy Hook families for suing Remington and decry the fact that people can't sue to hold a company responsible for what people who purchase its products could potentially do to others, but completely ignore the fact that we live in a country where no one is allowed to sue vaccine manufacturers directly for vaccine damage?
Also, can you imagine if every company could be sued for every time someone used their products in the commission of a crime to hurt someone else?
Knife manufacturers sued for stabbings... Car manufacturers and alcohol producers sued for DUI deaths... Companies who sell lighters sued if an arsonist decides to burn someone's house down... Shoelace manufacturers sued for someone being strangled by one... Swimming pool manufacturers being sued if someone drowns in one...
Personal responsibility be damned when there's an agenda, and this agenda is pretty obvious. If they can't get the laws passed to gut the Second Amendment, they'll just try to sue gun manufacturers out of existence instead.

Figure 2: Example of a document difficult to label [LOCO ID: C06962].

high expected values. Neither metric is useful for data with very high agreement and small sample size (Zhao et al., 2013). Given the results in Table 1, we decided to trust the retrieval strategy used for mainstream documents, with which the annotators agreed in most cases. For the CT documents, however, inter-annotator agreement was low, only for 9 out of the 20 documents did all 5 annotators agree, and Fleiss' kappa reached 0.466. Figure 1 shows a clear case of CT.

When discussing the documents on which the annotators did not agree, we found that in some cases, a conspiracy theory may be perpetuated, but the text itself did not show any evidence of the writer's belief in the CT. Other examples were unclear. One example for such a difficult decision is shown in Figure 2.

This article was particularly difficult to label as CT or non-CT: While the author is clearly opposed to the lawsuit against gun manufacturers, and while the document contains leading questions (e.g., "Also, can you imagine if every company could be sued for every time someone used their products in the commission of a crime to hurt someone else?") and mentions an "agenda", there is no indication of a belief in a conspiracy. After the discussion, all annotators agreed that this text should be classified as non-CT.

Many of those documents contain statements that were verifiably incorrect or misleading and that would indicate covert activities with malevolent intentions. An example of such a document is shown in Figure 3. In this example, the claim that the property records show

Over 30 Sandy Hook Homes "Gifted" In 2009
Newtown property records suggest that on December 25, 2009 a total of 35 properties located on and around Yogananda Street in Sandy Hook were transferred at zero value to new owners.
The transactions include the house belonging to mysterious figure Chris Manfredonia, who was apprehended by police on Sandy Hook School grounds on the morning of December 14, 2012.
"It's not just Yogananda Street that was given away on Christmas of '09," the researcher argues.
Yogananda addresses 6, 7, 8, 10, 11, 12, 13, 14, 15, 16, 21, and 23 all bear identical transactions to the ones exhibited here; 24 is owned by the town, while 18 is a normal transaction. On Charter ridge, 45, 47, 63, 71, and 72 appear normal and 61, 62, 64, 65, 66, 67, 68, 69, 70, and 73 are all December 25, 2009 transactions. All of these properties surround the Lanza home.

Figure 3: Example of a misinformation/fake news document [LOCO ID: C060d0].

Democrats Call For A Complete Ban on All Cryptocurrencies
Brad Sherman told a subcommittee for the House of Representatives Financial Services. Democrats are calling for a blanket ban on all forms of Cryptocurrencies including Bitcoin, claiming that digital money warrants heavy regulation by lawmakers. Congressman Brad Sherman told a subcommittee for the House of Representatives Financial Services that the American public should not be allowed to purchase any form of digital currency. "We should prohibit U.S. persons from buying or mining cryptocurrencies," the California Democrat said. According to Coindesk: He added that, beyond cryptocurrencies being potentially used as a form of money in the future, it can currently be used by tax evaders and rogue states seeking to bypass U.S. sanctions.

Figure 4: Example of an unrelated article [LOCO ID: C05e2a].

that 35 properties were transferred at zero value to new owners on the same day is technically correct but ignores that this was due to missing information in the computer system.
We decided that we would focus on the *language of conspiracy theories*, in the sense that a belief in the CT was shown in the language of the text. We consider fact checking a separate, but clearly related problem. When focusing on the language of CT, this document can be considered non-CT, even though the misinformation indicates a CT. This decision was made in order to keep the annotations feasible given time and budget constraints. A combination of fact checking and information about conspiracy beliefs anchored in the language will have to be addressed in the future.

5.2. Relatedness

From a cursory look at the CT documents, it became clear that solely distinguishing between conspiracy and non-conspiracy was not sufficient since we found that some documents, which were collected for a specific seed, may mention that seed, but were otherwise unrelated to the CT. For this reason, we added a *Relatedness* category, with three different labels: closely related, broadly related, and not related.
Figure 4 shows an extreme example. This is a text on cryptocurrencies, but the corpus groups it under the seed Sandy Hook. There is no mention of Sandy Hook in the whole document, and it is unclear how it was retrieved. We consider this document not related to the Sandy Hook CT.
The first two rows in Table 2 show the results of the first round of annotations. We see a similar picture to the annotations of CT vs. non-CT for the mainstream documents, Fleiss' kappa reaches 0.512. For the CT documents, the results are higher, with Fleiss' kappa reaching 0.655. A closer look at the documents where annotators disagreed shows that disagreements concern the hard boundaries between the labels. Is one cursory mention of Sandy Hook enough to make a document closely related? Does Sandy Hook need to be the only topic in a document for it to count as closely related? For the future, we will investigate a continuous scale for this type of annotation.

6. The New Annotation Scheme

After the first round of annotations and the discussion of the documents that had conflicting annotations, we updated the definition in (1) to the one in (2).

(2) A conspiracy belief is the belief that an organization made up of individuals or groups was or is acting covertly to achieve some malevolent end. It depicts causal narratives of an event as a covert plan orchestrated by a secret cabal of people or organizations instead of a random or natural happening.
A document is considered CT if and only if such a belief is manifested in the text via specific expressions. We explicitly exclude fact checking beyond obvious inconsistencies with information present in mainstream coverage of the event underlying the CT.

Given the retrieval strategies used in the creation of the LOCO corpus (see section 4), there are obvious differences since most of the mainstream documents are retrieved from news outlets while the CT documents tend to come from less official outlets. Thus, docu-

Topic	Category	Round	5 ann. agree	4+ ann. agree	Fleiss' kappa	Krippendorff's alpha
Sandy Hook	CT	1	11/20	16/20	0.655	0.657
Sandy Hook	Mainstream	1	8/20	13/20	0.512	0.508
Sandy Hook	CT	2	16/20	18/20	0.776	0.778
Sandy Hook	Mainstream	2	16/20	18/20	0.819	0.820
Coronavirus	CT		17/20	18/20	0.751	0.753
Coronavirus	Mainstream		13/20	19/20	0.517	0.518

Table 2: Inter-annotator agreement on relatedness for documents from two CT seeds

cue	example
contradictory	FBI says No One Killed at Sandy Hook [LOCO ID: C005a9]
	Watch Infowars explore why people believe the Sandy Hook shooting to be a hoax. [LOCO ID: C042fa]
	We at Prepare for Change (PFC) bring you information that is not offered by the mainstream news, and therefore may seem controversial. [LOCO ID: C0443c]
sensational	Americans Under Surveillance [LOCO ID: C00650]
	If you want more evidence of a government seeking control, look no further than the IRS scandal where the Obama administration was using the IRS to stop conservatives and religious groups from organizing opposition. [LOCO ID: C00650]
	MK-ULTRA is obsolete when private medical insurance plans are covering the costs of date-rape capsules [LOCO ID: C006b9]
other CT	Internet sleuths immediately took to the web to stitch together clues indicating the shooting could be a carefully-scripted false flag event, similar to the 9/11 terror attacks, the central tenet being that the event would be used to galvanize future support for gun control legislation [LOCO ID: C005a9]
all caps	RED ALERT: Google Censorship Is Destroying the Truth Movement [LOCO ID: C00775]
	They reported Fake numbers that they made up & don't even exist. WE WILL WIN AGAIN! [LOCO ID: C00775]
named entities	The Obama White House [LOCO ID: C00a2d]
	'Sleepy Joe' makes another gaffe on his campaign trail [LOCO ID: C0690d]
punctuation	Somebody is going to jail over this un-constitutional crime!!! [LOCO ID: C00a2d]
pronouns	I am aware of books by former insiders that describe the CIA's alliance with members of the media. When I was a member of the congressional staff, I was warned of the Washington Post's collaboration with the CIA. [LOCO ID : C0487a]
questions	Lauren Rousseau's Car Riddled With Bullet Holes In Sandy Hook Parking Lot? [...] how is it possible for a bullet hole to penetrate the side of her car at the trajectory shown above? Was there no car beside her? This is just one of the many mysteries about the official story. More research coming in different articles, stay tuned.[LOCO ID: C06689]
paraphrases	Recently released FBI crime statistics curiously show that no murders occurred in Newtown, Connecticut, in 2012, despite reports that numerous schoolchildren and faculty members were slaughtered during a shooting rampage in December of that year. [LOCO ID : C005a9]
	Mark Zuckerberg Says That Social Media Giant Facebook Will Continue To Give A Voice To Holocaust Deniers [LOCO ID : C00b0f]

Table 3: Verbal and textual cues for CTs.

ments grouped into the CT category tend to contain formatting, spelling, and sentence and discourse structure anomalies. For this reason, we created a set of cues that can help the annotators make decisions. The cues listed below are the ones that the annotators listed when asked what they noticed in CT texts. However, note that the cues individually or in their entirety do not constitute a justification for labeling a document as CT. Instead, these cues are used as *supporting evidence* in the decision process. In order to classify a document as CT, we need verbal signs of a conspiracy belief.

We use the content and textual cues described below. The first set of cues focuses on content, examples are shown in the upper half of Table 3.

1. Contradictory opinion to mainstream opinion

   Such cues consist of opinions that contradict opinions in the general domain. Note that this does not require elaborate fact checking.

2. Sensationalism

   Headlines and content are written to excite strong emotions, often at the expense of correctness.

If you're anything like me... as soon as you hear the news about a big shooting or a terrorist attack in Europe or America, you roll your eyes and yawn. Then you go pop some popcorn and kick back in your recliner to watch the amusing theatrics that ALWAYS follow. [...] "Nope... today in 2018... anything that makes simultaneous nationwide headlines and is covered non stop for a week or even a couple days... is ALWAYS a faked hoaxed event. [...] I know it's hard to swallow... that they would prefer to use a hoax model over just really killing ppl. But they've been using the "hoax false flag" now since about 2008. And here is why they fake all of these events instead of just sending a patsy in and really killing victims.
The deep state learned their lesson after really killing ppl in the false flag of 9-11. The victims families could not be controlled or managed to say the things they wanted them to say or push the agenda they wanted pushed. [...]
The McDonnell family – their daughter, Grace, was allegedly shot dead at Sandy Hook
Fake victims/no real deaths = crisis actors playing loved ones. Crisis actors instead of real heartbroken angry loved ones = no lawsuits and NO QUESTIONS. [...] [LOCO ID: C0443c]

Figure 5: Example of a CT document with clear CT language.

'Something's going on! Please!' Harrowing 911 calls from inside Sandy Hook Elementary School during massacre reveal staff desperately begging for help as dispatchers respond calmly. [LOCO ID: M1f6ae]

Figure 6: Example of a non-CT document with some of the verbal cues typical for CT.

3. Mentions of other conspiracy theories

   CT documents often draw connections between different conspiracy theories.

There are also textual cues that are indicative of CTs, many of these cues are typically also used in other social media (as opposed to news reports). Examples are shown in the lower half of Table 3.

1. Extensive use of all caps
2. Atypical named entities
3. Unconventional use of punctuation
4. Frequent use of 1st and 2nd person pronouns
5. Frequent questions directed at the reader
6. Paraphrasing instead of direct quoting

Several documents in the LOCO corpus were written by or reference prominent conspiracy theory proponents such as Alex Jones and Infowars. If we were interested in conspiracy theories in general, such documents should be labeled as CT. Given our definition in (2), such documents are labeled as non-CT since they do not contain any language showing the belief in a CT.
Figure 5 shows an example of a document that caused doubts based on our first definition in (1) but was considered a clear case of CT based on the new definition. In this document, we clearly see language relating to the conspiracy theory, e.g., "Fake victims/no real deaths = crisis actors playing loved ones. Crisis actors instead of real heartbroken angry loved ones = no lawsuits and NO QUESTIONS." Additionally, it shows a range of the cues we have identified: "The deep state", informal language, words in all caps to show emphasis, and repeatedly the hedge "allegedly".
In some cases, however, the verbal cues complicated the decision. Figure 6 shows an example containing verbal cues of emotional language, ("harrowing") and quotations indicating panic. This language seems to imply that the "calm" response was inappropriate in that situation. Within the remainder of the document, however, there is no claim of a secret plot, etc. Consequently, we annotated this document as non-CT.
The lack of clarity in these documents may allow readers to impose their pre-existing beliefs or worldview; in this way, the CT is perpetuated in part because it can mean different things to different people, thus contributing to the multi-faceted collection of beliefs centered around one CT.
After establishing our new annotation scheme, we conducted a second inter-annotator agreement experiment on 20 previously unseen documents from the CT subcorpus and 20 from mainstream. The inter-annotator agreement results are shown in rows 3 and 4 in Table 1 for the decision on CT vs. non-CT and in Table 2 for relatedness. Note that we reached a perfect agreement on the mainstream documents for CT vs. non-CT, thus corroborating our decision to trust the retrieval strategy for this subcorpus. For the CT documents, Fleiss' kappa increased from 0.466 to 0.696. For relatedness, we also see a marked improvement in Fleiss' kappa from 0.655 to 0.776 for CT documents and from 0.512 to 0.819 for mainstream documents, but we do not reach a perfect agreement. All scores correspond to substantial agreement based on Landis and Koch (1977).

7. Using the Annotation Scheme for Coronavirus Documents

The second round of annotation in Sandy Hook documents shows that annotators reach a high agreement in annotating for both conspiracy and relatedness. This leads to the next question, namely whether the annotation guidelines developed based on texts on Sandy Hook will also be relevant for the annotation of other

Seed	Category	# LOCO docs	# docs annotated	Conspiracy Rate	Related Rate
Sandy Hook	Conspiracy	364	364	0.615	0.615
Sandy Hook	Mainstream	1476	200	0.020	0.780
Coronavirus	Conspiracy	571	571	0.413	0.891
Coronavirus	Mainstream	1965	20	0	0.850

Table 4: Statistics of our annotations.

CTs, or whether we need to adapt the guidelines to new CTs.

To answer this question, we chose a second seed from the LOCO corpus: coronavirus. This choice was determined in the attempt to find a CT that is different enough from Sandy Hook. The coronavirus CT concerns ongoing events, unlike the Sandy Hook CT, where the focus event happened in 2012. Furthermore, while the majority of the narratives on Sandy Hook are centered around the event of the school shooting, there is no such core event for coronavirus. Our hypothesis is that the coronavirus texts are more diverse in topics than the Sandy Hook ones, therefore if the annotation guidelines are usable for coronavirus, they should also be usable for a wider range of CTs.

We conducted a third inter-annotator agreement experiment on 20 CT and 20 mainstream documents for the coronavirus seed. From the annotation results in rows 5 and 6 of Tables 1 and 2, we see a clear divergence. For CT vs. non-CT, both Fleiss' kappa and Krippendorff's alpha are considerably lower for these documents than for the second round of Sandy Hook documents (kappa: 0.577 vs. 0.696), clearly showing that the CT documents are structured differently in different CTs. For the mainstream documents, in contrast, the results are very similar to the second round of Sandy Hook annotations. For relatedness, the CT documents had similar trends to the second round of Sandy Hook while the mainstream documents reached lower scores (kappa: 0.517 vs. 0.751).

These differences can partly be explained by the differences in the success of the automatic retrieval strategies in LOCO (see below for more details): A much higher percentage of the documents in the CT subcorpus for the seed coronavirus are non-CT based on our definition. Additionally, in comparison to the Sandy Hook documents, a higher percentage of documents in both subcorpora for the coronovirus seed are related to the topic.

8. Overview of All Annotations

We re-annotated the documents from the first inter-annotator agreement experiment and continued annotating the remaining documents in the conspiracy subcorpus for both seeds. An overview of the complete set of annotations is shown in Table 4. Here the conspiracy rate refers to the percentage of documents of a subcorpus that were annotated as CT by our annotators. We see that for both seeds, the conspiracy rate is very low for mainstream documents (0.020 for Sandy Hook and 0.0 for coronavirus). However, the rate is also rather low for the CT documents, showing that less than 2/3 of the documents in the Sandy Hook CT subcorpus, and less than half of the documents in the coronavirus CT subcorpus, actually contain CT language. The relatedness rate refers to the percentage of documents that were labeled as closely or broadly related to the seed CT by the annotators. Here we see a similar trend to the Sandy Hook CT subcorpora, a much higher rate for the coronavirus CT subcorpus, and lower rates for the mainstream subcorpora: 0.780 for Sandy Hook and 0.850 for coronavirus. These numbers show very clearly that the two retrieval strategies work qualitatively differently for different CT seeds.

9. Conclusion and Future Work

We have investigated the annotation of documents in the LOCO corpus for the presence of language that indicated a belief in conspiracy theories. Our experiments show that the automatic retrieval methods used to create the LOCO corpus reach different levels of conspiracy content and relatedness for the two seeds that we used for our investigation. We also find that distinguishing between CT and non-CT is a difficult and subjective task. Our annotation guidelines can help with consistent decisions across different annotators and can be used across different CTs. We do notice a deterioration of inter-annotator agreement in some metrics, but these can be partly explained by the underlying differences in terms of the ratios of conspiracy content and relatedness. However, this needs deeper probing.

For the future, we are considering an extension of the CT annotation to include a concept similar to CThinking by Introne et al. (2020), to better handle documents such as the one in Figure 3. More generally, we plan to use the annotated texts for creating a classifier to detect CT language across different CTs. The annotations will be publicly available at `https://github.com/zytian9/locoAnnotations`.

10. Acknowledgments

This work is based on research supported by US National Science Foundation (NSF) Grants #2123635 and #2123618.

11. Bibliographical References

Banas, J. and Miller, G. (2013). Inducing resistance to conspiracy theory propaganda: Testing inoculation and metainoculation strategies. *Human Communication Research*, 39(2):184–207.

Barkum, M. (2013). *A Culture of Conspiracy*. University of California Press.

Baroni, M., Bernardini, S., Ferraresi, A., and Zanchetta, E. (2009). The WaCky wide web: A collection of very large linguistically processed web-crawled corpora. *Language Resources and Evaluation*, 43(3):209–226.

Castelo, S., Almeida, T., Elghafari, A., Santos, A., Pham, K., Nakamura, E., and Freire, J. (2019). A topic-agnostic approach for identifying fake news pages. In *Companion Proceedings of the 2019 World Wide Web Conference*, pages 975–980.

Douglas, K. M. and Sutton, R. M. (2018). Why conspiracy theories matter: A social psychological analysis. *European Review of Social Psychology*, 29(1):256–298.

Douglas, K. M., Uscinski, J. E., Sutton, R. M., Cichocka, A., Nefes, T., Ang, C. S., and Deravi, F. (2019). Understanding conspiracy theories. *Political Psychology*, 40:3–35.

Fong, A., Roozenbeek, J., Goldwert, D., Rathje, S., and van der Linden, S. (2021). The language of conspiracy: A psychological analysis of speech used by conspiracy theorists and their followers on Twitter. *Group Processes & Intergroup Relations*, 24(4):606–623.

Introne, J., Korsunska, A., Krsova, L., , and Zhang, Z. (2020). Mapping the narrative ecosystem of conspiracy theories in online anti-vaccination discussions. In *SMSociety'20: International Conference on Social Media and Society*, pages 184–192.

Kwon, S., Cha, M., and Jung, K. (2017). Rumor detection over varying time windows. *PloS one*, 12(1):e0168344.

Landis, J. R. and Koch, G. (1977). The measurement of observer agreement for categorical data. *Biometrics*, 33:159–268.

Lopez Long, H., O'Neil, A., and Kübler, S. (2021). On the interaction between annotation quality and classifier performance in abusive language detection. In *Proceedings of the Conference on Recent Advances in NLP (RANLP)*, Online.

Miani, A., Hills, T., and Bangerter, A. (2021). LOCO: The 88-million-word language of conspiracy corpus. *Behavior Research Methods*.

Papacharissi, Z. (2016). Affective publics and structures of storytelling: Sentiment, events and mediality. *Information, Communication & Society*, 19(3):307–324.

Samory, M. and Mitra, T. (2018). 'The government spies using our webcams': The language of conspiracy theories in online discussions. *Proceedings of the ACM on Human-Computer Interaction*, 2(CSCW):1–24.

Seelig, M., Funchion, J., Trego, R., Kübler, S., Verdear, D., Wuchty, S., Uscinski, J., Klofstad, C., Murthi, M., Premaratne, K., and Diekman, A. (2022). The dark side of Twitter: A framing analysis of conspiratorial rhetoric stoking fear. Presentation at the 72nd Annual ICA Conference: One World, One Network? Online.

Smith, N. and Graham, T. (2019). Mapping the anti-vaccination movement on Facebook. *Information, Communication & Society*, 22(9):1310–1327.

Uscinski, J. E., Parent, J., and Torres, B. (2011). Conspiracy theories are for losers. In *APSA 2011 Annual Meeting*.

Wood, M. J. (2018). Propagating and debunking conspiracy theories on Twitter during the 2015–2016 Zika virus outbreak. *Cyberpsychology, Behavior, and Social Networking*, 21(8):485–490.

Zhao, X., Liu, J. S., and Deng, K. (2013). Assumptions behind intercoder reliability indices. *Annals of the International Communication Association*, 36(1):419–480.

12. Language Resource References

Miani, A. et al. (2021). *Language Of Conspiracy Corpus (LOCO)*. Available from `https://osf.io/snpcg`.

Proceedings of the 16th Linguistic Annotation Workshop (LAW-XVI) @LREC 2022, pages 120–128
Marseille, 24 June 2022

Putting Context in SNACS: A 5-Way Classification of Adpositional Pragmatic Markers

Yang Janet Liu♣, Jena D. Hwang◇, Nathan Schneider♣, Vivek Srikumar♠,◇
♣Georgetown University, {yl879, nathan.schneider}@georgetown.edu
◇Allen Institute for AI, {jenah, viveks}@allenai.org
♠University of Utah, svivek@cs.utah.edu

Abstract

The SNACS framework provides a network of semantic labels called *supersenses* for annotating adpositional semantics in corpora. In this work, we consider English prepositions (and prepositional phrases) that are chiefly *pragmatic*, contributing extra-propositional contextual information such as speaker attitudes and discourse structure. We introduce a preliminary taxonomy of pragmatic meanings to supplement the semantic SNACS supersenses, with guidelines for the annotation of coherence connectives, commentary markers, and topic and focus markers. We also examine annotation disagreements, delve into the trickiest boundary cases, and offer a discussion of future improvements.

Keywords: adpositions, pragmatic markers, supersenses, context, discourse, annotation

1. Introduction

Sentence-level representations of meaning and compositionality in corpora tend to emphasize semantics, relegating pragmatics to the sidelines or sweeping it under the rug. Even pragmatics signaled explicitly with a lexical marker (*please*, *even*, *hopefully*, *however*) may be dumped into a miscellaneous category if the standard categories available to semantic elements are not a good fit: viz. UD's miscellaneous syntactic relation called `discourse` (de Marneffe et al., 2021) and UCCA's miscellaneous semantic category called `Ground` (Abend and Rappoport, 2013). Discourse-level representations, on the other hand, may explicate pragmatics in depth for certain kinds of markers: in particular, much work has targeted discourse connectives (e.g. Samy and González-Ledesma (2008)); some work has examined discourse particles (e.g. Stede and Birte (2000)); and few if any studies have attempted to examine the full range of pragmatic markers (§2).

Here we investigate whether a grammatically defined class of expressions (namely prepositions and idiomatic prepositional phrases in English, like *as for* and *in other words*) can be categorized at the token level with respect to their pragmatic status. We build on the SNACS framework and annotated data (Schneider et al., 2018). SNACS was designed to disambiguate adpositional *semantics* in corpora (§2.1). Expressions that cannot be assigned a semantic label were excluded from the regular SNACS supersenses (and annotated in corpora with a special "discourse" label, `d). Here we propose a small taxonomy to cover adpositional pragmatic markers in general (§3), with special designations for coherence connectives, commentary markers, and topic and focus markers (§4). A pilot study reveals that drawing boundaries is in some cases quite difficult (§5). We examine inter-annotator disagreements, diagnose some of the major problematic cases, and discuss possible improvements to the annotation guidelines (§6).

2. Background

Here we introduce the *semantic* framework for analyzing adpositions (§2.1), with an eye toward broadening it to include *pragmatic* meanings treated separately in the literature (§2.2 and §2.3).

2.1. SNACS Framework

The SNACS (Schneider et al., 2018, Semantic Network of Adposition and Case Supersenses) hierarchy is a multilingual annotation framework developed for annotating adpositional (i.e. prepositions and postpositions) and possessive markers. The hierarchy is an inventory of **supersenses**, categories designed to capture coarse-grained semantics while abstracting away from lexically particular meanings (e.g. the spatial difference between **inside** and **outside** is collapsed under the locative supersense, LOCUS).[1] Currently, the SNACS framework defines 50 supersenses that capture event participant or thematic roles (PARTICIPANT subhierarchy e.g. AGENT, RECIPIENT), circumstantial roles that define adjunct relations (CIRCUMSTANTIAL subhierarchy e.g. TIME, PURPOSE), and roles describing relations between entities (CONFIGURATION subhierarchy e.g. POSSESSOR, WHOLE).

Moreover, the SNACS framework makes use of an annotation mechanism called the **construal analysis** to handle meaning generalization across differing adpositional expressions (Hwang et al., 2017). In this approach, a token may receive two distinct supersenses. For example, both adpositions in "a slice **of** a cake" and "a page **in** a book" mediate a WHOLE relationship with respect to the governing nominal—but **in** contributes a distinctively locative framing. The generalization is captured by the **scene role**—semantic role associated with the scene (typically indicated by the predicate)—and al-

[1] The complete SNACS hierarchy is available at `http://www.xposition.org/supersenses/`.

lowing the **function** to specify the meaning more closely associated with the adpostion itself.[2] As detailed in §5.1, SNACS has been used to annotate multiple corpora in a handful of different languages. Extensive guidelines for English and expanded guidelines for other languages are publicly available.

2.2. Pragmatic Markers

Previous theoretical and sociolinguistic work has studied pragmatic and discourse markers in English and proposed several taxonomies. Fraser (1990) argued that pragmatic markers are linguistic devices to convey a speaker's potential communicative intentions, which do not belong to the content meaning of the proposition, as later categorized by Maschler and Schiffrin (2015). As Fraser (1996) further pointed out, pragmatic markers come in many different linguistic forms (e.g. syntactic, lexical, phonological), and their presence plays a crucial role in the interpretation of the utterances involved. Specifically, Fraser (1996) classified these pragmatic markers into four types: *basic pragmatic markers* (1a), *commentary pragmatic markers* (1b), *parallel pragmatic markers* (1c), and *discourse markers* (1d).[3]

(1) a. **I promise** that I will be there on time.
 b. **Amazingly**, Derrick passed the exam.
 c. Good evening **ladies and gentlemen**, welcome to the home of the Black Bears.
 d. Jane is here. **However**, she isn't going to stay.

Fraser (2009, p. 892) proposed a further taxonomy concerning "meta-comments" on the structure of the discourse under the fourth type above, namely *discourse markers*, called *discourse management markers*. This taxonomy consists of the following subtypes: *discourse structure markers* (e.g. *In summary*), used to highlight the contribution of the following discourse segment within the overall discourse structure; *topic orientation markers* (e.g. *by the way*), linguistic devices to foreshadow topic change; and *attention markers* (e.g. *in any case*), signaling a topic change is in the making. In particular, we are interested in the *topic orientation markers* and their uses from Fraser (2009) as they pertain to our discussion and observations on the pragmatic adpositional usages in English. Notable functions of *topic orientation markers* characterized by Fraser (2009) are as follows:

(2) a. return to a prior topic: **back** to my point
 b. continue with the present topic: speaking **of**
 c. digress from the present topic: **by** the way
 d. introduce a new topic: **on** a different note

Although the focus of the current work is on English pragmatic markers and in particular pragmatic uses of adpositions in English, it is worth pointing out that similar phenomena and linguistic devices are prevalent in other languages, such as discourse particles and their functions as well, for example, in German, as delineated in Stede and Birte (2000), and in a parallel corpus study for English, Spanish, and Arabic (Samy and González-Ledesma, 2008).

2.3. Pragmatic Markers vs. Discourse Markers

It is important to clarify that the categorization of pragmatic markers described in §2.2 is not mutually exclusive with contemporary computational approaches to discourse markers as in the Penn Discourse Treebank (Prasad et al., 2014, PDTB), nor are they subclasses of each other. While Fraser (1996) did not characterize pragmatic or discourse markers based on their syntactic categories, PDTB followed a well-defined set of syntactic classes to select explicit discourse markers,[4] one of which includes prepositional phrases such as ***as*** *a result* and ***on*** *the other hand* etc. (Prasad et al., 2014).

Adverbial discourse connectives, as recognized by PDTB, may be semantic and/or pragmatic. The following examples indicate a clear semantic relationship between events:

(3) a. **First**, preheat the oven to 350 degrees. **Then**, combine the ingredients in a saucepan. (`temporal`)
 b. We can go inside **if** it is raining. (`conditional`)
 c. The forecast was wrong. **As a result**, we got caught in the rain. (`causal`)

Adpositional expressions whose primary meaning is semantic would be covered by existing SNACS labels, even if the expression also functions as a discourse connective (see further discussion on this in §4.4).

Below we focus on expressions whose primary meaning is pragmatic. As we will demonstrate, a prepositional expression can even serve multiple pragmatic roles in English. In other words, a prototypical discourse marker considered by one discourse framework to signal a *coherence* relation between two propositions is not necessarily tied to that function invariably; instead, the interpretation of such markers depends on their specific use in context, and their contributions to a given discourse could be multi-dimensional, with some being primary and others being secondary.

[2] In other words, "a slice **of** a cake" would be annotated as plain WHOLE, while "a page **in** a book" would receive WHOLE⇝LOCUS (to be read as "WHOLE construed as LOCUS") in recognition of the locative meaning contributed by the preposition **in**.

[3] The examples used here were selected from the original paper. (Each type was further categorized into several subtypes.)

[4] PDTB uses the term *discourse connectives* to refer to the lexical items that connect discourse segments based on syntactic criteria. For our purposes, the terms *discourse connective* and *discourse marker* are used interchangeably to refer to any lexical item that adds extra-propositional meaning to the understanding of discourse.

3. Pragmatic Adpositional Usages

In contrast to the semantic usages where prepositions mediate a relationship between the two constituents (e.g. "The cat is **on** the mat"—the mat is the location of the cat), pragmatic uses of adpositions do not directly comment on the content of the sentence. Rather, they add contextual information that situates that content in discourse. For example, a prepositional expression may mediate the relationship between two propositions in a discourse as in (4), where the prepositional phrase idiom "**for** instance" does not add propositional content to the sentence. Rather, it links to a prior utterance and specifies that the current proposition ("Florida has no state income tax") is an example of the aforementioned situation.

(4) *Your state of domicile impacts financial matters.*
For instance, Florida has no state income tax.

Prepositional expressions can be deployed for a range of pragmatic meanings: signaling the speaker's opinion or perspective (5a); heralding a topical change in the discourse ((5b) switches the subtopic to snacks); or positioning the speaker's utterance with respect to the larger context ((5c) exemplifies digression from the main topic).

(5) a. **Without** a doubt, she's the best in her field.
b. **As for** snacks, I prefer pita chips.
c. This is a drugstore, **by** the way, not a pharmacy.

SNACS has excluded such usages from supersense annotation, directing annotators to tag them as non-semantic discourse markers (label `d) (Schneider et al., 2020).

A proposal for extending SNACS to pragmatic usages by introducing a new CONTEXT subhierarchy was made by the Korean SNACS project (Hwang et al., 2020, K-SNACS). K-SNACS has particularly focused on pragmatic adpositions that contribute meaning at the level of **information structure**, a level that includes the notions of focus, topic, and givenness (Lambrecht, 1994; Krifka, 2008; Lüdeling et al., 2016). For these pragmatic adpositions, K-SNACS has proposed the CONTEXT branch for adpositions whose meanings rely on contextual information either available in discourse or implicit in the shared knowledge between interlocutors. It places two labels within the CONTEXT tree: FOCUS and TOPICAL. FOCUS is assigned to usages where the adposition indicates the information structure focus of a sentence, contributing meanings of contrastiveness, likelihood, or value judgements (among others). TOPICAL markers apply to a phrase indicating a new subtopic, similar to (5b).[5] We will explore the details and usage of these labels in English and propose two additional labels for the CONTEXT subhierarchy in §4.

[5]The pragmatic label TOPICAL stands in contrast to SNACS TOPIC, which is the semantic role highlighted in locutions like *speak* **about** *something*.

4. Extending SNACS via Context

The current work extends upon the SNACS schema to include pragmatic relationships signaled by English prepositions. We build upon prior work by K-SNACS to introduce CONTEXT as a top-level *pragmatic* category on par with the existing *semantic* top-level categories: PARTICIPANT, CIRCUMSTANTIAL, and CONFIGURATION. For the purpose of SNACS, we note that an adpositional usage may qualify as **pragmatic** for one of two reasons:

- It provides ***extra-propositional*** reference to the interlocutors and/or their attitudes toward the propositional content or situation in which the conversation takes place.
- It mediates the relationship between sentences/utterances in the discourse, e.g. as a connective linking entire propositions, or as a marker that presupposes something was mentioned previously.

We propose four subcategories under CONTEXT: TOPICAL, FOCUS, COMMENTARY, and COHERENCE. These are expected to cover the lion's share of the pragmatic uses of adpositions; any miscellaneous pragmatic usages of adpositions that do not fit under these subtypes are to be directly labeled with CONTEXT.

It is also important to note that, for pragmatic uses of adpositions, we do not make use of the construal analysis (§2.1). For semantic relations, construals allow scene role and function labels to differ. For pragmatic uses requiring the CONTEXT hierarchy, we assume for now that only one label applies. We will revisit this assumption in §6.

4.1. Topical

TOPICAL annotates the adpositions that mark the information topic in a sentence. The information topic emphasizes the topic in a discourse that is presented in *contrast* to the available discourse referent, thereby signaling a change of topic in discourse. For example, the phrase "when it comes to..." puts forward a new topic in contrast to the old one. Adpositional examples of TOPICAL include:

(6) a. *Bill prefers beaches for vacations.*
As for me, I prefer the mountains.
b. *Jodi is a stickler about following directions.*
With regards to cooking, she never follows recipes.

4.2. Focus

The FOCUS label is used to mark the element of a sentence that contributes to information such as contrastiveness or likelihood, often evoking an implicitly understood pragmatic list (a set of alternatives or scale) pertinent to the object of the adposition. That is, FOCUS marks the tokens that emphasize an element of a sentence evoking an implicitly understood pragmatic scale pertinent to the object of the preposition. In English, the function of FOCUS is best exemplified by adverbials like *(not) only*, *(not) even*, and *also*.[6] In (7b), for example, by saying "*not even* Bill passed the test", we are implying that Bill, the likely was the candidate that was most likely to pass, failed along with many others less worthy candidates.

(7) a. **Only** Bill did a good job.
    b. **Not even** Bill passed the test.

Most prototypical English FOCUS usages are exemplified by adpositional phrases like "**as** well". In (8a), the phrase "**as** well" suggests that Bill is one of the many that would receive invitation. Modifying the utterance with "**in** itself", as in (8b), places a limitation to the stated proposition—that the idea may be problematic if other extraneous factors are considered.

(8) a. Don't forget to invite Bill **as** well.
    b. There's nothing wrong with the idea, **in** itself.

4.3. Commentary

The label COMMENTARY marks material with the speaker's orientation towards the main content, such as hedging, attributing it to themselves or someone else, or revealing their attitude (positive or negative) toward it or its veracity. Consider the following examples.

(9) a. Based **on** the latest reports, our cumulative spending is expected to continue rising.
    b. **In** my opinion, this is our only option.
    c. **Without** a doubt, she's the best in her field.
    d. **For** sure, we can change it.

In (9a), the prepositional phrase provides attribution for the statement or conclusion in the main proposition. Example (9b) does something similar—it attributes the proposition to the speaker's opinion, while also hedging the speaker's commitment to the proffered assertion. In (9c) and (9d), the prepositional phrases comment on the level of veracity of the propositions.

4.4. Coherence

COHERENCE signals how two propositions (i.e. clauses or sentences) are related in the discourse at a pragmatic level. Grammatically, markers of COHERENCE in English are usually attached to the second proposition. The broad label COHERENCE targets a coarser level of granularity than discourse annotation frameworks such as the Penn Discourse Treebank (Prasad et al., 2014, PDTB), Rhetorical Structure Theory (Mann and Thompson, 1988, RST), and Segmented Discourse Representation Theory (Asher and Lascarides, 2003, SDRT). Note, however, that discourse relations between sentences that are primarily semantic receive labels from the semantic parts of the hierarchy, rather than COHERENCE, such as PURPOSE or EXPLANATION shown below.[7]

(10) I need $10 (in order) **to:**PURPOSE see the movie. (Xposition_031)

(11) I will appoint him **as:**EXPLANATION he is most qualified for the job. (Xposition_008)

Although we do not formalize finer-grained coherence relations, we can illustrate some of the major subtypes that have been identified in English corpora following the aforementioned discourse formalisms such as the RST Discourse Treebank (Carlson et al., 2003; Carlson and Marcu, 2001, RST-DT) and PDTB 3.0 (Prasad et al., 2019):

- **JUXTAPOSITION**: The two propositions that the connective links contribute to the discourse jointly; that is, one proposition moves forward to the other proposition in a linear way: e.g. JOINT or SEQUENCE in RST-DT and CONJUNCTION in PDTB 3.0. Example: "**In** addition, we put in new floors."
- **ELABORATION**: one of the propositions is more specific than the other: e.g. one proposition provides further details for the other proposition such as elaborating or reinforcing a point, or narrowing or broadening the scope of discussion, as defined in RST-DT. Example: "**In** particular, we ..."
- **EXCEPTION**: One proposition describes a situation, and the other proposition describes or provides a counterargument or an exception, as defined in PDTB 3.0. Example: "**Outside** of my opinions about them, we ..."
- **INSTANTIATION**: One proposition describes a general situation or a group of things / issues etc., and the other proposition specifies one or more instances that belong to the aforementioned generic situation, as defined in PDTB 3.0 and is equivalent to ELABORATION-SET-MEMBER and EXAMPLE in RST-DT. Example: "**For** instance, we ..."
- **CONTRAST**: One or more differences are raised in the two propositions. Example: "**In** contrast to our expectations, we ..."
- **CONCESSION**: One proposition is acknowledged but the other proposition is still claimed. Example: "**Despite** recent fluctuations in stock price, we ..."

Again, these are merely illustrative examples of COHERENCE. At present we do not seek to distinguish them in our framework, but once an adpositional expression is tagged as COHERENCE, another framework can be invoked to clarify the nature of the coherence relation.

4.5. Context

The CONTEXT label is used directly for miscellaneous pragmatic meanings not covered by the aforementioned subtypes. This includes metadiscourse expressions that comment on the speaker's plan for the discourse such as

[6] Tor be clear, these adverbials are not annotated in SNACS as they are not adpositional. We provide these examples here with straightforward and unambiguous markers only to illustrate how focus can be marked lexically in English.

[7] The selected examples are from the SNACS project website, Xposition (Gessler et al., 2022): http://www.xposition.org.

by the way in (5c). Other prototypical uses in English include but are not limited to: on that note, speaking of, and moving on, which correspond to Fraser (2009)'s categorization of the topic orientation markers; and markers signaling something about the relationship between interlocutors such as politeness or formality (e.g. with all due respect).

5. Pilot Context Annotation

5.1. SNACS Corpora

A number of corpora in several languages have been annotated with SNACS such as English, Mandarin Chinese (Peng et al., 2020), Korean (Hwang et al., 2020), German (Prange and Schneider, 2021), and Hindi (Arora et al., 2022). Since the focus of the present pilot annotation effort is to annotate adpositional discourse elements in English, we extract such instances previously marked as discourse markers (`d) from the three English SNACS Corpora: PASTRIE (Kranzlein et al., 2020), STREUSLE (Schneider and Smith, 2015; Schneider et al., 2018), and The Little Prince (Schneider et al., 2020, LPP), amounting to 165 annotation instances. Specifically, PASTRIE contains data from Reddit produced by presumed speakers of four native languages (English, French, German, and Spanish).[8] STREUSLE contains web reviews from the Reviews section of the English Web Treebank (Bies et al., 2012). LPP contains an English translation of the fiction story *Le Petit Prince*. Albeit limited, the resulting annotated data could also provide insights into the use and distribution of adpositional pragmatic markers in English across different types of data.

5.2. Annotation Procedures

The STREUSLE data was used as development data for developing the guidelines: it formed the basis of preliminary discussions and attempts at categorization, culminating in a final round of annotation and joint adjudication by the four researchers developing the guidelines. In order to test the validity of the guidelines, two new annotators were recruited to independently annotate the STREUSLE data in comparison to the adjudicated version produced by the researchers developing the guidelines.

In the annotation workflow, each extracted `d element is presented in a sentence, with the `d element highlighted and the preceding and following sentences provided for additional context.[9] Annotations in (12)–(16) show prepositions (previously annotated with `d) updated to the appropriate CONTEXT labels.

(12) Tourists like the other reviewer might not appreciate their efficiency or quality, but I certainly do. This isn'ta TGIF or Cafe, its a lunch sandwich place and a good one **at:**FOCUS that. [END] (STREUSLE_reviews-317846-0008)

(13) Any ER would be the same. **As:**TOPICAL far as being treated like a drug seeker, that has not been my experience. As a nurse I know about drug seekers. (STREUSLE_reviews-169083-0005)

(14) We have used them for plumbing & A/C and they are affordable and get the work done right. Great place 5 stars **for:**COMMENTARY sure. Thanks From Bill (STREUSLE_reviews-359433-0003)

(15) And so you will love to watch all the stars in the heavens ... they will all be your friends . And , **besides:**COHERENCE , I am going to make you a present ... " He laughed again . (lpp_1943.1436)

(16) This store is a real gem and has much to offer the serious crafter or the occasional crafter. **By:**CONTEXT the way, Salmagundi (the store name) means something like smorgasbord; potpourri; motley; variety; mixed bag; miscellaneous assortment; mixture, a variety of many kinds of things. Great name for a great store! (STREUSLE_reviews-377347-0011)

In addition to the five labels described in §4 (i.e. FOCUS, TOPICAL, COMMENTARY, COHERENCE, CONTEXT), the annotators were also instructed to use a NOT_CONTEXT label if they think that no pragmatic use of the adposition is involved; in other words, the `d element in question only involves a semantic reading, and the existing SNACS framework should capture its meaning, as shown in (17) and (18) below as well as (10) and (11) in §4.4.

(17) They have messed up my order and.... The food was just not good! I had sonic in many other palces but **for:**EXPLANATION some reason this sonic is always just covered in grease and not good... :(I hope they get there act together... (STREUSLE_reviews-109263-0003)

(18) Then the desserts came, and they were hands down the best dessert we ever had. I will sum it up **with:**MEANS, it was worth every penny! [END] (STREUSLE_reviews-388799-0006)

5.3. Reliability of Annotation

In order to evaluate the reliability of the taxonomy and the complexity of the task, we conducted an inter-annotator agreement (IAA) study on each of the three English SNACS datasets, described in §5.1, which comprise 165 annotation instances. Each of the `d elements from each English SNACS dataset were annotated by two native speakers of American English using the guidelines described in §4. Overall, there were three annotators: STREUSLE was annotated by the same two annotators (Annotator 1 and Annotator 2), and PASTRIE and LPP were annotated by the same two

[8] See Section 3.1 of Rabinovich et al. (2018) for details on the identification of the native languages.

[9] If the sentence that contains the `d element is the beginning or the end of the document, a special token ([START] or [END]) is used to indicate this, as shown in (12).

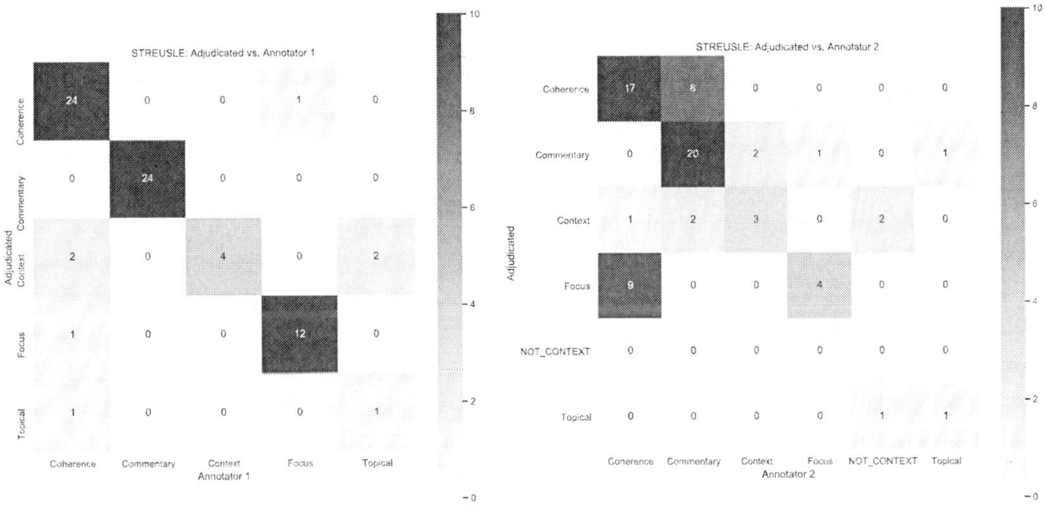

(a) ADJUDICATED vs. Annotator 1

(b) ADJUDICATED vs. Annotator 2

Figure 1: Confusion Matrices for STREUSLE Annotations.

annotators (Annotator 2 and Annotator 3), meaning that Annotator 2 annotated the STREUSLE, PASTRIE, and LPP data.

	#'d items	Raw Agreement	Cohen's Kappa
PASTRIE	74	56.8%	0.41
STREUSLE	72	59.7%	0.42
LPP	19	89.5%	0.83

Table 1: IAA of SNACS Context Annotation in English.

Table 1 shows raw agreement and Cohen's kappa scores between the two annotators for each dataset. Results show higher agreement levels for LPP than PASTRIE and STREUSLE. We attribute this to the fact that LPP is a formally written novella, while PASTRIE and STREUSLE are web or social media data written in a conversational style, in some cases with fragments or missing context from previous turns, which makes it much more difficult for the annotators to accurately gauge what was intended at the time of the writing. Feedback from the annotators indicated that for some cases the preceding and following sentences were insufficient context for interpreting the pragmatic markers.

We also note that the agreement for PASTRIE is slightly lower than that of STREUSLE. This is likely due to the fact that PASTRIE data contains Reddit discussions from a variety of topics, and some of the subreddits have their own jargon not readily understandable by annotators, as pointed out in Kranzlein et al. (2020). Another reason behind the complexity and difficulty of the PASTRIE annotations is that although the data is in English, 78.4% of the instances were produced by presumed native speakers of French, German, and Spanish. Though for the most part the text is fluent English, there may be instances where non-native speakers do not fully conform to native speakers' expectations in their use of pragmatic expressions.

For STREUSLE, we also noticed that Annotator 1 achieved higher agreement with the adjudicated version (i.e. the annotations produced by the researchers developing the guidelines) than Annotator 2, as shown in Figures 1a and 1b respectively. One possible interpretation is that Annotator 1 simply understood the annotation task better than Annotator 2, and thus the scores may indicate an issue with the guidelines instead of the categories themselves. Figure 2 also demonstrates that Annotator 2 underused the FOCUS label, which is unsurprising due to dearth of transparent and unambiguous cues in English. Additionally, the confusion matrices shown in Figure 1 also help identify some sources of confusion from the labels as well as the adpositonal markers associated with such labels such as FOCUS vs. COHERENCE (e.g. as well) and COHERENCE vs. COMMENTARY (e.g. in fact). We will discuss these cases in detail in §6 below.

6. Analysis

In this section, we take a closer look at some of the challenges posed by the annotation of adpositional pragmatic markers.

6.1. FOCUS vs. COHERENCE

The status of adpositional FOCUS is fairly clear-cut in languages like Korean, which features a small set of high-frequency focus markers (Hwang et al., 2020). In English, however, focus is less often cued adpositionally—and to the extent that it is, there is an apparent overlap between FOCUS and COHERENCE usages, which was a source of difficulty for annotators. Consider the following examples with pragmatic adverbs:

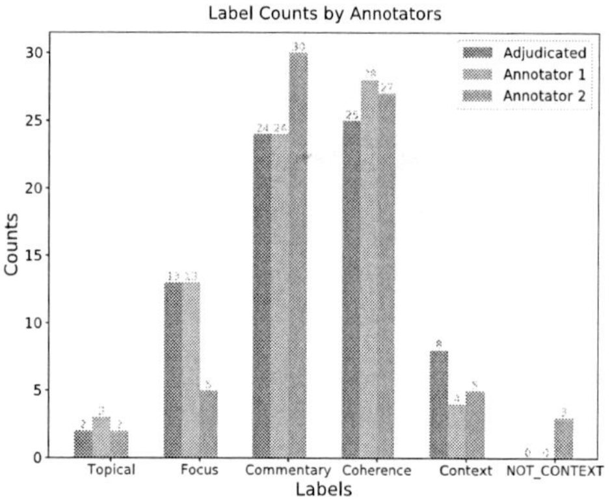

Figure 2: Distribution of Labels for STREUSLE Annotations.

(19) *It rained yesterday.*

a. **Additionally**, it hailed. [COHERENCE]

b. It **even** hailed. [FOCUS]

As a prototypical discourse connective, "additionally" in (19a) links the proposition "it hailed" to the previous utterance "It rained yesterday", advancing the content in a coherent manner. "Even" in (19b) brings focus to the marked proposition, expressing that the new information exceeds the expectation set by the information that is available in the context: it not only rained yesterday, but in a surprising turn of events, it hailed. The prepositional phrase "**as** well" seemingly does both, complicating the annotation.

(20) *It rained yesterday.* It hailed **as well**.

The phrase "**as** well" serves the role of a discourse connective linking the proposition to the previous utterance, but it also plays a focusing role like "even", in such a way that the *hailing* event is put forward as a surprising event that beyond contextual expectations. In other words, the interpretation of this piece of information is not contained in the semantics of the current proposition, nor does it inherit from the previous proposition. Rather, the focus reading here is extra-propositional.

As a means of addressing this issue, we considered the use of the construal analysis to resolve this semantic overlap was considered. That is, rather than having the annotators decide which label to go with, we would allow annotators to use both labels to annotate usages like "**as** well". However, this created yet another concern: which label, i.e. COHERENCE or FOCUS, should be assigned as scene role versus function? In SNACS annotation, the scene role is the meaning assigned by the *scene* of a sentence (e.g. head predicate, head nominal, or the construction). However, pragmatic labels are what they are by virtue of *not* being directly related to any of the aforementioned elements. To call either label as scene or function would essentially violate the construal analysis, by definition.

For this reason, in this pilot annotation study we only allowed one label per prepositional token, assigned at the annotator's discretion based on their interpretation of what meaning was most salient. For example, since the phrase "**as** well" in (21) functions as a connective between propositions (i.e. the beers were good *and* there were good choice of beers), it receives the label of COHERENCE. The phrase "**as** well" in (22), marked with the FOCUS label, implies the existence of other unmentioned incriminating aspects of the organization in question (presumably, a vet).

(21) Good place to be on a Sunday Night. The beers were good, nice choice of beers **as:**COHERENCE well, and as usual the mussels were great, the place upstairs is a nice addition to the bar downstairs. Filled up on too much beer and hence cannot comment on the food. (STREUSLE_reviews-366946-0003)

(22) They refused. Terrible communication **as:**FOCUS well. At one point they told me the dog had been fixed, the next day it hadn't. (STREUSLE_reviews-006970-0008)

We observe, however, that this practice does create annotation disagreements. (23) exemplifies a split between annotators. Annotator 1, who chose FOCUS, is cuing a perhaps more nuanced shade of meaning than Annotator 2, who chose COHERENCE. The extra-propositional meaning of "**as** well" would indicate the location to be an additional characteristic that further elevates their already high opinion of establishment. This suggests that the current guidelines will produce disagreements based on a variety of reasons: nuanced differences based on reading, familiarity with the topic of the text, or simple disagreement, to name a few.

(23) They are honest about 'immediate' concerns versus 'recommended' repairs and have very fair prices. Such a convenient location as well with coffee shop and bradley food and beverage right around corner. [END] (STREUSLE_reviews-303922-0005)

Thus, as alluded to in brief in §2.3, we also consider the possibility of introducing a modified version of construal analysis specifically for the CONTEXT tree whereby, when necessary, we recognize a secondary function (to the primary function) of pragmatic and discourse markers. That is, it is likely that multiple interpretations coexist, but they correspond to different aspects of the markers in question. Depending on the amount of available context provided and the common knowledge shared by the participants in a given discourse, some aspects and functions become more salient than the others.

6.2. COHERENCE vs. COMMENTARY

As can be seen from Figure 1b, another source of confusion comes from COMMENTARY and COHERENCE, corresponding to the discourse marker "in fact". Again, this is a prototypical discourse marker in English, but it mediates various types of relationships between discourse units, as attested in PDTB 3.0 (Prasad et al., 2019).[10,11] In the following example, "in fact" signals an elaboration or reinforcement of the previous proposition by describing a related event (i.e. vomiting) that happened.

(24) The sauce was dry and the enchiladas did not taste good.at all. <u>**In**:COHERENCE fact</u> my friend vomited after our meal. With higher than average prices to boot! (STREUSLE_reviews-150192-0004)

However, our annotation results indicate that "in fact" may project a pragmatic meaning beyond discourse linking. Consider the following examples:

(25) Practicing your joke is crucial . You do n't need to have it completely memorized — <u>in fact</u> , you " should n't " memorize it — but you need to be really comfortable with it , so comfortable that you can continue on with telling it even if you get nervous or sidetracked , which is very possible once you 're in front of an audience . (GUM_whow_joke)

(26) The question isn't about Is smoking Marijuana a progress ?. <u>**In** fact</u>, we don't care because we want to guarantee freedom not societal progress. In conclusion, we fight for the same results (on societal issues only). (PASTRIE_french-4c78c7ab-4fd2-4206-342f-22bae20cea4a-09)

Both of these examples of "in fact" manage the flow from one proposition to the next, consistent with the COHERENCE label. However, in addition to the coherence relationship they mediate, they inject a sense of the writer's attitude towards the topic. This is the most clearly evident in (25),[12] the writer uses "in fact" as a means of signaling their own commitment to the upcoming proposition (*not* memorizing a joke) with respect to a perhaps a more standardized advice (minimal memorization). In the same way, the prepositional phrase advances an attitude contrast in (26) between the previous proposition and upcoming proposition. In other words, "in fact" blurs the boundary between the COMMENTARY and COHERENCE categories.

Thus, it is clear that the assignment of COHERENCE to "in fact" is grounded in the criterion that COHERENCE marks the linking between the two propositions, according to the guidelines. The COMMENTARY reading depends on the interpretation of the single proposition that "in fact" is embedded in—i.e. whether it is also signaling something about the interlocutors' attitude towards the content. We believe that the current guidelines would benefit from a richer array of examples for multi-functional markers like "in fact". Additionally, the results from this pilot annotation work also suggest that for annotating adpositional pragmatic markers it may be necessary to either adopt a multi-label strategy (i.e. primary and secondary labels for different interpretations) or introduce a combined categorization (e.g. COHERENCE⇝COMMENTARY where the label on the left corresponds to the stronger reading) in order to better capture the pragmatic reading in context instead of imposing the constraint that only one single label is applicable.

7. Conclusion

In this paper, we presented a small taxonomy that aims to capture categories of pragmatic meaning associated with adpositional expressions in English. Our pilot annotation study sheds light on deficiencies in the guidelines that may explain annotator confusion and disagreements. These issues call for a deeper investigation of multi-functional uses of some of these pragmatic expressions. We intend to take these issues up in future work.

8. Acknowledgements

We thank anonymous reviewers for their feedback. We are grateful to Aryaman Arora and Shira Wein for their annotation work, Bonnie Webber for preliminary discussions of relevant issues, and Paul Portner and Amir Zeldes for their insightful feedback.

9. Bibliographical References

Abend, O. and Rappoport, A. (2013). UCCA: A semantics-based grammatical annotation scheme. In *Proceedings of the 10th International Conference on Computational Semantics (IWCS 2013) – Long Papers*, pages 1–12, Potsdam, Germany, March. Association for Computational Linguistics.

Arora, A., Venkateswaran, N., and Schneider, N. (2022). A corpus of Hindi adposition and case semantics. In *Proceedings of the 13th Language Resources and Evaluation Conference*, Marseille, France, June. European Language Resources Association.

Asher, N. and Lascarides, A. (2003). *Logics of Conversation*. Cambridge University Press, Cambridge.

Bies, A., Mott, J., Warner, C., and Kulick, S. (2012). English Web Treebank. LDC2012T13.

Carlson, L. and Marcu, D. (2001). Discourse tagging reference manual. Technical Report ISI-TR-545, University of Southern California Information Sciences Institute.

[10] Among those relations for "in fact" recognized by PDTB 3.0 are: EXPANSION.CONJUNCTION, EXPANSION.LEVEL-OF-DETAIL, COMPARISON.CONTRAST, and COMPARISON.CONCESSION.

[11] The PDTB 2.0 manual, however, registered doubts about the status of "in fact" as a discourse connective (The PDTB Research Group et al., 2007, p. 8, fn. 9). "Of course" is a similar expression that was not annotated in PDTB (Bonnie Webber, p.c.).

[12] This example is from the GUM corpus (Zeldes, 2017).

Carlson, L., Marcu, D., and Okurowski, M. E. (2003). Building a Discourse-Tagged Corpus in the Framework of Rhetorical Structure Theory. In *Current and New Directions in Discourse and Dialogue*, Text, Speech and Language Technology 22, pages 85–112. Kluwer, Dordrecht.

de Marneffe, M.-C., Manning, C. D., Nivre, J., and Zeman, D. (2021). Universal Dependencies. *Computational Linguistics*, 47(2):255–308, 07.

Fraser, B. (1990). An approach to discourse markers. *Journal of Pragmatics*, 14(3):383–398. Special Issue: 'Selected papers from The International Pragmatics Conference, Antwerp, 17-22 August, 1987'.

Fraser, B. (1996). Pragmatic markers. *Pragmatics*, 6(2):167–190.

Fraser, B. (2009). Topic orientation markers. *Journal of Pragmatics*, 41(5):892–898. Pragmatic Markers.

Gessler, L., Blodgett, A., Ledford, J., and Schneider, N. (2022). Xposition: An online multilingual database of adpositional semantics. In *Proc. of LREC*, Marseille, France, June. ELRA.

Hwang, J. D., Bhatia, A., Han, N.-R., O'Gorman, T., Srikumar, V., and Schneider, N. (2017). Double trouble: The problem of construal in semantic annotation of adpositions. In *Proceedings of the 6th Joint Conference on Lexical and Computational Semantics (*SEM 2017)*, pages 178–188, Vancouver, Canada, August. Association for Computational Linguistics.

Hwang, J. D., Choe, H., Han, N.-R., and Schneider, N. (2020). K-SNACS: Annotating Korean adposition semantics. In *Proceedings of the Second International Workshop on Designing Meaning Representations*, pages 53–66, Barcelona Spain (online), December. Association for Computational Linguistics.

Kranzlein, M., Manning, E., Peng, S., Wein, S., Arora, A., and Schneider, N. (2020). PASTRIE: A corpus of prepositions annotated with supersense tags in Reddit international English. In *Proceedings of the 14th Linguistic Annotation Workshop*, pages 105–116, Barcelona, Spain, December. Association for Computational Linguistics.

Krifka, M. (2008). Basic notions of information structure. *Acta Linguistica Hungarica*, 55(3-4):243 – 276.

Lambrecht, K. (1994). *Information Structure and Sentence Form: Topic, Focus, and the Mental Representations of Discourse Referents.* Cambridge Studies in Linguistics. Cambridge University Press.

Lüdeling, A., Ritz, J., Stede, M., and Zeldes, A., (2016). *Corpus Linguistics and Information Structure Research*, pages 599–617. Oxford University Press, 09.

Mann, W. C. and Thompson, S. A. (1988). Rhetorical Structure Theory: Toward a Functional Theory of Text Organization. *Text-Interdisciplinary Journal for the Study of Discourse*, 8(3):243–281.

Maschler, Y. and Schiffrin, D., (2015). *Discourse Markers Language, Meaning, and Context*, chapter 9, pages 189–221. John Wiley & Sons, Ltd.

Peng, S., Liu, Y., Zhu, Y., Blodgett, A., Zhao, Y., and Schneider, N. (2020). A corpus of adpositional supersenses for Mandarin Chinese. In *Proceedings of the 12th Language Resources and Evaluation Conference*, pages 5986–5994, Marseille, France, May. European Language Resources Association.

Prange, J. and Schneider, N. (2021). Draw mir a sheep: A supersense-based analysis of german case and adposition semantics. *Künstliche Intell.*, 35:291–306.

Prasad, R., Webber, B., and Joshi, A. (2014). Reflections on the Penn Discourse Treebank, Comparable Corpora, and Complementary A fnnotation. *Computational Linguistics*, 40(4):921–950.

Prasad, R., Webber, B., Lee, A., and Joshi, A. (2019). Penn Discourse Treebank Version 3.0. LDC2019T05.

Rabinovich, E., Tsvetkov, Y., and Wintner, S. (2018). Native language cognate effects on second language lexical choice. *Transactions of the Association for Computational Linguistics*, 6:329–342.

Samy, D. and González-Ledesma, A. (2008). Pragmatic annotation of discourse markers in a multilingual parallel corpus (Arabic- Spanish-English). In *Proceedings of the Sixth International Conference on Language Resources and Evaluation (LREC'08)*, Marrakech, Morocco, May. European Language Resources Association (ELRA).

Schneider, N. and Smith, N. A. (2015). A corpus and model integrating multiword expressions and supersenses. In *Proceedings of the 2015 Conference of the North American Chapter of the Association for Computational Linguistics: Human Language Technologies*, pages 1537–1547, Denver, Colorado, May–June. Association for Computational Linguistics.

Schneider, N., Hwang, J. D., Srikumar, V., Prange, J., Blodgett, A., Moeller, S. R., Stern, A., Bitan, A., and Abend, O. (2018). Comprehensive supersense disambiguation of English prepositions and possessives. In *Proc. of ACL*, pages 185–196, Melbourne, Australia, July.

Schneider, N., Hwang, J. D., Bhatia, A., Srikumar, V., Han, N., O'Gorman, T., Moeller, S. R., Abend, O., Shalev, A., Blodgett, A., and Prange, J. (2020). Adposition and Case Supersenses v2.5: Guidelines for English. *arXiv:1704.02134 [cs]*, April.

Stede, M. and Birte, S. (2000). Discourse particles and discourse functions. *Machine Translation*, 15:125–147, 06.

The PDTB Research Group, Prasad, R., Miltsakaki, E., Dinesh, N., Lee, A., Joshi, A., Robaldo, L., and Webber, B. (2007). The Penn Discourse Treebank 2.0 annotation manual. Technical Report IRCS-08-01, Institute for Research in Cognitive Science, University of Pennsylvania, Philadelphia, PA, December.

Zeldes, A. (2017). The GUM Corpus: Creating multilayer resources in the classroom. *Language Resources and Evaluation*, 51(3):581–612.

Proceedings of the 16th Linguistic Annotation Workshop (LAW-XVI) @LREC 2022, pages 129–138
Marseille, 24 June 2022

Building a Biomedical Full-Text Part-of-Speech Corpus Semi-Automatically

Nicholas Elder, Robert E. Mercer, Sudipta Singha Roy
The University of Western Ontario
London, Ontario, Canada
nelder@uwo.ca, mercer@csd.uwo.ca, ssinghar@uwo.ca

Abstract

This paper presents a method for semi-automatically building a corpus of full-text English-language biomedical articles annotated with part-of-speech tags. The outcomes are a semi-automatic procedure to create a large silver standard corpus of 5 million sentences drawn from a large corpus of full-text biomedical articles annotated for part-of-speech, and a robust, easy-to-use software tool that assists the investigation of differences in two tagged datasets. The method to build the corpus uses two part-of-speech taggers designed to tag biomedical abstracts followed by a human dispute settlement when the two taggers differ on the tagging of a token. The dispute resolution aspect is facilitated by the software tool which organizes and presents the disputed tags. The corpus and all of the software that has been implemented for this study are made publicly available.

Keywords: semi-automatic corpus annotation, biomedical document annotation, part-of-speech

1. Introduction

Training and evaluating machine learning Natural Language Processing (NLP) systems require benchmark corpora annotated for the NLP task being learned. Manually curated gold standard corpora, the language resources that are typically used to train and test such systems, are unfortunately, costly to produce especially in domains requiring specialized knowledge to understand the text.

Our goal is to provide a large corpus of biomedical text annotated with part-of-speech (POS) using the Penn Treebank Tagset to facilitate the training of a deep learning model. Our current corpus, which we call BioPOSTAg, drawn from full-text biomedical articles, has 5 million sentences and we continue to work toward a corpus containing 35 million sentences. Due to the size of this corpus, no completely manual annotation is possible. An alternative to a gold standard annotated corpus is a silver standard corpus (Rebholz-Schuhmann et al., 2010). Therefore we have decided on a silver standard approach. The silver standard was first proposed to be generated in a fully automatic way (Rebholz-Schuhmann et al., 2011) using annotation systems and some method to harmonize their resulting annotations. Researchers continue with this practice (Sousa et al., 2019), while others incorporate some manual annotations (Eckart and Gärtner, 2016). Because our building of the silver standard corpus uses only two automated annotators, we need to have some human intervention to make decisions when the annotators disagree. Since this human intervention is added, the process that is described herewith is termed semi-automatic.

The BioPOSTAg corpus is evaluated by comparing the performance of a model trained on the silver standard corpus versus the same model trained on a human-annotated gold standard corpus on a POS tagging task. We have chosen the CRAFT corpus (Verspoor et al., 2012) as the gold standard training and test sets for this comparison.

Our contributions can be summarized as follows: a semi-automatic procedure to create a large silver standard corpus; a large corpus of complete biomedical articles annotated for part-of-speech has been built and is made available to the research community; and a robust, easy-to-use software tool that assists the investigation of differences in two annotated datasets facilitating the human dispute resolution aspect of the semi-automated procedure.

2. Background

Part-of-speech (POS) tagging assigns a POS to each token in a text. Modern POS taggers are trained using some form of machine learning. Training requires an annotated corpus. Training of a deep learning model requires a corpus with a large number of samples, in this case sentences with the tokens annotated for POS. The manually tagged gold standard corpora that have been built, e.g., the GENIA corpus (1997 abstracts) (Kim et al., 2003) and the CRAFT corpus (97 full-text papers) (Verspoor et al., 2012) are reasonably small. Having larger tagged corpora may be beneficial. In addition, while part-of-speech tagging in the biomedical literature genre has long been a topic of research (Kim et al., 2003; Tateisi and Tsujii, 2004), the early focus has been on POS tagging of article abstracts. POS tagging of complete article texts provides some subtle differences due to sentence structure and other writing and content issues (Cohen et al., 2010).

Complete biomedical article datasets are becoming available to the research community, so having machine methods that work with full papers is both feasible and critically important given the large amount of literature produced in this socially significant research field. Because manual annotation is costly, especially in the biomedical domain since it requires specialized knowledge, large annotated corpora of full text biomedical articles do not currently exist. The focus of the current study is the semi-automatic curation of a sufficiently large silver standard corpus of complete article texts annotated with POS tags that might boost the performance of deep learning trained POS taggers. To provide the automatic aspect of this silver standard corpus curation task, this study uses two top ranked biomedical POS taggers: the popular Genia (Kim et al., 2003; Tateisi and Tsujii, 2004) and a variant of MedPost (Smith et al., 2004) that we call PostMed so as not to confuse it with the original but to pay homage to the original name and work. Genia was trained on a corpus of 1999 manually annotated MEDLINE abstracts. In addition to POS tagging, Genia's other abilities (named-entity tagging and chunk parsing) are not used in this study. MedPost is a POS tagger, but also of importance for this study, it can work with .nxml files: interpreting the xml tags, breaking the file into sentences, and performing tokenization. It was designed to work with MEDLINE abstracts, so a wrapper was provided by the second author giving PostMed, the modified version that works with full article texts (e.g., figures and tables are removed). These POS taggers have achieved over 98% and 97% accuracy, respectively, on MEDLINE citations.

Unlike other silver standard corpora building which use techniques developed for the type of data that is represented in the silver standard corpus, the techniques that we are using have been trained on MEDLINE abstracts whereas the data that we are annotating with our semi-automatic method are full-text articles. Full-text articles contain language that is not found in abstracts, such as references to figures and tables. So, the use of these two taggers could be considered akin to cross-domain tagging but obtaining good performance may not be as difficult as sometimes is the case with cross-domain tagging. Our hypothesis was that the outputs of these two part of speech taggers would perform reasonably well on this new type of data, that the number of differences would be manageable, and that human intervention would be able to enhance the final outcome. The second part of our hypothesis, that the number of differences would be manageable was overly optimistic. As a result, we developed a software tool, a data viewer, whose purpose was to organize these differences along different dimensions thereby facilitating our viewing of the differences in various ways.

3. Related Work

Research related to this study falls into three categories: corpora annotated for POS, POS taggers, and studies of the performance on full-text articles of taggers trained on article abstracts. Some small corpora annotated for POS based on clinical notes (Pakhomov et al., 2006) and on patient records (Huseth and Rost, 2007) have been built, the latter one being annotated semi-automatically. Because few biomedical corpora with POS annotations exist, methods such as cross-training have been used to circumvent this paucity of data, but the resulting performance tends to be low (Barrett and Weber-Jahnke, 2014). Adding a biomedical domain-specific corpus has been shown to improve results (Coden et al., 2005). MedPost (Smith et al., 2004) uses a lexicon that enumerates permitted POS tags for the most frequently occurring 10,000 words in MEDLINE to improve its performance (Smith et al., 2006). And, some improvements with cross-trained taggers have been reported by introducing specialized lexicons to address the problems associated with unknown words (Miller et al., 2007). It has been demonstrated (Tateisi et al., 2006) that because biomedicine has subdomains, performance drops when taggers are required to tag a subdomain that differs from the training subdomain. And, some results show excellent performance by off-the-shelf POS taggers (TnT (Brants, 2000)) for tagging clinical reports (Hahn and Wermter, 2004). Other POS taggers have been developed for the biomedical domain, some being better performers than others. dTagger (Divita et al., 2006), trained and tested on the MedPost corpus, performs with 95.1% accuracy. TcT (Barrett and Weber-Jahnke, 2014) performs with 96.7% accuracy on the MedPost corpus. These last two taggers have not been used in the present study because they are no longer available.

When using taggers that have been trained on biomedical article abstracts, it is important to know how well they scale up when they are used to tag full-text articles. Results suggest a 7-8 percentage point drop between testing the taggers on abstracts and testing them on full-text journal articles (Verspoor et al., 2012).

4. Data Set and Curated Corpus

The dataset used in this study is the complete article dataset that was first made available by The National Center for Biotechnology Information (PubMed Central) in 2009. It consists of the full text of articles published in 288 biomedical journals. Our goal is to build a corpus annotated for part-of-speech from the full set comprising approximately 35 million sentences. The current BioPOSTAg corpus[1] has been built from a set of 49 biomedical journals. The corpus comprises approximately 5 million sentences. These articles were POS tagged by Genia and PostMed.

The corpus is part-of-speech tagged using the biomedical update (Warner et al., 2012) of the Penn Treebank Tagset (Marcus et al., 1993). The updated tagset consists of the original 36 part-of-speech tags and 12 other tags for punctuation and currency symbols together with 4 additional tags added in the biomedical update. Tagging guidelines (Santorini, 1995; Warner et al., 2004; Warner et al., 2012) were consulted. The MedPost (and hence, PostMed) tagset used here is the original Penn Treebank Tagset. The Genia tagger uses the enlarged tagset.

[1] https://github.com/nelder/Biomedical-POS-Tagger/

5. Building the Corpus

The first step in the building of the corpus is to generate the tagging of Genia and PostMed. PostMed is used first to preprocess the .nxml files as described previously and to generate its tagged output. Genia then takes the tokenized output of PostMed and performs its tagging. These files can then be compared to discover the POS differences. We now direct our discussion in the next sections to how the POS differences are resolved with human intervention.

5.1. Part of Speech Tagging Difference

Because we were using only two POS taggers, our goal to produce a silver standard corpus could not use a scheme such as voting to decide a tagging outcome when the tags from the two taggers differed. So, we opted to have some human intervention to make decisions when this situation arose. Due to the volume of data and frequency of mismatch, it was not feasible to manually verify the tagged text produced by each of these taggers. As such we developed a software data viewer, using which, as humans, we could navigate and compare the outputs of these two taggers to identify where they disagreed. Implicit in this approach is the assumption that when Genia and PostMed specify the same tag for a particular word, then they are correct. While this might not be strictly true (see Section 6 for details), this assumption has seemed not to be deleterious. We harnessed the discord between these two taggers by assuming that one was correct and the other was incorrect. Our main focus thus, was the part of speech tagging difference (POSDiff). To illustrate, Genia and PostMed assigned the following tags:

Committee	for	Animal	Research
NNP	IN	NNP	NNP (Genia)
NN	IN	NN	NN (PostMed)

POSDiff instances exist, one for each of the words: Committee, Animal, and Research. The POSDiff allowed us to group like errors in an attempt to provide human solutions to classes of problems as opposed to individual instances of tagging errors. Our method to find and correct errors is described later.

5.2. POSDiffs Discovered

With all of our tools in hand we began the process of building a better corpus by analyzing the POSDiffs between Genia and PostMed tagged data for our 49 journal corpus. We discovered that 5% of POSDiffs account for 81% of the disagreements. This means that a small handful of the POSDiffs disproportionally are responsible for the tagging errors which also means that solutions to these POSDiffs would be highly valuable for overall corpus quality. We also noted that across our 5 million sentence corpus there were a total of 496 POSDiffs. As Table 1 outlines, the top 25 most frequent POSDiffs accounted for 81.38% of the disagreements. The full list of POSDiffs is included in https://github.com/nelder/Biomedical-POS-Tagger/ as a csv file.

5.2.1. Decision Making

With all of the information now in hand we began to look through the POSDiffs from most common to least common and apply human judgement to correct each of the POSDiffs. For each of the POSDiffs we assessed a random sample of instances from the most frequent words within each POSDiff to develop an understanding of the cause. We took into consideration the pattern, whether it be each example looking consistent or more sporadic to decide when to direct more energy into looking at additional examples. For each of the 13 most frequent POSDiffs listed in Table 1 we created a decision procedure which selected between the taggers. The encoded procedure (which is machine interpretable) indicates whether either of the taggers is globally correct for a given POSDiff. If not, it will indicate the preferred tagger and a procedure of specific interventions to apply before using the default preferred tagger. These interventions pattern match either words or word patterns and apply an intervention. These interventions can be a specific POS tag, a tagger to use, or a context specific procedure. For instance, "positive = mix : PRIOR_WORD_TAG@JJ|NN? postmed,genia". In this case the word "positive" is tagged using PostMed's tag when the tag on the prior word is either a JJ or NN, otherwise it uses Genia's tag. These decision procedures now exist for 70% of the POSDiff instances that occurred and as such we've eliminated many of the disagreements between the two taggers that were originally present with these procedures. The remaining 30% were eliminated by choosing the Genia tagger as providing the correct tag.

5.2.2. Sample Decision Procedures: Globally Correct Tagger

For Genia tagging VB (Verb, base form) and PostMed tagging VBP (Verb, non-3rd person singular present), we determined that Genia was tagging correctly in the vast majority of the sampled cases we examined. In all cases the syntactic structure involved a modal verb, then base case verb, followed up by the participle form of the verb. The issue was that PostMed was tensing the base form of the verb and then making a mistake on the main verb following this incorrectly tensed verb. An example is outlined in Figure 1, where this particular POSDiff is highlighted in black and other POSDiffs present in that selected sentence are highlighted in blue. Given the consistent cause we saw across the 10 sampled cases we assigned Genia to be the correct tagger globally for this POSDiff.

5.2.3. Sample Decision Procedures: Word Specific Solution

For Genia tagging NN (Noun, singular or mass) and PostMed tagging JJ (Adjective), we noted that neither tagger was exclusively correct. This tagging error was

Table 1: POSDiffs discovered (subset of most frequent 25).

POSDiff	Instances	Freq. (%)	Cumulative Freq. (%)	Unique Words	Instances per Word
G:NNP | P:NN	572,633	15.60%	15.60%	65607	9
G:JJ | P:NN	430,673	11.73%	27.33%	42387	10
G:VB | P:VBP	338,190	9.21%	36.54%	2312	146
G:VBN | P:JJ	270,197	7.36%	43.90%	4666	58
G:VBG | P:JJ	162,882	4.44%	48.34%	3727	44
G:NN | P:JJ	156,541	4.26%	52.60%	8360	19
G:NN | P:SYM	142,748	3.89%	56.49%	9	15861
G:VBG | P:NN	120,278	3.28%	59.77%	4290	28
G:VBN | P:VBD	91,012	2.48%	62.25%	1968	46
G:DT | P:PRP	87,779	2.39%	64.64%	22	3990
G:NNS | P:VBZ	63,313	1.72%	66.36%	2755	23
G:NNS | P:NN	54,028	1.47%	67.83%	4667	12
G:VBD | P:VBN	53,115	1.45%	69.28%	1762	30
G:RB | P:WRB	48,486	1.32%	70.60%	5	9697
G:NN | P:VBP	46,106	1.26%	71.86%	2090	22
G:FW | P:NN	46,018	1.25%	73.11%	1458	32
G:RBR | P:RB	44,569	1.21%	74.32%	22	2026
G:NNP | P:JJ	41,995	1.14%	75.46%	2586	16
G:CD | P:NN	36,809	1%	76.46%	7496	5
G:JJ | P:RB	35,246	0.96%	77.42%	2763	13
G:JJ | P:DT	32,357	0.88%	78.30%	11	2942
G:NNP | P:NNS	31,441	0.86%	79.16%	4178	8
G:VBD | P:JJ	28,888	0.79%	79.95%	1816	16
G:NN | P:NNS	27,213	0.74%	80.69%	2494	11
G:VBZ | P:NNS	25,422	0.69%	81.38%	2150	12

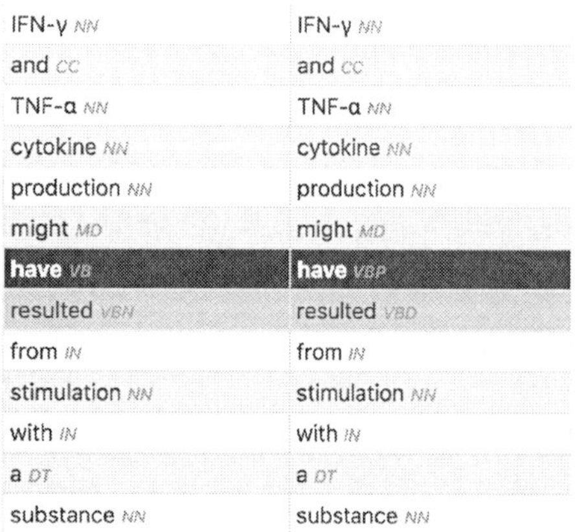

Figure 1: Example of a POSDiff that can be corrected globally

related to noun compounds: the use of a noun as a noun premodifier in English. In this case the noun acts as an adjective though is in fact a noun. In this case we sampled the more frequent words and assigned correct taggers on a word by word basis. We also noted that words ending in "ing" were in some cases (Manning, 2011) to be tagged as VBG (Verb, gerund or present participle) and as such we overrode both taggers and used our own tag. In this process we worked with a random sample of 5 examples for 10 different words. We noted that Genia was correct more often than PostMed and as such assigned it as the tagger to side with for less frequent words we were not able to assign a solution to. An example of this tagging error is illustrated in Figure 2, where the POSDiff of interest is highlighted in black and other POSDiffs present in that selected sentence are highlighted in blue. In this case our decision procedure for the correct tag is based upon the word within the POSDiff.

5.2.4. Sample Decision Procedures: Context Specific Solution

For Genia tagging NNS (Noun, plural) and PostMed tagging NN (Noun, singular or mass), we noted that there were cases in which both taggers were correct. This POSDiff was caused by tags for irregular plural forms of nouns. We selected correct taggers for 12 of the most common words, set a tag override to NNP (Noun, proper) for one word, but had a more complex pattern necessary for the word *bacteria*. After examin-

Genia	Postmed
This *DT*	This *PRP*
is *VBZ*	is *VBZ*
this *DT*	this *DT*
unexpected *JJ*	unexpected *JJ*
since *IN*	since *IN*
all *DT*	all *DT*
observers *NNS*	observers *NNS*
had *VBD*	had *VBD*
had *VBN*	had *VBD*
joint *JJ*	joint *JJ*
training *NN*	**training** *JJ*
sessions *NNS*	sessions *NNS*

Figure 2: Example of a word specific POSDiff

ing 5 samples for the word *bacteria* we concluded that if the following word after *bacteria* was either a NNP or NN we would use the PostMed tag, and otherwise use the Genia tag. These contextually based decision procedures were used in a number of other instances to handle complex errors. Genia was selected as the default tagger for words which were not captured by our rules.

5.2.5. Decision Procedure Language

In order to encode the decision procedure model we were building for each POSDiff we developed a machine interpretable language which was quick for us to type. This language was later interpreted by software when it was understanding the decisions we had made for each POSDiff so that we could build the new corpus. An example of this language was previously seen in Section 5.2.1.

5.3. The BioPOSTAg Corpus

The current BioPOSTAg corpus consists of 119,348,590 words, 4,790,737 sentences, part-of-speech annotated with the biomedical update (Warner et al., 2012) of the Penn Treebank Tagset (Marcus et al., 1993). It is publicly available at https://github.com/nelder/Biomedical-POS-Tagger/.

5.4. The Data Viewer

5.4.1. Comparison of Taggers

To construct this set of POSDiffs we built software which processed the tagged output from Genia and PostMed. The corpora these taggers had annotated was full-text data from 49 biomedical journals, as mentioned previously. We then kept track of each instance of a POSDiff, the particular word on which it occurred, and an address to the original article which would allow us to view the context in which this POSDiff occurred. In the example shown in abbreviated form in Figure 3 we can see the case where Genia tagged AFX and PostMed labeled JJ. This POSDiff occurred 12 times, 8 times on the word "non". We also can see the address of each instance of this difference in the form of a file path to the Genia and PostMed tagged journal papers including the line and word number (FILEPATH — line_number / word_number).

5.4.2. Complementary POSDiffs

Having collected this information we also considered the significance of the concept of a complementary part of speech difference (POSDiff-C). So far we have considered Genia saying tag A, and PostMed saying tag B to be entirely distinct from PostMed saying tag A and Genia saying tag B. While this was a valid assumption to make in pursuit of grouping likely similar errors together under each POSDiff (combining POSDiff & POSDiff-C likely would just create more complex decision criteria to pick the correct tagger later on) we may want to consider this data elsewhere in our assessment. As such we were interested in seeing the cardinality in terms of frequency of occurrence of each POSDiff versus its POSDiff-C. Within each POSDiff we also wanted to understand if particular words appeared in both POSDiff and POSDiff-C. If for example there was a case that for the word "web" Genia said common noun and PostMed said adjective as well as there existing cases where Genia said adjective and PostMed said common noun, then the decision criteria for selecting between taggers in these cases would need to be more nuanced. Otherwise if there were not many of these cases we could likely select with more basic criteria. The significance of this information was better understood as the decision making model is put together.

5.4.3. Context to POSDiff

We also constructed a tool to enable us to understand the window of context surrounding each POSDiff occurrence for a given POSDiff. By understanding the preceding and following words and POS tags around each instance, we were able to get a better understanding of the cause of each error. This information aided in our construction of a model for addressing the POSDiffs.

5.4.4. Data Explorer Tool

Having generated a large dataset of POSDiffs as well as a complementary data set around the number of occurrences of POSDiff-Cs we developed a viewing framework to enable easy traversal of this information. Using a HTML/CSS front-end, we were able to leverage libraries like JQuery and Bootstrap Data Tables to expedite our development process.

As illustrated in Figure 4 our table library made it easy to sort the information by any attribute and traverse our large data set. The first view enables a top level look at all POSDiffs. Clicking on any of the particular POSDiffs reveals information about the words on which a particular POSDiff occurred. This page also allows us to collect notes on which of the taggers was correct. This notes field will serve as the basis of our decision making model. Figure 5 reveals the frequency of each

```
"G:AFX|P:JJ": {
    "pos_frequency": 12,
    "words": [
        [
            "non",
            "Acta_Vet_Scand/
Acta_Vet_Scand-42-1-2202332.nxml.genia.tagged|31/29",
            "Acta_Vet_Scand/
Acta_Vet_Scand-42-1-2202332.nxml.postmed.tagged|31/29"
        ],
        [
            "non",
            "Acta_Vet_Scand/
Acta_Vet_Scand-43-2-1764189.nxml.genia.tagged|99/15",
            "Acta_Vet_Scand/
Acta_Vet_Scand-43-2-1764189.nxml.postmed.tagged|99/15"
        ],

.. abbreviated ..

    ],
    "words_freq": [
        [
            "non",
            8
        ],
        [
            "anti",
            4
        ]
    ],
    "words_freq_alpha": {
        "anti": 4,
        "non": 8
    }
},
```


Figure 3: View of the database containing the POSDiff information

Show 10 entries

Search:

Part of Speech	Frequency Count	Frequency %	Cumulative Frequency	Unique Words	Instances/Word	POSDiff-C Freq
G:NNP | P:NN	572633	15.6%	15.6%	65607	9	616
G:JJ | P:NN	430673	11.73%	27.33%	42387	10	156541
G:VB | P:VBP	338190	9.21%	36.54%	2312	146	16703
G:VBN | P:JJ	270197	7.36%	43.9%	4666	58	24337
G:VBG | P:JJ	162882	4.44%	48.34%	3727	44	4482
G:NN | P:JJ	156541	4.26%	52.6%	8360	19	430673
G:NN | P:SYM	142748	3.89%	56.49%	9	15861	8096
G:VBG | P:NN	120278	3.28%	59.77%	4290	28	12969
G:VBN | P:VBD	91012	2.48%	62.25%	1968	46	53115
G:DT | P:PRP	87779	2.39%	64.64%	22	3990	0

Showing 1 to 10 of 496 entries

Previous 1 2 3 4 5 ... 50 Next

Figure 4: Summary of the POSDiffs provided by the data viewer

word within this POSDiff as well as information about the POSDiff-C.

An additional page for each word provides links to view the particular source for each instance of a POSDiff which is displayed on a page as illustrated in Figure 6. Note this particular POSDiff is highlighted in black and other POSDiffs present in that selected sentence are highlighted in blue. Each word is followed by the POS tag it received from each of the taggers. Source data can be viewed at the bottom of this page.

Other views of the database have been presented earlier in Figures 1 and 2.

The software tool organizes and displays the differences in the tagging provided in two files. The tool

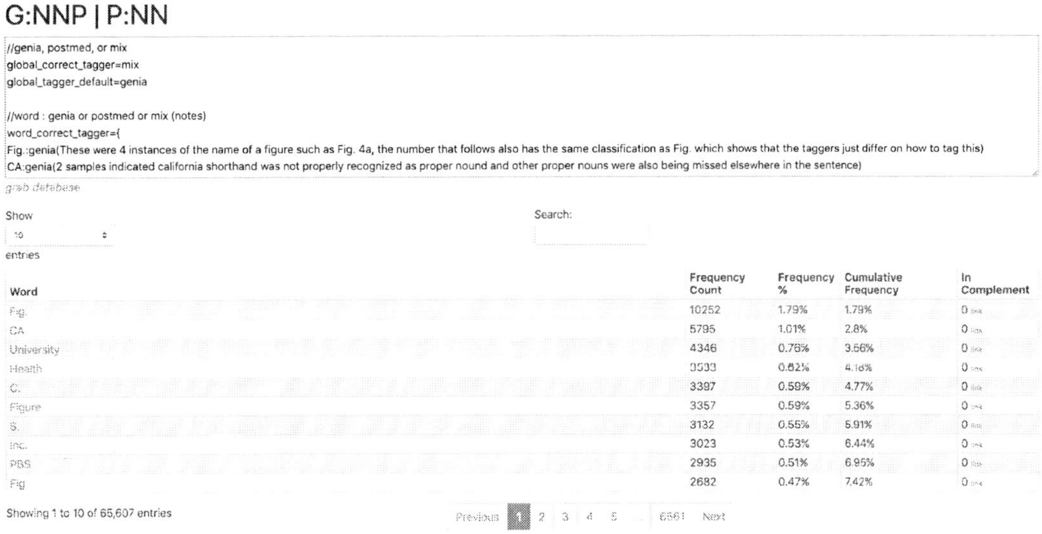

Figure 5: Example of a POSDiff view provided by the data viewer

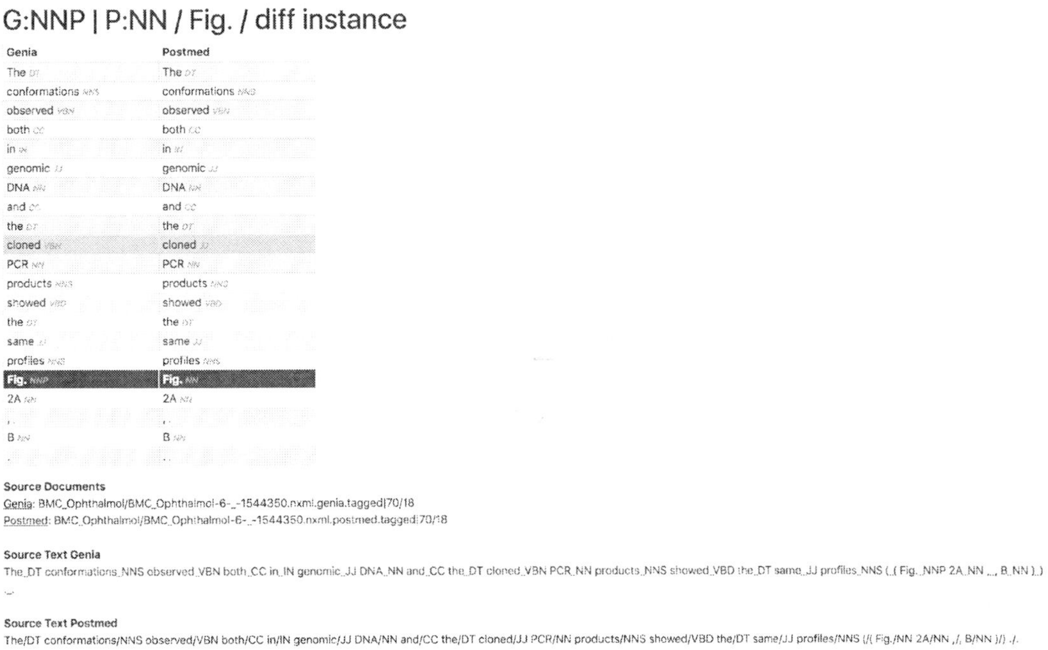

Figure 6: Example of a POSDiff, the document that it occurs in, and the Part-of-Speech tagging by Genia and PostMed

is very versatile. It was initially designed to compare the output given by two part-of-speech taggers but it is easily convertible to comparing any two files, so it can be used for human analysis of the differences between a machine tagged output and gold standard tags.

6. Evaluating the Quality and Effectiveness of the Corpus

Much interest in having POS taggers for biomedical text (Kim et al., 2003; Smith et al., 2004; Nguyen and Verspoor, 2019) and to have full-text corpora (Verspoor et al., 2012) to train from is evident. An in-depth manual study of a representative portion of the full-text silver standard corpus that we have developed here to determine the quality of the corpus is our ultimate goal and is our intention in future work. In the meantime, we have provided two evaluations of the silver standard corpus. First, we evaluate on a small sample, the percentage of correct tags provided by the Genia and PostMed taggers. In addition, we are interested in our assumption that the two taggers provide the correct tag when they agree. We have chosen a representative portion of the CRAFT corpus (Verspoor et al., 2012) for this test. The second evaluation method is to compare a model trained on the silver standard corpus compared to the same model trained on a human-annotated gold standard corpus on the downstream task of interest, i.e., POS tagging. We have chosen the CRAFT corpus (Verspoor et al., 2012) as the gold standard training and test sets for this comparison. There is no overlap between the papers in the CRAFT corpus and the papers used to build the silver standard corpus.

For the first test, we have chosen one paper from the CRAFT corpus consisting of approximately 8,700 tokens. With this subset of tokens the Genia tagger correctly predicts 87% and PostMed predicts 84%. These scores are approximately 10 percentage points below their scores when tagging abstracts. Of course, the human intervention that we have described previously improves this performance. When these two taggers agree, they disagree with the CRAFT corpus tag on about 1% of the tags. While this seems high (and higher than we expected), approximately half of these disagreements are between the JJ and NN tags when the word is used as a modifier. However, as we discuss below, this mistagging (since the human intervention does not correct these mistags) does not seem to be deleterious.

Second, to evaluate the effectiveness of this silver corpus, we have conducted two experiments to provide the comparison. In the first experiment, we have done a 5-fold cross-validation by training a third party BioRoBERTa-based POS-tagger (Trevett, 2021) with the training data portion of the CRAFT dataset and tested it against the test set portion of the CRAFT dataset. This experiment achieves an average 97.89% test set accuracy with a standard deviation of 0.04. In the second experiment, the same model is trained with the silver standard corpus and tested against the same five test set portions of the CRAFT corpus that were set aside in the 5-fold cross-validation evaluation. It achieves an average accuracy of 98.09% with a standard deviation of 0.05. The silver standard trained model outperforms the gold standard trained model used in the first experiment by a noteworthy, for this level of accuracy, 0.2 percentage point improvement. This performance gain is statistically significant, $p < 0.0001$. This evaluation is summarized in Table 2.

We provide the following information about the model and the training. The original BERT-based model (Trevett, 2021) consists of a BERT-based embedding layer followed by a linear layer to predict the POS tag of the input sentence. For the two biomedical text based experiments, we fine-tuned a BioRoBERTa embedding layer. The learning rate was initialized to 0.01 and it was decayed by 80% after any epoch if the validation accuracy decreased. The model was fine-tuned for 20 epochs in both experiments.

Tagger trained on:	Accuracy (mean and s.d.)
the CRAFT dataset	97.89 ± 0.04
the BioPOSTAg dataset	98.09 ± 0.05

Table 2: Evaluation on the CRAFT dataset of a third party BioRoBERTa-based POS-tagger (Trevett, 2021) trained on the CRAFT dataset and the BioPOSTAg dataset, mean and standard deviation from 5-fold cross-validations, $p < 0.0001$

7. Conclusions

Our goal to provide a large silver standard corpus of biomedical text annotated with part-of-speech using the Penn Treebank Tagset to facilitate the training of deep learning models has been partially fulfilled. Our current corpus, drawn from full-text biomedical articles, has 4,790,737 sentences comprised of 119,348,590 tokens annotated for part-of-speech, and we continue to work toward a corpus containing 35 million sentences. The corpus is available online at elder.ca/research/biomed_pos_corpus.txt. In addition to this language resource, we have also designed, implemented, and made available a robust, easy-to-use software tool that assists the investigation of differences in two tagged datasets. It is available at https://github.com/nelder/Biomedical-POS-Tagger/.

8. Future Work

As stated earlier, the goal is to completely annotate 35 million sentences drawn from 288 biomedical journals with POS tags. These journals represent both experimental and clinical research. Having a corpus comprised of writing styles across a wide variety of journals will facilitate having a more robust deep learning trained POS tagger.

When correcting the POSDiffs, some decisions were made for purposes of expediency. A more careful analysis of the word specific and context specific solutions needs to be carried out. As part of its functionality, the data viewer captures both the language that describes how modifications to the corpus are to be carried out by the associated software and notes discussing the rationale for these modifications. With these sources of information, the corpus can be easily modified after careful consideration of the discussion.

To enhance our understanding of quality of the corpus beyond the small study reported above, an in-depth manual study of a representative portion of the full-text silver standard corpus to provide measures of the quality of the corpus will be done.

9. Bibliographical References

Barrett, N. and Weber-Jahnke, J. (2014). A token centric part-of-speech tagger for biomedical text. *Artificial Intelligence in Medicine*, 61(1):11–20.

Brants, T. (2000). TnT – a statistical part-of-speech tagger. In *Sixth Applied Natural Language Processing Conference*, pages 224–231.

Coden, A. R., Pakhomov, S. V., Ando, R. K., Duffy, P. H., and Chuteb, C. G. (2005). Domain-specific language models and lexicons for tagging. *Journal of Biomedical Informatics*, 38(6):422–430.

Cohen, K. B., Johnson, H. L., Verspoor, K., Roeder, C., and Hunter, L. E. (2010). The structural and content aspects of abstracts versus bodies of full text journal articles are different. *BMC Bioinformatics*, 11:492.

Divita, G., Browne, A. C., and Loane, R. (2006). dTagger: A POS tagger. In *AMIA Annual Symposium Proceedings*, pages 200–203.

Eckart, K. and Gärtner, M. (2016). Creating silver standard annotations for a corpus of non-standard data. In *Proceedings of the 13th Conference on Natural Language Processing (KONVENS 2016)*, pages 90–96.

Hahn, U. and Wermter, J. (2004). High-performance tagging on medical texts. In *COLING 2004: Proceedings of the 20th International Conference on Computational Linguistics*, pages 973–979.

Huseth, O. and Rost, T. B. (2007). Developing an annotated corpus of patient histories from the primary care health record. In *Proceedings of the 2007 IEEE International Conference on Bioinformatics and Biomedicine Workshops (BIBMW)*, pages 165–173.

Kim, J.-D., Ohta, T., Tateisi, Y., and Tsujii, J. (2003). GENIA corpus—a semantically annotated corpus for bio-textmining. *Bioinformatics*, 19(suppl_1):i180–i182.

Manning, C. D. (2011). Part-of-speech tagging from 97% to 100%: Is it time for some linguistics? In Alexander F. Gelbukh, editor, *Computational Linguistics and Intelligent Text Processing*, pages 171–189.

Marcus, M. P., Santorini, B., and Marcinkiewicz, M. A. (1993). Building a large annotated corpus of English: The Penn Treebank. *Computational Linguistics*, 19(2):313–330.

Miller, J. E., Torii, M., and K., V.-S. (2007). Adaptation of POS tagging for multiple biomedical domains. In *Proceedings of the Workshop on BioNLP 2007: Biological, Translational, and Clinical Language Processing, (BioNLP'07)*, pages 179–180.

Nguyen, D. Q. and Verspoor, K. (2019). From POS tagging to dependency parsing for biomedical event extraction. *BMC Bioinformatics*, 20:72.

Pakhomov, S. V., Coden, A., and Chute, C. G. (2006). Developing a corpus of clinical notes manually annotated for part-of-speech. *International Journal of Medical Informatics*, 75(6):418–429. Recent Advances in Natural Language Processing for Biomedical Applications Special Issue.

Rebholz-Schuhmann, D., Jimeno Yepes, A. J., van Mulligen, E. M., Kang, N., Kors, J., Milward, D., Corbett, P., Buyko, E., Tomanek, K., Beisswanger, E., and Hahn, U. (2010). The CALBC silver standard corpus for biomedical named entities — a study in harmonizing the contributions from four independent named entity taggers. In *Proceedings of the Seventh International Conference on Language Resources and Evaluation (LREC'10)*, pages 568–573.

Rebholz-Schuhmann, D., Jimeno Yepes, A., Li, C., Kafkas, S., Lewin, I., Kang, N., Corbett, P., Milward, D., Buyko, E., Beisswanger, E., Hornbostel, K., Kouznetsov, A., Witte, R., Laurila, J. B., Baker, C. J. O., Kuo, C.-J., Clematide, S., Rinaldi, F., Farkas, R., Móra, G., Hara, K., Furlong, L. I., Rautschka, M., Neves, M. L., Pascual-Montano, A., Wei, Q., Collier, N., Chowdhury, M. F. M., Lavelli, A., Berlanga, R., Morante, R., Van Asch, V., Daelemans, W., Marina, J. L., van Mulligen, E., Kors, J., and Hahn, U. (2011). Assessment of NER solutions against the first and second CALBC Silver Standard Corpus. *Journal of Biomedical Semantics*, 2(S11).

Santorini, B. (1995). Part-of-speech tagging guidelines for the Penn Treebank Project (3rd Revision, 2nd printing). Technical report, University of Pennsylvania, February. Reprint of original June 1990 report updated and slightly reformatted by Robert MacIntyre.

Smith, L., Rindflesch, T., and Wilbur, W. J. (2004). MedPost: a part-of-speech tagger for bioMedical text. *Bioinformatics*, 20(14):2320–2321.

Smith, L., Rindflesch, T., and Wilbur, W. (2006). The importance of the lexicon in tagging biological text. *Natural Language Engineering*, 12(4):335–351.

Sousa, D., Lamurias, A., and Couto, F. M. (2019). A silver standard corpus of human phenotype-gene relations. In *Proceedings of the 2019 Conference of the North American Chapter of the Association for Computational Linguistics: Human Language Technologies, Volume 1 (Long and Short Papers)*, pages 1487–1492.

Tateisi, Y. and Tsujii, J. (2004). Part-of-speech annotation of biology research abstracts. In *Proceedings of the Fourth International Conference on Language Resources and Evaluation (LREC'04)*, pages 1267–1270.

Tateisi, Y., Tsuruoka, Y., and Tsujii, J. (2006). Subdomain adaptation of a POS tagger with a small corpus. In *Proceedings of the HLT-NAACL BioNLP Workshop on Linking Natural Language and Biology*, pages 136–137.

Trevett, B. (2021). Fine-tuning pretrained transformers for POS tagging. https://github.com/bentrevett/pytorch-pos-tagging/blob/master/2_transformer.ipynb. Accessed: 2021-12-30.

Verspoor, K., Cohen, K. B., Lanfranchi, A., Warner, C., Johnson, H. L., Christophe, R., Choi, J. D., Funk, C., Malenkiy, Y., Eckert, M., Xue, N., Baumgartner Jr, W. A., Bada, M., Palmer, M., and Hunter, L. E. (2012). A corpus of full-text journal articles is a robust evaluation tool for revealing differences in performance of biomedical natural language processing tools. *BMC Bioinformatics*, 13:207.

Warner, C., Bies, A., Brisson, C., and Mott, J. (2004). Addendum to the Penn Treebank II style bracketing guidelines: Biomedical treebank annotation. Technical report, University of Pennsylvania Linguistic Data Consortium, November.

Warner, C., Lanfranchi, A., O'Gorman, T., Howard, A., Gould, K., and Regan, M. (2012). Bracketing biomedical text: An addendum to Penn Treebank II guidelines. Technical report, Institute of Cognitive Science, University of Colorado at Boulder, January.

Proceedings of the 16th Linguistic Annotation Workshop (LAW-XVI) @LREC 2022, pages 139–150
Marseille, 24 June 2022

Human Schema Curation via Causal Association Rule Mining

Noah Weber[*,a], **Anton Belyy**[*,a], **Nils Holzenberger**[*,γ,a],
Rachel Rudinger[b], **Benjamin Van Durme**[a]

[a]Johns Hopkins University, 3400 N. Charles Street, Baltimore, Maryland, USA
[b]University of Maryland, College Park, 8125 Paint Branch Drive, College Park, Maryland, USA
{nweber6, abel, nilsh, vandurme}@jhu.edu   rudinger@umd.edu

Abstract

Event schemas are structured knowledge sources defining typical real-world scenarios (e.g., *going to an airport*). We present a framework for efficient human-in-the-loop construction of a *schema library*, based on a novel script induction system and a well-crafted interface that allows non-experts to "program" complex event structures. Associated with this work we release a schema library: a machine readable resource of 232 detailed event schemas, each of which describe a distinct typical scenario in terms of its relevant sub-event structure (*what* happens in the scenario), participants (*who* plays a role in the scenario), fine-grained typing of each participant, and the implied relational constraints between them. We make our schema library and the SchemaBlocks interface available online.[1 2]

Keywords: schemas, script induction, dataset curation, annotation interfaces

1. Introduction

What is implied by the invocation of a real-world scenario such as, say, a *criminal trial*? From one's knowledge of the world, one makes a myriad of inferences: the scenario typically starts with the *defendant* being accused and brought to court, it likely contains events such as the presentation of evidence by a *prosecutor*, and it ends with the *judge* announcing the final verdict. This type of scenario-level knowledge is recognized as being vital for text understanding (Schank and Abelson, 1977; Minsky, 1974; Bower et al., 1979; Abbott et al., 1985): scripts can help with coreference resolution, disambiguating word meaning, and making inferences (Lehnert et al., 1983). However, explicitly annotating this knowledge in a way useful to language processing systems has proven to be a difficult task. At one end, one may try to hand-engineer this knowledge in a richly detailed format (DeJong, 1983; Mooney and DeJong, 1985; Mueller, 1999). While this facilitates precise inferences, it requires an onerous annotation effort carried out by experts, and hence tends to be difficult to scale. On the other end, one may employ data-driven methods to automatically induce this knowledge (Chambers and Jurafsky, 2009; Balasubramanian et al., 2013; Rudinger et al., 2015), at the price of noise and a severe loss of detail. Wanzare et al. (2016) take a semi-automatic approach, taking advantage of both automatic and annotator-driven components. The authors use an initial human annotation to obtain high quality event sequence descriptions for a target scenario, before using semi-supervised clustering to aggregate these annotations (Wanzare et al., 2017; Regneri et al., 2010). In this paper, we also adopt a semi-automatic approach in order to facilitate the creation of a new annotated resource of structured, machine readable *event schemas*. As depicted in Figure 1, each event schema characterizes a real-world scenario, describing the *events* the scenario typically involves, the *participants* of these events, their role and typing information, and the implied *relations* between these participants. Our workflow follows two main steps. First, we automatically induce what we term as *skeleton schemas*: argumentless event sequences that form the outline of an event schema. Second, using our SchemaBlocks interface, we have human annotators "flesh out" the manually selected skeleton schemas

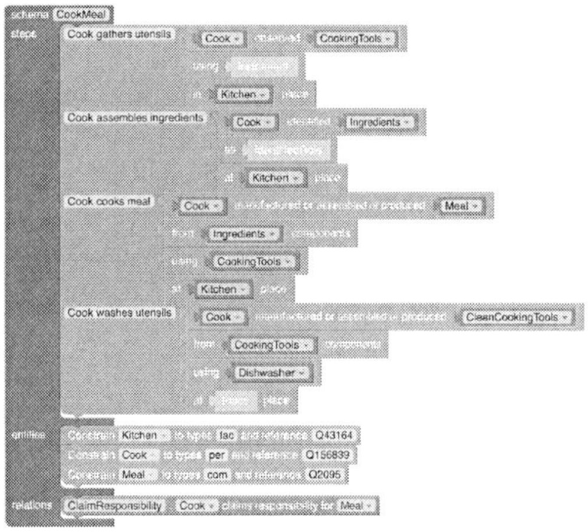

Figure 1: An example event schema from our library, induced from a skeleton mined by Causal Association Rule Mining (Section 3) and fully fleshed out by an annotator using our SchemaBlocks interface (Section 4).

*Equal contribution. Order decided via wheel.
γCorresponding author
[1]Schema library: https://nlp.jhu.edu/schemas/schemas.zip
[2]Interface: https://nlp.jhu.edu/demos/sb

by adding argument, role, typing, and relational information, in addition to a name and description of the scenario the schema describes.
The main contributions of this paper are:[3]

1. a new semi-automatic script induction system, which combines two recent advances in automatic script induction (Belyy and Van Durme, 2020; Weber et al., 2020) with a novel SchemaBlocks annotation interface, to elicit common sense knowledge from crowdworkers,

2. a resource of 232 schemas, 150 of which are semi-automatically induced, with the rest created manually from textual descriptions, and

3. two novel evaluation metrics for schemas: *corpus coverage*, an automatic metric which computes coverage of schemas on a text corpus, and *schema intrusion*, a human-based metric which quantifies the coherence of each schema, similarly to the word intrusion task (Chang et al., 2009).

2. The Anatomy of a Schema

Conceptualizations of what constitutes a *schema* differ across the literature. A schema in our resource is constructed from three basic elements:

1. events,

2. its *participants*, which are the entities that participate in these events, and

3. the relations between these participants.

The atomic types of events, entities, and relations are defined by the DARPA KAIROS Phase 1 (v3.0) ontology.[4] It consists of 67 event types, 24 coarse-grained entity types, and 46 relation types. The KAIROS ontology was selected because this work was carried out in the context of a larger effort, where collaborators used schemas for information extraction. While that choice influenced the content of the schemas produced here, our methods are ontology-agnostic, and our interface's building blocks (see Section 4.1) could easily be adjusted to elicit schemas from humans with any type of ontology, including more general and more flexible ontologies such as FrameNet (Baker et al., 1998).

Events In this work, the backbone for the meaning of a schema is the temporally ordered chain of events that it describes. The individual events that make up this chain are drawn from a taxonomy of event types (e.g., an *Acquit* event, a *Transportation* event). In addition, each event type has specific participants (e.g., the *Defendant* or *Transporter*), to be linked to entities. While we use the term "chain" to describe the sequence of events defined in a schema, the schemas presented here need not always be ordered as a linear chain. In our schemas, subsequences of events may be marked either as occurring in a linear temporal order, in an arbitrary temporal order, or as forming mutually exclusive branches.

Participants Participants fill the roles specified by each event in the schema. The same participant can (and usually will) be used to fill different roles across different events, indicating a co-referring relationship. All participants may also take on types: either coarse grained types defined in the KAIROS ontology (including types such as *person*, *organization*, *commercial item*, etc), or fine grained types defined as references to Wikidata: for instance, on Figure 1, Q156839 refers to a Wikidata entity for "cook", which substantially narrows down a more generic type *person*. Our annotated schemas utilize both KAIROS and Wikidata types.

Relations Relations between participating entities are the last ingredient of the schemas defined here. These relations are also drawn from the KAIROS ontology. As of now, all relations are defined between two entities, each of which participate in at least one event defined in the schema: e.g. ClaimResponsibility(*Cook*, *Meal*) in the "CookMeal" schema on Figure 1.

3. Induction of Skeleton Schemas

Our system first automatically induces what we term as *skeleton schemas*: argumentless event sequences forming an outline of a potential event schema. A selected group of these skeleton schemas is then passed to annotators to manually flesh out the full event schemas. By starting the schema creation with an automatic, data-driven step, we allow the data to "speak for itself" with regards to what kinds of topics and scenarios we might want to target given a specified domain. The fact that the base of the schemas has some connection to our targeted domain gives at least some assurance that the final schemas will be applicable towards making commonsense inferences when used in real-world applications. The automatic system for skeleton schema induction combines two recent advances in schema induction:

1. an Association Rule Mining (ARM) based algorithm presented in Belyy and Van Durme (2020), which efficiently finds all event subsequences with sufficient support in the data, and

2. a script compatibility scoring model presented in Weber et al. (2020), which finds high quality subsequences output by the ARM method, and combines them to form full skeleton schemas.

We give a brief overview of each of these approaches and how they are used in our system below.

3.1. Mining Associations for Script Induction

Belyy and Van Durme (2020) show how prior classic work in automatic script induction (primarily the line of

[3]Resources tied to this paper are grouped here: `https://nlp.jhu.edu/schemas`

[4]The ontology can be downloaded here: `https://nlp.jhu.edu/schemas/ont.xlsx`

work following Chambers and Jurafsky (2008)) can be better recast as a problem of Association Rule Mining. ARM works with a dataset where each datapoint is a set of items. In the script induction setting, an *item* is an event, and a datapoint is the set of events appearing in a document and sharing some co-referring argument. The ARM approach consists of two distinct stages:

1. **Frequent Itemset Mining**. This step searches for subsequences of events which have enough support in the dataset. What is considered "enough" is defined by a user-set hyperparameter. To do this efficiently, Belyy and Van Durme (2020) make use of the FP-growth algorithm (Han et al., 2000).
2. **Rule Mining**. This step uses the frequent itemsets mined from the previous step in order to define rules in a form similar to Horn clauses.

In our system, we make use of only step 1 of the process defined above, mining event subsequences which have enough support in our targeted domain data. We mine event subsequences from the NYTimes portion of Gigaword (Graff et al., 2003). The output of this step is a large set of potentially interesting event subsequences.

3.2. Building Schemas with a Causal Scorer

The step presented in the previous section leaves us with a fairly large inventory of event subsequences, not all of which may be useful or relevant for the creation of schemas. There are, hence, two problems at hand:

1. how to filter out lower quality subsequences, and
2. how to create skeleton schemas from the filtered inventory of event subsequences.

Both problems are handled via the causal inference based scoring approach of Weber et al. (2020). This approach defines a scoring function, cscore$(\cdot, \cdot)$ which, taking in two events e_1 and e_2, outputs a score proportional to the aptness of e_2 following e_1 in a script. As an example, "trip" and "fall" should take on high scores, while "trip" and "eat" should not. The approach builds upon reasonable assumptions on the data generation process to overcome conceptual weaknesses in prior approaches, and was shown to output scores more in line with human judgments of script knowledge. We refer readers to the paper for details.
In order to create our skeleton schemas, we first use the trained scoring module from Weber et al. (2020), which was trained on the Toronto Book corpus (Zhu et al., 2015; Kiros et al., 2015), to score all subsequences obtained via the process described in Section 3.1. Since the causal scoring module is only defined pairwise, we take the following average as the assigned score for a subsequence $S = (e_1, ..., e_N)$ of length N:

$$\text{score}(S) = \frac{2}{N(N-1)} \sum_{i=1}^{N-1} \sum_{j=i+1}^{N} \text{cscore}(e_i, e_j)$$

We take the top T of these subsequences. To ensure that a diverse set of events are selected in the subsequences, we remove those in which all event types in the sequence have been used at least 50 times by higher scoring subsequences.
The score function above is biased towards shorter subsequences: picking the highest scoring pair of events in a subsequence creates a higher-scoring subsequence. To mitigate this, our final step involves joining together subsequences to create larger chains. For each of these T subsequences, we find the highest scoring event that may be appended to the subsequence. We then find other subsequences that start with this event, and append the highest scoring one to the existing subsequence.
The top C of these larger subsequences are then given to a curator (one of the authors), who manually selects chains to be passed to human annotators as skeleton schemas. This is done as an expedient to ensure both the diversity and quality of the resulting schema annotations. We pick $C = 1{,}000$ as the upper feasible limit for a manual curator. To make sure there are enough potential merges, we set $T = 100C$. Finally, our annotation budget was enough to turn the top 150 of these C chains into schemas (see Section 4.3).

4. Annotation with SchemaBlocks

After skeleton schemas are induced, we want to include rich commonsense information (i.e. event participants, their types and relations) in addition to the event sequence. As the existing induction tools struggle to induce these fully automatically, we involve a human in this process. We describe the newly proposed schema annotation interface, SchemaBlocks, and show how it can be used to

1. create schemas from scratch (Section 4.2), and
2. flesh out skeleton schemas (Section 4.3).

We also share our annotation guide and some relevant statistics on the annotation process.

4.1. SchemaBlocks Annotation Interface

SchemaBlocks is a Web-based tool[5] that provides a way to display and modify the contents of a schema by representing its units – events and arguments, entity relations and types – as *blocks*, that can be stacked and nested. An example schema is shown in Figure 2. In addition to capturing schema events, participants, and their relations, the interface also allows for the representation of entity coreference, event ordering, and the mutual exclusivity of events.
To get started, an annotator needs to become familiar with the ontology, which defines the vocabulary of blocks used to build schemas. In the interface, this is displayed as the dashboard, organized hierarchically for

[5]Source code of SchemaBlocks:
https://github.com/AVBelyy/SchemaBlocks

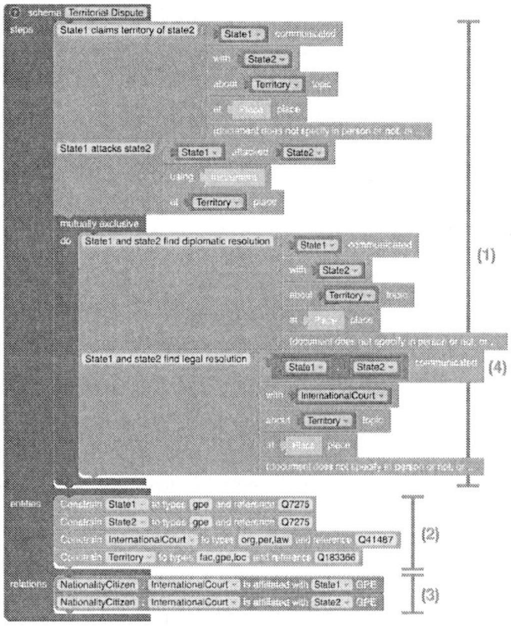

Figure 2: An excerpt from one of the released schemas, featuring: (1) mutually exclusive events, (2) entity types, (3) entity relations, and (4) a slot filled with more than one entity (*State1* and *State2*), reflecting that an event may include multiple participants under the same role. Participants left in light pink by the user are defined as part of the event type in KAIROS, but not instantiated (reified) in the event schema.

convenience. Figure 3 shows all levels of the ontology hierarchy for the "Medical" event category. The block interface is flexible and could be adapted to a similar event ontology, such as FrameNet (Baker et al., 1998), ACE (Doddington et al., 2004) and ERE (Song et al., 2015). For larger event ontologies, it may be helpful to implement search functionalities into the interface to facilitate quicker access to a specific event in the ontology. The core annotation process with SchemaBlocks would, however, remain the same. Such features may be worthwhile additions in future versions of SchemaBlocks.

SchemaBlocks' interface is primarily based on the Google Blockly library.[6] On top of the UI primitives provided by Blockly, we implement ontology-to-blocks and blocks-to-JSON converters. This allows to transform a structured ontology description into the set of Blockly blocks, which the user can manipulate to create a schema, and when they are done, transform their block-based schemas into a machine-readable format. During schema creation, we also continuously run type checking and type inference over schema entities, so that if a user breaks ontological type constraints, they will be notified and the relevant entity blocks will be highlighted until the error is fixed.

Our choice of block-based representation is inspired by

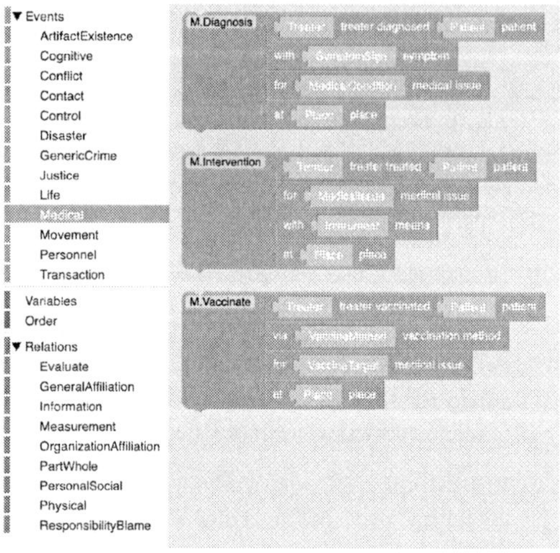

Figure 3: SchemaBlocks dashboard displaying high-level event and relation types from the KAIROS ontology. The "Medical" event category is further expanded to show subtypes. "Variables" and "Order" blocks allow to assign multiple entities to a single participant of an event, and to specify the ordering of events, respectively.

Scratch (Resnick et al., 2009), a prominent tool that engages children to learn the basics of computer programming. By enabling users to program schemas using ontology-specific blocks — as opposed to general-purpose text formats such as JSON or XML — we were able to engage annotators with non-programming backgrounds and annotate schemas at a faster rate. The annotators in our study (undergraduate students with non-CS majors) found the interface easy-to-use and left overall positive feedback. To familiarize annotators with the interface, we provided them with a guide prior to running the annotation: `https://nlp.jhu.edu/schemas/guide.pdf`.

4.2. Annotating Schemas from Scratch

In the first annotation round, annotators were provided with 82 textual descriptions of schemas from the KAIROS Schema Learning Corpus (LDC2020E25). This corpus contains textual definitions for 82 *complex events* (CEs), which we aim to transform into event schemas. Each complex event is given a title, a 2-3 sentence description, specifications of the scope of the complex event (i.e., when and where the complex event should be considered initiated or finished), and the series of steps that defines the complex event. Each step is defined with a title specifying the event type of the step, a short one sentence description, and expected high-level event types that may happen as subevents.[7]

The annotators are then tasked with translating these textual descriptions of schemas into a machine readable form via our SchemaBlocks interface. Relations and

[6] `https://github.com/google/blockly`

[7] All of this in natural language; no event ontology is used.

entity types are not specified in the textual descriptions, so annotators are instructed to annotate for relations that must be true throughout all steps of the schemas, as well as provide coarse- and fine-grained types. Annotators reported an average time of 30 minutes to annotate a CE into a schema, with 82 schemas being the product of this annotation task. The number of events in each of 82 schemas ranges from 2 to 10, with 6 being the median.

4.3. Fleshing out Skeleton Schemas

In the second annotation round, annotators were asked to "flesh out" the skeleton schemas from Section 3, into fully-fledged schemas. Given a skeleton schema, we import it into SchemaBlocks as a partially filled out schema, where only events are specified. We then present these partially filled out schemas to annotators and task them with determining:

- What scenario the partially filled out schema is describing. This includes naming the schema, as well as writing a brief textual description on what it is about.
- Who the participants of the given events are, what types (coarse- and fine-grained) they take on, and which roles are filled with co-referring participants.
- What relations hold between the above defined entities. The criteria for annotating relations here is the same as before.

Given that this annotation is designed to be similar to the one presented in Section 4.2, all annotators who participated in the first annotation effort required little extra training to complete this annotation (only a single one-hour training session). Again, annotators reported around a 30-minute average to annotate a schema. The end result of this fleshing out process is an additional 150 schemas. The number of events in this additional set ranges from 3 to 6, with 4 being the median.

5. Schema Library Evaluation

In this section, we evaluate our schema library[8], looking at schemas' internal coherence as well as usefulness of schemas for downstream tasks. Namely, we evaluate the coherence of the event sequence in a schema by measuring the accuracy on the *schema intrusion* task (Section 5.2). Then, we compute how many documents in a given corpus are "covered" by the schema library as a whole, using the *corpus coverage* metric (Section 5.3). Finally, we report the results on several ranking tasks, using event schemas as structured queries to rank multi-modal documents, and vice versa (Section 5.4).

We evaluate both the library of schemas created from scratch (Section 4.2, "82 schemas"), as well as the library created from schema skeletons (Section 4.3, "150 schemas"). The two methods used to obtain each library are not meant to be compared directly, because they are two different ways of eliciting schemas from humans. Each method relies on a different starting point for schemas: respectively, textual descriptions of schemas, and event chains induced from a corpus. Choosing which one to use depends on the resources available.

5.1. Evaluation Datasets

Gigaword We pick a random subset of 100K documents from the NYTimes portion of the Fifth Edition of the English Gigaword corpus (Graff et al., 2003), spanning the New York Times news articles from years 1994–2010. We use this corpus for corpus-based evaluation in the schema intrusion task (Section 5.2), as well as to compute corpus coverage (Section 5.3).

CC-News We pick a subset of 300K news articles from English, Russian, and Chinese CC-News (Nagel, 2016). To do that, we perform language ID over the original CC-news collection, using the cld3 library along with the "meta_lang" field from a particular news source. We then take a random subset of 100K documents for each language to evaluate corpus coverage (Section 5.3) in a cross-lingual scenario.

KAIROS SLC As part of the KAIROS Schema Learning Corpus (SLC), the Linguistic Data Consortium (LDC) has annotated 924 multilingual multimodal documents (covering images, audio, video, and text in English and Spanish) with KAIROS event types, labeling each document with one of 82 complex events mentioned earlier in Section 4.2.[9] The CE label indicates the complex event (from LDC2020E25) that best applies to a document. Each CE label is covered by 11 documents on average, one label per document. Out of 924 documents, 921 have partial event-only annotations and 36 have complete annotations (with identified and provenance linked entities and relations). Given the sparsity of complete annotations, we use the event-only annotated documents in order to compute ranking-based metrics (Section 5.4).

5.2. Schema Intrusion Task

To measure to what extent our schemas form meaningful units, and how much the content of one schema overlaps with that of another, we introduce the *schema intrusion* task. Schema intrusion is similar in spirit to *word intrusion* for topic models (Chang et al., 2009). At a high level, for each schema S from our library, we pick a step from a different schema S' and add it to S. We present S to a human evaluator with the task of picking the intruder. The more coherent and exhaustive each schema is, the more the intruder should stick out as being out of place, untypical, or at least irrelevant.

[8]At the time of writing, there were no other publicly available schema libraries using the KAIROS ontology, which limited the cross-library comparisons we could run.

[9]At the time of writing, these annotations have been split into three collections: LDC2020E24, LDC2020E31, and LDC2020E35. While rarely freely released, historically, such collections are eventually made available under a license to anyone, under some timeline established within a program.

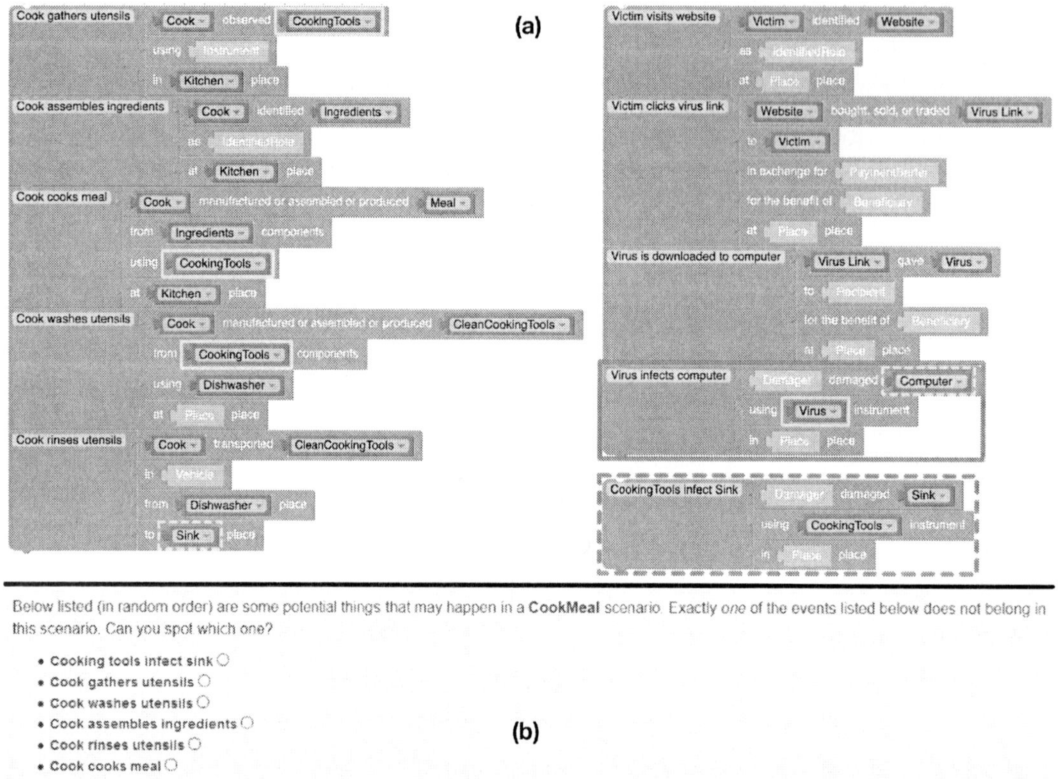

Figure 4: Example schema intrusion sample. (a) A step from the "Download Computer Virus" schema (right) is added to the "Cook Meal" schema (left). The step "Virus infects computer" (solid orange) is sampled, with "Computer" replaced with "Sink" (dashed yellow) and "Virus" replaced with "CookingTools" (solid yellow). This yields the intruder "Cooking Tools infect Sink" (dashed orange). (b) The schema with the intruder is presented to the human annotators.

Simply inserting a step from schema S' into schema S gives rise to artefacts, making it easy to spot the intruder without reasoning about the coherence of schema S. Consider Figure 4(a): inserting a step from "Download Computer Virus" into "Cook Meal" would introduce the participant "Computer" or "Virus", which gives the step away as the intruder, regardless of schema coherence. Thus, we need a way of renaming participants of the step we pick from "Cook Meal" before inserting it into "Download Computer Virus". To avoid any bias from the ordering of the steps, we shuffle the steps before showing them to the annotator.

Building instances of the intrusion task to present to annotators is a sampling procedure. In the following, we detail two ways to define the samples and their unnormalized weights: a *library-based* method and a *corpus-based* method. To sample an intruder for schema S with the library-based method, we need to sample a step e from a schema T, as well as a mapping $M = \{x \to y\}$ of the participants of e to participants of S. The mapping M is used to rename participants from e with names that come from S, camouflaging e's participants to look like participants from S, and mitigating the artifacts mentioned above. A sample is a tuple (T, e, M) with weight w. Let $\text{type}(x)$ be the set of types associated with participant x under the KAIROS ontology. For instance, in Figure 4(a), "Virus" is associated with the types $\{\texttt{abs}, \texttt{com}\}$. We use the Jaccard index $J(A, B) = \frac{|A \cap B|}{|A \cup B|}$ to measure overlap in types between participants, with $J(\varnothing, \varnothing) = 0$. We compute w as the geometric mean of type overlap between participants: $w = [\prod_{x,y \in M} J(\text{type}(x), \text{type}(y))]^{\frac{1}{|M|}}$. The use of the geometric mean is meant to exclude type incompatibilities, any of which would set the weight to 0. In addition, we reject any sample which, after renaming e's participants, would create a step already in S.

The corpus-based method finds candidate steps e by relying on documents. We first match schemas in the library with documents, in a process called *schema inference*. We describe a document using the events and participants from an ontology. We frame schemas as predicates over tuples of events, relying on that same ontology, and using Horn clauses to capture the relationships between schemas, events and their participants. Using the formalism and tools of Probabilistic

Soft Logic (Bach et al., 2017), schema inference is recast as a convex optimization problem, and solved. This procedure is further detailed in Appendix A.1. Here, a sample is (d, T, e, M) where d is a document such that both S and T match d. As part of matching with d, some of the participants in S and T will be matched with entities present in d. Let $\text{ent}(x, d)$ be the (possibly empty) set of entities associated with participant x in document d. For each tuple (d, T, e, M), similarly to the weight based on type mentioned above, we compute $w = [\prod_{x,y \in M} J(\text{ent}(x, d), \text{ent}(y, d))]^{\frac{1}{|M|}}$. For this corpus-based method, we used the Gigaword corpus mentioned in Section 5.1, only keeping documents that contain between 2 and 10 events, to be comparable to the number of events in our schemas.

The mapping $M = \{x \rightarrow y\}$ is used heuristically to modify the description of e, by replacing occurrences of string x by string y. We manually ensured that intruders would not be given away by artifacts that come up during this procedure, as follows. First, we normalized the form of the step descriptions in all schemas, standardizing verb inflection and syntax. Second, we reviewed each intruder instance and corrected any grammatical inconsistencies introduced by heuristically renaming participants. Finally, human evaluators for the task were only presented with the textual description of steps. As a result, any difference between schema curators in the use of the KAIROS ontology, the presence or absence of explanatory comments or any other SchemaBlocks feature, cannot have any influence on the human annotator's ability to spot the intruder. Figure 4(b) shows one instance of the task, as presented to the annotators.

Each intrusion task, consisting of one schema (as shown in Figure 4(b)), is completed by *three* separate annotators on the Mechanical Turk platform (see Appendix A.2). Results of this evaluation are shown in Table 1. The total accuracy for the task ("Total"), which considers each annotator separately, is far above the accuracy of randomly picking the intruder ("Random"). This shows that our schemas form units meaningful for humans. In addition, more than 85% of times, at least one out of the three annotators was able to spot the intruder ("1 Ann."), far above the corresponding accuracy of random picks ("Random 1"). Finally, even when we require all three annotators to agree on the intruder ("3 Ann."), the accuracy is still far above that of picking at random ("Random 3"). The differences in accuracy between "n Ann." and the corresponding "Random n" are significant (p-value $\ll 0.01$), as measured by the two-sided McNemar's test.

Contrasting both methods to sample the intruder, it seems both are roughly equally hard to spot. One would expect the corpus intruders to be more difficult to detect, since their sampling is informed by documents. While this is true for the 150 schemas, it is not for the 82 schemas. This can be explained by the fact that some schemas match many documents, while some match fewer documents. Similarly, some schema steps match more documents than others as certain events come up more often than others in the corpus. This likely induces a skew in the types of events that intruders typically cover, which in the case of the 82 schemas, introduces regularities that make the intruders stick out.

	Library			Corpus		
	82	150	232	82	150	232
Total	62.0	67.3	65.4	73.2	61.7	65.8
1 Ann.	84.1	86.7	85.8	93.0	83.3	86.6
2 Ann.	64.6	71.3	69.0	79.3	62.0	68.1
3 Ann.	36.6	44.0	41.4	48.0	40.0	43.0
Random	16.0	21.2	19.3	16.0	21.2	19.3
Random 1	40.2	50.8	47.1	40.2	50.8	47.1
Random 2	7.3	11.7	10.1	7.3	11.7	10.1
Random 3	0.5	1.0	0.8	0.5	1.0	0.8

Table 1: Human accuracy on the schema intrusion task, as %. "82", "150" and "232" refer to the size of the schema library used. "1 Ann." (resp. "2 Ann.") considers the intruder found if at least 1 (resp. 2) annotator(s) found the intruder. "3 Ann." counts an intruder as found only if it was found by all 3 annotators. "Total" considers each vote separately. "Random" is the expected accuracy of picking the intruder at random. "Random n" is the expected accuracy of picking three intruders at random with replacement, and having at least n of those be the correct answer.

5.3. Corpus Coverage

Event schemas are meant to provide missing pieces of knowledge (e.g., events and their participants) that are otherwise not stated explicitly in text, aiding document-level tasks such as coreference, summarization, and inference (Chambers and Jurafsky, 2010; Balasubramanian et al., 2013). When dealing with a large schema library L, one needs to first narrow down all schemas $s \in L$ to only those that apply to a given document d, depending on the task. We quantify this with a similarity function $sim(d, s)$ and a task-specific threshold t: namely, we say that s applies to d when $sim(d, s) \geq t$ for some task-specific t. Given t, we compute *coverage at t* (Cov@t) as a fraction of documents $d \in D$ such that at least one schema $s \subset L$ applies to d:

$$\text{Cov@}t = \frac{|\{d \in D \mid \exists s \in L : sim(d, s) \geq t\}|}{|D|}.$$

We compute Cov@t for the 82 schema subset, and for the full 232 schemas' library. We use $sim(d, s) = |E(d) \cap E(s)|/|E(d)|$, where $E(s)$ and $E(d)$ define all events mentioned in a schema s and extracted from a document d, respectively.[10] The events

[10]For our experiments, we treat both $E(s)$ and $E(d)$ as multisets of events. E.g., if a document d such that $E(d) = \{\text{LIFE.INFECT}, \text{LIFE.INFECT}, \text{MEDICAL.VACCINATE}\}$ is matched with a schema s such that $E(s) = \{\text{LIFE.INFECT}, \text{LIFE.DIE}\}$, then $sim(d, s) = 2/3$.

N_{events}	Schema ranking: Avg Rank↓	Schema ranking: MRR↑	Schema ranking: R@10↑	Document ranking: R@30↑	Document ranking: nDCG↑	Corpus coverage: Cov@0.5↑	Corpus coverage: Cov@0.7↑	Corpus coverage: Cov@0.9↑
$[1;5)$	26.4 *35.4*	.112 *.072*	.244 *.199*	.387 *.293*	.246 *.162*	.960 *.895*	.852 *.576*	.797 *.491*
$[5;10)$	23.8 *32.1*	.147 *.088*	.340 *.193*	.472 *.347*	.276 *.170*	.937 *.833*	.785 *.502*	.614 *.334*
$[10;\infty)$	20.8 *30.6*	.194 *.105*	.410 *.229*	.545 *.411*	.269 *.247*	.925 *.759*	.759 *.417*	.533 *.242*
$[1;\infty)$	21.1 *30.2*	.191 *.109*	.404 *.239*	.442 *.351*	.272 *.240*	.925 *.745*	.761 *.400*	.542 *.223*

Table 2: Summary of the ranking-based evaluation over 82 schemas and documents from **KAIROS SLC**. Numbers in regular font use gold events from the corpus, numbers in *italics* use events extracted with the LOME IE system.

N_{events}	82 schemas			232 schemas		
	0.5	0.7	0.9	0.5	0.7	0.9
$[1;5)$	.887	.531	.425	.975	.637	.509
$[5;10)$	.791	.391	.233	.892	.496	.278
$[10;\infty)$	.695	.313	.164	.807	.379	.195
$[1;\infty)$	.684	.303	.154	.798	.367	.183

Table 3: Corpus coverage Cov@t ($t \in \{0.5, 0.7, 0.9\}$) on the **Gigaword** corpus, using events extracted with the LOME IE system.

N_{events}	82 schemas			232 schemas		
	0.5	0.7	0.9	0.5	0.7	0.9
$[1;5)$	.874	.588	.529	.980	.719	.643
$[5;10)$	.784	.450	.303	.915	.558	.368
$[10;\infty)$	.708	.376	.224	.850	.472	.272
$[1;\infty)$	.720	.392	.246	.860	.490	.299

Table 4: Corpus coverage Cov@t ($t \in \{0.5, 0.7, 0.9\}$) on the **English** subset of the **CC-News** corpus, using events extracted with the LOME IE system.

N_{events}	82 schemas			232 schemas		
	0.5	0.7	0.9	0.5	0.7	0.9
$[1;5)$	.886	.612	.561	.983	.734	.670
$[5;10)$	.778	.465	.335	.921	.586	.408
$[10;\infty)$	.688	.387	.250	.839	.492	.306
$[1;\infty)$	.713	.414	.287	.858	.523	.349

Table 5: Corpus coverage Cov@t ($t \in \{0.5, 0.7, 0.9\}$) on the **Russian** subset of the **CC-News** corpus, using events extracted with the LOME IE system.

N_{events}	82 schemas			232 schemas		
	0.5	0.7	0.9	0.5	0.7	0.9
$[1;5)$	.875	.589	.528	.981	.718	.639
$[5;10)$	.776	.460	.314	.924	.582	.387
$[10;\infty)$	.699	.408	.251	.877	.531	.314
$[1;\infty)$	.713	.422	.271	.885	.545	.337

Table 6: Corpus coverage Cov@t ($t \in \{0.5, 0.7, 0.9\}$) on the **Chinese** subset of the **CC-News** corpus, using events extracted with the LOME IE system.

are automatically extracted using the pretrained multilingual FrameNet parser from the LOME IE system (Xia et al., 2021), which extracts FrameNet events and their arguments. To account for varying document lengths, we stratify the results by the number of extracted events N_{events} in each document. We map the extracted FrameNet events to the KAIROS ontology using a rule-based mapping.[11]

As a result, we observe (Tables 3 and 4) that the initial 82 schemas cover a meaningful part of Gigaword and CC-News: at least 15-25%, and up to 98.3% of documents, depending on corpus D and threshold t. Extending the library L by the additional 150 schemas improves corpus coverage by around 20%, thus suggesting these 150 schemas improve the diversity of the scenarios covered by the initial 82 schemas.

Comparing across multiple languages in CC-News (Tables 4 to 6), we notice the coverage on Chinese and Russian news articles does not drop and even improves, despite that schemas were originally mined using English-language resources. This suggests that the proposed schemas are robust and useful for cross-lingual scenarios, owing to its language-independent ontology and the advances in cross-lingual event extraction tools.

The difference between 82 and 232 schemas' coverage is significant (p-value $\ll 0.01$) for all compared variations of N_{events} and t, as measured by the two-sided Wilcoxon signed-rank test.

5.4. Ranking Evaluation

How sufficient is the event-only representation $E(d)$ of a document d to rank schemas $s \in L$ and predict the true complex event (CE), using $sim(d, s)$ as a ranking function? To answer this question, we conduct a ranking evaluation using KAIROS SLC, where each d has precisely one CE label. For each document d, we **rank schemas** according to $sim(d, s)$ and report the average rank (lower is better), mean reciprocal rank (MRR, higher is better), and recall@10 (R@10, higher is better) of the gold CE label. Similarly we ask, how well can we rank schema-salient documents $d \in D$ given event-only description $E(s)$ of a schema s? For each schema s, we **rank documents** according to $sim(d, s)$ and report

[11]The mapping rules can be accessed at this link: `https://nlp.jhu.edu/schemas/k2f.js`

recall@30 (higher is better) and normalized discounted cumulative gain (nDCG, higher is better) of the gold annotated documents. We also compute **corpus coverage**, which does not require ground-truth CE labels.

As a result (Table 2), we find that the event-only representation does provide useful signal for ranking documents and schemas, compared to e.g. a fully random ordering (where R@10 for schema ranking $= \frac{10}{82} \approx 0.122$ and R@30 for document ranking $= \frac{30}{921} \approx 0.033$). Including additional signal, like participants' types and relations, could potentially improve the ranking. However, this information is costly to annotate for, and was not provided for most of the documents in KAIROS SLC. Thus, improving annotation pipelines for complex events could not only boost schema induction, as argued throughout our paper, but also enable rapid data collection for schema-based information extraction, which in turn leads to more precise schema-supported inferences in downstream document-level tasks.

6. Conclusions

In this paper, we propose a novel semi-automatic script induction system and induce a dataset of 232 schemas. The automatic portion of our system is rooted in a new method, extending an ARM-based approach, which finds interesting subsequences, with a causal scoring metric for filtering out and fusing together these interesting subsequences. The interactive portion of our system is made possible through a new tool, SchemaBlocks, a block-based interface developed to make annotation of schema structures intuitive and easy.

We release both the SchemaBlocks interface and the induced 232 schemas to the community, which we believe will be useful broadly and will facilitate further efforts in what is traditionally an interminable pain for all looking to build robust AI systems: the annotation of robust commonsense knowledge structures.

7. Bibliographical References

Abbott, V., Black, J. B., and Smith, E. E. (1985). The representation of scripts in memory. *Journal of memory and language*, 24(2):179–199.

Bach, S. H., Broecheler, M., Huang, B., and Getoor, L. (2017). Hinge-loss Markov random fields and probabilistic soft logic. *Journal of Machine Learning Research (JMLR)*.

Baker, C. F., Fillmore, C. J., and Lowe, J. B. (1998). The berkeley framenet project. In Christian Boitet et al., editors, *36th Annual Meeting of the Association for Computational Linguistics and 17th International Conference on Computational Linguistics, COLING-ACL '98, August 10-14, 1998, Université de Montréal, Montréal, Quebec, Canada. Proceedings of the Conference*, pages 86–90.

Balasubramanian, N., Soderland, S., Mausam, O. E., and Etzioni, O. (2013). Generating coherent event schemas at scale. In *Proceedings of EMNLP*.

Belyy, A. and Van Durme, B. (2020). Script induction as association rule mining. In *Proceedings of the First Joint Workshop on Narrative Understanding, Storylines, and Events*, pages 55–62, Online, July. Association for Computational Linguistics.

Bower, G. H., Black, J. B., and Turner, T. J. (1979). Scripts in memory for text. *Cognitive psychology*, 11(2):177–220.

Chambers, N. and Jurafsky, D. (2008). Unsupervised learning of narrative event chains. In *Proceedings of the Association for Computational Linguistics (ACL)*, Hawaii, USA.

Chambers, N. and Jurafsky, D. (2009). Unsupervised learning of narrative schemas and their participants. In *Proceedings of the Association for Computational Linguistics (ACL)*, Singapore.

Chambers, N. and Jurafsky, D. (2010). A database of narrative schemas. In *LREC*.

Chang, J., Boyd-Graber, J. L., Gerrish, S., Wang, C., and Blei, D. M. (2009). Reading tea leaves: How humans interpret topic models. In Yoshua Bengio, et al., editors, *Advances in Neural Information Processing Systems 22: 23rd Annual Conference on Neural Information Processing Systems 2009. Proceedings of a meeting held 7-10 December 2009, Vancouver, British Columbia, Canada*, pages 288–296. Curran Associates, Inc.

DeJong, G. (1983). Acquiring schemata through understanding and generalizing plans. In *IJCAI*.

Doddington, G. R., Mitchell, A., Przybocki, M. A., Ramshaw, L. A., Strassel, S. M., and Weischedel, R. M. (2004). The automatic content extraction (ace) program-tasks, data, and evaluation. In *Lrec*, volume 2, pages 837–840. Lisbon.

Graff, D., Kong, J., Chen, K., and Maeda, K. (2003). English gigaword. *Linguistic Data Consortium, Philadelphia*, 4(1):34.

Han, J., Pei, J., and Yin, Y. (2000). Mining frequent patterns without candidate generation. *ACM sigmod record*, 29(2):1–12.

Kiros, R., Zhu, Y., Salakhutdinov, R., Zemel, R. S., Urtasun, R., Torralba, A., and Fidler, S. (2015). Skip-thought vectors. In Corinna Cortes, et al., editors, *Advances in Neural Information Processing Systems 28: Annual Conference on Neural Information Processing Systems 2015, December 7-12, 2015, Montreal, Quebec, Canada*, pages 3294–3302.

Lehnert, W. G., Dyer, M. G., Johnson, P. N., Yang, C. J., and Harley, S. (1983). BORIS - an experiment in in-depth understanding of narratives. *Artif. Intell.*, 20(1):15–62.

Minsky, M. (1974). A framework for representing knowledge. MIT Laboratory Memo 306.

Mooney, R. and DeJong, G. (1985). Learning schemata for natural language processing. In *Ninth International Joint Conference on Artificial Intelligence (IJCAI)*, pages 681–687.

Mueller, E. T. (1999). A database and lexicon of scripts for thoughttreasure.

Nagel, S. (2016). Cc-news. https://commoncrawl.org/2016/10/news-dataset-available.

Regneri, M., Koller, A., and Pinkal, M. (2010). Learning script knowledge with web experiments. In *Proceedings of the 48th Annual Meeting of the Association for Computational Linguistics*, pages 979–988. Association for Computational Linguistics.

Resnick, M., Maloney, J., Monroy-Hernández, A., Rusk, N., Eastmond, E., Brennan, K., Millner, A., Rosenbaum, E., Silver, J., Silverman, B., et al. (2009). Scratch: programming for all. *Communications of the ACM*, 52(11):60–67.

Rudinger, R., Rastogi, P., Ferraro, F., and Van Durme, B. (2015). Script induction as language modeling. In *Proceedings of the 2015 Conference on Empirical Methods in Natural Language Processing*, pages 1681–1686.

Schank, R. C. and Abelson, R. P. (1977). *Scripts, plans, goals, and understanding: An inquiry into human knowledge structures*. Psychology Press.

Song, Z., Bies, A., Strassel, S., Riese, T., Mott, J., Ellis, J., Wright, J., Kulick, S., Ryant, N., and Ma, X. (2015). From light to rich ere: annotation of entities, relations, and events. In *Proceedings of the the 3rd Workshop on EVENTS: Definition, Detection, Coreference, and Representation*, pages 89–98.

Wanzare, L. D. A., Zarcone, A., Thater, S., and Pinkal, M. (2016). A crowdsourced database of event sequence descriptions for the acquisition of high-quality script knowledge. In *Proceedings of the Tenth International Conference on Language Resources and Evaluation (LREC'16)*, pages 3494–3501, Portorož, Slovenia, May. European Language Resources Association (ELRA).

Wanzare, L., Zarcone, A., Thater, S., and Pinkal, M. (2017). Inducing script structure from crowdsourced event descriptions via semi-supervised clustering. In *Proceedings of the 2nd Workshop on Linking Models of Lexical, Sentential and Discourse-level Semantics*, pages 1–11, Valencia, Spain, April. Association for Computational Linguistics.

Weber, N., Rudinger, R., and Van Durme, B. (2020). Causal inference of script knowledge. In *Proceedings of the 2020 Conference on Empirical Methods in Natural Language Processing (EMNLP)*, pages 7583–7596, Online, November. Association for Computational Linguistics.

Xia, P., Qin, G., Vashishtha, S., Chen, Y., Chen, T., May, C., Harman, C., Rawlins, K., White, A. S., and Durme, B. V. (2021). LOME: large ontology multilingual extraction. In Dimitra Gkatzia et al., editors, *Proceedings of the 16th Conference of the European Chapter of the Association for Computational Linguistics: System Demonstrations, EACL 2021, Online, April 19-23, 2021*, pages 149–159. Association for Computational Linguistics.

Zhu, Y., Kiros, R., Zemel, R. S., Salakhutdinov, R., Urtasun, R., Torralba, A., and Fidler, S. (2015). Aligning books and movies: Towards story-like visual explanations by watching movies and reading books. In *2015 IEEE International Conference on Computer Vision, ICCV 2015, Santiago, Chile, December 7-13, 2015*, pages 19–27. IEEE Computer Society.

A. Schema Intrusion Task Details

A.1. Schema Inference

Here, we describe how we match schemas with documents in the schema intrusion task. There are 3 main parts to the Schema Inference system:

1. representations for events and participants,
2. representations for schemas, and
3. the inference mechanism based on Probabilistic Soft Logic (PSL) (Bach et al., 2017).

Throughout the following, we will use the example depicted in Figure 2.

Events and participants Each document is turned into a knowledge graph using a FrameNet parser, as described in Section 5. Knowledge graphs are then flattened to unary or binary relations, following neo-Davidsonian semantics. For instance,

```
{ "@id": "K0C03N60D.7.2",
  "@type": "kairos:Primitives/Events/
           Movement.Transportation.Unspecified",
  "confidence": 0.9,
  "participants": [
    { "@id": "K0C03N60D.7.2.P1.1",
      "role": "kairos:Primitives/Events/
              Movement.Transportation.Unspecified/
              Slots/Destination",
      "values": [{ "confidence": 1.0,
                   "entity": "e2323a3", }]},
    { "@id": "K0C03N60D.7.2.P3.1",
      "role": "kairos:Primitives/Events/
              Movement.Transportation.Unspecified/
              Slots/PassengerArtifact",
      "values": [{ "confidence": 0.8,
                   "entity": "e2323a1", }]}
  ],
}
```

is turned into

```
Movement.Transportation.Unspecified(K0C03N60D.7.2) .9

Destination(K0C03N60D.7.2, e2323a3) 1.

PassengerArtifact(K0C03N60D.7.2, e2323a1) .8
```

We omit common prefixes for readability. We collect those predicates in dedicated files, together with confidence values, which constitute PSL's observation files.

Schemas We frame each step in a schema as a predicate, whose arguments are an event and a number of participants. We frame a schema as a predicate, whose arguments are a set of events, where each is an argument to one of its steps. Using Horn clauses, we define the schema as a conjunction of its steps.
Concretely, the example from Figure 2 turns into:

```
Territorial_Dispute(Claim_event, Attack_event,
        Diplomatic_event)
    <- Claim(Claim_event, State1, State2, Territory)
    & Attack(Attack_event, State1,
        State2, Territory)
    & Diplomatic_Resolution(Diplomatic_event,
        State1, State2, Territory)

Territorial_Dispute(Claim_event, Attack_event,
        Resolution_event)
    <- Claim(Claim_event, State1, State2, Territory)
    & Attack(Attack_event, State1,
        State2, Territory)
    & Legal_Resolution(Resolution_event, State1,
        State2, InternationalCourt, Territory)

Claim(Contact_event, State1, State2, Territory)
    <- Contact.Contact.Unspecified(Contact_event)
    & Participant(Contact_event, State1)
    & Participant(Contact_event, State2)
    & Topic(Contact_event, Territory)

Attack(Attack_event, State1, State2, Territory)
    <- Conflict.Attack.Unspecified(Attack_event)
    & Attacker(Attack_event, State1)
    & Target(Attack_event, State2)
    & Place(Attack_event, Territory)

Diplomatic_Resolution(Contact_event, State1,
        State2, Territory)
    <- Contact.Contact.Unspecified(Contact_event)
    & Participant(Contact_event, State1)
    & Participant(Contact_event, State2)
    & Topic(Contact_event, Territory)

Legal_Resolution(Contact_event, State1, State2,
        InternationalCourt, Territory)
    <- Contact.Contact.Unspecified(Contact_event)
    & Participant(Contact_event, State1)
    & Participant(Contact_event, State2)
    & Participant(Contact_event, InternationalCourt)
    & Topic(Contact_event, Territory)
```

We include negative priors for each step and schema predicate. We give each rule a weight: 100 for step definitions, 10 for schema definitions, and 1 for negative priors. The negative priors and the weights jointly ensure that with a rule of the form `A & B -> C` where `A` and `B` are ground expressions, `C` will be assigned the probability assigned to `A & B`. Primitive events from the ontology and typing predicates are set to closed predicates. Other predicates are set to open.

PSL Inference PSL is a formalism and a tool to assign probabilities to ground expressions. To perform schema inference, we enumerate all the possible groundings for schemas and steps, i.e. all possible combinations of predicates and arguments. The set of possible arguments is taken as the set of entities and events from the knowledge graph. The set of possible predicates is that of all possible events and slots from the KAIROS ontology. PSL associates a continuous variable to each of those targets, and uses the observation files and the rule file to produce a convex optimization problem involving those variables. Solving this optimization problem results in values for the variables, which we interpret as the probability, for individual events, steps and schemas, that they have happened. To be able to partially match a schema, we need to be able to ground any subset of its events and participants. We do this by introducing "UNK" events and entities, which can fill any event and participant role, and co-refer with any entity.
We post-process PSL's results to obtain instantiated schemas, using the confidence values provided by PSL. Any event whose value is an "UNK" event, we consider as unmatched, and interpret this as an event that was not found in the documents, but that is predicted by the schema to have happened. We re-scale the confidence of a schema by the proportion of matched events it contains.

To simplify the matching process, we filter the schema library using an Apache Lucene index. Schemas and knowledge graphs are represented as bags-of-events. We build a Lucene index for the schema library, and given a knowledge graph, query it for relevant schemas.

A.2. Human Evaluation

We use Mechanical Turk to collect responses for the schema intrusion task. Each Mechanical Turk assignment consists of a *single* intrusion task (i.e. a single schema with an intruder, see Figure 4(b)). Each task is completed by three separate annotators who are paid \$0.20 per assignment. Instructions shown to the annotators can be seen on Figures 5 and 6.

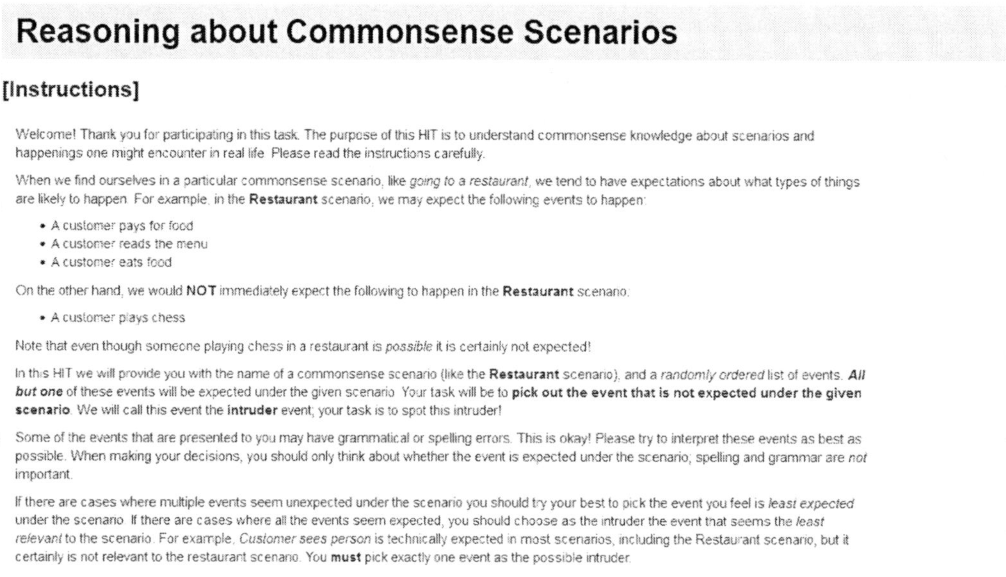

Reasoning about Commonsense Scenarios

[Instructions]

Welcome! Thank you for participating in this task. The purpose of this HIT is to understand commonsense knowledge about scenarios and happenings one might encounter in real life. Please read the instructions carefully.

When we find ourselves in a particular commonsense scenario, like *going to a restaurant*, we tend to have expectations about what types of things are likely to happen. For example, in the **Restaurant** scenario, we may expect the following events to happen:

- A customer pays for food
- A customer reads the menu
- A customer eats food

On the other hand, we would **NOT** immediately expect the following to happen in the **Restaurant** scenario:

- A customer plays chess

Note that even though someone playing chess in a restaurant is *possible* it is certainly not expected!

In this HIT we will provide you with the name of a commonsense scenario (like the **Restaurant** scenario), and a *randomly ordered* list of events. ***All but one*** of these events will be expected under the given scenario. Your task will be to **pick out the event that is not expected under the given scenario**. We will call this event the **intruder** event; your task is to spot this intruder!

Some of the events that are presented to you may have grammatical or spelling errors. This is okay! Please try to interpret these events as best as possible. When making your decisions, you should only think about whether the event is expected under the scenario; spelling and grammar are *not* important.

If there are cases where multiple events seem unexpected under the scenario you should try your best to pick the event you feel is *least expected* under the scenario. If there are cases where all the events seem expected, you should choose as the intruder the event that seems the *least relevant* to the scenario. For example, *Customer sees person* is technically expected in most scenarios, including the Restaurant scenario, but it certainly is not relevant to the restaurant scenario. You **must** pick exactly one event as the possible intruder.

Figure 5: Instructions for the schema intrusion task shown to the Amazon Mechanical Turk workers.

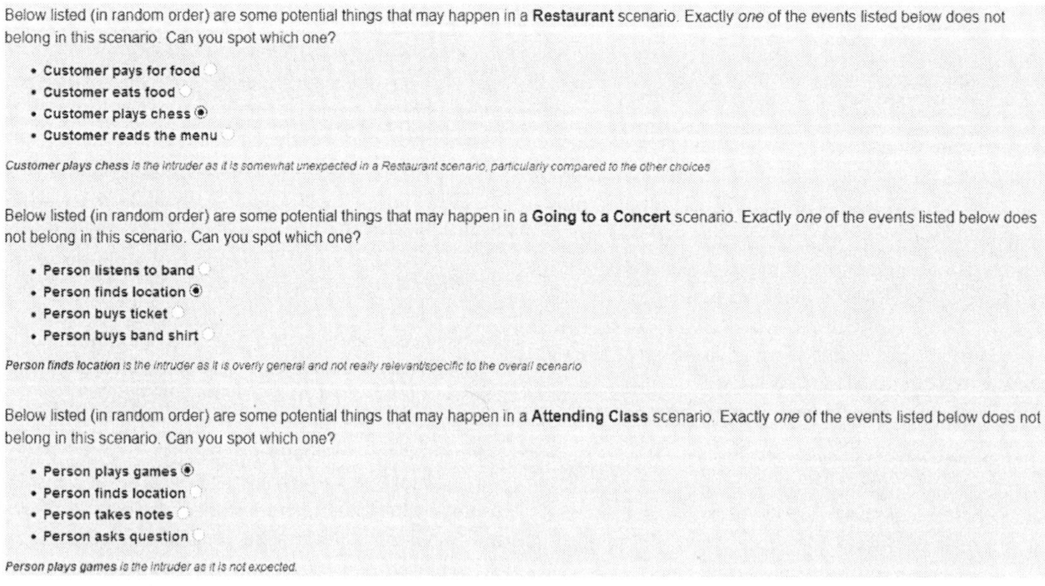

Below listed (in random order) are some potential things that may happen in a **Restaurant** scenario. Exactly *one* of the events listed below does not belong in this scenario. Can you spot which one?

- **Customer pays for food**
- **Customer eats food**
- **Customer plays chess**
- **Customer reads the menu**

Customer plays chess *is the intruder as it is somewhat unexpected in a Restaurant scenario, particularly compared to the other choices*

Below listed (in random order) are some potential things that may happen in a **Going to a Concert** scenario. Exactly *one* of the events listed below does not belong in this scenario. Can you spot which one?

- **Person listens to band**
- **Person finds location**
- **Person buys ticket**
- **Person buys band shirt**

Person finds location *is the intruder as it is overly general and not really relevant/specific to the overall scenario*

Below listed (in random order) are some potential things that may happen in a **Attending Class** scenario. Exactly *one* of the events listed below does not belong in this scenario. Can you spot which one?

- **Person plays games**
- **Person finds location**
- **Person takes notes**
- **Person asks question**

Person plays games *is the intruder as it is not expected.*

Figure 6: Examples of schemas along with intruder events shown to the Amazon Mechanical Turk workers.

Proceedings of the 16th Linguistic Annotation Workshop (LAW-XVI) @LREC 2022, pages 151–159
Marseille, 24 June 2022

A Cognitive Approach to Annotating Causal Constructions in a Cross-Genre Corpus

Angela Cao, Gregor Williamson, Jinho D. Choi
Emory University
Atlanta, GA 30322, USA
Department of Computer Science
{angela.yuan.cao, gregor.jude.williamson, jinho.choi}@emory.edu

Abstract

We present a scheme for annotating causal language in various genres of text. Our annotation scheme is built on the popular categories of CAUSE, ENABLE, and PREVENT. These vague categories have many edge cases in natural language, and as such can prove difficult for annotators to consistently identify in practice. We introduce a decision based annotation method for handling these edge cases. We demonstrate that, by utilizing this method, annotators are able to achieve inter-annotator agreement which is comparable to that of previous studies. Furthermore, our method performs equally well across genres, highlighting the robustness of our annotation scheme. Finally, we observe notable variation in usage and frequency of causal language across different genres.

Keywords: causal annotation, cross-genre annotation, manual annotation, semantic relations

1. Introduction

The way we comprehend the world through notions of *causer* and *caused* dominates how we form notions of responsibility, make decisions based on world knowledge, and relate events to one another. For example, are the addictive properties of nicotine or genetics to blame for the correlation between lung cancer and smoking (Gundle et al., 2010)? Do language patterns limit channels of thought, or do channels of thought limit language patterns (Whorf, 1956)? Did Eve make Adam eat the apple (Pearl, 2009)? In line with previous work on annotating causal relations in text, which makes the author's internal causal reasoning primed for the purpose of analysis, this paper presents the Constructions of CAUSE, ENABLE, and PREVENT (CCEP) corpus. This project builds mainly upon the Bank of Effects and Causes Stated Explicitly (BECauSE) of Dunietz (2018), Dunietz et al. (2017b), and Dunietz et al. (2015) while incorporating a force dynamics approach to causation categorization first introduced by Wolff et al. (2005) and defined in Table 1. We provide a multi-test approach for annotators in order to ground intuitions about the vague concepts of CAUSE, ENABLE and PREVENT (abbreviated as C, E, and P, respectively) in a straightforward and accurate manner. Unlike the majority of previous annotation studies on causal language, which typically work with news data, the CCEP is annotated on a cross-genre dataset including short stories, Reddit posts, in addition to news data, to provide insights into how causal relations are described differently across genres. In the next section, we provide a brief overview of the theoretical motivation behind the categories of CAUSE, ENABLE, and PREVENT. Following this, in section 3, we provide an overview of related causal annotation research in order to contextualize the present study. Next, in section 4, we provide a description of our annotation guidelines and supporting materials[1]. In section 5, we describe the training methods and tools used during annotation. Section 6 presents our IAA scores, comparing them to other causal annotation projects, which demonstrates the robustness and reliability of the present scheme. Finally, we discuss future directions for research as well as outstanding practical and theoretical issues in section 7, before concluding in section 8.

2. Theoretical motivation

The force dynamics theory of causation (Wolff et al., 2005; Wolff, 2007) is an approach to knowledge representation that encodes how causal judgements may be formed in human cognition (Wolff and Thorstad, 2017). The concepts of CAUSE, ENABLE, and PREVENT are distinguished according to "various patterns of tendency, relative strength, rest, and motion between an *affector* and a *patient*" (Wolff and Zettergren, 2002, p.2). More specifically, these notions are defined in terms of whether the affector and the patient act in concordance, whether there is a tendency for the patient toward the result, and whether the result occurs or not. The specific attributes of each category are given in Table 1.

	Patient tendency toward result	Affector-Patient Concordance	Occurrence of result
CAUSE	N	N	Y
ENABLE	Y	Y	Y
PREVENT	Y	N	N

Table 1: Wolff et al.'s (2005) force dynamics theory of causation.

While useful, this table is somewhat misleading, as boundaries between the three classes are often unclear.

[1]Publicly available at: https://github.com/emorynlp/LAW-2022-Causal

A more appropriate way of understanding these classes is as products of various force vectors, as in Figure 1.

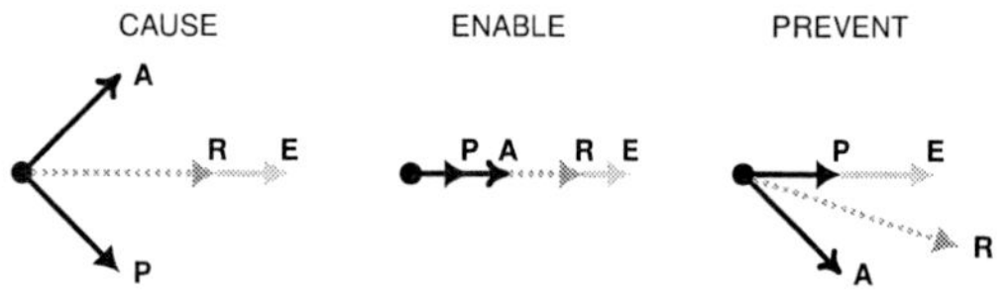

Figure 1: Representation of CAUSE, ENABLE, and PREVENT from Wolff (2007), where forces associated with the affector (A), forces associated with the patient (P) combine to form the resultant force (R) that may or may not be directed towards the endstate (E).

These vector diagrams represent the various forces at play in a causal relation. The patient is viewed as having a *tendency* for the endstate when the force associated with the patient is in the same direction as the endstate. Furthermore, the patient and affector act in *concordance* when the patient's force is in the same direction as the affector's force. The endstate may only *occur* when both the resultant's force and the force of the endstate are collinear. In PREVENT relations, the resultant force and the endstate are not collinear, and so the endstate that the patient tends toward does not occur. Understood as complex interactions of various factors, it is clear that there are numerous edge cases where affector and patient work more or less in concordance. As Wolff (2007) observes, people use qualitative assessments when deciding whether the resultant force could have been produced from the affector and patient forces. Accordingly, it would be unreasonable to ask annotators to consider complex vector operations when annotating text. With this in mind, two questions arise. Firstly, how can we enable annotators to resolve instances which lie at the edges of these categories? And secondly, how can we design intuitive guidelines to aid annotators in recognizing these relations, helping them identify the appropriate category when annotating causal language?

3. Related Research

Table 2 summarizes a number of influential studies on causal annotation. Among these works there are those in which annotations are performed manually (Mostafazadeh et al., 2016b; Caselli and Vossen, 2017; Dunietz et al., 2017a; Dunietz, 2018), those in which events are pre-identified (Mirza et al., 2014; Mirza and Tonelli, 2016; Caselli and Vossen, 2017), those in which additional temporal relations are annotated (Mirza et al., 2014; Mirza and Tonelli, 2016; Mostafazadeh et al., 2016b; Caselli and Vossen, 2017; Dunietz, 2018), as well as those that categorize the causal relation into the three CEP categories (Mirza et al., 2014; Mirza and Tonelli, 2016; Mostafazadeh et al., 2016b; Caselli and Vossen, 2017).

We identify three improvements that could be implemented in annotation schemes of causal relations. Firstly, most of the previous annotation schemes that aim to implement the CEP categories use simple counterfactual tests to discern between them. However, counterfactual reasoning by itself is often cognitively taxing and these rather simplistic counterfactual tests are not always ideal since, as mentioned in section 2, there are many edge cases which are hard to reason about. For example, consider the Causal and Temporal Relation Scheme's (CaTeRS) definitions of A CAUSE B, which is: *In the textual context, if A occurs, B most probably occurs as a result*, and A ENABLE B, which is: *In the textual context, if A does not occur, B most probably does not occur*. These definitions are concerned with only one facet of the CEP relations—namely, necessity and sufficiency. However, Wolff et al. (2005) does not define *necessity* as an attribute of ENABLE nor *sufficiency* for CAUSE or PREVENT. Not only are the notions of sufficiency and necessity a point of contention in literature (Lauer and Nadathur, 2020; Baglini and Siegal, 2020; Bar-Asher Siegal and Boneh, 2019), but these characteristics of CEP arguably arise as a byproduct of the core attributes of CAUSE, ENABLE, and PREVENT as shown in Figure 1.

Secondly, causal language encompasses a wide variety of lexical items. Much previous work in annotation of causal language ties causal meaning to a closed class of *triggers*. For example, the Penn Discourse Treebank's (PDTB) triggers are limited to conjunctions and adverbials, while PropBank limits its annotation of causal language to arguments of verbs. Furthermore, since the arguments of causal relations are usually taken to be events, as in Mostafazadeh et al. (2016b), some schemes do not annotate causal relations where only the agent in the Cause is specified. Thus, a richer representation of causal language enabled by a wide variety of identified triggers would improve the field's understanding of causal language.

Finally, the majority of causal annotation has been carried out on data from news sources. As such, there is a clear need for causal annotation of different genres and text types.

3.1. BECauSE

Of most relevance to the present study is the BECauSE corpus of causal relations developed in Dunietz et al. (2015), Dunietz et al. (2017b) and Dunietz (2018). The causal relations in this corpus are annotated based on pre-identified connectives between a Cause argument and an Effect argument listed in the Constructicon, a spreadsheet containing 191 pre-identified causal constructions and other relevant information. The causal relations are identified in 3x2 dimensions, including `Purpose`, `Motivation`, `Consequence` and `Facilitate` vs. `Inhibit`. However, he notes that the combination of both `Inhibit` and `Purpose` is not possible. Furthermore, since the identification choice between `Inhibit` and `Facilitate` relationships were pre-identified in Dunietz's Constructicon, the

Annotation scheme	Manual annotation	Pre-identified events	Temporal relations	Discourse relations	CEP
PDTB (Prasad et al., 2008; Prasad et al., 2006)	✓			✓	
PropBank (Kingsbury and Palmer, 2003; Bonial et al., 2014)	✓			✓	
Causal TempEval-3 (Mirza et al., 2014)		✓	✓		✓
CATENA (Mirza and Tonelli, 2016)		✓	✓		✓
CaTeRS (Mostafazadeh et al., 2016b)	✓		✓		✓
Storyline Extraction (Caselli and Vossen, 2017)	✓	✓	✓		✓
BECauSE 2.1 (Dunietz et al., 2017b; Dunietz, 2018)	✓		✓		*

*BECauSE uses `Facilitate` and `Inhibit`, where `Facilitate` maps onto CAUSE/ENABLE and `Inhibit` to PREVENT.

Table 2: Previous causal annotation schemes.

project's annotators' decision-making was constrained to the dimension of `Purpose`, `Motivation`, and `Consequence`. Notably, Dunietz expresses a desire to attempt more fine-grained distinctions based on Wolff et al. (2005)'s aforementioned CEP categories, although he is unable to achieve sufficiently stable inter-annotator agreement.

4. The CCEP Annotation Scheme

The Constructions of CAUSE, ENABLE, and PREVENT (CCEP) annotation scheme includes the annotation guidelines which utilizes the Constructicon as an annotation tool. Included in the annotation guidelines is a flowchart (named the Causal Relation Decision Tree abbreviated as CRDT, presented as Figure 2) designed to guide the annotators' decision process. These three components are adapted from Dunietz (2018).
In this section we describe the main features of both the Constructicon and the Annotation Scheme. Annotating instances of "causal language" within the CCEP scheme consists of labelling clauses or phrases which denote an event, state, action, or entity, the Cause, which is *explicitly presented as* promoting or hindering another, the Effect. The Cause and Effect must be textually connected through an explicit trigger, referred to as the "connective".

4.1. Parts of an annotatable causal instance

Annotation of an instance is prompted by the appearance of a causal connective, which can be related with up to three other spans of text of which any may be disjoint. Annotation spans are thus one of four types: (i) The Causal Connective which functions as the basis of all annotation instances and signifies the possibility of a causal construction (e.g. *for...to*, *because*), (ii) The Cause span which is generally an event or state involving an entity and is ideally expressed as a propositional clause or phrase, (iii) The Effect span which is also generally an event or state, ideally expressed as a propositional clause or phrase, and (iv) The Means span which includes an action that serves the purpose of differentiating between the agent of the Cause and the action by which that agent induces the Effect.

4.2. The Constructicon

Causal connectives are pre-identified in the Constructicon which is provided to annotators to actively use as they annotate. It is adapted from Dunietz (2018) with the addition of three causal connectives identified during annotation (*'due to'*, *'stop'*, and *'caused by'*). We also deleted six columns containing information which is not pertinent to the CEP classification task, including 'WordNet senses included', 'Type', 'Degree', 'Notable restrictions on type', 'Possible overlapping categories' (since these are only relevant with Dunietz's roles), and 'Number of distinct construction variants' (which was deemed unimportant for annotators). The Constructicon grounds the backbone of this scheme in Construction Grammar, meaning that *constructions* are taken as the fundamental units of language. On this account, constructions pair directly with meanings. As such, causal relations should be easily observable in specific lexical constructions, following the surface construction labeling approach. The Constructicon is provided as a searchable spreadsheet of 194 causal connective patterns, and was designed to minimize the decision-making burden placed on annotators. Examples of constructions include *for <Effect> to <Effect>*, *<Cause>* and *<Effect> because <Cause>*.

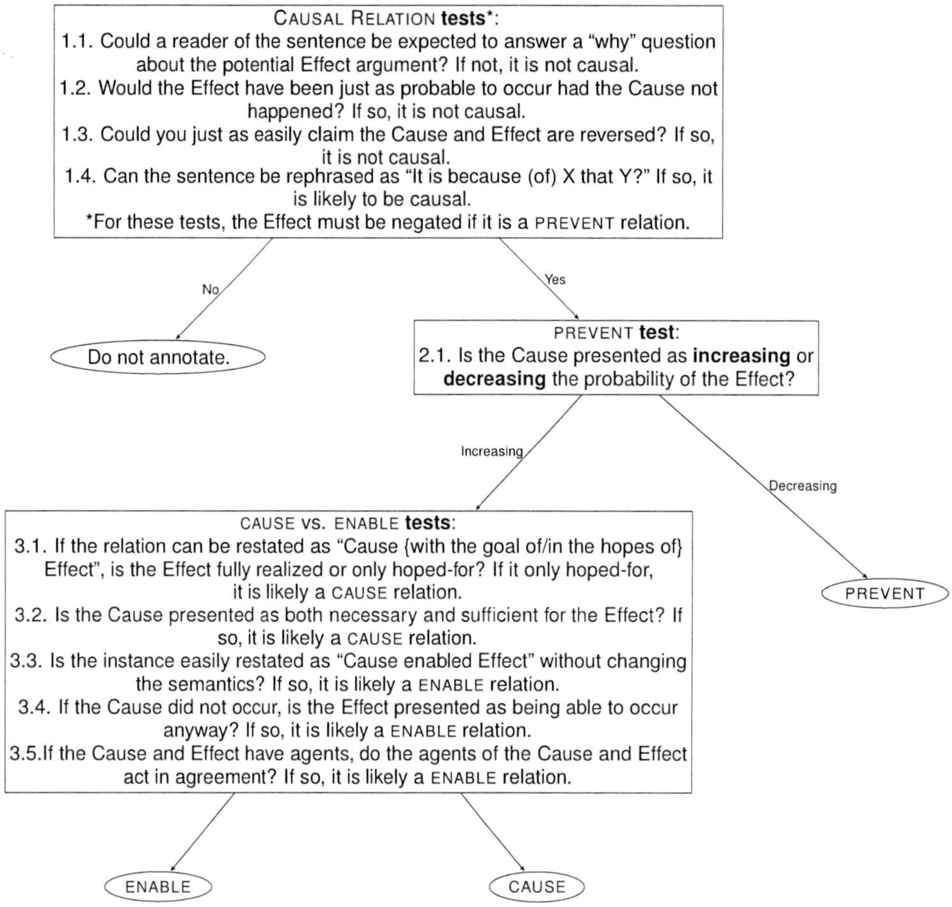

Figure 2: Decision tree for causation categorization (the CRDT).

4.3. Causation in CCEP

While Dunietz focuses on causal categories of `Purpose`, `Motivation`, and `Consequence`, as well as `Facilitate` and `Inhibit`, we aim to extend the applicability of his tools to categorize CAUSE, ENABLE, and PREVENT, which is a more nuanced exploration of his second dimension. Dunietz (2018) discusses a preliminary attempt to have a 3x3 categorization including CEP; unfortunately, he is unable to reach satisfactory IAA scores. His solution is to collapse CAUSE and ENABLE into `Facilitate`, leaving PREVENT to map to `Inhibit`, where in the 3x2 combination of possible relations, relations of both `Inhibit` and `Purpose`-types were not possible.

As discussed above, the CCEP scheme is built on the force dynamics model of causation from Wolff and Song (2003). Consequently, annotators are tasked with identifying causal relations as CAUSE, ENABLE, or PREVENT-type. Since the Constructicon specifies when a connective is PREVENT-type, the core task for annotators of the CCEP scheme is to distinguish between instances of CAUSE and ENABLE. To this end, we provide the following tests presented in the annotator's decision flow as depicted in the CRDT in Figure 2.

Test 3.1. If the relation can be restated as "⟨Cause⟩ {with the goal of / in the hopes of} ⟨Effect⟩", is the Effect fully realized or only hoped-for? If it is only hoped-for, it is likely a CAUSE relation.

Test 3.2. Is the Cause presented as both necessary and sufficient for the Effect? If so, it is likely a CAUSE relation.

Test 3.3. Is the instance easily restated as "⟨Cause⟩ enabled ⟨Effect⟩" without changing the meaning? If so, it is likely a ENABLE relation.

Test 3.4. If the Cause did not occur, is the Effect presented as being able to occur anyway? If so, it is likely a ENABLE relation.

Test 3.5. If the Cause and Effect have agents, do the agents of the Cause and Effect act in agreement? If so, it is likely an ENABLE relation.

These tests are ordered hierarchically, so passing test 3.1 holds more weight than passing test 3.5. However, tests are not necessarily definitive. For instance, if a relation does not pass test 3.1, this does not guarantee it is an

ENABLE relation. As such, annotators are instructed to work through each test and make a judgement that takes into account the greater weight of the earlier tests over the later tests.

Test 3.1 is intended to capture causal relations of purpose. Specifically, when an agent acts in a way to bring about a desired state of affairs, that desire causes the agent to act.

Test 3.2 reflects the fact that Causes of ENABLE are not sufficient alone for the Effect to occur given the patient tendency towards the endstate. Therefore, if the Cause is presented as necessary and sufficient, it must be a Cause of a CAUSE relation (by contraposition). For example, if the author writes, *'I failed the test only because the professor dislikes me'*, the span of *'the professor dislikes me'* is to be interpreted as the sole Cause, sufficient for bringing about the author's failure, and should thus be annotated as a CAUSE relation.

Test 3.3 is motivated by the observation that while not all instances of the use of lexical *cause* are of CAUSE-type (e.g., *'a cause of her death were her poor eating habits'*), uses of *enable* are generally of ENABLE-type.

Test 3.4. is grounded in similar reasoning to the point made for Test 3.3, but holds for cases where a force relevant to the causal relation is not captured within the span of the Cause or Effect, but may or may not be mentioned elsewhere in the document. If all relevant forces act toward the same endstate, it may be possible for one of the forces to compensate for the lack of an alternate force moving in the same direction.

Finally, test 3.5 is designed to determine the cases in which the affector and patient act in concordance, tracking Wolff's notion of ENABLE.

To conclude, these diagnostics aid in clarifying the vague notions of CEP for annotators in a way that sufficiently retains the original prototypical notions of CAUSE, ENABLE, and PREVENT characterized by Wolff and Song (2003).

5. Methodology

5.1. Data

The CCEP is a corpus of 150 documents (totalling 22,558 tokens) taken from three different sources: Aesops Fables[2], CNN newswire from the cnn_dailymail corpus[3], and Reddit posts taken from popular college subreddits[4]. Posts are filtered using the Profanity-Check Python library[5]. All data from these sources are tokenized using the ELIT Tokenizer[6] and then filtered to a length between 100 and 200 tokens.

[2]https://www.gutenberg.org/cache/epub/21/pg21.txt

[3]https://huggingface.co/datasets/cnn_dailymail

[4]https://github.com/emorynlp/RedditData accessed on 14th February 2022.

[5]https://github.com/vzhou842/profanity-check

[6]https://github.com/emorynlp/elit-tokenizer

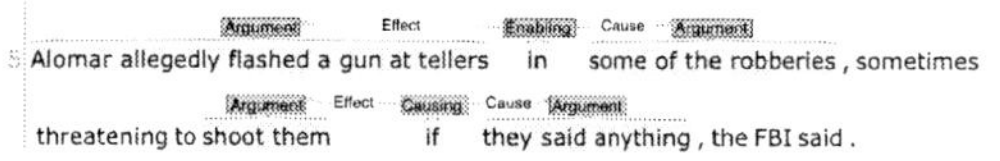

Figure 3: A sample annotation instance in INCEpTION.

5.2. Training

To guarantee that annotators understand the guidelines and meet a standard of performance, they undergo extensive training prior to undertaking annotation. The training consists of three stages: (i) annotators read the guidelines and view an instructional video, (ii) they take 10 online quizzes[7] consisting of 10 questions each on span identification, argument labelling, and relation labelling, and (iii) they must achieve a satisfactory inter-annotator agreement (IAA) score with gold-standard annotation of 10 practice documents. We began the training process with four annotators, consisting of three undergraduate students and a postdoctoral researcher who are all experienced annotators. Of these four, two progressed into the annotation process. Annotators are instructed to rotate through the various data sources in batches of 5 to ensure that any difference in IAA scores is not a result of familiarity with the annotation tool or experience following the annotation scheme.

5.3. Annotation Tool

Annotation was performed using the INCEpTION tool[8] (illustrated in Figure 3) developed by Technische Universität Darmstadt (Klie et al., 2018). This tool enabled the coordination of CCEP with two other parallel annotation projects in multiple layers including coreference and temporal relation annotation.

6. Results from the CCEP corpus

6.1. Inter-Annotator Agreement

We used F_1 to measure span agreement and Cohen's Kappa to measure causation type and argument labels in order to be able to compare our performance to Dunietz (2018)'s, as shown in Table 3. As demonstrated in Table 4, our overall corpus of causal annotations yields an F_1 score of 0.77 for connective identification, which is an improvement on the 0.70 of Dunietz (2018). Allowing for partial overlap, our F_1 score of 0.83 also improves upon Dunietz's 0.78. For agreed connective spans, the corpus also yielded a κ score of 0.83 for types of causation. This is similar to Dunietz's 0.80 for the causation categories of `Purpose`, `Motivation`, and `Consequence`. However, our argument span score of 0.71 was lower than Dunietz's at 0.86 (excluding overlap) and his 0.96 compared to our 0.86 including overlap. This was likely due to argument length disagreement, as all three document types contained very

[7]Training quizzes were created using Google Forms.

[8]https://inception-project.github.io/

Annotation scheme	Relation types	Arguments IAA	Arguments metric	Connectives IAA	Connectives metric	Relation IAA	Relation metric	Corpus size
PDTB	1	0.90* (Miltsakaki et al., 2004)	Percent	n/a	n/a	0.53† (Pitler et al., 2008)	F_1	2499 (news) (Prasad et al., 2019)
PropBank	1	0.93	Cohen's Kappa	0.93	Cohen's Kappa	0.91	Cohen's Kappa	2499 (news) (Palmer et al., 2005)
Causal TimeEval-3	3	n/a	n/a	0.55	F_1	0.3	F_1	20 (news)
CATENA	3	n/a	n/a	n/a	n/a	0.622	F_1	276 (news) (Pustejovsky et al., 2006) (Graff, 2002) (UzZaman et al., 2012)
CaTeRS	9**	0.91	Fleiss' Kappa	n/a	n/a	0.51	Fleiss' Kappa	320 (stories) (Mostafazadeh et al., 2016a)
StoryLine Extraction	2	n/a	n/a	n/a	n/a	0.638	Dice Coefficient	258 (news)
BECauSE 2.1	5	0.86‡	F_1	0.70	F_1	0.80	Cohen's Kappa	>116 (news) (Sandhaus, 2008) (Marcus et al., 1994) (Ide et al., 2010) (Smith et al., 2014)

* Calculated for 3103 tokens. † Only for CONTINGENCY relations. ** Only 4 of 9 are causal. ‡ Spans only.

Table 3: Results from previous causal annotation studies.

different writing styles, ranging from the wordy, rant-like style of Reddit documents to more succinct news reporting.

	Reddit	News	Fables	Overall
Connective spans (F_1)	0.82	0.75	0.75	0.77
Connectives + overlap (F_1)	0.86	0.81	0.81	0.83
Types of causation (κ)	0.78	0.89	0.82	0.83
Argument spans (F_1)	0.76	0.72	0.68	0.71
Arguments + overlap (F_1)	0.91	0.83	0.85	0.86
Argument labels (κ)	0.93	0.86	0.91	0.90

Table 4: Annotation performance across different text types, with and without partial overlap for span identification. κ = Cohen's Kappa.

Since the main obstacle faced by the present study is to provide a means of establishing agreement on instances of vague CEP categories—and specifically distinguishing between CAUSE and ENABLE—we provide the percentage of how often annotators agreed on the CAUSE and ENABLE labels in Table 5. These scores demonstrate that annotators were able to reliably differentiate between these categories across different document types.

	CAUSE vs. ENABLE agreement
Reddit	78.57%
News	89.25%
Fables	80.95%
Overall	82.48%

Table 5: Percentage of agreement in cause type between CAUSE and ENABLE across the various genres.

Finally, we perform a one-way ANOVA comparing overall F_1 scores across genres for all documents, which yields a p-value of 0.29 showing no significant effect of data type on IAA. This demonstrates the robustness of our guidelines across genres, which included specific instructions for genre-specific idiosyncrasies such as the appearances of abbreviations and shorthands in Reddit posts.

6.2. Statistics

The analysis of our corpus provides numerous interesting insights. The corpus contains a total of 150 doubly-annotated documents, which featured 870 annotations of causal constructions between both annotators, with 22 of our 300 annotated documents containing no causal annotation at all. As shown in Figure 4, CAUSE-type instances dominated all instances of annotated causal language. This was to be expected since test 3.2 of the CRDT tests for CAUSE-type instances asks annotators whether the textual context presents the Cause as necessary and sufficient for the Effect. In the limited context of a 200-token document, many authors present the Cause as contextually necessary and sufficient in some way for the Effect to occur.

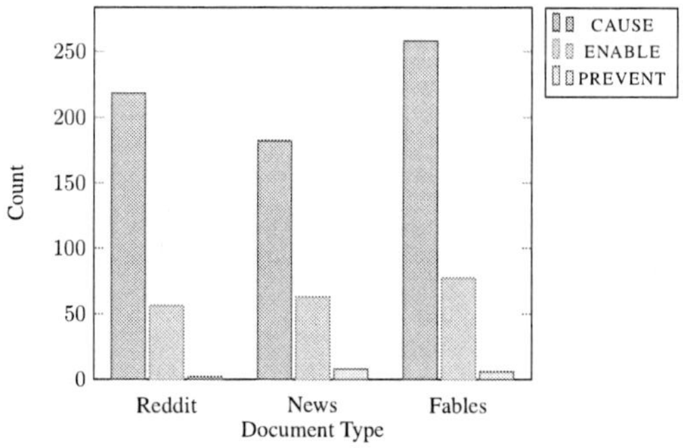

Figure 4: Counts of CEP across document types.

Table 6 is also of interest because it demonstrates that Fables had the most annotations of causal language, while News contained the least. We hypothesize that this is because of the narrative, event-driven structure of Fables, which have been popularly used for temporal annotations for this reason (Bethard et al., 2012). The same reasoning may explain the less frequent use of causal relations in news data—news articles are more concerned with reporting states of affairs than making attributions of causality.

Category	Reddit n	Reddit %	News n	News %	Fables n	Fables %	Total n
CAUSE	218	79	182	71.9	258	75.7	658
ENABLE	56	20.3	63	24.9	77	22.5	196
PREVENT	2	0.7	8	3.2	6	1.8	16
Total	276	100	253	100	341	100	870

Table 6: Counts of CEP across document types.

Table 7 reports the most popular connectives across the different document types. Firstly, note that the most frequent five connectives account for approximately half of all instances of annotated causal language. While our findings generally align with Dunietz's counts of connective patterns in the BECauSE corpus (our most frequent five appear in his top seven), it is interesting to note that their frequencies vary across document type. For example, the conditional only appears 8 times in the CNN news data, highlighting the factual nature of news reporting. Furthermore, while *'after'* appears as our fourth most popular connective pattern, these instance occur almost exclusively in the CNN data (with 41 counts, compared to only 4 in Reddit and 6 in Fables). Similarly, while *'because'* occurs in the top five most frequently appearing connectives, 77.8% of these appearances were in Reddit. This is most likely due to the stream-of-consciousness style of Reddit writing, where writers are not so concerned with diversifying their word choice. Finally, Table 8 lists the connectives that were used exclusively for either CAUSE or ENABLE throughout the entire corpus. While some pairings seem intuitive (e.g., *'let'* and *'allow'* denoting ENABLE relations), others are less so (e.g., *'with'* denoting CAUSE relations).

6.3. Summary of findings

In summary, this project reached IAA scores of $F_1 = 0.77$ for connective spans, $\kappa = 0.83$ for causation categorization of connectives, $F_1 = 0.71$ for argument spans, and $\kappa = 0.90$ for argument labels. Also observe that allowing for partial overlap only increases connective identification F_1 from 0.82 to 0.86, while argument identification improves from 0.71 to 0.86. This is to be expected, since connective spans are pre-delimited in the Constructicon for annotators, while argument spans are not. Furthermore, the most frequently annotated connectives in our corpus aligned with those in the BECauSE corpus. The sub-corpus of Fables contained the most occurrences of causal language, while News had the least. Finally, analysis of the connectives and their types across different sub-corpora reveal some interesting trends, such as connectives that appear frequently in one document type but not another, or connectives that only appear as CAUSE or ENABLE.

7. Discussion

A limitation of the surface construction labeling approach is its inability to represent long-distant, document-level causal relations. Consider the following text taken from one of the Reddit posts: *'I'm pretty much being called a liar and a cheat. Happened to anyone else? So, I literally cried when my TA told me.'* Intuitively, the accusation of plagiarism described in the first sentence could be construed as a Cause of the narrator *'literally crying'*. However, this causal relation is not annotatable according to our guidelines because (i) it is not demarcated by a lexical connective, and (ii) even with the connective *'so'* before *'I literally cried...'*, the span is not enough to fit into the construction of *<Cause>, so <Effect>* as the left argument of *'so'* is not the accusation of plagiarism.

A potential direction for future researchers may be to annotate a wider, more varied datasets when choosing text to annotate. While the straightforward and clean language used in news and short stories may enable higher IAA, using noisy data such as Reddit posts test the robustness of annotation schemes.

Finally, the IAA of our project demonstrates the feasibility of using CEP categorization in causal relation annotation. However, we did not include Dunietz's other causal dimensions of `Motivation`, `Purpose`, and `Consequence`. Thus, a natural next step in future research would be to integrate these aforementioned three categories and CEP into a single scheme. This expansion of dimensions annotated in the same layer would provide more insight into how causal relations are described in text.

8. Conclusion

In this paper, we introduced a decision based method for annotating causal categories across various genres of text. Our annotation scheme was designed to capture the categories of CAUSE, ENABLE, and PREVENT, and their many edge cases which are difficult for annotators to consistently identify in practice. We showed that, by using this method, annotators can achieve IAA which is comparable to previous studies. Furthermore, our method performs equally well across genres, highlighting the robustness of our annotation scheme. Finally, we observed a number of interesting differences in usage and frequency of causal language across different genres.

9. Acknowledgements

We gratefully acknowledge the support of the Amazon Alexa AI grant. Any opinions, findings, and conclusions or recommendations expressed in this material are those of the authors and do not necessarily reflect the views of the Alexa AI. We also thank Yingying Chen, Yuxin (Jessica) Ji, Claire Fenton, and Yifeng Wu for feedback on the annotation guidelines.

Causal Connective	Reddit		News		Fables			
	n	Frequency	n	Frequency	n	Frequency	Total	Overall %
to	48	17.39%	24	9.49%	46	13.49%	118	13.56%
for	29	10.51%	30	11.86%	42	12.32%	101	11.61%
if	30	10.87%	8	3.16%	47	13.78%	85	9.77%
after	4	1.45%	41	16.21%	2	0.59%	47	5.40%
because	35	12.68%	4	1.58%	6	1.76%	45	5.17%
Total	146	52.90%	107	42.30%	143	41.94%	396	45.52%

Table 7: Comparison of popular connectives across different document types.

Causal Connective	Type	Reddit	News	Fables	Total
make	CAUSE	6	8	15	29
with	CAUSE	4	4	10	18
cause	CAUSE	4	6	0	10
let	ENABLE	0	0	6	6
allow	ENABLE	2	3	0	5
have	CAUSE	0	2	3	5

Table 8: Count of connectives annotated exclusively as either CAUSE or ENABLE and $n \geq 5$.

10. Bibliographical References

Baglini, R. and Siegal, E. A. B.-A. (2020). Direct causation: A new approach to an old question. *University of Pennsylvania Working Papers in Linguistics*, 26:19–28.

Bar-Asher Siegal, E. and Boneh, N. (2019). Sufficient and necessary conditions for a non-unified analysis of causation. *Proceedings of the 36th West Coast Conference on Formal Linguistics*, pages 55–60.

Bethard, S., Kolomiyets, O., and Moens, M.-F. (2012). Annotating story timelines as temporal dependency structures. In *Proceedings of the Eighth International Conference on Language Resources and Evaluation (LREC'12)*, pages 2721–2726, Istanbul, Turkey, May. European Language Resources Association (ELRA).

Bonial, C., Bonn, J., Conger, K., Hwang, J. D., and Palmer, M. (2014). PropBank: Semantics of new predicate types. In *Proceedings of the Ninth International Conference on Language Resources and Evaluation (LREC'14)*, pages 3013–3019. European Language Resources Association (ELRA).

Caselli, T. and Vossen, P. (2017). The event StoryLine corpus: A new benchmark for causal and temporal relation extraction. In *Proceedings of the Events and Stories in the News Workshop*, pages 77–86, Vancouver, Canada, August. Association for Computational Linguistics.

Dunietz, J., Levin, L., and Carbonell, J. G. (2015). Annotating causal language using corpus lexicography of constructions. In *Proceedings of The 9th Linguistic Annotation Workshop*, pages 188–196.

Dunietz, J., Levin, L., and Carbonell, J. (2017a). Automatically Tagging Constructions of Causation and Their Slot-Fillers. *Transactions of the Association for Computational Linguistics*, 5:117–133, 06.

Dunietz, J., Levin, L., and Carbonell, J. (2017b). The BECauSE corpus 2.0: Annotating causality and overlapping relations. In *Proceedings of the 11th Linguistic Annotation Workshop*, pages 95–104, Valencia, Spain, April. Association for Computational Linguistics.

Dunietz, J. (2018). *Annotating and Automatically Tagging Constructions of Causal Language*. Ph.D. thesis, Carnegie Mellon University.

Graff, D. (2002). *The AQUAINT Corpus of English News Text*. 09.

Gundle, K., Dingel, M., and Koenig, B. (2010). "to prove this is the industry's best hope": Big tobacco's support of research on the genetics of nicotine addiction. *Addiction*, 105(6):974–983.

Ide, N., Baker, C., Fellbaum, C., and Passonneau, R. (2010). The manually annotated sub-corpus: A community resource for and by the people. In *Proceedings of the ACL 2010 Conference Short Papers*, pages 68–73, Uppsala, Sweden, July. Association for Computational Linguistics.

Kingsbury, P. R. and Palmer, M. (2003). Propbank: the next level of treebank.

Klie, J.-C., Bugert, M., Boullosa, B., Eckart de Castilho, R., and Gurevych, I. (2018). The INCEpTION platform: Machine-assisted and knowledge-oriented interactive annotation. In *Proceedings of the 27th International Conference on Computational Linguistics: System Demonstrations*, pages 5–9, Santa Fe, New Mexico, August. Association for Computational Linguistics.

Lauer, S. and Nadathur, P. (2020). Causal necessity, causal sufficiency, and the implications of causative verbs. *Glossa: a journal of general linguistics*, 5:49–105.

Marcus, M., Kim, G., Marcinkiewicz, M. A., MacIntyre, R., Bies, A., Ferguson, M., Katz, K., and Schasberger, B. (1994). The Penn Treebank: Annotating predicate argument structure. In *Human Language Technology: Proceedings of a Workshop held at Plainsboro, New Jersey, March 8-11, 1994*.

Miltsakaki, E., Prasad, R., Joshi, A., and Webber, B. (2004). The Penn Discourse Treebank. In *Proceedings of the Fourth International Conference on Language Resources and Evaluation (LREC'04)*, Lisbon, Portugal, May. European Language Resources Association (ELRA).

Mirza, P. and Tonelli, S. (2016). CATENA: CAusal and TEmporal relation extraction from NAtural language texts. In *Proceedings of COLING 2016, the 26th International Conference on Computational Linguistics: Technical Papers*, pages 64–75, Osaka, Japan, December. The COLING 2016 Organizing Committee.

Mirza, P., Sprugnoli, R., Tonelli, S., and Speranza, M. (2014). Annotating causality in the TempEval-3 corpus. In *Proceedings of the EACL 2014 Workshop on Computational Approaches to Causality in Language (CAtoCL)*, pages 10–19, Gothenburg, Sweden, April. Association for Computational Linguistics.

Mostafazadeh, N., Chambers, N., He, X., Parikh, D., Batra, D., Vanderwende, L., Kohli, P., and Allen, J. (2016a). A corpus and cloze evaluation for deeper understanding of commonsense stories. In *Proceedings of the 2016 Conference of the North American Chapter of the Association for Computational Linguistics: Human Language Technologies*, pages 839–849, San Diego, California, June. Association for Computational Linguistics.

Mostafazadeh, N., Grealish, A., Chambers, N., Allen, J., and Vanderwende, L. (2016b). CaTeRS: Causal and temporal relation scheme for semantic annotation of event structures. In *Proceedings of the Fourth Workshop on Events*, pages 51–61, San Diego, California, June. Association for Computational Linguistics.

Palmer, M., Gildea, D., and Kingsbury, P. (2005). The Proposition Bank: An annotated corpus of semantic roles. *Computational Linguistics*, 31(1):71–106.

Pearl, J. (2009). *Causality*. Cambridge University Press, Cambridge, UK, 2 edition.

Pitler, E., Raghupathy, M., Mehta, H., Nenkova, A., Lee, A., and Joshi, A. (2008). Easily identifiable discourse relations. In *Coling 2008: Companion volume: Posters*, pages 87–90, Manchester, UK, August. Coling 2008 Organizing Committee.

Prasad, R., Miltsakaki, E., Dinesh, N., Lee, A., Joshi, A. K., Robaldo, L., and Webber, B. L. (2006). The penn discourse treebank 2.0 annotation manual.

Prasad, R., Dinesh, N., Lee, A., Miltsakaki, E., Robaldo, L., Joshi, A., and Webber, B. (2008). The Penn Discourse TreeBank 2.0. In *Proceedings of the Sixth International Conference on Language Resources and Evaluation (LREC'08)*, Marrakech, Morocco, May. European Language Resources Association (ELRA).

Prasad, R., Webber, B., Lee, A., and Joshi, A. (2019). Penn Discourse Treebank Version 3.0.

Pustejovsky, J., Verhagen, M., Saurí, R., Moszkowicz, J., Gaizauskas, R., Katz, G., Mani, I., Knippen, R., and Setzer, A. (2006). *TimeBank 1.2*. 01.

Sandhaus, E. (2008). The New York Times Annotated Corpus.

Smith, N. A., Cardie, C., Washington, A., and Wilkerson, J. (2014). Overview of the 2014 NLP unshared task in PoliInformatics. In *Proceedings of the ACL 2014 Workshop on Language Technologies and Computational Social Science*, pages 5–7, Baltimore, MD, USA, June. Association for Computational Linguistics.

UzZaman, N., Llorens, H., Allen, J., Derczynski, L., Verhagen, M., and Pustejovsky, J. (2012). Tempeval-3: Evaluating events, time expressions, and temporal relations.

Whorf, B. L. (1956). *Language, Thought, and Reality: Selected Writings of Benjamin Lee Whorf*. MIT Press.

Wolff, P. and Song, G. (2003). Models of causation and causal verbs. *Cognitive Psychology*, 47:276–332.

Wolff, P. and Thorstad, R. (2017). Force dynamics. *The Oxford handbook of causal reasoning*, pages 147–168.

Wolff, P. and Zettergren, M. (2002). A vector model of causal meaning. In *Proceedings of the twenty-fifth annual conference of the cognitive science society*. Erlbaum.

Wolff, P., Klettke, B., Ventura, T., and Song, G. (2005). Expressing causation in english and other languages.

Wolff, P. (2007). Representing causation. *Journal of experimental psychology. General*, 136:82–111, 03.

Proceedings of the 16th Linguistic Annotation Workshop (LAW-XVI) @LREC 2022, pages 160–169
Marseille, 24 June 2022

Automatic Enrichment of Abstract Meaning Representations

Yuxin Ji[†], Gregor Williamson[‡], Jinho D. Choi[‡]
Emory University
Atlanta, GA 30322, USA
† Department of Quantitative Theory and Methods
‡ Department of Computer Science
{jessica.ji, gregor.jude.williamson, jinho.choi}@emory.edu

Abstract

Abstract Meaning Representation (AMR) is a semantic graph framework which inadequately represent a number of important semantic features including number, (in)definiteness, quantifiers, and intensional contexts. Several proposals have been made to improve the representational adequacy of AMR by enriching its graph structure. However, these modifications are rarely added to existing AMR corpora due to the labor costs associated with manual annotation. In this paper, we develop an automated annotation tool which algorithmically enriches AMR graphs to better represent number, (in)definite articles, quantificational determiners, and intensional arguments. We compare our automatically produced annotations to gold-standard manual annotations and show that our automatic annotator achieves impressive results. All code for this paper, including our automatic annotation tool, is publicly available at `https://github.com/emorynlp/EnrichedAMR/`

Keywords: Abstract Meaning Representation (AMR), automatic annotation, automatic data enrichment

1. Introduction

Abstract Meaning Representation (AMR) is a semantic graph framework that represents natural language sentences in directed, acyclic graphs (Banarescu et al., 2013). Nodes represent concepts, and labeled edges represent relations between concepts (1-b). AMRs are most commonly written in PENMAN format (Matthiessen and Bateman, 1991), as shown in (1-c).

(1) a. *The boy wants the girl to believe him.*

b.

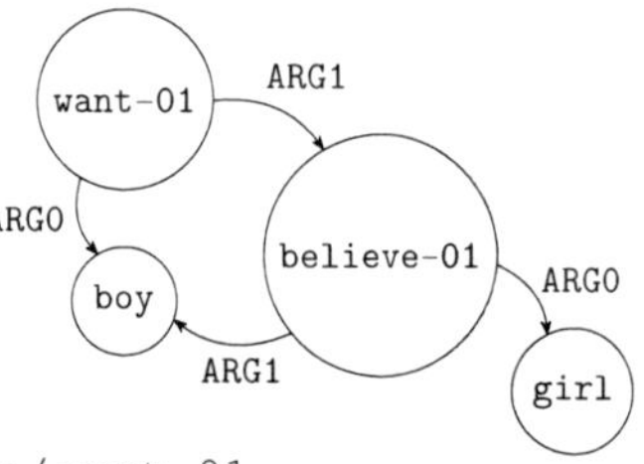

c.

```
(w / want-01
   :ARG0 (b / boy)
   :ARG1 (b2 / believe-01
      :ARG0 (g / girl)
      :ARG1 b))
```

The primary function of AMR is to capture argument structure. Features of the graph need not be anchored to grammatical features of the natural language sentence. This has the advantage of allowing succinct representation of non-compositional aspects of meaning. A major disadvantage, however, is that it can give rise to inter-annotator disagreement (Bender et al., 2015), as well as making the task of parsing harder (Buys and Blunsom, 2017; Lin and Xue, 2019; Oepen et al., 2019; Oepen et al., 2020). Moreover, evidence show that more explicit grammatical information might improve AMR parsing performance. For example, bridging the gap between natural language and AMR, via preprocessing with an Elementary Dependency Structures (EDS) (Oepen and Lønning, 2006) parser, has been shown to improve AMR parsing results (Shou and Lin, 2021).

In addition to being abstract, AMR is under-specified with respect to a number of important semantic features. A consequence of this design choice is that AMR introduces ambiguity which is absent from the source sentence. For instance, the graph depicted in (1-b)/(1-c) is also the representation for (i) *'a boy wanted girls to have believed him'*, (ii) *'the boys will want a girl to believe them'*, etc. This radical under-specification can be problematic for NLU tasks beyond identifying argument structure.

In this paper, we report results from our Automatic (enriched) AMR Annotator, A^3. In section 2, we provide a background on existing approaches to improving the expressive capacity and representational adequacy of AMR. In section 3, we outline the proposed enrichments to be made by A^3. In section 4, we describe how the automatic annotator enriches existing graph structures, starting with the base cases before discussing more challenging constructions which arise as a result of AMR's abstraction from grammatical form. In section 5 we report two annotation experiments. In the first experiment, we calculate Inter-Annotator Agreement (IAA) scores for gold-standard manual annotations, demonstrating the reliability of the enrichment scheme. In the second, we compare the output of A^3 to manually produced annotations. Section 6 provides a comprehensive analysis of error types produced by A^3. Finally, in section 7, we discuss implications of the present approach on data production, before concluding in section 8.

2. Related Work

There has been a concerted effort towards improving the representational adequacy of AMR, as well as its recent

Translation		**Richer Graph Structure**	
Artzi et al. (2015)	*(coreference)*	Bonial et al. (2018)	*(comparatives)*
Bos (2016)	*(quantifier scope)*	Donatelli et al. (2018)	*(tense and aspect)*
Stabler (2017)	*(number, determiners)*	Donatelli et al. (2019)	*(tense and aspect)*
Lai et al. (2020)	*(quantifier scope)*	Pustejovsky et al. (2019)	*(quantifier scope)*
Williamson et al. (2021)	*(Intensionality)*	Bonial et al. (2020)	*(speech acts)*
		Bos (2020)	*(quantifier scope)*
		Van Gysel et al. (2021)	*(quantifier scope)*

Table 1: Approaches to improving the representational adequacy of AMR

offspring, Uniform Meaning Representation (UMR) (Van Gysel et al., 2021). This strand of research endeavors to improve the expressive power of AMR either in terms of enriching its graphical structure (Bonial et al., 2018; Donatelli et al., 2018; Donatelli et al., 2019; Pustejovsky et al., 2019; Bonial et al., 2020; Bos, 2020; Van Gysel et al., 2021) or by adding information during a subsequent translation step into a logical form (LF) in first-order logic or lambda-calculus (Artzi et al., 2015; Bos, 2016; Stabler, 2017; Lai et al., 2020; Williamson et al., 2021). Table 1 lists the phenomena addressed in these representative works.

Both of these approaches have their own merits. On the one hand, developing a richer graph structure allows us to directly represent meaning in the AMRs. However, revision of existing resources, such as the AMR 3.0 corpus (Knight et al., 2020), is costly and time-consuming. Moreover, unless the resulting graph structure can be mapped to a coherent model theoretical semantics, the enriched graph will not be any more representationally adequate than the original structure. On the other hand, making use of a translation function with minimal revision to the graphical structure allows us to work with existing corpora after translation into symbolic logical. However, we would ultimately like to work with AMR graphs directly, avoiding the need for translation into a logical language such as lambda calculus which can often be cumbersome for the purposes of computation. For these reasons, we take enriching the graph structure to be the ultimate goal, with the caveat that the graphs should have a model-theoretic semantic interpretation with as few ad-hoc interpretation rules as possible.

Despite various theoretical works on enriching AMR's graphical structure, there are no large-scale annotated corpora which implement these design features. The gold standard AMR 3.0 corpus (Knight et al., 2020) remains the major resource for parser training and evaluation. Considering the size of the AMR 3.0 corpus and the extensive cost for manual annotation, there is a clear need for efficient automatic annotation methods to augment the pre-existing data. The challenge, therefore, is to design graph structure which is not only suitably expressive but also tractable for automatic annotation.

While some previous work has focused on classifying AMR labels for natural language sentences (Chen et al., 2021), there has been no attempt to systematically add these labels to the graph structure. Enriching AMR graphs requires additional steps in mapping the semantic features from sentence tokens to the abstract (or unanchored) graphs. The methodology of this paper is inspired by Chen et al. (2021), who introduce a rule-based classifier for labeling aspect based on the UMR guidelines. The classifier uses part-of-speech (POS) tagging and lexical frames such VerbNet (Kipper et al., 2002; Kipper, 2005). It takes a sentence and returns a list of events labeled with aspectual information. Like Chen et al. (2021), we develop a rule-based classifier. However, our classifier performs the additional step of fitting the labels onto the corresponding AMR graph.

In this paper, we focus on the representation of grammatical number (singular/plural), (in)definite articles, quantifiers, and intensional arguments, all of which can provide important quantificational and referential cues for semantic scope, coreference resolution, and natural language inference tasks.

3. Enriched Graph Structure

In this section, we outline the enriched graph structure adopted in the present study. Here, we describe simple cases for each feature, reserving discussion of exceptional cases for section 4.5.

3.1. Representation of Number

In many cases, number marking adds important information because it is the only indicator of quantity. Even for noun phrases with a quantificational determiner, plurality is often informative. For example, the two cases in (2) can be differentiated only if plurality is marked.

(2) a. *Some boys painted the wall.*
    b. *Some boy painted the wall.*

As such, plurality should ideally be represented in AMR to avoid the introduction of unwanted ambiguity. Stabler (2017) represents both plural and singular nouns by appending a marker to the corresponding concept matching the noun's grammatical number, as in (3).

(3) a. *The boy wants to go to the museums.*
    b.
```
(w / want-01
    :ARG0 (b / boy.sg)
    :ARG1 (g / go-01
        :ARG0 b
        :ARG1 (m / museum.pl)))
```

However, this exact implementation is potentially problematic for a few reasons. Firstly, it is redundant to annotate both singular and plural explicitly. Instead, we can leave singular as the unmarked form, marking only plurals. Secondly, it is not uncommon for plural nouns to be represented by a predicate sense (e.g., *'the attempts'* ⇒ `attempt-01.pl`). However, most evaluation and processing scripts will be unable to process this notation since they rely on regex patterns to detect predicate senses.

We propose instead to add number as an additional attribute introduced by a `:number` role. We also do not abbreviate the marking, to better exploit the familiarity of AMR parsers built on pre-trained language models with natural language descriptions such as `plural` as opposed to the abbreviated `.sg` and `.pl`.

(4) **Enriched AMR: Number**

a. *The boy wants to go to the museums.*

b.
```
(w / want-01
    :ARG0 (b / boy)
    :ARG1 (g / go-01
        :ARG0 b
        :ARG1 (m / museum
            :number plural)))
```

This representation is also able to represent dual number marking, present in languages such as Slovene and Hebrew, with an additional attribute `dual`.

3.2. Representation of Definiteness

Definite and indefinite articles convey information which is useful for coreference resolution. While indefinite articles occasionally express quantity information (e.g., '*They could buy everyone a house*'), definite and indefinite articles are typically referential. To avoid confounding the role of articles and quantificational determiners, we introduce a new `:definite` role with the attribute + for definite and – for indefinite articles, as in (5).

(5) **Enriched AMR: Articles**

a. *The boy gave a girl some cookies.*

b.
```
(g / give-01
    :ARG0 (b / boy
        :definite +)
    :ARG1 (c / cookie
        :quant (s / some
        :number plural))
    :ARG2 (g / girl
        :definite -))
```

3.3. Representation of Quantifiers

The majority of work on quantifiers in AMR treats them as constants as opposed to concepts (Bos, 2016; Stabler, 2017; Lai et al., 2020; Williamson et al., 2021). As such, we aim to replace quantificational arguments of a `:quant` role with a quantificational constant. It is also common in existing corpora to see quantifiers annotated using the `:mod` role, in which case we replace it with `:quant` to maintain consistency, as in (6).

(6) **Enriched AMR: Quantifiers I**

a. *Every dog*

b.
```
(d / dog
    :mod (e / every))
```

c.
```
(d / dog
    :quant every)
```

Unlike Bos (2016) and (Lai et al., 2020), we do not conflate universal quantifiers such as *every*, *all*, and *each*, as these may vary in distributivity. Information which could be useful for downstream NLI tasks.

Next, AMR represents generalized quantifiers such as *someone*, *somebody*, *something*, *everyone*, *everybody*, *everything*, *no one*, *nobody*, and *nothing* as atomic concepts (7-b). However, this representation obscures the quantificational force of these noun phrases, so we decompose them as in (7-c).

(7) **Enriched AMR: Quantifiers II**

a. *Everyone*

b.
```
(e / everyone)
```

c.
```
(p / person
    :quant every)
```

We do not take a stance on whether or how to represent quantifier scope in the AMR graph structure. Unlike with the previous semantic features, if AMRs are left underspecified for scope, no information is lost since the corresponding natural language sentence is also scopally ambiguous. Provided there is some independent mechanism of scope taking, AMR can remain underspecified for scope as in Minimal Recursion Semantics Copestake et al. (2005), Hole Semantics Blackburn and Bos (2005), or Glue Semantics Asudeh and Crouch (2002), without loss of information. The scope of quantifier phrases could either be represented in an additional scope node layer (Pustejovsky et al., 2019; Van Gysel et al., 2021) or could be generated deterministically and filtered (Stabler, 2017). This could be done either manually or by training a parser on a large scope-disambiguated corpus. Unfortunately, the several existing scope-disambiguated corpora are either too small in size for robust machine learning and are not representative of complex scope interactions (Higgins and Sadock, 2003; Andrew and MacCartney, 2004; Srinivasan and Yates, 2009; Manshadi et al., 2011), or are not yet publicly available (Bunt, 2020). In anticipation of developments on this front, our changes to the representation of quantifier phrases remains flexible.

3.4. Representation of Intensionality

Finally, Crouch and Kalouli (2018) note that AMR is unable to represent non-veridical environments. For example, the following AMR will give rise to the inferences that there is a girl, and that she is sick.

(8) a. *The boy believes a girl is sick.*

b. (b / believe-01
    :ARG0 (b2 / boy)
    :ARG1 (s / sick-05
        :ARG1 (g / girl)))

However, these inferences are not valid given the intensional nature of the attitude verb *'believe'*. To remedy this, Williamson et al. (2021) propose the addition of a :content role which is interpreted as an intensional operator responsible for representing the scope of modal predicates such as attitude verbs.

(9) $[\![\texttt{(x / P :content A)}]\!] = \lambda w. \exists x. P(x) \wedge \text{content}(x)(\lambda w'. [\![\texttt{A}]\!](w')))$

We adopt Williamson et al. (2021)'s proposal to replace numbered arguments with the :content role where appropriate.

(10) **Enriched AMR: Intensionality**

a. *The boy believes a girl is sick.*

b. (b / believe-01
    :ARG0 (b2 / boy)
    :content (s / sick-05
        :ARG1 (g / girl)))

Following the scheme just described, the sentence in (11-a) is represented as in (11-b).

(11) **Enriched AMR**

a. *A boy believes that the girls gave everyone some cookies.*

b. (b / believe-01
    :ARG0 (b2 / boy
        :definite -)
    :content (g / give-01
        :ARG1 (g2 / girl
            :definite +)
        :ARG1 (c / cookie
            :quant some
            :number plural)
        :ARG2 (p / person
            :quant every)))

4. The Automatic Annotator

Our automatic annotator, A^3 uses a combination of cues from the natural language sentence as well as its AMR in order to classify and map the target labels to the graph using the PENMAN parser (Goodman, 2020).[1] In sections 4.1-4.4, we describe the simpler cases of classification and mapping, before describing some of the numerous challenges in section 4.5.

4.1. Annotating Number

A^3 searches for tokens identified by the Stanford CoreNLP parser[2] (Manning et al., 2014) as having the plural *noun* part-of-speech (POS) tag. The plural noun is then mapped to the corresponding alignment in the AMR graph and the plural number attribute is appended to the triple. However, several abstract structures of AMR require special treatment. These are discussed in section 4.5.

4.2. Annotating Definiteness

Articles are identified through using a POS tag match. A string match for definite (*'the'*) and indefinite (*'a/an'*) articles is then used for tokens that are classified with a *DET* tag. A^3 then locates the span of head noun using the Stanford CoreNLP constituency parser (Manning et al., 2014) which was chosen due to it's performance, after experimenting with different constituency parsers including ELIT (He et al., 2021) and the Berkely Neural Parser (Kitaev and Klein, 2018). Finally, an appropriate :definite attribute is attached to the concept corresponding to the span of the head noun.

4.3. Annotating Quantifiers

The conversion for quantifiers utilize cues from the AMR graph alone and contains two steps. First, we identify quantifier concepts which are arguments of either a :quant or :mod role, before converting the quantificational concept to a constant. The second step decomposes generalized quantifiers by separating the concept and quantifier through a string match. The instance assignment for the original generalized quantifier is modified to the corresponding concept and the quantifier is attached to it as the attribute of the :quant role.

4.4. Annotating Intensionality

A^3 identifies intensionality through relevant lists of verbs and constituency structures. In most cases, appropriate uses of the :content role are identified using the MegaVeridicality dataset (White et al., 2018). Finite clauses are identified using MegaVeridicality version 1 (White and Rawlins, 2018), and non-finite clauses using version 2 (White et al., 2018). A^3 loops through the lemmatized tokens and searches for lemmas that are in the MegaVeridicality dataset. We compared the NLTK (Bird and Loper, 2004) and LemmInflect[3] lemmatizer and found that LemmInflect performs better. An intensional context is identified by checking if the matched verb is followed by a sentential complement, signified by a corresponding verb phrase constituent containing an SBAR or S label.

For speech verbs such as *'say'* or *'report'*, the sentence structure is not correctly identified by the parser when the complement clause has been fronted (e.g. *'The stock price doubled yesterday, as reported by the newspaper'*), which is not uncommon in the dataset, especially since AMR is sourced from news and broadcast data. To deal with these cases, A^3 instead looks for sentences where the verb is not followed by a noun phrase and annotates the object argument with a :content role.

[1] https://github.com/goodmami/penman

[2] https://github.com/stanfordnlp/CoreNLP

[3] https://github.com/bjascob/LemmInflect

4.5. Mapping Difficulties

Here, we list some non-canonical cases of each phenomena which are handled by A^3, but which require additional mapping instructions. We reserve discussion of cases which are not presently handled by our annotator to section 6.

4.5.1. Relational and Agentive/Patient Nouns

When enriching AMR with grammatical number and (in)definiteness, there are numerous non-trivial mapping problems posed by AMR's abstraction away from surface form. Most notably, AMR opts to express concepts using disambiguated predicate senses from PropBank (Kingsbury and Palmer, 2002) wherever possible. For instance, AMR uses a `person` concept to represent agentive nouns (12) and patient nouns (13).

(12) a. *Teacher*
b.
```
(p / person
    :ARG0-of (t / teach-01))
```

(13) a. *Employee*
b.
```
(p / person
    :ARG1-of (e / employ-01))
```

Other deverbal nouns may be represented through the use of an implicit `thing` argument.

(14) a. *An apology*
b.
```
(t / thing
    :ARG3-of (a / apologize-01))
```

Finally, AMR represents relational nouns using specialized concepts such as `have-rel-role-91` or `have-org-role-91`.

(15) a. *My uncles*
b.
```
(p / person
    :ARG0-of (h / have-rel-role-91
        :ARG1 (u / uncle)
        :ARG2 (i / i)))
```

These design choices create obvious problems for a naive mapping from grammatical features onto graph structure. In each case, we want to mark the root node of each of these (sub)-trees with a `plural` attribute, `:definite +/-` attribute, or `:quant` constant. However, the concept which most transparently corresponds to the surface string is not the root, for example *uncle* in (15-b). To solve this, A^3 tracks back through the directed edges of the sub-graph to find the root node, before marking it with the relevant attribute.

4.5.2. Name, Date, and Quantity Entities

We also observe exceptions for plural and definite markings for `name` and `date-entity` concepts, as well as `X-quantity` concepts. The `X-quantity` concept is typically introduced as a `:unit` and explicit quantity information is provided in the form of a real number. Similarly, for the case of `name` and `date-entity` concepts, the addition of a `:definite` or `:number` attribute is redundant.

(16) a. *Five dollars*
b.
```
(m / monetary-quantity
    :quant 5
    :unit (d / dollar))
```

4.5.3. Intensional Transitive Verbs

In addition to attitude predicates present in the MegaVeridicality dataset, A^3 is designed to map the numbered arguments of several Intensional Transitive Verbs (ITVs) to a `:content` role. ITVs are verbs that combine with a nominal direct object, but which do not permit an inference to the existence of the direct object in the world of evaluation (Schwarz, 2020). This can be seen in the following examples, which are semantically coherent despite the non-existence of unicorns in the actual world.

(17) *I {wanted/expected/desired/looked for} a unicorn.*

Since object arguments of ITVs are intensional regardless of whether their complement is a noun phrase or a sentential complement, A^3 converts the object argument of these predicates to a `:content` role. This mapping is defined for a non-exhaustive dictionary of the most common intensional transitive verbs (e.g. '*want*') and their intensional numbered argument as defined in their PropBank argument structure (Palmer et al., 2004).

4.5.4. Other Intensional Operators

Besides attitude predicates and ITVs, A^3 is designed to handle modal auxiliaries, modal verbs, and intensional raising predicates. Consequently, A^3 uniformly converts specific numbered arguments of modal predicate senses onto a `:content` role. These are summarized in Table 2.

Lexical item	Predicate Sense	Argument
need	`need-01`	`:ARG1`
can, might, could	`possible-01`	`:ARG1`
must (deontic)	`obligate-01`	`:ARG2`
must (epistemic)	`infer-01`	`:ARG1`
can	`capable-01`	`:ARG2`
seem	`seem-01`	`:ARG1`
allow	`allow-01`	`:ARG1`
permit	`permit-01`	`:ARG1`
should	`recommend-01`	`:ARG1`[4]

Table 2: Numbered arguments of modal concepts which are converted to `:content`.

5. Annotation Experiments

In this section, we report the methodology and results of two annotation experiments. In the first experiment, we measure Inter-Annotator Agreement (IAA) on the

[4] A^3 converts `:ARG1` of `recommend-01` to `:content` specifically when aligned with *'should'*, as this role may also used for non-intensional arguments of *'recommend'* e.g., *'I recommend this drink'*.

enrichment guidelines by doubly annotating 66 PENMAN graphs selected from the AMR 3.0 corpus. In the second experiment, we singly annotate an additional 60 graphs and compare the 126 manually annotated graphs to the output of our automatic annotation tool.

5.1. Method

To build our dataset, we first select up to 8 PENMAN graphs from each of the 12 datasets making up the (unsplit) AMR 3.0 corpus (excluding the guidelines). To ensure that the graphs contain relevant features, we restrict our dataset to graphs associated with a sentence of good-length (between 30 and 40 tokens), totalling 96 AMR graphs. We then select 30 additional graphs, from the same corpus (including the guidelines), which contain the relevant quantificational determiners or generalized quantifiers.

For the first experiment, we manually enrich 56 graphs from the good-length dataset and 10 graphs from the quantifier dataset for grammatical number, (in)definite articles, quantifiers, and the `:content` role. We compare IAA between the gold standard annotation by calculating F1 scores for the features of interest.

For the second experiment, we singly annotate the remaining 60 graphs and adjudicate among the doubly annotated graphs, creating a dataset of 126 gold-standard human annotations. We then processes the same 126 graphs using A^3 and we compare the output with our gold-standard annotations.

All annotations were carried out by the first and second authors using StreamSide[5] an open-source annotation tool for producing graph-based meaning representations (Choi and Williamson, 2021).

5.2. Manual Annotation Results

In the first experiment, two experienced annotators doubly annotate 56 graphs from our good-length dataset and a further 10 graphs from our quantifier dataset. The standard agreement metric for AMR graphs is the Smatch score of Cai and Knight (2013). However, this metric compares similarity between entire graphs. Calculating this score on our enriched graphs will give inflated scores due to the underlying similarity of the graphs used as the foundation for our annotations. Consequently, we present specific F1 scores calculated for each of the relevant features covered by the guidelines. Table 3 presents the F1 scores and the statistics for the 66 double annotations. This dataset contains around 1.7 grammatical number and article each per graph and one quantifier and intensional role per 2-3 graphs. The F1 scores range from 90.05 for (in)definite articles to 97.35 for the marking of plurals, demonstrating the robustness of our annotation guidelines for human annotation. The IAA for intensionality is surprisingly high (91.43) given the increased difficulty associated with correctly identifying intensional contexts. Unlike with number, articles, and quantifiers, there are a wide range of lexical items responsible for introducing a `:content` argument, as attitude predicates are a relatively open-class.

Task	F1	Count	Per-Annotation
Number	97.35	114	1.73
Articles	90.05	113	1.71
Quantifiers	95.45	20	0.30
Intensionality	91.43	53	0.80
All	93.52	300	4.55

Table 3: Inter-annotator agreement and count of enrichment types in the 66 doubly annotated AMR graphs.

5.3. Automatic Annotation Results

In the second experiment, we compare the output of the automatic annotator, A^3, to 126 singly annotated gold-standard annotations. Average count per annotation for each feature is provided in Table 4. The frequent occurrence of these semantic features highlight the need for representing them in meaning representations.

Task	Count	Per-Annotation
Number (Plural)	173	1.37
Articles	214	1.70
Quantifiers	41	0.33
Intensionality	102	0.81
All	530	4.21

Table 4: Count of enrichment types in the 126 gold-standard annotations.

Table 5 presents the precision, recall, and F1 scores for the automatic annotator.

Task	FP	FN	Precision	Recall	F1
Number	14	17	91.76	90.17	90.96
Articles	8	34	95.72	84.04	89.50
Quantifiers	2	2	96.00	96.00	96.00
Intensionality	15	24	84.54	77.36	80.79
All	39	77	92.26	85.79	88.91

Table 5: The performance of A^3 on 126 gold standard AMR graphs.

For the 173 plurals identified in the gold annotations, A^3 failed to identify 17 of them. It also labeled 14 extra cases with plural that are not marked in the gold annotations, yielding an F1 of 90.96. The sources of error originated mostly from incorrect alignment information and the parser's failure to identify the correct POS tags (see Table 6 in section 6). The F1 score for articles is 89.50, with high precision (95.72) and lower recall (84.04). A^3 failed to attach 34 out of the 214 (in)definite articles to the AMR graph and inserted 8 additional articles. Potential causes for the false negatives include failure to identify the correct head noun, incorrect alignment of the head noun, missing alignment of the head noun that disables attachment of articles, as well as incorrect article location due to mapping problems mentioned in

[5] https://github.com/emorynlp/StreamSide

section 4.5. The performance for quantifiers is the best among the features and scores highly for both precision and recall. Finally, A^3 achieves an F1 score of 80.79 for intensionality. While this score is lower than that of the other features, it is nonetheless quite high considering the degree of complexity of this classification task. Overall, the results demonstrate the efficacy of A^3 in enriching AMR graphs for the targeted features.

6. Analysis of Errors

In this section, we report on the errors made by A^3. These limitations stem from a number of issues. Among them are: imperfect annotation or alignment, limitations of the parsers, abstractness of the AMR graph, non-canonical or ungrammatical syntax, discrepancies between annotator judgements and the verb list, and inadequacies of certain PropBank argument structures. A percentage of error types made by A^3 is provided in Table 6, with specific examples provided in the text.

Limitations of the POS tagger caused A^3 to occasionally fail to label irregular plurals. For example, the tool correctly marks `person` for plural when aligned with *people*, but it fails to mark `phenomenon` for plural when aligned with *phenomena*. Moreover, *mathematics* is marked as plural by the automatic annotator even though it is associated with the concept `mathematics`. Lastly, the POS tagger fails to identify the head noun in *'the welfare rolls'* since *'rolls'* is treated as a verb instead of a plural noun.

The constituency parser struggles with dialogue when it features an interruption with a filler word, such as *'umm'* or *'err'*, producing a disjoint constituency tree. It may also struggle to correctly resolve syntactically ambiguous sentences. Lastly, there are a number of ungrammatical sentences in the dataset (e.g., *'For the time before everything is officially opened, opened, all , no cars can enter unless they have special permission'*) which lead to parsing errors.

The abstract and un-anchored nature of AMR can sometimes present difficulties for A^3 to map tokens to the corresponding concepts in the graph. For instance, *'according to'* is represented with the predicate `say-01` in AMR due to their similarity in meaning, though the token *'say'* does not appear anywhere in the sentence. Another example occurs with the noun phrase *'two men, deadly enemies to each other'* which is represented with two separate `man` concepts and thus should not be marked as plural in the graph.

Another source of error is discrepancies between the MegaVeridicality dataset and human annotator judgments about whether to mark an argument as intensional. For instance, the MegaVereridicality dataset contains some aspectual verbs which are not intensional such as *'continue'*.

Finally, certain ITVs have overloaded predicate senses in PropBank. For example, the ITV *'look for'* has an intensional object position which is annotated as `:ARG1` of `look-01`. However, the same numbered argument is used to annotate the non-intensional object argument of *'look at'*, as shown in the description tag of its PropBank argument structure (18).

(18)
```
look.01
  <role descr="thing looked at
   or for or on" f="gol" n="1">
```

7. Discussion

While the agreement scores of A^3 are impressive, there is nonetheless a gap in quality between the annotation tool's output and our manual annotations. Nevertheless, we expect this gap to inevitably shrink with the development of better parsers, and several of the remaining problems can be solved through the production of handwritten mapping dictionaries, similar to the ones we created for modal auxiliaries and common ITVs but at a larger scale.

Given its baseline performance A^3 can already be used to enrich a large number of graphs, which can then be quality checked by trained human annotators. This semi-automated approach affords a means of producing gold-standard meaning representations at a rate which far surpasses creating manual annotations from scratch (Oepen and Lønning, 2006; Abzianidze et al., 2017; Abzianidze and Bos, 2019).

8. Conclusion

Recent work on improving the representational adequacy of AMR has focused on enriching its graph structure. In this paper, we presented an automatic AMR annotation tool, A^3, designed to enrich AMR graphs to better represent a number of important semantic features including number, (in)indefiniteness, quantificational determiners, and intensional arguments. This task involves correctly identifying an appropriate label, before mapping it onto an existing AMR graph. This task is often non-trivial due to the abstract, or un-anchored, nature of AMR graphs. Our tool thus utilizes a number of cues provided by several state of the art parsers.

To demonstrate the effectiveness of the enrichment scheme as well as that of A^3, we presented two annotation experiments. The first involves manually producing doubly annotated graphs which are enriched for the semantic features mentioned above. IAA was calculated for specific labels, showing a high rate of agreement. Secondly, we compared the output of A^3 to gold-standard manual annotations. The F1 scores of the automatic annotator are close to that of human annotators except when identifying intensional arguments which is by far the hardest classification task. It is our hope that the present paper encourages further efforts to automatically augment existing AMR corpora, with the aim of producing large corpora of representationally adequate Abstract Meaning Representations. All code for this paper is publicly available on our repository at `https://github.com/emorynlp/EnrichedAMR/`.

Source of Error	Plural	Article	Quantifier	Intensionality
Incorrect or missing alignment	32.26%	19.05%		2.56%
POS tagger fails to identify correct tag	48.39%	16.67%		
Constituency parser error		50.00%		33.33%
Ambiguous/ungrammatical syntax			25.00%	
Abstractness of AMR graph	19.35%	14.28%	75.00%	30.77%
Verb list discrepancies				23.08%
Overloaded predicate sense for ITV				10.26%
Total	100%	100%	100%	100%

Table 6: Percentages of error types made by A^3

9. Acknowledgements

We gratefully acknowledge the support of the Amazon Alexa AI grant. Any opinions, findings, and conclusions or recommendations expressed in this material are those of the authors and do not necessarily reflect the views of the Alexa AI.

10. Bibliographical References

Abzianidze, L. and Bos, J. (2019). Thirty musts for meaning banking. In *Proceedings of the First International Workshop on Designing Meaning Representations*, pages 15–27, Florence, Italy, August. Association for Computational Linguistics.

Abzianidze, L., Bjerva, J., Evang, K., Haagsma, H., van Noord, R., Ludmann, P., Nguyen, D.-D., and Bos, J. (2017). The Parallel Meaning Bank: Towards a multilingual corpus of translations annotated with compositional meaning representations. In *Proceedings of the 15th Conference of the European Chapter of the Association for Computational Linguistics: Volume 2, Short Papers*, pages 242–247, Valencia, Spain, April. Association for Computational Linguistics.

Andrew, G. and MacCartney, B. (2004). Statistical resolution of scope ambiguity in natural language. *Unpublished manuscript.*

Artzi, Y., Lee, K., and Zettlemoyer, L. (2015). Broad-coverage CCG semantic parsing with AMR. In *Proceedings of the 2015 Conference on Empirical Methods in Natural Language Processing*, pages 1699–1710, Lisbon, Portugal, September. Association for Computational Linguistics.

Asudeh, A. and Crouch, R. (2002). Glue semantics for hpsg. In *Proceedings of the 8th international HPSG conference, Stanford, CA. CSLI Publications.*

Banarescu, L., Bonial, C., Cai, S., Georgescu, M., Griffitt, K., Hermjakob, U., Knight, K., Koehn, P., Palmer, M., and Schneider, N. (2013). Abstract Meaning Representation for sembanking. In *Proceedings of the 7th Linguistic Annotation Workshop and Interoperability with Discourse*, pages 178–186, Sofia, Bulgaria, August. Association for Computational Linguistics.

Bender, E. M., Flickinger, D., Oepen, S., Packard, W., and Copestake, A. (2015). Layers of interpretation: On grammar and compositionality. In *Proceedings of the 11th International Conference on Computational Semantics*, pages 239–249, London, UK, April. Association for Computational Linguistics.

Bird, S. and Loper, E. (2004). Nltk: The natural language toolkit. In *Proceedings of the ACL Interactive Poster and Demonstration Sessions*, pages 214–217.

Blackburn, P. and Bos, J. (2005). *Representation and inference for natural language: A first course in computational semantics.* Center for the Study of Language and Information Amsterdam.

Bonial, C., Badarau, B., Griffitt, K., Hermjakob, U., Knight, K., O'Gorman, T., Palmer, M., and Schneider, N. (2018). Abstract Meaning Representation of constructions: The more we include, the better the representation. In *Proceedings of the Eleventh International Conference on Language Resources and Evaluation (LREC 2018)*, Miyazaki, Japan, May. European Language Resources Association (ELRA).

Bonial, C., Donatelli, L., Abrams, M., Lukin, S. M., Tratz, S., Marge, M., Artstein, R., Traum, D., and Voss, C. (2020). Dialogue-AMR: Abstract Meaning Representation for dialogue. In *Proceedings of the 12th Language Resources and Evaluation Conference*, pages 684–695, Marseille, France, May. European Language Resources Association.

Bos, J. (2016). Squib: Expressive power of Abstract Meaning Representations. *Computational Linguistics*, 42(3):527–535, September.

Bos, J. (2020). Separating argument structure from logical structure in AMR. In *Proceedings of the Second International Workshop on Designing Meaning Representations*, pages 13–20, Barcelona Spain (online), December. Association for Computational Linguistics.

Bunt, H. (2020). Annotation of quantification: The current state of ISO 24617-12. In *16th Joint ACL - ISO Workshop on Interoperable Semantic Annotation PROCEEDINGS*, pages 1–12, Marseille, May. European Language Resources Association.

Buys, J. and Blunsom, P. (2017). Robust incremental neural semantic graph parsing. In *Proceedings of the 55th Annual Meeting of the Association for Computational Linguistics (Volume 1: Long Papers)*, pages 1215–1226, Vancouver, Canada, July. Association for Computational Linguistics.

Cai, S. and Knight, K. (2013). Smatch: an evaluation metric for semantic feature structures. In *Proceedings of the 51st Annual Meeting of the Association for Computational Linguistics (Volume 2: Short Papers)*, pages 748–752, Sofia, Bulgaria, August. Association for Computational Linguistics.

Chen, D., Palmer, M., and Vigus, M. (2021). AutoAspect: Automatic annotation of tense and aspect for uniform meaning representations. In *Proceedings of The Joint 15th Linguistic Annotation Workshop (LAW) and 3rd Designing Meaning Representations (DMR) Workshop*, pages 36–45, Punta Cana, Dominican Republic, November 11. Association for Computational Linguistics.

Choi, J. D. and Williamson, G. (2021). Streamside: A fully-customizable open-source toolkit for efficient annotation of meaning representations.

Copestake, A., Flickinger, D., Pollard, C., and Sag, I. A. (2005). Minimal recursion semantics: An introduction. *Research on language and computation*, 3(2):281–332.

Crouch, R. and Kalouli, A.-L. (2018). Named graphs for semantic representation. In *Proceedings of the Seventh Joint Conference on Lexical and Computational Semantics*, pages 113–118, New Orleans, Louisiana. Association for Computational Linguistics.

Donatelli, L., Regan, M., Croft, W., and Schneider, N. (2018). Annotation of tense and aspect semantics for sentential AMR. In *Proceedings of the Joint Workshop on Linguistic Annotation, Multiword Expressions and Constructions (LAW-MWE-CxG-2018)*, pages 96–108, Santa Fe, New Mexico, USA, August. Association for Computational Linguistics.

Donatelli, L., Schneider, N., Croft, W., and Regan, M. (2019). Tense and aspect semantics for sentential AMR. *Proceedings of the Society for Computation in Linguistics*, 2(1):346–348.

Goodman, M. W. (2020). Penman: An open-source library and tool for AMR graphs. In *Proceedings of the 58th Annual Meeting of the Association for Computational Linguistics: System Demonstrations*, pages 312–319, Online, July. Association for Computational Linguistics.

He, H., Xu, L., and Choi, J. D. (2021). ELIT: Emory Language and Information Toolkit. *arXiv*, 2109.03903.

Higgins, D. and Sadock, J. M. (2003). A machine learning approach to modeling scope preferences. *Computational Linguistics*, 29(1):73–96.

Kingsbury, P. R. and Palmer, M. (2002). From treebank to propbank. In *LREC*, pages 1989–1993. Citeseer.

Kipper, K., Palmer, M., and Rambow, O. (2002). Extending PropBank with VerbNet Semantic Predicates. In *Proceedings of the AMTA Workshop on Applied Interlinguas*.

Kipper, K. (2005). Verbnet: A Broad-Coverage, Comprehensive Verb Lexicon. Master's thesis, University of Pennsylvania.

Kitaev, N. and Klein, D. (2018). Constituency parsing with a self-attentive encoder. In *Proceedings of the 56th Annual Meeting of the Association for Computational Linguistics (Volume 1: Long Papers)*, pages 2676–2686.

Lai, K., Donatelli, L., and Pustejovsky, J. (2020). A continuation semantics for Abstract Meaning Representation. In *Proceedings of the Second International Workshop on Designing Meaning Representations*, pages 1–12, Barcelona Spain (online), December. Association for Computational Linguistics.

Lin, Z. and Xue, N. (2019). Parsing meaning representations: Is easier always better? In *Proceedings of the First International Workshop on Designing Meaning Representations*, pages 34–43, Florence, Italy, August. Association for Computational Linguistics.

Manning, C. D., Surdeanu, M., Bauer, J., Finkel, J. R., Bethard, S., and McClosky, D. (2014). The stanford corenlp natural language processing toolkit. In *Proceedings of 52nd annual meeting of the association for computational linguistics: system demonstrations*, pages 55–60.

Manshadi, M., Allen, J., and Swift, M. (2011). A corpus of scope-disambiguated English text. In *Proceedings of the 49th Annual Meeting of the Association for Computational Linguistics: Human Language Technologies*, pages 141–146, Portland, Oregon, USA, June. Association for Computational Linguistics.

Matthiessen, C. M. I. M. and Bateman, J. A. (1991). *Text generation and systemic-functional linguistics: experiences from English and Japanese*. Pinter.

Oepen, S. and Lønning, J. T. (2006). Discriminant-based MRS banking. In *Proceedings of the Fifth International Conference on Language Resources and Evaluation (LREC'06)*, Genoa, Italy, May. European Language Resources Association (ELRA).

Oepen, S., Abend, O., Hajic, J., Hershcovich, D., Kuhlmann, M., O'Gorman, T., Xue, N., Chun, J., Straka, M., and Uresova, Z. (2019). MRP 2019: Cross-framework meaning representation parsing. In *Proceedings of the Shared Task on Cross-Framework Meaning Representation Parsing at the 2019 Conference on Natural Language Learning*, pages 1–27, Hong Kong, November. Association for Computational Linguistics.

Oepen, S., Abend, O., Abzianidze, L., Bos, J., Hajic, J., Hershcovich, D., Li, B., O'Gorman, T., Xue, N., and Zeman, D. (2020). MRP 2020: The second shared task on cross-framework and cross-lingual meaning representation parsing. In *Proceedings of the CoNLL 2020 Shared Task: Cross-Framework Meaning Representation Parsing*, pages 1–22, Online, November. Association for Computational Linguistics.

Pustejovsky, J., Lai, K., and Xue, N. (2019). Modeling quantification and scope in Abstract Meaning Representations. In *Proceedings of the First International*

Workshop on Designing Meaning Representations, pages 28–33, Florence, Italy, August. Association for Computational Linguistics.

Schwarz, F. (2020). Intensional transitive verbs: I owe you a horse. *The Wiley Blackwell Companion to Semantics*, pages 1–33.

Shou, Z. and Lin, F. (2021). Incorporating eds graph for amr parsing. In *Proceedings of* SEM 2021: The Tenth Joint Conference on Lexical and Computational Semantics*, pages 202–211.

Srinivasan, P. and Yates, A. (2009). Quantifier scope disambiguation using extracted pragmatic knowledge: Preliminary results. In *Proceedings of the 2009 conference on empirical methods in natural language processing*, pages 1465–1474.

Stabler, E. (2017). Reforming AMR. *International Conference on Formal Grammar*, pages 72–87.

Van Gysel, J. E., Vigus, M., Chun, J., Lai, K., Moeller, S., Yao, J., O'Gorman, T., Cowell, A., Croft, W., Huang, C.-R., et al. (2021). Designing a uniform meaning representation for natural language processing. *KI-Künstliche Intelligenz*, pages 1–18.

White, A. S. and Rawlins, K. (2018). The role of veridicality and factivity in clause selection. In *Proceedings of the 48th Annual Meeting of the North East Linguistic Society*, pages 221–234.

White, A. S., Rudinger, R., Rawlins, K., and Van Durme, B. (2018). Lexicosyntactic inference in neural models. *arXiv preprint arXiv:1808.06232*.

Williamson, G., Elliott, P., and Ji, Y. (2021). Intensionalizing Abstract Meaning Representations: Non-veridicality and scope. In *Proceedings of The Joint 15th Linguistic Annotation Workshop (LAW) and 3rd Designing Meaning Representations (DMR) Workshop*, pages 160–169, Punta Cana, Dominican Republic, November 11. Association for Computational Linguistics.

11. Language Resource References

Knight et al. (2020). *Abstract Meaning Representation (AMR) Annotation Release 3.0.* distributed via Linguistic Data Consortium, ISLRN 676-697-177-821-8.

Palmer et al. (2004). *Proposition Bank (PropBank) I.* distributed via Linguistic Data Consortium, ISLRN 874-058-423-080-1.

White et al. (2018). *The MegaVeridicality Dataset.* available at: `http://megaattitude.io/projects/mega-veridicality/`.

Proceedings of the 16th Linguistic Annotation Workshop (LAW-XVI) @LREC 2022, pages 170–181
Marseille, 24 June 2022

GRAIL—A Generalized Representation and Aggregation of Information Layers

Sameer Pradhan[1,4] **and Mark Liberman**[1,2,3]
[1]Linguistic Data Consortium,
[2]Department of Linguistics,
[3]Department of Computer Science,
University of Pennsylvania, Philadelphia, USA
[4]`cemantix.org`
`spradhan@` $\frac{\texttt{upenn.edu}}{\texttt{cemantix.org}}$

Abstract

This paper identifies novel characteristics necessary to successfully represent, search, and modify natural language information shared simultaneously across multiple modalities such as text, speech, image, video, etc. We propose a multi-tiered system that implements these characteristics centered around a declarative configuration. The system facilitates easy incremental extension by allowing the creation of composable workflows of loosely coupled components, or plugins. This will allow simple initial systems to be extended to accommodate rich representations while providing mechanisms for maintaining high data integrity. Key to this is leveraging established tools and technologies. We demonstrate using a small example.

Keywords: Annotation, Representation, Corpora, Framework

1. Introduction

In this paper, we propose a novel representation that is capable of addressing some frequent use cases that arise during the manipulation of data and annotations spanning multiple modalities. To the best of our knowledge, none of the existing systems are capable of gracefully addressing them. The proposed approach is capable of handling multiple modalities of information. However, for the purposes of this article, we will restrict ourselves to areas of research that deal with three modalities: i) Natural Language Processing (NLP) (a.k.a. Computational Linguistics (CL)); ii) Automatic Speech Recognition (ASR); iii) Computer Vision (CV). A fortunate side-effect of neural network methods is an exponential growth in research on multimodal data across various disciplines (Ramachandram and Taylor, 2017). In addition, the availability of large datasets, and fast GPUs has made it possible for an individual without explicit linguistic, acoustic, image processing, or other forms of knowledge, to assemble a system demonstrating state of the art performance across a wide array of "understanding" tasks. However, all these advances have not (yet) made redundant the need for some level of task-specific supervision. Such supervision is typically provided through a combination of gold standard and predicted annotation layers. Over the past two or three decades, each community has made significant progress in terms of the tools and representations that allow the capture of multiple layers of annotations *within* their subdomain. However, the problem identified by Bird and Liberman (2001), the lack of standards to guarantee interoperable representations across the input signals and associated annotation remains *largely unsolved*.

Many existing tools and methods tend to be fragmented and brittle. Small changes in the information aggregate can impose a substantial toll on orchestrating the harmony across multiple annotation layers. The typical approach for addressing this disconnect is an *ad-hoc* manipulation of information (either content or annotations) at a stage lying somewhere *after* it is captured and *before* being used for training; or pre-processing information *before* the application of trained models to unseen cases in order to ensure maximum compatibility with the assumptions made during training.

We start by reviewing the state of frameworks in Section 2. In Section 3 we look at the collection of serializations that have been proposed over the years with a quick look at the available tooling in Section 4 before presenting the need for a generalized architecture in Section 5, followed by details of the architecture in Section 6 with a Subsection 6.3 demonstrating some core capabilities using concrete use case. We conclude in Section 7.

2. State of Frameworks

Over time many types of annotations have been created within as well as across the three modalities. While some layers of annotations can be independent of others, they typically tend to be interdependent. These dependencies can range from very simple to very complex. Many annotation frameworks[1] have been proposed over the years to enable the capture, storage and manipulation of this information aggregate. Due to space limitation, we will highlight only some of them[2]. Following are a few notable frameworks de-

[1]A framework is a collection of (software) tools, libraries and methodologies to help manage the data and annotations.

[2]For a more detailed information on the evolution of various frameworks, the reader can refer to the Handbook of Lin-

veloped over the past two decades:

- **ATLAS**: A Flexible and Extensible Architecture Linguistic Annotations (Bird et al., 2000; Bird and Liberman, 2001; Maeda et al., 2006)
- **GATE**: General Architecture for Text Engineering (Cunningham, 2002)
- **UIMA**: Unstructured Information Management Architecture (Ferrucci and Lally, 2004)
- **LAF**: The Linguistic Annotation Framework: A Standard for Annotation Interchange and Merging (Ide and Suderman, 2014)
- **ELAN**: A Professional Framework for Multimodality Research (Wittenburg et al., 2006)
- **EMU**: Advanced Speech Database Management and Analysis (Winkelmann and Raess, 2014; Winkelmann et al., 2017; Jochim, 2017)
- **ANNIS**; Complex Multilevel Annotations in a Linguistic Database (Dipper et al., 2004; Götze and Dipper, 2006; Zeldes et al., 2009; Rosenfeld, 2010; Zipser et al., 2015; Krause and Zeldes, 2016)

GATE was probably one of the first comprehensive suite of tools that could be used to annotate and tag linguistic information on text. It was created during the heyday of the Java programming language. The GATE ecosystem has evolved over time and is currently being overhauled to use cloud architecture. Unfortunately, the new version is not available for testing yet.

As for UIMA, its strong coupling with the Java programming language has had a severely negative impact on its user base as Python has emerged as the language of choice for most popular frameworks across NLP, speech and video. The underlying Common Annotation Structure (CAS) which claimed to address various interoperability issues through the creation of a type system did not live up to the hype.

The Linguistic Annotation Framework (which includes GrAF) is designed with the assumption that all annotations should be represented as graphs and manipulated using various graph algorithms of minimization, transduction, etc. LAF (and GrAF) framework is not being actively developed but is being adopted by the Text-Fabric[3] that is using it for curating corpora of ancient texts.

ANNIS, in combination with PAULA XML and Salt-NPepper has an active, large community. The Salt-NPepper modules play a similar role in the ANNIS framework—somewhat akin to the role SQL plays in the database landscape. It handles multiple modalities using a *pluriverse* approach where multiple disparate layers of different annotations and variations within annotation schemata for similar phenomena.

One other notable example is the OntoNotes corpus (Weischedel et al., 2011) which used a relational data model (Pradhan et al., 2007), to capture inter- and intra- layer connections and delegated constraint checks to its ACID[4] conformant engine. Individual layers of annotations were independently serialized in separate files with minimum inter-layer data coupling (Pradhan and Ramshaw, 2017). Unfortunately, it did not see adoption outside the project itself. Recent introduction of data versioning systems (DVS) and the use of Data Frames for representing such information, seem to reinforce the importance of an underlying relational data model.

guistic Annotation (Ide and Pustejovsky, 2017)

[3]https://github.com/annotation/text-fabric

3. State of Representations

In the previous section we looked at some annotation frameworks. Over the years, there have been large scale initiatives such as the Text Encoding Initiative (TEI) (Ide and Véronis, 1995) and international standardization efforts such as the ISO TC37 SC4. The NLP community has seen numerous annotation formats over the years, with the general consensus that they are best represented using some graph formalism. The requirements of such formats can vary quite a bit depending on whether it is being used during the creation of complex annotations or whether a stable version of this is used for training machine learning models, or for purposes of teaching. In the first case where the users are creators of some complex set of annotation, it is important to have a rich set of tools and representations to address the issues that creep over a lifetime of an annotation project, such as evolution in guidelines which can necessitate retroactive updates to annotations in order to create a consistent body of annotations. On the other hand, (typically read-only) consumers of annotations don't need to understand or deal with data complexities that don't impact its use. We cannot cover a complete history of work in this area, but will discuss a few notable cases.

- **The LAF, GrAF, TCF and LIF family**—The Linguistic Annotation Format (LAF) (Ide and Romary, 2004) and its successor—Graph Annotation Format (GrAF) (Ide and Suderman, 2007) primarily used XML.
- **NXT**—Short for NITE XML Toolkit (Calhoun et al., 2010; Carletta et al., 2005), where NITE stands for Natural Interactivity Tools Engineering, is a multi-level, cross-level and cross-modality annotation representation, retrieval and exploitation of multi-party natural interactive human-human and human-machine dialogue data.
- **EAF**—ELAN Annotation Format (EAF), is an XML based data serialization format is part of a larger Abstract Corpus Model[5] (ACM).
- **AG**—This is the annotation graph XML format used by various tools to create and manipulate in-

[4]In computer science, ACID (atomicity, consistency, isolation, durability) is a set of properties of database transactions intended to guarantee data validity despite errors, power failures, and other mishaps.

[5]http://emeld.org/workshop/2003/brugman-paper.html

ternally to store various corpora by the Linguistic Data Consortium which are typically released as simpler representations.

- **TextGrid**—This is the underlying format for files created and used by the Praat tool[6] (Boersma and others, 2014)—probably the most popular tool used by researchers and students for the study of computational phonetics.
- **CHAT**—This is the serialization used by the CLAN programs that have evolved over the years as part of the CHILDES project (MacWhinney, 2014) which has grown to become a larger collection—the TalkBank. This also has a task specific nature.
- **The CoNLL-* family**—The Computational Natural Language Learning (CoNLL) shared tasks initiated a culture of yearly international evaluations, starting in 2002, to promote consistent and replicable research. The initial data representation was in the form of a space (or, tab) separated table of columns one of which being the words and the other being a sequence of labels that identified various annotation classes such as base phrases, named entities, etc. Each year, a new task *typically* added one or more columns to this table creating what came to be widely recognized as CoNLL (column) format.

  The Universal Dependencies effort (De Marneffe et al., 2021) started as a project for representing dependencies across many languages in a consistent fashion. This group embellished the CoNLL format, starting with version that represented dependency trees, and gave it a new moniker CoNLL-U (Universal). The Universal Dependencies effort has spawned off-shoots in coreference, morphological layers, named entities, etc. and has become the consumer favorite. Notable *extensions* to this are CoNLL-UA (Universal Anaphora) and CoNLL-UP (Universal Propositions). There have been recent updates to this format to allow the injection of useful metadata.
- **Symbolic Expressions**—One of the oldest, large scale and successful annotation projects—The Penn Treebank (Marcus et al., 1993) used Lisp-like symbolic expressions (S-Expressions or `sexp`) to represent syntax trees. A variation of such formalism called the PENMAN (Kasper, 1989) notation was used for defining the Suggested Upper Merged Ontology (SUMO) (Bateman, 1990; Bateman et al., 1990). This has seen a recent revival in the Abstract Meaning Representation (AMR) project (Banarescu et al., 2013).

We can see that over the years many task agnostic formats were based on a larger ecosystem of serialization technologies such as XML, and have recently seen some evolution to use JSON, as a result of the growth and significance of the world wide web. Two of these formats—TextGrid and CHAT—addressed specific tasks in the humanities discipline. They were not designed to be extensible which led to some backwards incompatibilities. Also since they don't have a formal grammar, it is harder to write tools to manipulate them. Finally, somewhat surprisingly, defying all principles of database theory, the CoNLL family of formats, which are essentially a collection of single *unnormalized*, tables of data, has become the most widely used format by most NLP researchers. And we are seeing some resurgence in the use of symbolic-expressions to represent rich graph structures.

The data formats for storing binary data such as audio and video signals is a completely different branch that has seen various proprietary and open source standardizations somewhat akin to the evolution of the Unicode standard for text. Most of the annotation formats that deal with audio and video information use offsets into this data typically as time points/intervals possibly along with a spatial specification commonly in the form of a pair of coordinates bounding box (or, bounding rectangle) for two dimensional signals which are the most commonly used ones[7].

4. State of Tooling

Although we are going to focus on *architecture* in this article, it is very important to acknowledge the fact that availability of *right tools* and *libraries* plays a crucial role in minimizing the inertia in its adoption and evolution. Unfortunately, creation of novel architectures and toolings is also one of the least funded areas[8]. For a very recent and thorough survey of of tools that are available for various document annotation phenomena we refer the reader to Neves and Seva (2021). They list some 60 tools and thoroughly evaluate 15 of them using 26 criteria that cover multiple aspects of the annotation and tooling requirements. It is evident that many tools have been moving to use the web and cloud based architectures but are mostly centered on a graphical user interface. One tool—SLATE- (Kummerfeld, 2019)–that stands out from others by catering to a niche user base—*an expert*—someone who prefers a command line interface.

5. Case for a Generalized Architecture

It would be helpful to reiterate that one of the important lessons that the community–specifically the ones evolving a science of annotation–has learned over the past couple of decades is that the most robust abstract representation of a many different kinds of (or, layers of) annotations has roots in a graph formalism. The LAF framework attempts at a representation that can capture conflicting variations in annotation schemas for

[6] `https://praat.org`

[7] The discussion of three dimensional signals such as lidar data used for autonomous driving is beyond the scope of this discussion.

[8] We can only speak from experience in the area of tooling in natural language processing research

a given layer of annotation—the classic example being that of difference in word segmentation across guidelines. They propose a way forward for merging across layers with such variations through the use of *dummy nodes* that can be resolved in multiple ways while reading or serializing a specific version. The LAF architecture, however, only deals with text sources. Chiarcos et al. (2012) provide an elaborate discussion on the potential complexities introduced by minor differences in representational decisions made by individual annotation schemas in a multi-layered annotation corpus. They provide an algorithm for merging annotations using the case of conflicting token representations across such layers. The problem gets further complicated when the notion of temporal intervals is introduced as described in the ExMARaLDA effort (Schmidt, 2004). Both these efforts address special case of a class of problems that are expected to multiply with the addition of additional modalities such as speech signals that are a function of time; and visual information which adds a spatial dimension to the mix. The algorithms presented in these are engineered for many such eventualities on an as-needed basis. This approach is likely to prove prohibitive in the long run. Most approaches poorly address the need for capturing metadata associated with the data itself.

Using *declarative constraint specifications*, for example, an *interval algebra* in the temporal domain, or using constraints on transformation of *graphic primitives* in a spatial domain, could allow one to generalize the solutions at a higher level of abstraction which could allow the creation of a class of solutions that would reasonably manage a potential explosion of checks across possible constraint violations. Furthermore leveraging developments in *version control* and *fully persistent data structures* (Driscoll et al., 1989) and *conflict-free replicated data types* (Preguiça, 2018) which have standard implementations in many languages that are very efficient in time and space could allow room for better integration across schema evolutions. One other issue with the existing frameworks is their typically monolithic nature that results in a steep learning curve. An architecture that attempts to decompose the typical domains into smaller sub-domains can facilitate selective and *incremental adoption* by end users and also allow for creation of flexible extensions to address edge cases specific to a particular sub-domain.

6. Proposed Architecture

A way to handle various slices of the representations, maybe even an individual layers locally while still allowing global consistency guarantees could substantially relive the cognitive load on the user, or in other words could go a long way in managing the *incidental* and *accidental complexities* of the tooling, which would be even more important given the significant *essential* complexities arising from the integration across multiple modalities.

The architecture we propose here does claim to be a new invention. Rather our design approach can be compared with the evolution of the concept of the *blockchain*, which as detailed by Narayanan (2017) is a careful selection and assembling of a collection of conceptual and technological innovations that happened over the past fifty some years. The UNIX operating system designers made a very similar claim[9] (Ritchie and Thompson, 1974). We have identified existing tools, technologies and propose to follow well established design principles such as, for example, *separation of concerns*, the liberal use of *open/closed principle*, and a decomposition of the domain into modules that can be composed together in various declarative configurations, as opposed to a monolithic design.

6.1. Design Requirements

All the design requirements that we will discuss are assumed to operate over a corpus with the following general characteristic of the underlying data and annotations:

- Multiple layers of span-*ed* or span-*less*[10]; time-*ed* or time-*less*[11]; annotations
- Multiple media types and encodings
- Different annotation guidelines
- Produced using different tools

6.1.1. Functional Requirements

Here we list some functional requirements that the formalism absolutely has to satisfy.

- **Selective Disassembly and Reassembly**—This is an important requirement that we address in our architecture as the example we discuss later will highlight.
- **Structured Querying Capability**—One should be able to perform structured queries spanning media and layers.
- **Ensure Synchronization after Modifications to Layer(s)**—For example, it should be *reasonably easy* to propagate changes in one layer to other layers while maintaining certain core constraints,

[9]"The success of UNIX lies not so much in new inventions but rather in the full exploitation of a carefully selected set of fertile ideas, and especially in showing that they can be keys to the implementation of a small yet powerful operating system."—Ritchie and Thomson (1974)

[10]A span-*ed* annotation is one that is associated with a specific text span. Named-entities, base phrases, sentences, etc. fall in this category. Whereas span-*less* annotations are ones that are not *directly* associated with one specific span. Typically they tend to capture relation between two or more annotations that themselves may be span-*ed* or span-*less*. For example, an identify coreference relation between a set of span-*ed* entities and/or events in a text.

[11]A classic example of time-*less* annotation is punctuation in a transcript; The space between words in a transcript on the other hand can represent many different time durations. It can be almost negligible (given some lower duration threshold) with an effective duration of zero, or could range from several milliseconds to several seconds or more with a positive value of time duration.

- **Customized Aggregation**—Allow modular and customized information aggregation strategies.

6.1.2. Non-Functional Requirements

we have identified various capabilities that would be expected of this architecture. We have identified a few of these that we consider to be salient and concepts that have not *so far* been sufficiently exploited by existing frameworks.

- Prefer **convention** and **configuration** over writing custom code.
- A focus on **functional decomposition** across different modalities at both the level of data and multiple layers to promote incremental adoption.
- Allow the capture of **metadata** at various levels—including metadata on the annotations themselves.
- **Retain rich source context** to allow for its potential regeneration.
- Allow **declarative specification** of entities, constraints and transformations.
- Rely on **functional data structures** which are the underpinnings of modern **version control** systems
- **Delegate** complex constraint satisfaction requirements to tools like **relational database engines**
- Build on an ecosystem of established **data abstractions and libraries** rather than from scratch.
- Allow customizations through special **modes**, **hooks** and **plugins** .
- Adopt **literate annotation** practices
- Easy but powerful **data importing and exporting** mechanism.

6.2. An Implementation

In this section we will cover some details of the choices we made over possible implementations that let us adhere to the list of criteria that we listed in the earlier section.

6.2.1. Convention and Configuration over Code

Convention can go a long ways in keeping information easily understandable and shareable. Our architecture makes very few assumptions about the data, and allows the creation of a *multi-tier configuration* with sensible defaults for a small class of typical set of roles expected of a user, or a typical combination of modalities. The user can decide to tune the configuration as they become more comfortable using the system and in a way that allows them to be most effective at a given task. We will look at two example abstraction that can go a long way in reducing task complexity and allowing for better data consistency.

A case <u>specialized</u> MIME

When dealing with multiple modalities of data and a mix of text, binary or mixed content in files, it becomes important to use some notations that allow the interpretation of the file content. This is one of the main reasons for the creation of a Multipurpose Internet Mail Extensions (MIME) standard. The purpose for creating this standard was initially to identify multimedia contents and to support non-ASCII text characters. However, the degree of specification that such formalism provides globally across all data can be too general for a specific domain. In specialized domains as in the case of natural language processing, indication that a file contains text does not add very much information. In the absence of standard mechanisms, the differentiation between file formats containing various information is made through the use of various conventional names or multiple file extensions. Let's take a look at a few historical cases: i) The ATLAS XML files were traditionally named with an `.aif.xml` file extension; ii) The original *merged* representation of the Penn Treebank parses were stored in files with extension `.mrg`; iii) The CoNLL shared task tabular format used a `.conll` extension. The variability introduced using (sometimes) arbitrary naming conventions flies in the face of the concept of *namespaces* with a likely origin in programming language literature, but significant enough to have been exported in other fields of study such as computer networking, *area codes* and *country codes* in phone numbers, *zip codes*, etc. The cases are too numerous and common place to need further justification. However, so far as we are aware, there has not been a way of specifying important information of the quality, source, version, etc. of information found in various annotation files—either gold standard or manual. Typically a file containing a syntactic parse is commonly named with the `.parse` or `.tree` extension. There was a time when the landscape of parses was limited to Penn Treebank parses, and a few more bits of information was enough to disambiguate the contents for the end user.

It could be a predicted parse, or a gold standard parse; a constituent parse, or a dependency parses, etc. Even if one knows the answers to these questions the precise provenance might be impossible to trace as it could be predicted parse using a specific version of a specific parser trained on a specific corpus and which (as is traditionally the case with off-the-shelf parses) was trained on parses after removing *empty category* nodes from them.

We propose the use of a system of *tags* and such taxonomy itself can be grouped under the meta tag (prefix) "NLP-" to form a category of MIME types called NLP-MIME and possibly ASR-MIME for speech data and CV-MIME for vision data. Most of the data represented in other modalities such as image, videos, etc. tends to be containers of binary data, and the mechanism that has been in use for decades is by creating a plethora of file types such as `.wav`, `.au`, `.mp3` for audio, and `.png`, `jpeg`, etc. for images, and so on and so forth. A common solution for such content was the specification of a header at the beginning of the file which conveyed the salient invariants for that representation. For example, a `.wav` file would have a header specifying the sampling rate to be 16K, a bit precision of 16-bit and containing a single channel. We propose a content hash-like framework of 10 character hashes which can capture the important characteristic of a file, say a `.parse` file.

We will use an extension of signature `.uughtzzzzz_-parse` to indicate exactly what kind of parse it contains. In this case we use a ten character coding scheme where the first two characters map to a table indicating the source file—if any. And the following few indicate the value of one specific property each as shown below:

`01` (word formed using first two characters `[0,1]`)
This is reserved for the tag for the file that was used as the source file and was transformed—either automatically or manually—to form the current version. If this is the source file, then these have a special value of `uu`. Letter `u` standing for *unset*.

`2` (character at index `2`)
Whether the parse is a gold standard (`g` or an automatic `c, C, d`

- `g` Gold standard Penn Treebank parse
- `c` Output of Charniak Parser
- `b` Output of Berkeley Parser
- ...

`3` (character at index **3**)
How the hyphenization was represented in the schema for these parses

- `h` Tokens split at most hyphens (e.g., Treebank parses using guidelines version ...)
- `s` Tokens split at some hyphens (e.g., an intermediate inconsistent version)
- `n` Tokens split at none of the hyphens (e.g., the original Treebank v3 parses)
- ...

`4` (character at index **4**)
Whether the parse used the NML phrase tag which was added in later versions of Treebank guidelines

- `t` Yes, it did
- `f` No, it did not.

...

...

If one devises a reasonable strategy of creating such tags, and once the crucial properties of the contents are specified in the six character tag, then the user of the data can make several sensible assumptions about the contents. In fact, when there is a one-to-one conversion between two such tags, it can be used in a build system that would provide various guarantee—whether the verifiable features in the contents match the tag; exactly what function or transformations one needs to apply to a source tag to generate the contents for another tag, likely within the same layer. Such a system can substantially reduce the cognitive overhead on uses of the system and also allow modular functions to be written that only rely on the specific localized information for a particular layer.

If it feels like creating a whole category of new MIME types is going too far, then one might want consider the

Line No.	A Typical Editor	Emacs
1	`# coding=utf-8`	`#!/usr/bin/python`
2		`# -*- coding: utf-8 -*-`

Figure 1: An established convention (from the early days of UNIX, and further expanded over time) for adding useful metadata on the first two lines of source code.

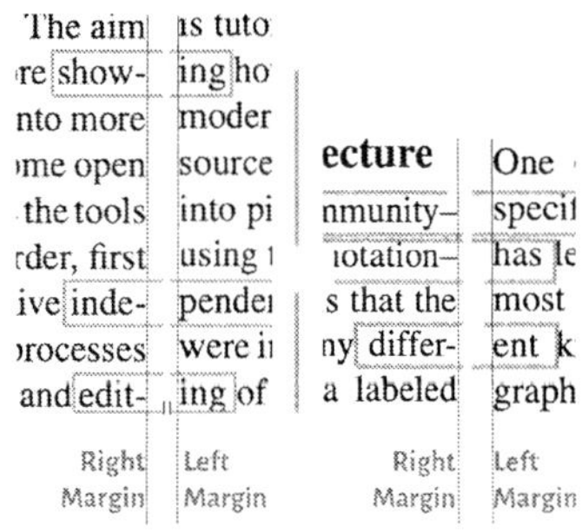

Figure 2: Example of hyphenation near right margin in a typical typeset document. There are two parts or columns in this figure. The left column is a snapshot of portion of text adjacent to the right page margin. And the right column shows the part that is adjacent to the left margin and on the following line. Three out of nine lines have these hyphenation artifacts marking the continuation of words on the following line.

creation of *molecular file formats*[12] which includes a `chemical/MIME` specification.

A case for <u>magic</u> comments

We recommend the use of magic comments to provide more detailed information, potentially richer and complimentary to the tag classes. One of the practices or conventions that goes long back in time is the concept known as *shebang*, which would be immediately recognized by UNIX/GNU-Linux users as the interpreter that should be involved to run the contents of that file as a *script* provided the *executable bit* is set for that file. This concept, which can be considered somewhat akin to the headers in binary files, has found its way into being used for many other scenarios—one of them being the specification of the text encoding used in a file as part of the UNICODE standard. A few bits of (visually) *invisible* sequence of bytes, called the Byte Order Marker[13] (BOM) is used to indicate the specific encoding used by a text file. The mechanics in various situations are complex and described in the UNICODE standard. The same design principle was used in other systems such as by the Python programming language to indicate the text encoding of the source code used in a Python script.

It matters <u>where</u> and <u>in what form</u> data originates

NLP is a relatively new field that has seen an explosion in interest over the past several years. Most researchers made a very simplifying assumption that source text is born as tokens. This recently raised interesting issues leading to the introduction of shared tasks that started with raw text.

[12] `https://en.wikipedia.org/wiki/Chemical_file_format`

[13] `https://www.unicode.org/faq/utf_bom.html#BOM`

Raw text in its unsegmented/untokenized form is still not usually the root source of the text. Much of the text that is part of the word layer of various corpora typically is in the form of some markup which is interpreted by the end application and is not visible on the interface. To take a few examples, most PubMed articles are available as a XML documents that adhere to a specific schema. This text can contain various details such as emphasis markers, subscripts, superscript, formula, tables, etc. However, most annotation projects strip that out while preparing data for annotation. A result of this is that the consuming learning algorithm or system often does not have access to all the information encoded in the source document. This can be good in some cases but in many cases it results in the prediction algorithm having to re-learn structure and properties of the text which it could have otherwise used to learn useful patterns. Recent iterations of CoNLL-U files have started keeping such information in the headers.
Figure 2 demonstrates another special case that is typically encountered when annotating scanned text. When scanned text is used as a source of annotation, it is a typical practice to *clean up* such artifacts. However that results in loss of useful information.
What we propose to do is keep track of all such information in a way that it can be cleaned when necessary, but can also be accessible to the learning algorithms.

6.2.2. Appropriate Level of Functional Decomposition

We use the *command design pattern* that has been central to generations of version control systems, but was likely made popular, and has been expanded by the `git` version control tool. This allows for a creation of tools that focus on several top-level domain decomposed (potentially hierarchically) reasonably independently of each other while ensuring that the resulting artifacts can be aggregated to form a consistent whole. One can design custom workflows that take into consideration the nature of segmentation of a typical user base such as the annotator, the data consumer (e.g., for training machine learning models), a linguist, a phonetician, the schema designer (with less programming expertise), the power user (who can write new plugins and custom workflows), to name a few. For the power user the architecture allows for creating and storing frequently used or infrequent but complex stages of data transformations or searches that can be executed easily later.

6.2.3. Built on top of Giants—Emacs, Emacs-Lisp, Org-mode, Babel, etc.

We decided to use the time tested decisions on representing text and other media that went into the design of the **programmable editor**—Emacs[14]. It is important to clarify that the architecture is not tied to the Emacs editor. Emacs-Lisp[15] (Monnier and Sperber, 2020) is a dialect of lisp with a special focus on programmatic text editing capabilities. Its extensive documentation[16] details the numerous text and data encoding decisions that were made with its evolution and which we can simply adopt.
We try to highlight some aspects of emacs-lisp that are of particular import in this context:

- **Homoiconicity**—This is a fortunate side effect of using a lisp dialect. The ability to treat data and code interchangeably can be very powerful.
- **Extreme Configurability**—As part of its core design principle, the data represented and processed using emacs-lisp is extremely configurable. There are several layers of configurability that can be a very powerful tool.
- **Hooks**—One of the fundamental design principles which also is its strength is the care taken in capturing various events that alter states of data and which allow for insertion of *hooks* that get automatically triggered helping one create an automated way of describing and ensuring validity of constraints.

Another important component is the *orgmode*[17] library that can be used to represent *active documents* which is touted to be a great format/library for conducting reproducible research(Schulte and Davison, 2011). It's core functionality can provide many features that could a general framework such as this one. Given the space limitations, We will highlight a few functionalities that directly contribute towards our goal.

- **Rich Document Representation**—orgmode is sometimes referred to as Org Document as one can consider it to be a set of tools to create rich, structured documents.
- **(Programmable) Structured Editing**—It is a kind-of markdown language that is designed with structured editing in mind
- **Rich API**—The `org-element.el` library provides a rich set of functions and allows for customizing connections between various pieces of information through a mechanism of mixing and matching (hierarchical) inheritance of information (properties or key-value pairs) with a hierarchical *tag* structure that can provide an immensely powerful representation of information.
- **Rich Set of Plugins**—It has a very rich set of plugins that provide a rich collection of search and filtering libraries that can be used to search and manipulate the data structures.
- **Literate Programming (and therefore Literate Annotation)**—Another sub-ecosystem of plugins are based on the babel library (another important component of the emacs ecosystem.) This combination opens up potential for a practice of *literate annotation* where one can potentially *annotate*

[14] `https://emacs.org`
[15] `https://cemantix.org/links/emacs-lisp.html`
[16] The emacs-lisp manual is very comprehensive spanning some 1200 pages and regularly maintained.
[17] `https://orgmode.org`

Rich Transcript	`Um {lipsmack} and that's it. {laugh}`
Input to Syntactic Parser	`Um and that 's it .`
Output of the Parser	`(S (INTJ (UH Um)) (CC and) (NP (DT that)) (VP (VBZ 's) (NP (PRP it))) (. .))`

Figure 3: Level of information from a syntactic parse as expected by a syntactician.

annotations—among other capabilities.

We refer to the specification using a recursive acronym YAMR[18]—YAMR Ain't Meaning Representation.

6.2.4. Relational Data Model—The Force is Still Strong

Separation of concerns is another important design decision that plays a part in this architecture. One can incorporate local constraints easily through the use of `hooks` but complex constraints are best delegated to a database engine using a database schema. There was a time when NoSQL database seemed to promise the world, but history has shown that an absence of schema does not make schema go away. It just reappears in places where it is not convenient to maintain and share. The move by Google engineers to switch Spanner, their distributed database, from NoSQL to SQL (Bacon et al., 2017) architecture is a good indicator that relational models still have their place in the world of distributed computing.

6.3. Illustrating the Architecture

We will try to illustrate the richness and flexibility of our architecture using two short sentences.

6.3.1. An Example Task

Let's assume that a syntactician would like to parse the utterance shown on the first line of Figure 3 (among many others). In its most raw form, this string reflects the guidelines used for transcription that marks *non-word* sounds in curly braces as shown. Most of the off-the-shelf parsers are not trained on such special tokens representing *non-words*. Let's assume that the parser expects pre-tokenized text as input. The second line shows a cleaned, tokenized string that can be fed to the parser. Following that is its likely parse.

Let's say that a phonetician would like to take a closer look at the relation between syntax and the duration of words, pauses, etc. In order to accomplish that, first the utterance needs to be processed through a *forced alignment* routine that tries to align audio segments to words, non-words in the transcript and also pauses that are longer than a certain threshold. A typical aligner does not care about the *punctuation's* in the input, and some even expect that to be part of the data *clean up* process. The forced aligner produces two new *layers* of information—a sequence of *timed words* and a *phone-level word alignment* of the audio with respect to the transcript. The next step is to integrate the *syntax* layer with the *phone-level alignment*. Figure 4 depicts the same transcript but in a tabular form.

[18] `https://yamr.org`

For the purposes of this discussion the top level header represents four *layers* of information. The caption describes the notations used in the table. A closer look at the table tells us that the alignment of sequence of *symbols* across the layers is not quite straight forward. Especially the fact that the *time aligned* words layer does not insert an `sp` (pause duration) marker when the duration is below a certain threshold. It should also be noted that the *phone-level alignment* layer uses a different scale than the use of *seconds* by the *timed word* layer. It is not hard to convince the reader that some non-trivial mechanism needs to be in place for one to integrate the syntax layer in this richer layer of information. One could write one time script to deal with a particular set of examples, but as far as we know there is no good general purpose solution available to anyone wanting to do such analysis.

The set of tools that we provide makes it easier for one to address such cases only by filling in some configurational parameters, such as the fact that {`LG`} and {`laugh`} are to be considered equivalent. In the worst case one might have to write a few lines of custom code if all such cases are not addressable using the configuration.

6.3.2. A Serialized Representation

In this section we will try to describe and illustrate how the serialization of the information looks like through snapshots of the file view. One important piece to know about `orgmode` is that it started as outline mode and so there is an innate ability (when opened in `emacs`) of folding (or, hiding) various levels of hierarchical information under a specific *node* (called *entry* or *headline*) in the `orgmode` lingua. Figure 5 shows a small cross section of a file with a top-level *Session* node and its first child that is the first *utterance*. The utterance itself has multiple children nodes. The child nodes are represent either a *word*, a *token*, a *whitespace* or a *metanode*. Whitespace is shown as a single underscore (_). These are identified using *tags* in the `orgmode` lingua which is a alphanumeric sequence within two colons (`:`). When a word and token are the same, the node can have both tags `:word:token:`. Tags can be concatenated to one other to indicate a set.

This structure somewhat represents a variation of an abstract syntax tree. The nodes that are tagged as `:metanode:` have an associated operator. In this case it is shows as `[OR]` and `[AND]` They are used when traversing the tree to get a sequence of tokens that match the users requirement. For example the three nodes (`I`, `_`, `'m`) that are children of `[AND]` will all be selected during the traversal provided each of them represents a specific signature—in this case a `:token:` tag—if one is trying to read the tokenized version of the utterance.

One of the powerful features of the *orgmode* data structure is that one can assign arbitrary number of (potential *hierarchy* of) *tags* AND *property*, *name-value* tuples and configure their *inheritability*. A node with many associated properties is shown in Figure 6. We

Tokens				Timed Words			Phone Alignment					Transcript
Token (index)	Start (char)	End (char)	Word	Start Time (seconds)	End Time (seconds)	Word	Start (sample)	End (sample)	Phone	Score	Word	
0	0	2	Um	30.082	30.952	um	300700000	302300000	AH1	-597.189941	UM	um
							302300000	309400000	M	517.626770		
	2	3	sp			sp	309400000	309400000	sp	-0.156736	sp	
			{LS}	30.952	31.312	{LS}	309400000	313000000	ls	-896.665771	{LS}	{lipsmack}
			sp	31.312	31.502	sp	313000000	314900000	sp	-76.367462	sp	
0	3	6	and	31.502	32.102	and	314900000	316300000	AE1	-131.814972	AND	and
							316300000	320600000	N	248.685242		
							320600000	320900000	D	-30.130604		
	6	7	sp			sp	320900000	320900000	sp	-0.156736	sp	
1	7	11	that	32.102	32.402	that's	320900000	321700000	DH	-34.681316	THAT'S	that's
2	11	13	's				321700000	322000000	AE1	-109.149544		
							322000000	322500000	T	-150.791061		
							322500000	323900000	S	45.310963		
	13	14	sp	32.402	32.702	sp	323900000	326900000	sp	-517.184387	sp	
3	14	16	it	32.702	33.182	it.	326900000	328400000	AH0	-507.279114	IT	it.
4	16	17	.				328400000	331700000	T	-731.196716		
			sp			sp	331700000	331700000	sp	-0.156736	sp	
			{LG}	33.182	33.692	{LG}	331700000	336800000	lg	-160.172989	{LG}	
				33.692	33.782	sp	336800000	337700000	sp	1.512673	sp	

Figure 4: Further details (in addition to the syntactic parse) expected by a phonetician. sp represents tokens identifying space character. These are explicitly marked in the output of the aligner; {LS} and {LG} respectively are equivalent to {lipsmack} and {laugh} as understood by the aligner. Greyed out tokens represent that they are missing from that layer. We have not identified space characters in the transcript column as they are typically invisible to the eye.

```
* Session                          :session:...
  * What I'm I'm tr- # telling now. :utterance:...
    * What                         :word:token:...
    * _                            :whitespace:...
    * [OR]                         :metanode:...
      * [AND]                      :metanode:...
        * I'm                      :word:...
      * [AND]                      :metanode:...
        * I                        :token:...
        * _                        :whitespace:...
        * 'm                       :token:...
    * tr-                          :word:token:...
    * _
    * #                            :word:token:...
    * _
    * [OR]                         :metanode:...
      * [AND]                      :metanode:...
        * I'm                      :word:...
        * _
      * [AND]                      :metanode:...
        * I                        :token:...
        * _
        * 'm                       :token:...
        * _
    * telling                      :word:token:...
    * _
    * [OR]                         :metanode:
      * [AND]                      :metanode:
        * now.                     :word:...
      * [AND]                      :metanode:
        * now                      :token:...
        * _
        * .                        :token:...
```

Figure 5: The abstract tree representation of an utterance with both the raw and tokenized versions available using appropriate means of traversal.

have added some comments (not part of the org syntax) along with the properties so that the reader can better interpret their meaning. This framework makes use of the concept that hypergraphs are better than just graphs for modeling relational data (Wolf et al., 2016).

Finally, Figure 7 shows how one can switch to a tabular view where a selected group of properties are displayed as columns and are editable similar to a spreadsheet. Lack of space prohibits us to go into much details but one can customize the values for a given property to belong to a certain list of values which makes it easier to change them while adhering to those constraints.

In essence this forms a stream of rich nodes interconnected to form *hypergraphs* where a *hyperedges* can represent the sequence of nodes satisfying a specific use case *without destroying* its *relation with other annotations, data and metadata*, thus allowing one to potentially re-insert a transformed/enriched version of those nodes into the (richer) consistent whole.

7. Conclusion

In this article we have outlined a novel architecture that uses established tools and technologies as well as various time tested design principles that could streamline and simplify the management of multiple layers of annotations across various media while keeping the barrier to entry quite minimal without sacrificing future extensibility while allowing multiple versions of data and annotations to stay alongside each other and allow easy export of meaningful slices of the whole that are of interest to the end user.

8. Acknowledgements

We would like to thank Prof. Mitch Marcus for providing invaluable feedback on various design decisions. He suggested the acronym GRAIL connecting this work with the Treebank parser evaluation metric—PARSEVAL[19]. Thanks also to Dr. Richard Stallman (rms), founder of the Free Software Foundation, Chief GNUisance of the GNU Project for creating GNU Emacs, one of the oldest, extensible *free* software still under active development. This work builds on its many, carefully designed data structures and rich design concepts. Numerous discussions with him influenced the design of this representation.

9. Bibliographical References

Bacon, D. F., Bales, N., Bruno, N., Cooper, B. F., Dickinson, A., Fikes, A., Fraser, C., Gubarev, A., Joshi, M., Kogan, E., et al. (2017). Spanner: Becoming a sql system. In *Proceedings of the 2017 ACM International Conference on Management of Data*, pages 331–343.

[19] Percival was one of the Grail knights in numerous medieval and modern stories of the Grail quest.

```
* Session                                                                    :session:...
  * What I'm I'm tr- # telling now.                                          :uid_00:utterance:...
    * What                                                                   :word:token:
      :PROPERTIES:
      :IS_WORD:                 t                 # t/f     -- Whether node is a span of type WORD
      :IS_TOKEN:                t                 # t/f     -- Whether node is a span of type TOKEN
      :WORD_INDEX:              0                 # int     -- Value of  word index if node is a WORD
      :TOKEN_INDEX:             0:0               # int:int -- Value of token index if node is a TOKEN
      :IS_WHITESPACE:           f                 # t/f     -- Whether WORD (or, TOKEN) represents whitespace (ws)
      :WHITESPACE_VALUE:        -                 # string  -- Type of WHITESPACE (ws) represented by span
      :NODE_ID:                 nid_02            # string  -- Unique ID of the node
      :NODE_TYPE:               0                 # int     -- Type of node: 0) non_ws; 1) ws; 2) inserted_ws; 3) or_....
      :NODE_DESCRIPTION:        non_whitespace    # string  -- Description of the node type
      :SPAN_START:              0                 # int     -- Value of start character offset for WORD (or TOKEN)
      :SPAN_END:                4                 # int     -- Value of   end character offset for WORD (or TOKEN)
      :INCOMPLETE_WORD:         f                 # t/f     -- Whether WORD (or, TOKEN) is incomplete (e.g., partially spoken)
      :RESTART_MARKER:          f                 # t/f     -- Whether WORD (or, TOKEN) is a marks a resetart event
      :PARSE_IGNORE:            f                 # t/f     -- Whether WORD (or, TOKEN) should be ignored during parsing
      :IS_REPEATED:             f                 # t/f     -- Whether WORD (or, TOKEN) is repeated
      :IS_HIDDEN:               t                 # t/f     -- Whether WORD (or, TOKEN) should be hidden from the view by default
      :CAN_HAVE_DURATION:       t                 # t/f     --     Can WORD (or, TOKEN) has a time duration
      :HAS_DURATION:            t                 # t/f     --    Does WORD (or, TOKEN) have a time duration
      :START_TIME:              5.01              # float   -- Start time in fraction of seconds
      :END_TIME:                7.56              # float   --   End time in fraction of seconds
      :COMPUTED:                f                 # t/f     -- Whether the value of this node was computed or present in the source
      :END:
    * _                                                                      :whitespace:
      :PROPERTIES:
      :IS_WHITESPACE:           t
      :WHITESPACE_VALUE:        " "
      :NODE_ID:                 nid_03
      :NODE_TYPE:               1
      :NODE_DESCRIPTION:        whitespace
      :CAN_HAVE_DURATION:       t
      :HAS_DURATION:            f
```

Figure 6: The properties associated with one particular node—the word "What"

ITEM	NODE_ID	NODE_TYPE	NODE_DESCRIPTION	WORD_INDEX	TOKEN_INDEX	INCOMPLETE_WORD	IS_REPEATED	ALLTAGS
* Session	nid_00	0	non_whitespace	.	.			:session:
* What I'm I'm tr- # tellin..	nid_01	0	non_whitespace	.	.			:uid_00:utterance:
* What	nid_02	0	non_whitespace	0	0:0			:uid_00:word:token:
* _	nid_03	1	whitespace	.	.			:uid_00:whitespace:
* [OR]	nid_04	3	metanode_or	.	.			:uid_00:metanode:
* [AND]	nid_05	4	metanode_and	.	.			:uid_00:metanode:
* I'm	nid_06	0	non_whitespace	1	.			:uid_00:metanode:word:
* [AND]	nid_07	3	metanode_and	.	.			:uid_00:metanode:
* I	nid_08	0	non_whitespace	.	1:0			:uid_00:metanode:token:
* _	nid_09	3	inserted_whitespace	.	.			:uid_00:metanode:whitespace:
* 'm	nid_10	0	non_whitespace	.	1:1			:uid_00:metanode:token:
* [OR]	nid_11	3	or_metanode	.	.			:uid_00:metanode:
* [AND]	nid_12	4	and_metanode	.	.			:uid_00:metanode:
* I'm	nid_13	0	non_whitespace	2	.		t	:uid_00:metanode:word:
* [AND]	nid_14	4	and_metanode	.	.			:uid_00:metanode:
* I	nid_15	0	non_whitespace	.	2:0		t	:uid_00:metanode:token:
* _	nid_16	2	inserted_whitespace	.	.		t	:uid_00:metanode:whitespace:
* 'm	nid_17	0	non_whitespace	.	2:1		t	:uid_00:metanode:token:
* tr-	nid_18	0	non_whitespace	3	3:0	t		:uid_00:word:token:
* _	nid_19	3	inserted_whitespace	.	.			:uid_00:whitespace:
* #	nid_20	0	non_whitespace	4	4:0			:uid_00:word:token:
* _	nid_21	1	whitespace	.	.			:uid_00:whitespace:
* _	nid_22	1	whitespace	.	.			:uid_00:whitespace:
* telling	nid_23	0	non_whitespace	5	5:0			:uid_00:word:token:
* _	nid_24	1	whitespace	.	.			:uid_00:whitespace:
* [OR]	nid_25	3	and_metanode	.	.			:uid_00:metanode:
* [AND]	nid_26	4	and_metanode	.	.			:uid_00:metanode:
* now.	nid_27	0	non_whitespace	6	.			:uid_00:metanode:word:
* [AND]	nid_28	4	and_metanode	.	.			:uid_00:metanode:
* now	nid_29	0	non_whitespace	.	6:0			:uid_00:metanode:token:
* _	nid_30	3	inserted_whitespace	.	.			:uid_00:metanode:whitespace:
* .	nid_31	0	non_whitespace	.	6:1			:uid_00:metanode:token:

Figure 7: The `column view` which allows a columnar representation of the nodes and properties. A hyperedge with set of node IDs 02, [03,] 06, [22,] 23, [24,] 27 represent the untokenized sentence and 02, [03,] 08, [09,] 10, [22,] 23, [24,] 29, [30,] 31 represent the tokenized version. The node IDs inside square brackets represent the whitespace nodes.

Banarescu, L., Bonial, C., Cai, S., Georgescu, M., Griffitt, K., Hermjakob, U., Knight, K., Koehn, P., Palmer, M., and Schneider, N. (2013). Abstract meaning representation for sembanking. In *Proceedings of the 7th linguistic annotation workshop and interoperability with discourse*, pages 178–186.

Bateman, J. A., Kasper, R. T., Moore, J. D., and Whitney, R. A. (1990). A general organization of knowledge for natural language processing: the penman upper model. Technical report, Technical report, USC/Information Sciences Institute, Marina del Rey, CA.

Bateman, J. A. (1990). Upper modeling: Organizing knowledge for natural language processing. Technical report, University of Southern California Marina del Rey Information Sciences Institute.

Bird, S. and Liberman, M. (2001). A formal framework for linguistic annotation. *Speech Commun.*, 33(1-2):23–60.

Bird, S., Day, D., Garofolo, J. S., Henderson, J., Laprun, C., and Liberman, M. (2000). ATLAS: A flexible and extensible architecture for linguistic annotation. In *Proceedings of the Second International Conference on Language Resources and Evaluation, LREC 2000, 31 May - June 2, 2000, Athens, Greece*.

Boersma, P. et al. (2014). The use of praat in corpus research. *The Oxford handbook of corpus phonology*, pages 342–360.

Calhoun, S., Carletta, J., Brenier, J. M., Mayo, N., Jurafsky, D., Steedman, M., and Beaver, D. (2010). The nxt-format switchboard corpus: a rich resource for investigating the syntax, semantics, pragmatics and prosody of dialogue. *Language resources and evaluation*, 44(4):387–419.

Carletta, J., Evert, S., Heid, U., and Kilgour, J. (2005). The nite xml toolkit: data model and query language. *Language resources and evaluation*, 39(4):313–334.

Chiarcos, C., Ritz, J., and Stede, M. (2012). By all these lovely tokens... merging conflicting tokenizations. *Language resources and evaluation*, 46(1):53–74.

Cunningham, H. (2002). Gate, a general architecture for text engineering. *Computers and the Humanities*, 36(2):223–254.

De Marneffe, M.-C., Manning, C. D., Nivre, J., and Zeman, D. (2021). Universal dependencies. *Computational linguistics*, 47(2):255–308.

Dipper, S., Götze, M., Stede, M., and Wegst, T. (2004). Annis. *Interdisciplinary studies on information structure: ISIS; working papers of the SFB 632*, (1):245–279.

Driscoll, J. R., Sarnak, N., Sleator, D. D., and Tarjan, R. E. (1989). Making data structures persistent. *Journal of computer and system sciences*, 38(1):86–124.

Ferrucci, D. and Lally, A. (2004). Uima: an architectural approach to unstructured information processing in the corporate research environment. *Natural Language Engineering*, 10(3-4):327–348.

Götze, M. and Dipper, S. (2006). Annis: Complex multilevel annotations in a linguistic database. In *Proceedings of the 5th Workshop on NLP and XML (NLPXML-2006): Multi-Dimensional Markup in Natural Language Processing*.

Ide, N. and Pustejovsky, J. (2017). *Handbook of linguistic annotation*, volume 1. Springer.

Ide, N. and Romary, L. (2004). International standard for a linguistic annotation framework. *Natural language engineering*, 10(3-4):211–225.

Ide, N. and Suderman, K. (2007). Graf: A graph-based format for linguistic annotations. In *proceedings of the Linguistic Annotation Workshop*, pages 1–8.

Ide, N. and Suderman, K. (2014). The linguistic annotation framework: a standard for annotation interchange and merging. *Language Resources and Evaluation*, 48(3):395–418.

Ide, N. and Véronis, J. (1995). *Text encoding initiative: Background and contexts*, volume 29. Springer Science & Business Media.

Jochim, M. (2017). Extending the emu speech database management system: Cloud hosting, team collaboration, automatic revision control. In *INTERSPEECH*, pages 813–814.

Kasper, R. T. (1989). A flexible interface for linking applications to penman's sentence generator. In *Speech and Natural Language: Proceedings of a Workshop Held at Philadelphia, Pennsylvania, February 21-23, 1989*.

Krause, T. and Zeldes, A. (2016). Annis3: A new architecture for generic corpus query and visualization. *Digital Scholarship in the Humanities*, 31(1):118–139.

Kummerfeld, J. K. (2019). SLATE: A super-lightweight annotation tool for experts. In *Proceedings of the 57th Annual Meeting of the Association for Computational Linguistics: System Demonstrations*, pages 7–12, Florence, Italy, July. Association for Computational Linguistics.

MacWhinney, B. (2014). *The CHILDES project: Tools for analyzing talk, Volume II: The database*. Psychology Press.

Maeda, K., Lee, H., Medero, J., and Strassel, S. M. (2006). A new phase in annotation tool development at the linguistic data consortium: The evolution of the annotation graph toolkit. In *Proceedings of the Fifth International Conference on Language Resources and Evaluation, LREC 2006, Genoa, Italy, May 22-28, 2006*, pages 1570–1573.

Marcus, M. P., Santorini, B., and Marcinkiewicz, M. A. (1993). Building a large annotated corpus of english: The penn treebank. *Comput. Linguistics*, 19(2):313–330.

Monnier, S. and Sperber, M. (2020). Evolution of emacs lisp. *Proceedings of the ACM on Programming Languages*, 4(HOPL):1–55.

Narayanan, A. and Clark, J. (2017). Bitcoin's academic pedigree: The concept of cryptocurrencies is built from forgotten ideas in research literature. *Queue*, 15(4):20–49.

Neves, M. and Ševa, J. (2021). An extensive review of tools for manual annotation of documents. *Briefings in bioinformatics*, 22(1):146–163.

Pradhan, S. and Ramshaw, L. (2017). Ontonotes: Large scale multi-layer, multi-lingual, distributed annotation. In *Handbook of linguistic annotation*, pages 521–554. Springer.

Pradhan, S. S., Hovy, E., Marcus, M., Palmer, M., Ramshaw, L., and Weischedel, R. (2007). Ontonotes: A unified relational semantic representation. In *International Conference on Semantic Computing (ICSC 2007)*, pages 517–526. IEEE.

Preguiça, N. (2018). Conflict-free replicated data types: An overview. *arXiv preprint arXiv:1806.10254*.

Ramachandram, D. and Taylor, G. W. (2017). Deep multimodal learning: A survey on recent advances and trends. *IEEE signal processing magazine*, 34(6):96–108.

Ritchie, D. M. and Thompson, K. (1974). The unix time-sharing system. *Commun. ACM*, 17(7):365–375, jul.

Rosenfeld, V. (2010). An implementation of the annis 2 query language. *Berlin: Humboldt-Universität zu Berlin*.

Schmidt, T. (2004). Transcribing and annotating spoken language with exmaralda. In *Proceedings of the LREC-Workshop on XML based richly annotated corpora*, Lisbon.

Schulte, E. and Davison, D. (2011). Active documents with org-mode. *Computing in Science & Engineering*, 13(3):66–73.

Weischedel, R., Hovy, E., Marcus, M., Palmer, M., Ramshaw, L., Belvin, R., Pradhan, S., and Xue, N. (2011). Ontonotes: A large training corpus for enhanced processing. *Joseph Olive, Caitlin Christianson, andJohn McCary, editors, Handbook of Natural LanguageProcessing and Machine Translation: DARPA GlobalAutonomous Language Exploitation*.

Winkelmann, R. and Raess, G. (2014). Introducing a web application for labeling, visualizing speech and correcting derived speech signals. In *Proceedings of the Ninth International Conference on Language*

Resources and Evaluation (LREC'14), pages 4129–4133.

Winkelmann, R., Harrington, J., and Jänsch, K. (2017). Emu-sdms: Advanced speech database management and analysis in r. *Computer Speech & Language*, 45:392–410.

Wittenburg, P., Brugman, H., Russel, A., Klassmann, A., and Sloetjes, H. (2006). Elan: A professional framework for multimodality research. In *5th international conference on language resources and evaluation (LREC 2006)*, pages 1556–1559.

Wolf, M. M., Klinvex, A. M., and Dunlavy, D. M. (2016). Advantages to modeling relational data using hypergraphs versus graphs. In *2016 IEEE High Performance Extreme Computing Conference (HPEC)*, pages 1–7. IEEE.

Zeldes, A., Lüdeling, A., Ritz, J., and Chiarcos, C. (2009). Annis: a search tool for multi-layer annotated corpora. In *Proceedings of Corpus Linguistics*.

Zipser, F., Krause, T., Lüdeling, A., Neumann, A., Stede, M., and Zeldes, A. (2015). Annis, saltnpepper & paula: A multilayer corpus infrastructure. In *Final Conference of the SFB*, volume 632.

Author Index

Association for Computational Linguistics
209 N. Eighth Street
Stroudsburg, Pennsylvania 18360

ISBN 978-1-7138-6125-6

CURRAN ASSOCIATES INC.
proceedings.com